THE JO
Pastor's Library

COUNSELING

HOW *to* COUNSEL BIBLICALLY

JOHN MACARTHUR

and THE MASTER'S COLLEGE FACULTY

THOMAS NELSON
Since 1798

Counseling: How to Counsel Biblically

Copyright © 2005 by John MacArthur.

Published in Nashville, Tennessee, by Thomas Nelson. Thomas Nelson is a registered trademark of HarperCollins Christian Publishing, Inc.

Published in association with the literary agency of Wolgemuth & Associates, Inc.

ISBN 978-0-310-14125-9 (softcover)

ISBN 978-0-785-21520-2 (eBook)

Library of Congress Cataloging-in-Publication Data

MacArthur, John 1939–
 Counseling / by John MacArthur and Wayne A. Mack with the Master's College Faculty
  p. cm.
 Includes bibliographical references and index.
 ISBN 1-4185-0005-4
 1. Pastoral counseling 2. Discipling (Christianity) 3. Pastoral psychology—
Controversial literature. I. Mack, Wayne, A. II. The Master's College III. Title.
 BV4012.M32 1994
 253.5—dc20   92–10306
                      CIP

Printed in the United States of America

Dedicated to
Biblical Counselors-in-Training
at
The Master's College
and Seminary

Contents

Preface

This book is written to present a system of biblical truth that brings together people, their problems, and the living God. *Counseling* is based on the convictions that (1) God's Word should be our counseling authority, (2) counseling is a part of the basic discipling ministry of the local church, and (3) God's people can and should be trained to counsel effectively.

Counseling is written for all of God's people: pastors, elders, and laypeople. We foresee the book as a potential textbook in biblical counseling or pastoral theology at the Christian college and seminary levels. Veteran pastors with a great deal of training and experience and pastors without seminary training or much practical experience can all profit from this volume. Sincere laypeople who want to improve their skills in serving Christ and His people will also find many useful, practical, and stimulating insights in this publication.

In preparing this book, we have labored to present material that is accurately biblical rather than humanistic or secular, basically proactive rather than reactive or polemic, practical rather than theoretical and abstract, and easily understood rather than technical or complicated. We have written to inform, to excite, to instruct, to confirm, to enlarge, and to promote spiritual and ministerial growth in the readers.

This book has been written with eleven objectives in mind:

1. To enlarge and reinforce the confidence of God's people in the sufficiency, superiority, and practicality of Scripture for dealing with all of the issues of life, and to convince Christians that the resources we have in Christ and His Word are not only sufficient for handling and solving all of the personal and interpersonal problems of life but are superior to the resources that are found in the world; that is, to answer the questions, "Do we need more than what the Scriptures offer to be effective in our counseling ministries? What do the Scriptures say about counseling? What is the biblical basis for using Scriptures in counseling?"

2. To encourage Christians to think biblically about all counseling-related issues; that is, to answer the question, "What does it mean to think biblically, and how can we develop a biblical mind-set or consistently biblical worldview?"[1]

3. To help Christians understand people and their problems through the lens of Scripture; that is, to answer the question, "What do the Scriptures say about who and what people are and why they have the problems they have?"

4. To demonstrate how our counseling methods must be consistent with our theological convictions; that is, to answer the question, "How should what we believe interface with and relate to our counseling ministry?"

5. To provide biblical guidelines to counsel people effectively who are struggling with problems; that is, to answer the question, "How does one do biblical counseling?"

6. To motivate Christians to be more involved in the ministry of counseling and to equip them to be more competent in this work; that is, to answer the question, "Why should I be concerned about biblical counseling, and how can I become a more effective counselor?"

7. To give Christians specific biblical principles for discerning the difference between counseling that purports to be biblical and counseling that actually is; that is, to answer the question, "What are the distinctives of biblical counseling?"

8. To foster an approach to Scripture that is both exegetically correct and extremely practical; that is, to answer the questions, "What should our attitude be as we study and interact with the Bible? How should we study and apply the Scriptures?"

9. To present a brief historical perspective on the ministry of counseling; to discuss how secular psychology filtered into and influenced the church during the twentieth century; and to relate how the biblical counseling movement is progressing; that is, to answer the questions, "Who have been some of the promoters and practitioners of biblical counseling? How did the Church become enamored with the insights of secular psychology in the twentieth century? How was the emphasis on and concern for true biblical counseling recovered? What progress is being made in the movement?"

10. To encourage the church to accept its God-given responsibility to do counseling and to present a method for developing a counseling ministry; that is, to answer the questions, "Where does counseling fit in the church's ministry? Who should be involved in counseling? How does a church develop a biblical counseling ministry?"

11. To respond to some of the objections that are raised against biblical counseling and to clarify what is meant by biblical counseling; that is, to answer questions such as, "Isn't it simplistic to insist that the Bible gives us all that we need to deal with the problems of people? Can the Bible provide everything that is necessary to counsel people with serious problems? Don't some people need an expert, someone with a lot of psychological training, to understand and help them?"

The book is arranged in four parts. The first part, devoted to the historical perspectives on biblical counseling, sets the tone and provides some of the rationale for the book. The second part presents the crucial theological issues that function as underpinnings for biblical counseling. The third part of the book focuses on the practical implementation of biblical counseling. The fourth part places biblical counseling in the context of other ministries in the local church. Indexes of authors, Scripture, and subjects are provided at the end of the volume.

We who serve Christ at The Master's College and have had a part in producing this book, dedicate *Counseling* to the honor and glory of Christ and pray that our God will use it for the good of His people, whom He loved and for whom He gave Himself. Our prayer is that He will use this material to equip pastors and laypeople for the work of the ministry in building up the body of Christ. May He be pleased to utilize the concepts and information presented in this book in making us more skillful in preparing and repairing the saints so that He might receive the praise and glory He so richly deserves.

John MacArthur
Wayne A. Mack

Introduction

The November 29, 1993, issue of *Time* featured a series of articles on the turmoil in modern psychology. The magazine's cover featured a retouched photograph of Sigmund Freud—his head a hollow, incomplete, three-dimensional jigsaw puzzle—and the caption, "IS FREUD DEAD?"

One of the articles inside raised the question, "What if Freud was wrong?" Noting that the twentieth century had already seen the sudden collapse of Marxism, the article suggested that we might be about to witness a similarly dramatic toppling of "the complex Freudian monument."[1]

Evangelicals not so long ago would have roundly cheered such news. But, alas, we live in strange times. Ironically, while the secular world has grown increasingly disaffected with the professional psychotherapy industry, the evangelical world has been frantically trying to marry secular psychology and biblical truth. While the world becomes more and more suspicious of psychology, Christians seem to be growing more and more committed to it. Perhaps it is fair to say that many in the church are addicted to psychotherapy.

The rush to embrace psychology within the church is frankly mystifying. Psychology and Christianity have been enemies from the beginning. Freud's presuppositions were atheistic and cynical. He called religion a "universal, obsessional neurosis."[2] To him, religion was an illusion that derived its strength from irrational, wishful thinking rooted in human instinct.[3] Those who followed Freud at first were uniformly hostile to biblical belief. The foundational doctrines of the movement were therefore based on blatantly anti-Christian presuppositions. To Freud and his followers the human being was nothing but an animal motivated by the sex drive and other ego needs.

The church was naturally wary of these ideas, and justifiably so. Freudianism was one of several atheistic hypotheses, along with Darwinism and Marxism, that were gaining popularity at the dawn of the twentieth century. The church's greatest battlefield at that time, however, was against another insidious enemy: theological liberalism, a pseudo-Christianity that denied the authority of Scripture and questioned the supernatural. This was yet another doctrine that was contributing to the rapid secularization of society.

Among professing Christians, only theological liberals found allies among the atheistic psychologists. Carl Jung wrote much about religion. In his system, however, the human unconscious was divine. William James, father of modern pragmatism, also blended behavioral theory and religion into a humanistic creed that made lavish use of theological terminology. But these men were by no means Christians. They utterly rejected supernaturalism, repudiated the authority of Scripture, and discarded most of the central tenets of historic Christian belief.

Psychology was thus ideally suited for an increasingly secular age. By the middle of this century, the new discipline was accepted by the popular mind as a full-fledged science, even though the movement was already beginning to fragment into dozens of competing schools and philosophies, and even though its hypotheses could not be tested or its results verified through any of the traditional means of true science. None of that could slow psychology's acceptance in an age that had grown hostile to the notion of absolute truth.

Within a few short decades, the psychotherapy industry and evangelicals settled into a more or less guarded coexistence. Christians seemed intimidated by the world's overwhelming acceptance of psychotherapy as a true science. The psychotherapists believed they were privy to a higher knowledge and more effective therapies than traditional spiritual counsel could ever offer. They stated in no uncertain terms that spiritual counselors and the clergy should stay off their turf.

One textbook on pastoral psychology written in the 1950s summed up the professional therapists' attitude to pastoral counsel:

> It is [the pastor's] duty not to try to enact the role of the psychiatrist, but *as quickly as possible, he must refer the sick person to the professional man.* Oftentimes he must secure the judgment of the psychiatrist regarding the symptoms which a petitioner displays. Moreover, *the clergyman, in such instances, must place himself under the direction of the psychiatrist,* in the event that the latter believes his assistance as a religionist is helpful. Psychotherapy and religio-therapy demand consistent, patient treatment, over long periods of time, and the clergyman rarely finds the hours to furnish this. Therefore he must have a specialist as a member of the staff of his church or synagogue, to whom he can refer cases. Or if such a professional is not a member of the institution's staff, he may be a friend and advisor of the clergyman when required. All this entails the expenditure of time and money, and it must not be forgotten that while the clergyman is willing to give his time freely, the professional psychiatrist must make his hours count in monetary terms. *Too often distressed persons come to the clergyman when they have been unsuc-*

cessful in their consultations with the psychiatrist, but it is an astute pastor who immediately turns them back to their psychiatrist.

Frequently the clergyman and the psychiatrist can work hand in hand, especially in the case of parishioners who, at one time, will accept guidance from the clergyman, and, at another moment, from the psychiatrist. Husbands and wives have been brought together as a consequence of this technique. Sometimes the psychiatrist will recommend to the clergyman that he accept a convalescent youth as a member of the religious institution's young people's organization, in the hope that social opportunities will accelerate the cure. Sometimes the psychiatrist will appreciate the value of attendance at divine worship, the reading of religious literature, and the performance of traditional rites and ceremonies. *In every such instance, the psychiatrist must be the mentor and the director of the treatment.*[4]

Too many pastors capitulated to such thinking, and over the past forty years or so, counseling has steadily moved out of the church and into the clinics. Now "Christian" psychology is a billion-dollar business. Yet has the spiritual and emotional state of believers been improved by this trend? Surely no one would argue seriously that it has.

One of the promising trends in the evangelical world today is the emergence of a renewed emphasis on counseling that is *biblical;* not mere psychology colored with biblical words and phrases but an earnest effort to help people solve their problems by turning them to the objective, life-changing truth of Scripture.

Scripture does, after all, claim to be the only reliable resource to which we can turn to solve our spiritual problems:

- How can a young man keep his way pure? By keeping it according to Thy word (Ps. 119:9).
- Thy testimonies also are my delight; They are my counselors (Ps. 119:24).
- Thy commandments make me wiser than my enemies, for they are ever mine. I have more insight than all my teachers, for Thy testimonies are my meditation. I understand more than the aged, because I have observed Thy precepts (Ps. 119:98–100).
- All Scripture is inspired by God and profitable for teaching, for reproof, for correction, for training in righteousness; that the man of God may be adequate, equipped for every good work (2 Tim. 3:16–17).

Dozens of similar passages could be quoted to demonstrate the utter superiority and absolute sufficiency Scripture claims for itself. Either we believe what God's Word teaches in this regard, or we open ourselves to all kinds of corrupt influences from worldly thinking. The choice is as simple as that.

I am encouraged to see a large movement of Christians returning to Scripture as the sole source of wisdom and correction for the human soul. I am grateful to God for the men and women He is using to awaken the church to this need.

Wayne Mack is one of those who have been at the forefront of this issue for many years. Under his wise leadership, The Master's College is building a biblical counseling program that is unequalled anywhere. While carrying out that task, Dr. Mack has also found time to compile and edit this book. It is the realization of a longtime desire of mine to have a comprehensive textbook on the issues that Christian counselors struggle with, a guidebook for those who want to offer truly *biblical* counsel, not just warmed-over concepts from the scrap heap of secular psychology. I believe this book will effectively equip and embolden Christian counselors who have been intimidated or confused by the claims of modern psychology. It will also instruct and assist those who are already committed to biblical counseling, so that they can be more effective.

Whether you are a seasoned biblical counselor or someone just starting out, I know you will find much to help and encourage you in this volume. My prayer is that it will be a major catalyst in moving the Church away from the toxic, false counsel of worldly wisdom and back to the pure milk of the Word.

John MacArthur

Part I

The Historical Background of Biblical Counseling

1

Rediscovering Biblical Counseling

John MacArthur[1]

Ever since apostolic times, counseling has occurred in the church as a natural function of corporate spiritual life. After all, the New Testament itself *commands* believers to "admonish one another" (Rom. 15:14); "encourage one another" (Heb. 3:13, KJV); "comfort one another with these words" (1 Thess. 4:18); "encourage one another, and build up one another" (1 Thess. 5:11); "confess your sins to one another, and pray for one another, so that you may be healed" (James 5:16).

The apostle Paul wrote, "We who are strong ought to bear the weaknesses of those without strength and not just please ourselves" (Rom. 15:1). And, "Even if a man is caught in any trespass, you who are spiritual, restore such a one in a spirit of gentleness; each one looking to yourself, lest you too be tempted. Bear one another's burdens, and thus fulfill the law of Christ" (Gal. 6:1–2).

All those instructions apply to rank-and-file church members, not only to some priestly caste of experts. Counseling, particularly counseling that skillfully employs and applies God's Word, is a necessary duty of Christian life and fellowship. It is also the expected result of true spiritual maturity: "Let the word of Christ richly dwell within you, with all wisdom teaching and admonishing one another with psalms and hymns and spiritual songs, singing with thankfulness in your hearts to God" (Col. 3:16).

In recent years, however, there has been a strong and very influential movement within the church attempting to replace biblical counseling in the church body with "Christian psychology"—techniques and wisdom gleaned from secular therapies and dispensed primarily by paid professionals. Those who have championed this movement often *sound* vaguely biblical. That is, they quote Scripture and often blend theological ideas with the teachings of Freud, Rogers, Jung, or whatever school of secular psychology they follow. But the movement itself is certainly *not* taking the church in a biblical direction. It has conditioned Christians to think of counseling as something best left to trained experts. It has opened the door to a whole range of extrabiblical theories and therapies. Indeed, it has left many with the feeling that God's Word is incomplete, insufficient, unsophisticated, and unable to offer help for people's deepest emotional and spiritual problems. It has directed millions of Christians seeking spiritual help away from their pastors and fellow believers and into psychological clinics. It has given many the impression that adapting secular methods such as twelve-step recovery plans can be more helpful than spiritual means in weaning people from their sins. In short, it has diminished the church's confidence in Scripture, prayer, fellowship, and preaching as means through which the Spirit of God works to change lives.

If the presuppositions behind this movement were sound, we might expect that Christians today would be the most well-adjusted and mentally healthy generation who ever lived. After all, they have the benefit of several generations of psychological expertise, applied by men and women who claim to be able to synthesize such knowledge with Scripture and make it "Christian."

But, clearly, that is not the case. Record numbers of people are seeking psychological treatment. More Christians than ever before are lining up at the doors of clinics and professional counselors. Christian psychologists offering live counsel are now heard daily on thousands of Christian radio stations around the country. In the past decade and a half, Christian psychology has become a billion-dollar industry. Millions of evangelical Christians, it seems, are addicted to therapy.

In contrast to those trends, however, another movement has been gaining strength among evangelicals. Clear voices are beginning to call the church back to the Scriptures as a sufficient help for people's spiritual problems. A groundswell of support has been building for a return to biblical counseling in the church. Every week I hear from pastors and church leaders who are rediscovering the importance of biblical counseling. They are realizing what they have actually always believed: that Scripture is superior to human wisdom (1 Cor. 3:19); that the Word of God is a more effective discerner of the human heart than any earthly means (Heb. 4:12); that the Spirit of God is the only effective agent of recovery and regeneration (Eph. 5:18–19); and that all the treasures of wisdom and knowledge are found in Christ Himself (Col. 2:3).

Those truths are so basic to Christian belief that it is astonishing to think they would ever come under fire from within the church itself. But of course that is precisely what has happened over and over in church history. And it is happening even now as psychology is being peddled in the church as a necessary, and even superior, solution to spiritual problems.

I was first thrust into the forefront of the battle between psychology and biblical counseling in 1980, when our church was hit with the first ever "clergy malpractice" lawsuit. The suit charged that the pastors on our staff were negligent because we tried to help a suicidal young member of our church by giving him biblical truth. It was the first such case ever heard in the American court system. The secular media had a field day as the case dragged on for years. Some national news sources even alleged that our church had encouraged the young man to kill himself, teaching him that suicide was a sure way to heaven. Of course, that was not true. We showed him from Scripture that suicide is wrong. We urged him to let the Word of God lead him to intimate knowledge and appropriation of the resources available in the One who wanted to heal his troubled mind. Tragically, he refused our counsel and took his own life.

The case raised the question of whether churches should have the legal right to counsel troubled people using only the Bible. The plaintiffs argued that giving a depressed or suicidal person advice from Scripture is a simplistic and irresponsible approach to counseling. They brought forward several "experts" who testified that spiritual counsel is not appropriate for people who have *real* problems. Victims of chronic depression, suicidal tendencies, and similar emotional and mental problems should be referred to a psychological expert, they claimed. Pastors and church counselors should be *required* to refer such people to mental-health professionals, the lawsuit contended. Their basic charge was that attempting to counsel troubled people from the Bible amounts to recklessness and negligence for which church counselors must be held morally and legally culpable. Had they won the case, *any* church that practiced biblical counseling would be taking a huge liability risk.

The facts of the case that came out in court received little or no coverage on the network news. Testimony showed that this young man *was* under the care of professional psychiatrists. In addition to the biblical direction he received from our pastoral staff, he had sought psychiatric treatment. Moreover, our staff had seen to it that he was examined by several medical doctors, to rule out organic or chemical causes for his depression. He was receiving every kind of therapy available, but he chose to end his life anyway. We did all we could to help him; he rejected our counsel and turned his back on his spiritual sufficiency in Christ.

Three different courts actually heard evidence in the case, and all three ruled in favor of the church. Twice those rulings were overturned on appeal because of technicalities, but every court that actually tried the case agreed in the verdict absolving the church from any blame. Eventually, the case was appealed to the United States Supreme Court. The High Court refused to hear the case, thereby letting stand the California State Supreme Court's ruling that finally vindicated the church.

All three times the case was heard and a ruling was given, the judges also expressed the opinion that the church had *not* failed in its responsibility to give proper care. Their judgment was that our staff had more than fulfilled their legal and moral obligations in how we had attempted to help this young man who had sought our counsel. But even more important, the courts affirmed every church's constitutional right to counsel from the Bible. The case established a legal precedent upholding an important first-amendment right of freedom of religion. The court's ruling means that secular courts have no right to encroach on the area of counseling in the church.

<h2 align="center">PSYCHOLOGIZING THE CHURCH</h2>

That clergy malpractice trial thrust me into the midst of the debate about psychology and biblical counseling. Before that, I had noticed that Christian psychologists, once unheard of, were becoming more and more common, more and more outspoken. Unfortunately, I had paid little attention to the trend and was not listening closely to how they were marketing psychology in the church.

But during the trial itself, a surprising number of the "experts" who were called to argue against biblical counseling were professional Christian counselors. I was startled and dismayed during the trial to hear men who identified themselves as evangelicals testifying that the Bible alone does not contain sufficient help to meet people's deepest personal and emotional needs. These people were actually arguing before a secular court that God's Word is not an adequate resource for dealing with people's spiritual problems! What is truly appalling is the number of evangelicals who are willing to accept the word of such professionals.

There is no denying that psychology has made incredible inroads into evangelical culture over the past twenty-five years. The influence of psychology is reflected in the kind of sermons that are preached from evangelical pulpits, in the kind of counseling that is being offered over the radio airwaves, in the proliferation of psychologists who cater primarily to evangelical Christians, and in the books that are being offered by many evangelical publishers.[2]

Over the past decades a host of evangelical psychological clinics have sprung up. Though almost all of them claim to offer biblical counsel, most merely dispense secular psychology disguised in spiritual terminology. This can be seen clearly in the literature spawned by the movement. As Jay Adams observed, "Nearly all recent counseling books for ministers, even conservative ones, are written from the Freudian perspective in the sense that they rest largely upon the presuppositions of the Freudian ethic of non-responsibility."[3]

The rise of counseling clinics poses another problem for the church: the trend has removed the counseling ministry from its proper arena in the church body and conditioned most Christians to think of themselves as incompetent to counsel. Many pastors, feeling inadequate and perhaps afraid of possible malpractice litigation, are perfectly willing to let "professionals" take over what used to be seen as a vital pastoral responsibility.[4] Too many have bought the lie that a crucial realm of spiritual wisdom exists outside Scripture, and that some idea or technique from that extrabiblical realm holds the real key to helping people with their deep problems.

What Is Wrong with Psychology?

The word *psychology* literally means "the study of the soul." True soul-study cannot be done by unbelievers. After all, only Christians have the resources for comprehending the nature of the human soul and understanding how it can be transformed. The secular discipline of psychology is based on godless assumptions and evolutionary foundations and is capable of dealing with people only superficially and only on the temporal level. Sigmund Freud, the father of modern psychology, was an unbelieving humanist who devised psychology as a substitute for religion.

Before Freud, the study of the soul was thought of as a spiritual discipline. In other words, it was inherently associated with religion. Freud's chief contribution was to define the human soul and the study of human behavior in wholly secular terms. He utterly divorced anthropology (the study of human beings) from the spiritual realm and thus made way for atheistic, humanistic, and rationalistic theories about human behavior.

Those fundamentally antibiblical theories became the basis of all modern psychology. Of course, today's psychologists use hundreds of counseling models and techniques based on a myriad of conflicting theories, so it is impossible to speak of psychotherapy as if it were a unified and consistent science.[5] But the basis of modern psychology can be summarized in several commonly held ideas that have their roots in early Freudian humanism. These are the very same ideas many Christians are zealously attempting to synthesize with biblical truth:

- Human nature is basically good.
- People have the answers to their problems inside them.
- The key to understanding and correcting a person's attitudes and actions lies somewhere in that person's past.
- Individuals' problems are the result of what someone else has done to them.
- Human problems can be purely psychological in nature, unrelated to any spiritual or physical condition.
- Deep-seated problems can be solved only by professional counselors using therapy.
- Scripture, prayer, and the Holy Spirit are inadequate and simplistic resources for solving certain types of problems.

Those and other similar godless theories have filtered down into the church from the assorted stuff in the psychological tank and are having a profound and disturbing effect on its approach to helping people. Many sincere Christians are seriously off track in their understanding of what counseling is and what it is supposed to accomplish.

Some basic reminders might be helpful. For example, Scripture is the only reliable manual for true soul-study. It is so comprehensive in the diagnosis and treatment of every spiritual matter that, energized by the Holy Spirit in the believer, it leads to making one like Jesus Christ. This is the process of biblical sanctification. It is the goal of biblical counseling.

The Puritans, by the way, referred to the counseling ministry as "soul work." They spoke of the minister's responsibility as "the cure of souls." They understood that the only reliable help for the human soul is the infallible truth of Scripture applied by the Spirit of God. They knew that the only genuine, effective, or permanent cure for the soul's maladies is the transformation wrought by God's grace in the heart of a believer.

ARE PSYCHOLOGICAL TECHNIQUES EVER ADVISABLE?

Does that mean the modern behavioral sciences offer nothing of value in treating emotional or behavioral problems? Do not medication, shock therapy, group therapy, and other techniques help in some cases? Are not some soul-sicknesses actually medical problems that should be treated by skilled psychiatrists?

Certainly, it is reasonable for people to seek medical help for medical problems. We would send someone to the doctor for a broken leg, dysfunctional kidney, tooth cavity, or other physical malady. And it is true that certain kinds of depression actually have physical causes requiring medical treatment. D. Martyn Lloyd-Jones, best known for his powerful expository preaching ministry, was actually trained as a physician. He pointed out that depression and certain mental illnesses often have causes that are physical rather than spiritual. Pernicious anemia, arteriosclerosis, porphyria, and even gout are all examples Lloyd-Jones suggested of physical diseases that can cause dementia or produce depression.[6] It is entirely appropriate, even advisable, for the counselor to advise the counselee suffering from such symptoms to seek medical advice or get a thorough physical examination to rule out such causes.

It is also sensible for someone who is alcoholic, drug addicted, learning disabled, traumatized by rape, incest, or severe battering, to seek help in trying to cope with their trauma. Some kinds of therapy or medical treatment can serve to lessen trauma or dependency. In extreme situations medication might be needed to stabilize an otherwise dangerous person.

It must be noted that these are relatively rare problems, however, and should not be used as examples to justify the indiscriminate use of secular psychological techniques for essentially spiritual problems. Dealing with the psychological and emotional issues of life in such ways is *not* sanctification. That is why such techniques are equally effective in modifying behavior in both Christians and non-Christians.

WHAT ABOUT "CHRISTIAN PSYCHOLOGY"?

"Christian psychology" as the term is used today is an oxymoron. The word *psychology* employed in that expression no longer speaks of studying the soul; instead, it describes a diverse menagerie of therapies and theories that are fundamentally humanistic. The presuppositions and most of the doctrine of psychology cannot be successfully integrated with Christian truth.[7] Moreover, the infusion of psychology into the teaching of the church has blurred the line between behavior modification and sanctification.

The path to wholeness is the path of spiritual sanctification. Would we foolishly turn our backs on the Wonderful Counselor, the spring of living water, for the sensual wisdom of earth and the stagnant water of behaviorism?

Our Lord Jesus reacted in a perfect and holy way to every temptation, trial, and trauma in life, and they were more severe than any human could ever suffer. Therefore, it should be clear that perfect victory over all life's troubles must be the result of being like Christ. No "soul worker" can lift another above the level of spiritual maturity he is on. So the supreme qualification for all soul-work is Christlikeness.

The truly Christian counselor must be doing soul work in the realm of the deep things of the Word and the Spirit, not fooling around in the shallows of behavior modification. Why should believers choose to do behavior modification when we have the tools for spiritual transformation (like a surgeon wreaking havoc with a butter knife instead of using a scalpel)? The most skilled counselor is the one who most carefully, prayerfully, and faithfully applies the divine spiritual resources to the process of sanctification, shaping another into the image of Jesus Christ.

There may be no more serious threat to the life of the church today than the stampede to embrace the doctrines of secular psychology. They are a mass of human ideas that Satan has placed in the church as if they were powerful, life-changing truths from God. Most psychologists epitomize neo-gnosticism, claiming to have secret knowledge for solving people's real problems. Though many psychologists call their techniques "Christian counseling," most of them are merely using secular theory to treat spiritual problems with biblical references tacked on.[8]

Unfortunately, such thinking dominates most of the counseling theories that have pervaded contemporary evangelicalism. The distressing result is that pastors, biblical scholars, teachers of Scripture, and caring believers using the Word of God have been made to feel they are not qualified to counsel people.

That very opinion is often at the heart of the message conveyed in some of the most widely read textbooks on Christian counseling. One best-seller claims that Christian counselors who believe the Bible is a sufficient guide for counseling are frequently guilty of "a nonthinking and simplistic understanding of life and its problems."[9] Thus those who attempt to limit their counsel to the questions Scripture answers are disdained as naive, superficial, and altogether inadequate counselors.

The literature of Christian psychology commonly belittles Bible reading and prayer as pat answers or incomplete solutions for someone struggling with depression or anxiety. Scripture, the Holy Spirit, Christ, prayer, and grace—these are the traditional solutions Christian counselors have pointed people to. But Christian psychology now tells us that none of them *really* offers the cure for people's woes.

In fact, many would have us believe that secular psychology can help people *more* effectively than the counselor armed only with spiritual weapons. The same popular Christian bestseller I quoted above claims the church "promote superficial adjustments while psychotherapists, with or without biblical foundations, . . . do a better job than the church of restoring troubled people to more effective functioning."[10] Later, that same author adds, "Secularists sometimes seem to have a corner on honestly facing the disturbing complexity of life while Christians recite clichés that push away real questions of the heart. As a result, nonbelievers often help people with emotional problems more effectively than Christians [do]."[11]

HOW SCIENTIFIC ARE THE BEHAVIORAL SCIENCES?

As we noted earlier, psychology is not a uniform body of scientific knowledge like thermodynamics or organic chemistry. When we speak of psychology, we refer to a complex menagerie of ideas and theories, many of which are contradictory. Psychology has not even proved capable of dealing effectively with the human mind and with mental and emotional processes. Thus it can hardly be regarded as a science. Karl Kraus, a Viennese journalist, made this perceptive comment: "Despite its deceptive terminology, psychoanalysis is not a science but a religion—the faith of a generation incapable of any other."[12]

Most advocates of psychology simply assume that psychology is a true science.[13] But it is not. It is a pseudo-science, the most recent of several human inventions designed to explain, diagnose, and treat behavioral problems without dealing with moral and spiritual issues. Little more than a century ago debate was raging over a different kind of behavioral science called phrenology. Phrenology held that personality characteristics were determined by the shape of someone's skull. You have probably seen old phrenologists' diagrams; they were maps of the head with specific areas labeled, showing which zone of the brain determined a particular emotion or characteristic. A phrenologist would feel people's skulls, diagnosing their problems by the location of bumps on their head.

If you think behavioral science has advanced greatly since then, ask yourself how reasonable it is to surround an adult in the fetal position with pillows so he can get back in touch with his prenatal anxieties. Or consider the type of treatment suggested by those who advocate primal scream therapy, a methodology that teaches people to let out their frustrations by screaming mindlessly at the top of their lungs.[14] Combine that idea with group therapy and imagine the result! Group members hold hands and shriek at each other to work out their problems. Believe it or not, some psychologists are already using precisely that form of therapy, and arguing that it is the most dramatically effective treatment psychology has yet discovered![15] Given the choice, I believe I would opt for a phrenologist poking around on my head!

Jay Adams quoted a paper written for a Harvard symposium more than twenty-five years ago. The author of the paper raised the question, "Where will psychoanalysis be even 25 years from now?" His bold prediction was: "It will take its place along with phrenology and mesmerism."[16] Unfortunately, the prediction proved overly optimistic. And strangely enough, psychology seems to owe its survival to an unholy alliance between the church and popular culture.

At about the same time the church was becoming infatuated with behavioral science, those who knew psychology best were beginning to voice aloud the question of whether it was a science at all. Eleven years ago, *Time* magazine ran a cover story called "Psychiatry on the Couch." It said this:

> On every front, psychiatry seems to be on the defensive. . . . Many psychiatrists want to abandon treatment of ordinary, everyday neurotics ("the worried well") to psychologists and the amateur Pop therapists. After all, does it take a hard-won M.D. degree . . . to chat sympathetically and tell a patient you're-much-too-hard-on-yourself? And if psychiatry is a medical treatment, why can its practitioners not provide measurable scientific results like those obtained by other doctors?
>
> Psychiatrists themselves acknowledge that their profession often smacks of modern alchemy full of jargon, obfuscation and mystification, but precious little real knowledge. . . .
>
> As always, psychiatrists are their own severest critics. Thomas Szasz, long the most outspoken gadfly of his profession, insists that there is really no such thing as mental illness, only normal problems of

living. E. Fuller Torrey, another antipsychiatry psychiatrist, is willing to concede that there are a few brain diseases, like schizophrenia, but says they can be treated with only a handful of drugs that could be administered by general practitioners or internists. . . . By contrast, the Scottish psychiatrist and poet R. D. Laing is sure that schizophrenia is real and that it is good for you. Explains Laing: it is a kind of psychedelic epiphany, far superior to normal experience.

Even mainline practitioners are uncertain that psychiatry can tell the insane from the sane.[17]

The article went on to chronicle the failures of psychiatry, noting that "of all patients, one-third are eventually 'cured,' one-third are helped somewhat, and one-third are not helped at all."[18] But as the article further stated,

The trouble is that most therapies, including some outlandish ones, also claim some improvement for two-thirds of their patients. Critics argue that many patients go into analysis after a traumatic experience, such as divorce or a loved one's death, and are bound to do better anyway when the shock wears off. One study shows improvement for people merely on a waiting list for psychoanalytic treatment; presumably the simple decision to seek treatment is helpful.[19]

The article concludes with a pessimistic forecast by Ross Baldessarini, a psychiatrist and biochemist at the Mailman Research Center. He told *Time,* "We are not going to find the causes and cures of mental illness in the foreseeable future."[20]

Several years later, a conference in Phoenix, Arizona, brought together the world's leading experts on psychotherapy for what was billed as the largest meeting ever on the subject. The conference, called "The Evolution of Psychotherapy," drew seven thousand mental-health experts from all over the world. It was the largest such gathering in history, billed by its organizer as the Woodstock of psychotherapy. Out of it came several stunning revelations.

The Los Angeles Times, for example, quoted Laing, who "said that he couldn't think of any fundamental insight into human relations that has resulted from a century of psychotherapy. 'I don't think we've gone beyond Socrates, Shakespeare, Tolstoy, or even Flaubert by the age of 15.'"[21] Laing added,

"I don't think psychiatry is a science at all. It's not like chemistry or physics where we build up a body of knowledge and progress."

He said that in his current personal struggle with depression, humming a favorite tune to himself (he favors one called "Keep Right On to the End of the Road") sometimes is of greater help than anything psychotherapy offers.[22]

Time magazine, reporting on the conference, noted that in a panel discussion on schizophrenia, three out of four experts said there is no such disease.[23]

> R. D. Laing, the favorite shrink of student rebels in the '60s, retains his romantic opinion of schizophrenics as brave victims who are defying a cruel culture. He suggested that many people are diagnosed as schizophrenic simply because they sleep during the day and stay awake at night. Schizophrenia did not exist until the word was invented, he said. . . . At a later panel, a woman in the audience asked Laing how he would deal with schizophrenics. Laing bobbed and weaved for 27 minutes and finally offered the only treatment possible for people he does not view as sick: "I treat them exactly the same way I treat anybody else. I conduct myself by the ordinary rules of courtesy and politeness."[24]

One truth came out clearly in the conference: among therapists there is little agreement. There is no unified science of psychotherapy, only a cacophony of clashing theories and therapies. Dr. Joseph Wolpe, a leading pioneer of behavioral therapy, characterized the Phoenix conference as "a babel of conflicting voices."[25]

And indeed it was. One specialist, Jay Haley, described what he called his "shaggy dog" technique. Evidently he means it is like a fluffy animal that appears to be fat until it gets wet; there seems to be more substance than really exists. This is his approach to therapy:

> Get the patient to make an absolute commitment to change, then guarantee a cure but do not tell the patient what it is for several weeks. "Once you postpone, you never lose them as patients," he said. "They have to find out what the cure is." One bulimic who ate in binges and threw up five to 25 times a day was told she would be cured if she gave the therapist a penny the first time she vomited and doubled the sum each time she threw up. Says Haley: "They quickly figure out that it doubles so fast that they can owe the therapist hundreds of thousands of dollars in a few days, so they stop."[26]

Jeffrey Zeig, organizer of the conference, said there may be as many as a hundred different theories in the United States alone. Most of them, he said, are "doomed to fizzle."[27]

Not only do psychologists sell supposed cures for a high price, but they also invent diseases for which the cures are needed. Their marketing strategy has been effective. Invent problems or difficulties, harp on them until people think they are hopelessly afflicted, then peddle a remedy. Some of the supposed problems of our culture are pathetically trite: self-image, looks, co-dependency, emotional abuse, mid-life crisis, and unfulfilled expectations.

Today's "infirmities" were once seen more accurately as the pains of self-ishness. Egocentricity has become a major market strategy for psychotherapists. By fostering people's natural tendency toward self-indulgence, psychology has sold itself to an eager public. And the church has witlessly jumped on the bandwagon.

Psychology is no more a science than the atheistic evolutionary theory upon which it is based. Like theistic evolution, "Christian psychology" is an attempt to harmonize two inherently contradictory systems of thought. Modern psychology and the Bible cannot be blended without serious compromise to or utter abandonment of the principle of Scripture's sufficiency.

Though it has become a lucrative business, psychotherapy cannot solve anyone's spiritual problems. At best it can occasionally use human insight to superficially modify behavior. It succeeds or fails for Christians and non-Christians equally because it is only a temporal adjustment, a sort of mental chiropractic. It cannot change the human heart, and even the experts admit that.

THE FAILURE OF CHRISTIAN PSYCHOLOGY

Meanwhile, however, the attitude within the church is more accepting of psychotherapy than ever. If the Christian media serve as a barometer of the whole church, a dramatic shift is taking place. Christian radio, for example, once a bastion of Bible teaching and Christian music, is overrun with talk shows, pop psychology, and phone-in psychotherapy. Preaching the Bible is passé. Psychologists and radio counselors are the new heroes of evangelicalism. And Christian radio is the major advertising tool for the selling of psychology, which is pulling in money by the billions.

The church is thereby ingesting heavy doses of dogma from psychology, adopting secular wisdom, and attempting to sanctify it by calling it Christian. Evangelicalism's most fundamental values are thus being redefined. "Mental and emotional health" is the new buzzword. It is not a biblical concept, though many seem to equate it with spiritual wholeness. Sin is called sickness, so people think it requires therapy, not repentance. Habitual sin is called addictive or compulsive behavior, and many surmise its solution is medical care rather than moral correction.[28]

Human therapies are embraced most eagerly by the spiritually weak, those who are shallow or ignorant of biblical truth and who are unwilling to accept the path of suffering that leads to spiritual maturity and deeper communion with God. The unfortunate effect is that these people remain immature, held back by a self-imposed dependence on some pseudo-Christian method or psycho-quackery that actually stifles real growth.

The more secular psychology influences the church, the further people move from a biblical perspective on problems and solutions. One-on-one therapists are replacing the Bible, God's chief means of sanctifying grace

(John 15:3; 1 Cor. 1:21; Heb. 4:12). The counsel these professionals dispense is often spiritually disastrous. Not long ago, I listened aghast as a Christian psychologist on live radio counseled a caller to express anger at his therapist by making an obscene gesture at him. "Go ahead!" he told the caller. "It's an honest expression of your feelings. Don't try to keep your anger inside."

"What about my friends?" the caller asked. "Should I react that way to all of them when I'm angry?"

"Why, sure!" this counselor said. "You can do it to anyone, whenever you feel like it. Except those who you think won't understand—they won't be good therapists for you." That is a paraphrase. I have a tape of the entire broadcast, and what the counselor actually suggested was much more explicit, even to the point of being inappropriate to print.

That same week, I heard another popular Christian broadcast that offers live counseling to callers nationwide. A woman called and said she had had a problem with compulsive fornication for years. She said she went to bed with "anyone and everyone" and felt powerless to change her behavior.

The counselor suggested that her conduct was her way of striking back, a result of wounds inflicted by her passive father and overbearing mother. "There's no simple road to recovery," this radio therapist told her. "Your problem won't go away immediately—it's an addiction, and these things require extended counseling. You will need years of therapy to overcome your need for illicit sex." The suggestion was then made for the caller to find a church that would be tolerant while she worked her way out of the "painful wounds" that were "making" her fornicate.

What kind of advice is that? First, the counselor in effect gave that woman permission to defer obedience to a clear command of Scripture: "Flee immorality" (1 Cor. 6:18; see also 1 Thess. 4:3). Second, he blamed her parents and justified her vengeance toward them. Third, he seemed to be suggesting she could taper off gradually from her sin, under therapy, of course.

Furthermore, he gave his nationwide audience the clear message that he has no real confidence in the Holy Spirit's power to immediately transform a person's heart and behavior. Worse, he encouraged churches to tolerate a person's sexual sin until therapy begins to work.

Contrast both of those radio counselors' advice with the profound simplicity of Galatians 5:16: "Walk by the Spirit, and you will not carry out the desire of the flesh." Do we really think years of therapy can bring people to the point where they walk by the Spirit? Certainly not if the therapist is someone who recommends obscene gestures, delayed repentance, and churches tolerant of chronic immorality! There is no biblical justification for such counsel; in fact, it flatly contradicts God's Word. The apostle Paul told the Corinthian church to turn an adulterer over to Satan, putting him out of the church (1 Corinthians 5).

I thank God for men and women in the church who depend on the Bible when counseling others. I am grateful for godly counselors who urge troubled people to pray and who point them to Scripture, to God, and to the fullness of His resources for every need.

I have no quarrel with those who use either common sense or social sciences as a helpful observer's platform to look on human conduct and develop tools to assist people in getting some external controls in their behavior. That may be useful as a first step for getting to the real spiritual cure. But a wise counselor realizes that all behavioral therapy stops on the surface, far short of actual solutions to the real needs of the soul, which are resolved only in Christ.

On the other hand, I have no tolerance for those who exalt psychology above Scripture, intercession, and the perfect sufficiency of our God. And I have no encouragement for people who wish to mix psychology with the divine resources and sell the mixture as a spiritual elixir. Their methodology amounts to a tacit admission that what God has given us in Christ is not really adequate to meet our deepest needs and salve our troubled lives.

God Himself does not think very highly of counselors who claim to represent Him but rely instead on human wisdom. Job 12:17–20 says:

> He makes counselors walk barefoot [a sign of humiliation],
> And makes fools of judges.
> He loosens the bond of kings,
> And binds their loins with a girdle.
> He makes priests walk barefoot,
> And overthrows the secure ones.
> He deprives the trusted ones of speech,
> And takes away the discernment of the elders.

God's wisdom is so vastly superior to man's that the greatest human counselors are made into a spectacle. Verses 24–25 add,

> He deprives of intelligence the chiefs of the earth's people,
> And makes them wander in a pathless waste.
> They grope in darkness with no light,
> And He makes them stagger like a drunken man.

If anyone had to endure the folly of well-intentioned human counselors it was Job. Their irrelevant, useless advice was as much a grief to him as the satanic afflictions he suffered.

The depth to which sanctified psychotherapy can sink is really quite profound. A local newspaper recently featured an article about a thirty-four-bed clinic that has opened up in Southern California to treat "Christian sex addicts."[29] (The reason for beds in this kind of clinic escapes me.) According to the article, the clinic is affiliated with a large and well-known Protestant church in the area. Its staff comprises specialists described as "real pioneers in the area [of sexual addictions]. These are all legitimate, licensed psychotherapists who happen to have a strong Christian orientation to therapy," according to the center's director.[30]

Does their "Christian" orientation happen to be solid enough to allow these psychotherapists to admit that lasciviousness is sin? Evidently not. Several were interviewed for the article. They consistently used the terms *illness, problem, conflict,* and *compulsive behavior, treatment,* and *therapy.* Words with moral overtones were carefully avoided. Sin and repentance were never mentioned.

Worse, these so-called experts scoffed at the power of God's Word to transform a heart and break the bondage of sexual sin. The article quoted the center's program director, who explained why he believes his treatment center specifically for Christians is so crucial: "There are some groups of Christians who believe the Bible is all you need."[31]

That statement is the echo of neo-gnosticism. Belittling those who believe the Bible is sufficient, these latter-day "clouds without water" (Jude 12) insist that they are privy to a higher, more sophisticated secret knowledge that holds the real answer to what troubles the human soul. Do not be intimidated by their false claims. No higher knowledge, no hidden truth, nothing besides the all-sufficient resources that we find in Christ exists that can change the human heart.

The church must recover her confidence in the spiritual resources God provides. We must return to the conviction that Scripture alone is "inspired by God and profitable for teaching, for reproof, for correction, for training in righteousness" (2 Tim. 3:16). I am convinced that far more is at stake than the average Christian realizes. If evangelicals do not rediscover biblical counseling and reinstate God's Word to its rightful place as the supreme discerner and mender of the thoughts and intents of the heart (see Heb. 4:12), we will lose our testimony to the world, and the church itself will die. These matters are that critical.

2

Biblical Counseling in Recent Times

David Powlison

Happily, in the past thirty-five years the church of Jesus Christ has rediscovered biblical counseling. Now in order to rediscover something, it must have been lost. How was biblical counseling lost in the church? In order to understand how this happened we need to turn back the pages of history.

English-speaking believers have a long history of case-wise pastoral care. Many of the greatest Protestant writings are marked by an ability to bring Scripture to bear sensitively on varied "cases"; Thomas Brooks' *Precious Remedies Against Satan's Devices,* Richard Baxter's *A Christian Directory,* John Bunyan's *The Pilgrim's Progress,* and Jonathan Edwards' *A Treatise Concerning Religious Affections* all stand out. Each of these pastoral writers had God's burning concern for doctrinal correctness, moral uprightness, a disciplined devotional life, and Christian service. But these pastors also possessed a rich measure of the Shepherd's discerning love: not only did they know people intimately, but they had a feel for the road of progressive sanctification.[1]

Edwards' classic is almost 250 years old, the others more than 300 years old; so, identifiable biblical counseling could be found well into the 1800s. Jay Adams cited Ichabod Spencer as "a sample of one sort of pastoral counseling that was done by a Presbyterian preacher prior to the near capitulation of the Christian ministry to psychiatry. In his *Sketches,* Spencer discussed a large variety of problems and how he handled them."[2] Spencer wrote in the 1850s, but the well of biblical counseling wisdom that had been trickling for years gradually went dry in subsequent decades.

In the nineteenth and twentieth centuries, American Christians basically lost the use of truths and skills they formerly possessed. That is, practical wisdom in the cure of souls waned, even while the conservative church, by definition, retained its grasp upon orthodox doctrine, biblical moral absolutes, the spiritual disciplines, and the missionary calling. The church lost that crucial component of pastoral skill that can be called *case-wisdom:* wisdom that knows people, knows how people change, and knows how to help people change. A shepherd's skill is an *applied* art and science; it is a form of love that abounds in knowledge and discernment in working with people. Yet this ability to apply truth to specific "cases" atrophied. In fact, by the early twentieth century, liberal theology and secular psychology were ascendant in the counseling domain.[3] Only dim echoes and shadows of former wisdom could be heard and seen among conservative Christians.[4]

Instead, secular psychologies claimed the turf of counseling expertise and of insight into human nature. Conservative Christians may have retained parts of Jonathan Edwards' formal theology, but psychologist William James was heir to Edwards' style of careful observation and reflection.[5] The Christians took the Bible, and the psychologists took people; not a happy situation for needy people in either camp! The growing edge of pastoral care occurred not among ministers of the gospel of Jesus but among ministers of a secular or liberal gospel. Freud's psychoanalysis and other nascent psychotherapies were adapted to shepherd a people without the Shepherd: the mental hygiene movement, Harry Emerson Fosdick's pulpit, and Carl Rogers' therapeutic gospel of self are landmarks in the first half of the twentieth century.

The psychologies not only claimed the turf of counseling; they made good their claim. Sociologist Philip Rieff accurately titled his book on twentieth-century America *The Triumph of the Therapeutic* and noted astutely, "Religious man was born to be saved; psychological man is born to be pleased. . . . If the therapeutic is to win out, then surely the psychotherapist will be his secular spiritual guide."[6] Rieff nostalgically mourned the death of Christian culture, but he was a modern man making do, not a prophet calling people back to the living God.[7] The goals, the truths, the methods, even the possibility of biblical counseling vanished in the psychological revolution. In fact, biblical counseling not only disappeared, it became unthinkable.

By the mid-1960s when biblical counseling was rediscovered, it emerged as an alien discipline in the midst of three psychologized communities. The cultural setting of the activity called counseling or psychotherapy could be likened to three nested circles whose differences, even sharp differences, occurred within a fundamental consensus. The huge and dominating outer circle was secular psychology. Within this circle the pioneering theory-builders, the university graduate and undergraduate programs, the credentials, the mental health system, the journals, and the books set the intellectual and methodological pace. The middle circle consisted of liberal pastoral theology, which defined the field of pastoral counseling, even in conservative seminaries. The smallest circle contained professing believers who were psychologists and therapists.

The larger circle dominated the intellectual agenda and therapeutic methods of the two lesser circles. Thus, religious counselors joined clinical psychologists, social workers, guidance counselors, and psychiatric nurses in a vast army of practitioners within the "enlisted" ranks of the cure-of-souls professions. The "officers" were the psychiatrists and personality theorists who provided cognitive content and philosophical rationale for the mental health endeavor. Anyone who wanted to talk about counseling, or read counseling, or join an association of counselors, or go to school in counseling, or do counseling, did it somewhere within the big circle. Biblical counseling emerged as a stranger in a foreign land.

Secular psychology dominated counseling, defining discourse about people and their problems. The social, behavioral, and medical sciences attained enormous social power, intellectual prestige, and self-confidence. As a result, the entire practice of counseling in the twentieth century became encircled by and permeated with secular versions of how to understand and help people. Various forms of psychotherapy—secular pastoral work— overwhelmed the biblical cure of souls; various theoretical psychologies— secular theologies—overwhelmed biblical understandings of human nature and functioning; various therapeutic institutions—secular church communities—overwhelmed the church as the primary location for helping people with their troubles.

The most perceptive psychologists recognized and frankly stated what they were doing. Even Freud, contrary to most of his disciples, denied that the psychoanalyst's role was a distinctly medical role. He stated that the psychoanalyst was a "secular pastoral worker" and need not be a doctor.[8] For example, Freud's noted disciple Erik Erikson had his professional training in art! Carl Jung commented in similar fashion, "Patients force the psychotherapist into the role of a priest, and expect and demand of him that he shall free them from their distress. That is why we psychotherapists must occupy ourselves with problems which, strictly speaking, belong to the theologian."[9] B. F. Skinner's *Walden Two* consciously and specifically offered substitutes for the truths, techniques, and institutions of the Christian faith. In fact, behavioral psychologists are the priest-equivalents in Skinner's heaven on earth.[10] The big circle of secular psychology posited a secular universe. The leading psychologists and psychiatrists were secular people who wanted to help secular people. It is no surprise that they offered a substitute religion, because the problems they dealt with were fundamentally religious.[11]

Unfortunately, the liberal churches were wedded to this psychotherapeutic revolution from its beginning; thus the development of the second circle, liberal pastoral theology. In their abandonment of biblical truth and authority, leaders within these churches looked to the social sciences to provide authority and efficacy. Harry Emerson Fosdick, whose theological liberalism was one trip wire for the fundamentalist-modernist splits of the 1920s, was, not by coincidence, simultaneously a leader in the mental hygiene movement. Using his pulpit to expound a new psychotherapeutic version of Christianity, his psychologism was the flip side of his unbelief in the "fundamentals." The very idea of pastoral counseling was defined by liberal theology's integration of secular psychologists, especially Carl Rogers and Alfred Adler, from World War I into the 1960s.

In general, conservative Christians simply did not talk or write about counseling.[12] And when they did begin to think about and practice counseling, they adopted the powerful paradigms of the encircling secular psychologies and liberal pastoral theologies. The presuppositions for both practice and thought were neither exposed by nor subjected to biblical analysis. There was no attempt to build a biblical practical theology of counseling from the ground up. The big circle of secular psychology and psychotherapy was always the dominant partner in the discussions. Meanwhile, the middle-sized circle, an implicitly or explicitly liberal theology, was always tugging at evangelical thought and practice. Fuller Theological Seminary's Graduate School of Psychology (founded in 1965) exemplified the hold secular and liberalizing paradigms had on professing Bible-believers.[13]

The Rediscovery of Biblical Counseling

Godly people, wise and experienced in living the Word, have applied God's Word to the problems of life in all times and places. In this sense, wherever wise Christians have sought to encourage and admonish one another, biblical counseling has occurred. Although truths that are not systematized are jeopardized, it is to God's praise that informal wisdom has always operated. God has always enabled wise pastors to approach their people with love and patience, and to open their Bibles to the right places to "comfort the disturbed and disturb the comfortable." In spite of the fact that the systematic approaches to counseling recorded in books and taught in classrooms during the twentieth century have not been biblically based, there has been a rediscovery of biblical counseling. From the human point of view, that rediscovery is linked primarily to the life and efforts of one man: Jay E. Adams. He began to see, discuss, and do counseling in ways that he and others had not been seeing, discussing, or doing previously.

Jay Adams (born 1929) grew up in Baltimore, the only child of a policeman and a secretary. Converted to Christ in high school, he obtained a Bachelor of Divinity from Reformed Episcopal Seminary (Philadelphia) and a Bachelor of Arts in classics from Johns Hopkins University (Baltimore) in 1952. Adams served as an area director of Youth for Christ in the early 1950s, was ordained in 1952, and over the next thirteen years pastored several Presbyterian congregations. He also received a Masters in Sacred Theology from Temple University (Philadelphia) in 1958 and a Ph.D. in speech from the University of Missouri in 1969. Bible, theology, Greek, and preaching formed the heart of his education. But as a pastor, the problems of people's lives continually troubled and weighed on him. "It bothered Jay so much during those years that he never could help people with their problems. He'd say, 'Psychology is just as bad as the liberals. It isn't right and doesn't work. But how do you really help people?'"[14]

Adams continually sought to upgrade his counseling skills. He read voraciously from all three circles of counseling: the leading twentieth-century psychologists, the standard works in pastoral counseling (which mediated Carl Rogers through liberal or neo-orthodox theology), and Clyde Narramore and other evangelicals who had begun to publish from either a Freudian or an eclectic point of view. While at Temple, he took two courses in counseling with a psychiatrist of Freudian bent.[15] Adams was disappointed and frustrated with this training. Indeed, he felt it was full of theory-driven speculations, was ineffective in practice, and was contrary to basic biblical truths. The approaches offered did not make sense of people, they did not help people, and they were overtly unbiblical. He had no coherent alternative, but muddled along doing what little he could in pastoral counseling situations. Workshops for pastors, which were regularly sponsored by mental health agencies, reiterated the litany that the pastor should not attempt much but should "defer and refer" to secular mental health experts. The bottom line message to pastors was, "Leave things to the professionals. There is little you can do besides provide an accepting atmosphere for people. Troubled people are not violators of conscience but morally neutral victims of an accusing conscience. They need professional help. Pastors shouldn't do more than refer."[16] Such propaganda was intimidating to thousands of conservative pastors.

In 1963, Adams was invited to teach practical theology at Westminster Theological Seminary. His responsibilities focused on preaching, but included a course in pastoral theology that contained a segment on pastoral counseling. This course raised the stakes. What should he teach? Adams happened to hear of psychologist O. Hobart Mowrer and went to hear him speak. That speech, Mowrer's book *The Crisis in Psychiatry and Religion,* (Princeton: Van Nostrand, 1961), and a six-week intensive course with Mowrer that summer had a catalytic effect on Adams. Mowrer "cleared the field of rubble for me. He destroyed Freud, which was the reigning system, and he shook up faith in mental health professionals. His positive system was completely unbiblical, but he gave me the confidence to go forward."[17] Mowrer shook loose the death grip of secular propaganda. This freed Adams to challenge the reigning psychological orthodoxy and to follow his nose biblically. As a result, Adams did intensive Bible study about the conscience, guilt, anthropology, and change. He described the next two years as "night and day, counseling and studying: studying people, studying counseling books, studying the Bible."[18]

Adams' first rough outline of biblical counseling began to emerge during that small segment of the pastoral theology course. At first it was little more than "sin is the problem, the Bible has the answers," incorporating a few case studies. Problems were addressed on an *ad hoc* basis as they arose in counseling or from a study of Scripture. But by 1967 Adams' thinking about counseling had jelled into a system, and he expanded the counseling segment of the theology course into a counseling course. Then when he published his first book in 1970, Adams' personal rediscovery of biblical counseling initiated a widespread rediscovery for the entire church.

Adams has written prolifically to create and develop a system of biblical counseling. He considers four of his books to be basic texts. *Competent to Counsel,* his first book, dropped a bombshell on the conservative Christian world. It was both polemical and positive. The polemics attacked the preeminence of pagan psychology and psychiatry in the field of counseling, and the positive methods set forth an ideal of "nouthetic confrontation."[19] Adams saw the Bible's way of counseling as radically dependent on the work of the Holy Spirit to apply the Word of God to people's lives: the promises encourage and empower, the commands convict and guide, and the stories make application. The Bible calls for human counselors to be frank, loving, humble about their own failings, and change-oriented. They are to be servants of the Holy Spirit's agenda, not autonomous professionals or gurus. In Adams' shorthand, nouthetic counseling is confrontation that is done out of concern for the purposes of changing something God wants to change.[20] That something can involve attitudes, beliefs, behavior, motives, decisions, and so forth.

Adams' second book, *The Christian Counselor's Manual,* fine-tuned the philosophy of biblical counseling and provided counseling methods, including a discussion on how to understand and solve particular problems. A third book, *Lectures on Counseling,* brought together a number of essays on foundational topics, and a fourth book, *More Than Redemption* (republished as *A Theology of Christian Counseling*), expanded the systematic base of biblical counseling.

Throughout his prolific written works, Adams challenged biblical counselors not to fall prey to rigid ways of thinking or to mechanical techniques. He insisted that counselors must do justice both to the fundamental commonalities and to the diverse particulars of counseling situations and life situations.

> "*Insight* into the inner workings of sinful human beings, into their outer circumstances and problems, and into the correct meaning and applicability of appropriate Bible passages is absolutely essential to counseling. Likewise, the importance of *creativity* cannot be minimized. It is creativity that particularizes the common, fitting together the usual and the unusual in each situation. Without it, people are crammed into

molds they don't fit; rather, the truth must be adapted and applied (but not accommodated) to each person as he is."[21]

Not only did Adams write abundant resources for the development of biblical counseling, but he also pioneered settings where biblical counseling was the *modus operandi* and agenda. As noted above, his first rudimentary courses in biblical counseling took place at Westminster Theological Seminary in the mid-1960s. Though Adams left Westminster in 1976 to devote himself to research and writing, the program continued to develop under the leadership of Adams' colleague, John Bettler. A residential Doctor of Ministry in Counseling was begun in 1980 with a dozen courses offered in biblical counseling. When the residential program was replaced by a modular program, most of the courses migrated into the regular Westminster curriculum as electives. A Master of Arts and Religion with a counseling major was begun in 1984.[22]

Adams was concerned for pastors, even more than for students who might one day become pastors. He felt pastors needed a site where counseling was taking place, where they could learn to counsel and then return to their congregations and communities. Thus in 1967, Adams and several associates made plans to develop a counseling center that would offer both counseling and a place for pastors to observe and train. These plans crystallized in 1968 when Adams and John Bettler began the Christian Counseling and Educational Foundation (CCEF) in Hatboro, Pennsylvania. Counseling was offered to needy people, and education was offered to would-be helpers of needy people. During the first course, trainees sat in on counseling sessions during the day and evening and then discussed cases over supper. In 1974, John Bettler became CCEF's director and first full-time employee. As CCEF continued to grow, counseling sites were opened in San Diego, California, and at several places in Pennsylvania and New Jersey. The CCEF faculty currently teaches courses at Westminster Theological Seminary and Biblical Theological Seminary.[23]

As biblical-nouthetic counseling gained adherents, the need for a professional association became evident. Concerns for the growing group of practitioners included certification for biblical counselors, accountability for standards of biblical commitment and ethics, fellowship and interaction among biblical counselors, ongoing in-service training, and protection from lawsuits. To meet these and other needs, Adams joined with several men to found the National Association of Nouthetic Counselors (NANC) in 1976. Today, NANC publishes a quarterly newsletter, *The Biblical Counselor,* and coordinates a large annual conference.[24]

Adams also wanted a forum where ideas could be shared and discussed, and where writers could try their wings. So in 1977 he founded *The Journal of Pastoral Practice,* published through CCEF. As JPP's editor for the next fifteen years, his purpose was to develop a journal that would adhere to scholarly standards but would be "intensely practical" and would meet "the needs of men serving in the pastoral ministry."[25] This journal embodied a unique vision in at least three respects. First, counseling was not isolated from the rest of pastoral practice: preaching, Christian education, missions, worship, and evangelism. The mere act of embedding private ministry in the context of a comprehensive vision counteracts the common vision of counseling as discrete from the rest of the ministry of the Word of God. Second, the counseling articles (and counseling articles always constituted the bulk of the journal's contents) took a distinctively biblical point of view. Third, the journal sought to be practical. It sought to address and influence practice, not simply theology or theory. In 1992 the name of the journal was changed to *The Journal of Biblical Counseling.* The concern to meet the needs of pastors has continued but has broadened to include the needs of trained laypeople who seek to counsel biblically.[26]

Jay Adams, his writings, and the institutions he founded have led to a proliferation of biblical counseling ministries and training centers both in the United States and abroad. For example, a growing ministry for training laypeople grew out of lectures Adams gave in Washington, D.C. (1973) when John Broger, a Christian layman active in ministry in the Pentagon, had a deep concern that discipleship address and solve the counseling issues in people's lives. He took Adams's materials and in 1974 founded the Biblical Counseling Foundation (BCF), which continues to grow as a ministry that trains laypeople and pastors in discipleship methods largely flavored by biblical counseling.[27]

Various local churches have founded biblical counseling ministries, taking many different forms: formal or informal, pastor or lay, focusing on congregational needs or reaching out to the community. Particularly noteworthy is Faith Baptist Church in Lafayette, Indiana. This church has founded a thriving counseling center and built church life around the concepts of progressive sanctification and mutual counsel that are at the heart of biblical counseling. Faith Baptist Counseling Ministries (FBCM) was started in 1977 by Rev. Bill Goode and Dr. Bob Smith. It has grown to offer training throughout the Midwest. Randy Patton is the executive director of NANC, and FBCM has served as the location for the NANC offices. Faith Baptist Church has hosted the NANC national conference several times in recent years.[28]

The biblical counseling agenda has also become established in The Master's College (www.masters.edu) and The Master's Seminary (www.tms.edu) in California. In the late 1980s, John MacArthur and his co-laborers turned their attention closely to the issues of biblical counseling and secular psychology. They restructured the curriculum at both undergraduate and seminary levels to reflect a commitment to use biblical truth to explain people's needs and to offer them help. Two of Jay Adams' longstanding associates, Bob Smith (from FBCM) and Wayne Mack (from CCEF) have been instrumental in designing and building the program.[29]

The notion of doing distinctively biblical counseling has also been planted in a number of countries around the world. Whenever and wherever Christians counsel wisely in obedience to the Scriptures, biblical counseling happens, whether it is so titled or not. But it is a great advantage to identify self-consciously what one aims to do and to rally like-minded believers to the cause. For this reason, there are nascent biblical counseling movements in Germany, Switzerland, Great Britain, and South Africa, taking the form of associations and/or counseling and training centers.

QUESTIONS FOR THE TWENTY-FIRST CENTURY

One of the results of tracing the rediscovery of biblical counseling has been the challenge to think towards the future. Church history bears testimony to the uncertain fortunes of ministries and movements. Some thrive. Some miscarry early on. Some grow, then collapse. Some prosper awhile and then stagnate. Some go soft and drift into compromise. Some go the other way, becoming sectarian and self-righteous. Some are renewed when things look bleak. Some go off the tracks into error or irrelevancy. How can biblical counseling continue to grow in wisdom and stature as it faces the challenges of the future? Without doubt, the biblical counseling movement faces three fundamental tasks at the beginning of the twernty-first century: (1) the task of defining, (2) the task of edifying, and (3) the task of evangelizing.

The Task of Defining

How will biblical counseling be defined? A creedal circle needs to be drawn delineating the boundaries of a biblical counseling confession of faith and practice. What commitments and practices mark one as a biblical counselor? What commitments and practices mark one as some other sort of counselor? Why does this next decade demand creedal development? Defining the boundaries is important for three reasons.

First, through the first twenty-five years of development, Jay Adams's personal influence and his network of friendships provided a rough guide to the definition of biblical counseling. But the movement is growing rapidly, and the next generation will not necessarily know Jay Adams personally. The content of an allegiance to the biblical counseling vision and cause must be more precisely defined. Creedal definition and consolidation is a necessary phase of any healthy movement of reformation in the church.

Second, the integration movement of Christian psychotherapists increasingly employs the adjective "biblical" and calls for theological renewal within their point of view. While we applaud any genuine increase of biblical consciousness and practice among integrationists, it remains to be seen whether the increase in Bible talk, God talk, and Jesus talk represents a substantive shift. In the meantime, the higher degree of verbal similarity between integrationist and biblical counseling has the potential to confuse many. Defining core biblical commitments will help weed out the theories and practices that claim to be biblical but deviate substantively from the Bible's teachings about people, about change, and about ministry.

Third, the biblical counseling movement from the beginning has pulled together an otherwise diverse group of Christians. We have never been monolithic, but have embraced Bible-believers of many shades: reformed, fundamentalist, and evangelical. The founders and developers of biblical counseling have held diverse opinions on many specific counseling issues, as well as wider theological issues. What has held the movement together has been the judgment that these differences were secondary differences of application or emphasis, not matters of core commitment. Nailing down the primary areas of agreement becomes increasingly important as the movement expands. One way to phrase the boundary question is, "What is the size of the teapot within which there are allowable tempests?" Defining primary areas of agreement creates the freedom for the iron-sharpening-iron discussion of differences. The alternatives are either fragmentation or drift.

What are the common commitments? What are the rudiments of biblical counseling? Every reader of the Scriptures and of Adams's efforts to systematize the Scriptures would generate a slightly different list. Here we will highlight seven core elements that Adams rediscovered, articulated, and defended.

1. God is at the center of counseling. God is sovereign, active, speaking, merciful, commanding, and powerful. The Lord and Savior, Jesus Christ, is the central focus of counseling and the exemplar of the Wonderful Counselor. The Word of God and the work of the Holy Spirit are foundational to all significant and lasting life change. The Word of God is about counseling, giving both understanding of people and methods of ministering to people. The Bible is authoritative, relevant, and comprehensively sufficient for counseling. God has spoken truly to every basic issue of human nature and to the problems in living. His Word establishes the goal of counseling, how people can change, the role of the counselor, counseling methods, and so forth. Christians have the only authoritative source for counseling wisdom: the Holy Spirit speaking through the Word of God. The fear of the Lord is the beginning of wisdom, and wisdom is the only worthy goal of counseling.

2. Commitment to God has epistemological consequences. First, other sources of knowledge must be submitted to the authority of Scripture. The sciences, personal experience, literature, and so forth may be useful, but may not play a constitutive role in counseling. Second, there is a conflict of counsel built into human life. Genesis 3, Psalm 1, and Jeremiah 23 are paradigmatic. Counsel that contradicts God's counsel has existed since the garden of Eden, challenging God's counsel and building from other presuppositions and towards other goals. Such false counsel must be noted and opposed. Specifically, in our time and place, secular psychology has intruded into the domain of biblical truth and practice. Secular theories and therapies substitute for biblical wisdom and deceive people both inside and outside the church. The false claimants to authority must be exposed and opposed.

3. *Sin, in all its dimensions* (for example, both motive and behavior; both the sins we do and the sins done against us; both the consequences of personal sin and the consequences of Adam's sin) *is the primary problem counselors must deal with.* Sin includes wrong behavior, distorted thinking, an orientation to follow personal desires, and bad attitudes. Sin is habitual and deceptive, and much of the difficulty of counseling consists in bringing specific sin to awareness and breaking its hold. The problems in living that necessitate counseling are not matters of unmet psychological needs, indwelling demons of sin, poor socialization, inborn temperament, genetic predisposition, or anything else that removes attention from the responsible human being. The problem in believers is remnant sin; the problem in unbelievers is reigning sin. Sin is the problem.

4. *The gospel of Jesus Christ is the answer.* Forgiveness for sin and power to change into Christ's image are the greatest needs of mankind. The orthodox gospel of Jesus Christ is the answer to the problem. Christ deals with sin: the guilt, the power, the deception, and the misery of sin. He was crucified for sinners, He reigns over hearts by the power of the Holy Spirit, and He will return to complete the redemption of His people from their sins and sufferings. These core truths must infuse the counseling process.

5. *The biblical change process which counseling must aim at is progressive sanctification.* While there are many ways of changing people, biblical counseling aims for nothing less than transformation into the image of Jesus Christ amid the rough and tumble of daily life. Change is not instantaneous, but progresses throughout life. This progressive view of sanctification has many implications. For example, the process of change is only metaphorically, not actually, healing. The metaphor is meant to capture the process of sanctification: ongoing repentance, renewal of mind unto biblical truth, and obedience in the power of the Spirit.

6. *The situational difficulties people face are not the random cause of problems in living.* These difficulties operate within the sovereign design of God. They are the context in which hearts are revealed, and faith and obedience are purified through the battle between the Spirit and the flesh. Influential aspects of one's life situation do not cause sin. Heredity, temperament, personality, culture, oppression and evil, bereavement, handicaps,

old age, Satan, physical illness, and so forth are significant for counseling, but are not ultimately causative of sin.

7. *Counseling is fundamentally a pastoral activity and must be church-based.* It must be regulated under the authority of God's appointed under-shepherds. Counseling is connected both structurally and in content to other aspects of the pastoral task: teaching, preaching, prayer, church discipline, use of gifts, missions, worship, and so forth. Counseling is the private ministry of the Word of God, tailored specifically to the individuals involved. The differences between preaching and counseling are not conceptual but only methodological. The same truths are applied in diverse ways.

These seven commitments have unified the biblical counseling movement. They have provided a framework within which many secondary differences of Bible interpretation, of theological commitment, of setting for counseling, of personality have been able to exist constructively rather than destructively. But there are numerous other issues that demand clear biblical thinking and firm commitment: the place of the past, the place of feelings, the biblical view of human motivation, the relationship of biblical truth to secular psychology, the place of suffering, how to apply various aspects of biblical truth and methods of biblical ministry to different kinds of problems, etc. Will biblical counselors draw the boundaries in the right places? Or will the lines be drawn too narrowly, creating a sectarian party spirit? Or will the lines be drawn too widely, inviting compromise and drift? Only within properly drawn creedal boundaries can energies for edification and evangelization be guided and released.

The Task of Edifying

How will biblical counselors develop greater skill in the cure of souls? How will we become wiser practitioners, thinkers, apologists, and Christian men and women? The task of edifying biblical counselors demands advances that are both exegetically sound and case-tried. It demands that we think well about many issues. One of the often ignored aspects of Jay Adams' work has been his repeated observation that his work is a starting place, and that much work remains to be done to build on the foundation.

Biblical counseling has been rediscovered. But perhaps it is more accurate to say that the *idea* of biblical counseling and the *call* to do biblical counseling have been rediscovered. This has brought into focus many fresh discoveries and new insights into the cure of souls. For example, the concern to specify counseling methodology (such as techniques of asking questions, building relationships, setting goals, speaking the truth, and using homework) has produced helpful developments. And the concern to translate general biblical truths into a specific renewal of both inward and outward life (Rom. 13:12–14), tailor-made both to the counselee and the life situation, is refreshingly new. Will biblical counseling continue to develop intellectually and practically?[30] Or will we stagnate and turn yesterday's breakthroughs into tomorrow's formulaic-truisms and techniques?

The Task of Evangelizing

How will biblical counselors propagate the cause of biblical counseling? The task of persuasion must be undertaken with three distinct groups of people: (1) the great bulk of the believing church, both in the United States and internationally; (2) the integrationist community here in the United States and abroad; and (3) the members of the secular psychological culture. Many people remain ignorant of the existence of biblical counseling, while others dismiss it on the basis of a caricature that bears no resemblance to anything the Bible teaches or anything wise counselors think and do. Biblical counseling needs evangelists and apologists with sensitivities and passions for each of these communities. We have answers people need; answers that are better than those they already have. Biblical counselors must think well, pray pointedly, and discuss actively to develop energetic and creative apologetic and evangelistic efforts to help people find these answers.

3

Why Biblical Counseling and Not Psychology?

John Street

Biblically informed Christians ought to be sanctified skeptics. They should direct a justified cynicism toward any discipline or epistemological scheme that seeks obligatory authority as it relates to counseling of personal problems. A natural antagonism has always existed between biblical counselors and therapeutic practitioners because psychotherapeutic theories have aggressively encroached upon the jurisdiction of soul-care.[1] Christians are fully warranted in casting a wary eye in psychology's direction for its Enlightenment-inspired dismissal of the Bible's veracity and its *carte blanche* rejection of the jurisdictional authority which Scripture claims in the matters of the soul.

For the Christian counselor, the Word of God must be more than an interpretative grid for the acceptance or denial of psychological truth claims; it is the operative domain from which the counselor derives his/her functional and final authority,[2] being accepted as the determinative authority in anthropology. Scripture serves as the only reliable resource for the Christian counselor's diagnostic terminology and remedy. The Word of God possesses the exclusive theoretical framework from which soul-problems can be properly interpreted and resolved.[3] More importantly, it claims exclusive authority in defining the significance of and purpose for the life of man.[4] When placed in juxtaposition with the counsel of man, the comprehensive superiority of the Word is unmistakable. God's purposes in the life of man will prevail. The psalmist stated:

> The LORD nullifies the counsel of the nations;
> He frustrates the plans of the peoples.
> The counsel of the LORD stands forever,
> The plans of His heart from generation to generation.
> (Ps. 33:10–11)

THEOLOGY AND PSYCHOLOGY

The historical distrust and innate hostility between psychology and theology exist because each calls into question the legitimacy of the other's

Weltanschauung.[5] The imperialistic intrusion of the psychotherapeutic into Christianity has attempted to undermine and redefine the supremacy of the Word of God among Christians. Nowhere has its effects been more intrusive and dramatic than in the ministry of the Word in relation to pastoral soul-care.

For over a century, graduate schools and seminaries have trained an army of pastoral students in a variety of psychologies under the label "pastoral counseling." This training often assumed the tenets of some renowned psychologist or psychotherapist, or worse, taught an academic smorgasbord of psychological methods and theories from which the pastor could draw as he saw fit.[6] Some of the most influential, early psychologies in theological graduate schools included the psychoanalysis of Sigmund Freud, the analytical psychology of Carl Jung, the non-directive psychotherapeutic counseling of Carl Rogers, the physiological psychology of the liberal theologian-turned-psychologist G. T. Ladd,[7] and the existential psychology of Søren Kierkegaard. Pastors, trained under these psychologies, influenced an entire generation of parishioners to think and act according to the therapeutic instead of according to the gospel. Even the authorial intent of Scripture was replaced by a psychological hermeneutic that loaded biblical terminology with psychotherapeutic meaning. Where the Bible was not replaced by a psychology, it was redefined by it.

Few psychologists or psychiatrists today claim to follow these older psychologies exclusively. This underscores the fact that psychology is in constant flux and is far from being a mature science. Psychological theories are frequently replacing other psychological theories. In the spirit of German innovationism, academic psychology relentlessly quests for elusive insight, only to resign itself (eventually) to postmodern relativism. Sigmund Koch expressed his frustration with psychology when he wrote:

> The idea that psychology—like the natural sciences on which it is modeled—is cumulative or progressive is simply not borne out by history. Indeed, the hard knowledge gained by one generation typically disenfranchises the theoretical fictions of the last . . . Throughout psychology's history as "science" the *hard* knowledge it has deposited has been uniformly negative.[8]

Nevertheless, Christians continue to be taught the essentials of psychology overtly or inadvertently, in sermons, Sunday school lessons, marriage seminars, self-help books, radio programs, missionary training, and Christian universities. The principles of psychology are presented as though they were on the same authoritative level as Scripture and compete for its jurisdiction as the sole authority in determining the well-being of the soul. Mission organizations persist in using psychological assessment tools,[9] built upon secular normality research of unbelievers' attitudes and opinions, to determine the fitness and potential adjustment of prospective candidates. Furthermore, as

John MacArthur has observed, "Over the past decade a host of evangelical psychological clinics have sprung up. Though almost all of them claim to offer biblical counsel, most merely dispense secular psychology disguised in spiritual terminology."[10] Many Christian colleges, universities, and seminaries have taken their psychology programs and relabeled them "Biblical Counseling Programs," while maintaining an essentially psychological core of subjects. Because of this, Christians have good reason to be skeptical toward any type of counseling that is not thoroughly biblical.

PSYCHOLOGY IN THE BIBLE?

Some believe and even teach that the English term "psychology" is of biblical extraction because of its transliterated Greek original. It is a compound consisting of two Greek words, *psychē* (soul, mind)[11] and *logos* (word, law). The united etymology of this word became *the study or science of the mind or soul.* Actually, this word has closer etymological ties to Classical Greek than to New Testament *Koinē* Greek.[12]

The word "psychology" does not occur in the Bible, even though there are endless eisegetical efforts to discover the presence of its earliest meanings. Reading ideas of modern psychology into the biblical term *psychē* is like equating the contemporary idea of dynamite with the New Testament Greek word *dunamis*.[13] D. A. Carson referred to this as a "semantic anachronism."

> Our word dynamite is etymologically derived from δύναμις (power, or even miracle). I do not know how many times I have heard preachers offer some such rendering of Romans 1:16 as this: "I am not ashamed of the gospel, for it is the dynamite of God unto salvation for everyone who believes"—often with a knowing tilt of the head as if something profound or even esoteric has been uttered. This is not just the old root fallacy revisited. It is worse: it is an appeal to a kind of reverse etymology, the root fallacy compounded by anachronism. Did Paul think dynamite when he penned this word? . . . Dynamite blows things up, tears things down, rips out rock, gouges holes, destroys things.[14]

In the first century, Paul was not thinking of the explosive type of dynamite invented by the Swedish industrialist, Alfred Nobel (A.D. 1833–1896), and patented in 1867. He was thinking of the supernatural salvific ability of God the Father. The tendency to assume a contemporary word meaning and impose it upon a biblical word, often in hopes of claiming a dynamic insight or legitimizing a questionable practice, is a common, misleading ploy of interpreters today. In fact, reading various contemporary meanings back into the inspired text, foreign to the authorial intent, is a treacherous postmodern phenomenon.

Therefore, Scripture's usage of the term *psychē* does not biblically validate the supplemental practice of psychoanalysis in Christian counseling.[15] Nor can overtones of psychoanalytic theory, such as the superego, id and ego, be found latently in this term. Yet, it is not uncommon for Christians, psychologists, and others to read neo-Freudian notions of a layered subconscious into the biblical word, *psychē*.

Furthermore, the typical bifurcation between the soul and the spirit made by some Christian psychologists cannot be biblically sustained. One Christian psychiatrist offered this explanation: "The soul is the psychological aspect of man, whereas the spirit is spiritual. . . . The mind alone lies in the psychological aspect of man and not the spiritual."[16] Such an artificial distinction grows from reading psychological meaning into biblical terms. Both "soul" and "spirit" speak of the same intangible aspect of the inner man, the part of man that only God sees. A concordance study of *psychē* shows that when Scripture uses the term "soul" in relation to man, it refers to that aspect of the inner man *in connection* with his body. When it uses the term "spirit," it is that aspect of the inner man *out of connection* with his body.[17] No distinction exists in Scripture between the psychologically oriented and the spiritually oriented inner man.

The whole of the inner man comes under the dominion of the spiritual. In this arena the Bible reigns not only as a sufficient source for addressing soul-problems, but also as the supreme source. As Agur plainly warned in Proverbs, "Every word of God is tested; / He is a shield to those who take refuge in Him. / Do not add to His words / Lest He reprove you, and you be proved a liar."[18] Importing late twentieth century psychological significance into biblical English (or the original Hebrew, Aramaic, or Greek for that matter) denies the divine intent of its authorship. In fact, anachronistic efforts to legitimize psychotherapeutic practices among Christians by appealing to similar biblical terminology are linguistically fallacious, presumptuous, and misleading.

Using the Bible to justify psychological practices can only be attempted through the broadest of definitions. One author painted his definition with wide strokes before he described the psychological insights he saw in Matthew 5: "But the study of character, the aspects of its well-being, and the change of character for the better seem to be a sort of psychology and psychotherapy in a broad sense of these words."[19] "Broad sense" implies "simple sense," or something lacking the complexity of contemporary psychological research. Christian psychology views Scripture as the "fountainhead of Christian ideas, including psychological ones."[20] In other words, the Bible is good for introductory thoughts and the germination of new ideas, but it is not sufficiently comprehensive to give substantive assistance to the intricacies of serious soul-problems. Scripture, according to so-called Christian psychology, is a primitive catalog of Christian character development and change; psychology and psychotherapy, however, provide exhaustive ideas for refining character and promoting well-being. So the "fountainhead of Christian ideas" merely moistens the palate but does not quench deep thirst. Supposedly, additional psychological canals must irrigate Scripture's trickle of truth if the counselor is to assuage the thirsty soul-problems of life. According to Christian psychology, the Sermon on the Mount has a form of pathology, personality distinctives, and therapeutic involvement, but only in an unsophisticated composition.

While secular psychologists contemptuously dismiss the Bible as an archaic and mistaken psychology, their Christian colleagues desperately labor to prop up its fledgling therapeutic with an apologetic of psychological naivete. Christian psychologists often act embarrassed, like the illegitimate child of its larger, more sophisticated psychological family: the American Psychological Association (APA) and the International Psychoanalytical Association (IPA). Driven by a deep desire to impress its more affluent parents, it ignominiously acknowledges the dangers of total reliance upon the Bible. Organizations such as the Christian Association of Psychological Studies (CAPS), and to a lesser extent, the American Association of Christian Counselors (AACC), have viewed psychology as a supplemental resource to the Bible. As one Christian who functions as a psychologist explained:

> Despite its wealth of information about human beings, their universe, and their God, the Bible is not intended to be a psychology textbook. . . . The Bible does not tell us about . . . the developmental stages of infancy, the fine points of conflict resolution, or the ways to treat dyslexia or paranoia. Psychology focuses on issues like these.[21]

In other words, the biblical text is a shallow and imprecise psychology and must only be seen as the starting gate of a more informed therapeutic. The APA sneers at Christians who are "deluded" with religious myths but finds the myths potentially helpful if the Christian psychologist does not take his Bible too seriously when dealing with them. Trying to keep one foot in the Bible and another in the intrusive discipline of psychology presents a precarious balancing challenge. Those who do not slip from the Christian faith are often torn apart. Subjugating Jesus and the disciples to an early, unrefined psychology undermines the Christian's complete confidence in the Bible, and this subjugation is, at best, a tacit acknowledgment of an alleged biblical insufficiency.

PSYCHOLOGY IN THE DICTIONARY

What is psychology? Although a common and often used term, its connotation is misleading. Popular and scholastic definitions cover a wide semantic continuum from scientific research to therapeutic theory and practice, from the biological to clinical mental health. Systems include biopsychology, experimental psychology, cognitive psychology, developmental psychology, clinical psychology, social psychology, industrial-organizational psychology, and cross-cultural psychology. In addition, an assortment of psychotherapeutic theories drives many of the psychological systems: psychodynamic, humanistic, existential, family systems, cognitive-behavioral, and postmodern psychotherapy. As mentioned earlier, the brief history of psychology is littered with an untold number of discarded models. In other words, psychology is far from being a unified discipline. It would be better to refer to "psychologies,"[22] since a plethora of theories and systems, current and past, abound.

The more common and basic definition of psychology used by the overwhelming majority of teaching institutions maintains a close connection between psychology and science. According to these institutions, "Psychology is the scientific study of behavior and mental processes."[23] But is this true? Is psychology a scientific discipline? If it is scientific, how can anyone object to its truth-claims? The initial chapters in most freshman-level introductory psychology textbooks draw heavily upon the natural sciences: biology, biochemistry, neurology, the limbic system, the endocrine system, and sensory organs. However, the remaining chapters of the book often move farther and farther from the hard sciences into personality theory, motivation, emotions, human development, sexual orientation, abnormal psychology, social psychology, and psychotherapies.

Serious questions arise concerning the true scientific nature of psychology as greater reliance is placed upon the so-called "behavioral" sciences. Much of the espoused scientific evidence is no better than opinion research. Psychology's relationship to the natural sciences is like margarine's relationship to real butter. Margarine looks and spreads like the real thing, but anyone who tastes it can tell the difference. Karl Popper detected a major problem in psychology when he wrote, "Psychological theories of human behavior 'though posing as sciences,' had in fact more in common with primitive myths than with science. . . . They contain most interesting psychological suggestions, but not in testable form."[24] A similar note of caution from Scott Lilienfeld concerns the practice of mental health:

> Over the past several decades, the fields of clinical psychology, psychiatry, and social work have borne witness to a widening and deeply troubling gap between science and practice (see Lilienfeld, 1998, for a discussion). Carol Tavris (1998) has written eloquently of the increasing gulf between the academic laboratory and the couch and of the worrisome discrepancy between what we have learned about the psychology of memory; hypnosis; suggestibility; clinical judgment and assessment;

and the causes, diagnosis, and treatment of mental disorders, on the one hand, and routine clinical practice, on the other.[25]

Herein lies an epistemological problem at the heart of the *a priori* truth-claims of psycho-science: it is not as scientific as it claims to be. If psychology and psychiatry maintained a strict code of cause-and-effect science instead of research built on causes that appear to be related to effects, they could be credible authorities for biblical pastors and counselors. However, when psychology encroaches upon biblical territory by claiming jurisdictional authority in the counseling arena of what man "ought" to do, it is usurping God's domain. Psychology's illegitimate efforts cannot come to absolute conclusions about life, since at its heart psychology is only one fallible man telling another fallible man what to do. Arrogance abounds in such an environment. Only the divinely inspired Word of God has authority to do that.

Another problem arises with the science of psychology. Even if psychology withdrew from its pseudo-scientific subjectivism and fully relied upon the natural sciences, it would still draw inaccurate conclusions. Why? The *a priori* presupposition of the overwhelming majority of natural sciences is an evolutionary one. Freud (A.D. 1856–1939) was a Darwin devotee. All the psychological textbooks since his time, graduate and otherwise, espouse that man is an evolved animal. Psychological research studies about the biology of man interacting with his environment are frequently based on animal studies. For example, concrete inferences were made concerning the emotional attachment between a child and his mother through the study of how infant monkeys became attached to soft, warm terry-cloth "mother-monkeys" instead of to wire "mother-monkeys" who gave milk.[26] The obvious assumption is that human infants, because of their evolutionary heritage, are identical or remarkably similar in development to infant monkeys in their attachment-responses. From these foundational studies that garner considerable credibility, psychologists establish sweeping developmental standards that affect governmental and educational child-welfare policies. Even more importantly, therapeutic advice given to parents is based upon the same evolutionary research.

Evolutionary biopsychology defines man as nothing more than the sum total of his chemical components. An understanding of the advanced complexity of the highly evolved animal called man, illuminates what makes him tick. Every psychology textbook has an account of the unfortunate mishap of Phineas Gage, the twenty-five-year-old railroad employee, who in 1848 had a one-inch-diameter metal spike driven through his skull while blasting rock. Remarkably he lived, but he was a radically changed man. Before the accident, he was a responsible, hardworking, mostly moral, and smart employee. After the accident he transformed into a cussing, carousing, irresponsible man who could not hold down a job or maintain good relationships with others. According to the theories in most psychology texts, the association areas of the cerebral cortex of Mr. Gage's brain were destroyed, an area where higher mental processes like thinking, language, memory, and speech occur. In other words, the texts make a case that morality is not a spiritual issue after all; it is an organic issue. According to them, man is moral because his brain has evolved over millennia from a central core (the "old brain") to a higher reasoning capacity in the cerebral cortex (the "new brain"). What was destroyed in Mr. Gage's brain was a portion of the highly evolved association areas of the cortex where morality is determined. Then the question must be asked, "Is morality an issue for biology and not the Bible?" Will organic solutions suffice? Could pedophiles be given a pill in the future to stop their molestation of children? Would a prescription end the thievery of a kleptomaniac? Maybe drugs could be added to the water supply to finally rid society of criminals? Evolutionary biopsychology focuses in this direction.

The cases of traumatically brain-injured people like Phineas Gage and others prove nothing. Again, psychology has made associations that appear to be related to causes, but there is no direct cause and effect between injury and immoral behavior. A strong relationship is made because evolutionary psychiatry is committed to a materialistic worldview that assumes the uniformity of natural cause in a closed system. Sudden changes toward wickedness, like that evidenced by Gage, are also evident in cases where no brain damage has been sustained. Conversely, some who have suffered serious brain damage to the associational areas of the brain have not changed morally. Regardless, the sheer trauma of such an accident could sufficiently expose wickedness in the heart of someone like Gage who had suppressed it previously.

Often, years of hostility and anger can surface in a counselee who had previously lived a rather moral lifestyle. As Ed Welch explained, an injury can make it harder to think clearly and resist latent wickedness: "When affected by underlying sin, cognitive problems are often translated into childish behavior, unwillingness to be taught, irresponsibility, impulsiveness (especially financial), unusual emotional fluctuations, depression, and irritability."[27] Trauma only magnifies the need to keep the heart pure. Elderly counselees who are suffering from early forms of Alzheimer's or dementia will often have a difficult time restraining ungodly desires, especially if the inner man has not been nurtured over the years. Biblical counselors believe in a uniformity of natural cause in an *open* system. This means that these problems have supernatural/spiritual dimensions. The supernatural work of the Spirit of God through the Word of God can bring about a renewed life of holiness and righteousness in spite of brain damage or disease. Evolutionary materialism ends in nihilism, devoid of such hope.

Is psychology a scientific discipline? The answer to this previously posed question is, at best, debatable. Certainly, there are aspects of this discipline that carefully use rigid scientific reasoning. Even then, however, the *a priori* presuppositions necessary to bring about some meaningful significance are blatantly evolutionary. Psychology is better viewed as a philosophical system of thought disseminated as a materialistic worldview that expresses itself variously as behaviorism, humanism, determinism, existentialism, epiphenomenalism, and simple pragmatic utilitarianism.

Biblical counseling is not a scientific discipline either. And, does not claim to be, even though it is quick to affirm valid medical science and biological research as applied to genuinely organic problems. Biblical counseling fully acknowledges that its epistemology grows out of a theistic presupposition of a self-revelatory Creator who "has granted to us everything pertaining to life and godliness, through the true knowledge of Him who called us by His own glory and excellence" (2 Pet. 1:3). The Bible is not an encyclopedia of counseling topics that lists every particular counseling problem, but it does contain sufficient revelatory data to establish an effective worldview framework for the diagnosis and remedy of every soul problem. An extended explanation by David Powlison illustrates this point:

> Biblical counselors who fail to think through carefully the nature of biblical epistemology run the danger of acting as if Scripture were exhaustive, rather than comprehensive; as if Scripture were an encyclopedic catalogue of all significant facts, rather than God's revelation of the crucial facts, richly illustrated, that yield a world view sufficient to interpret whatever other facts we encounter; as if Scripture were the whole bag of marbles rather than the eyeglasses through which we interpret all marbles; as if our current grasp of Scripture and people were triumphant and final. Integrationists view Scripture as a small bag of marbles and psychology as a large bag of marbles. The logic of integrationist epistemology is this: Put the two bags together, weeding out the obviously bad marbles in psychology, and you have more marbles.[28]

Some biblical counselors err in believing the Bible is the whole bag of marbles. On the other hand, Christian psychologists with an integrationist epistemology do not believe that the Bible has sufficient marbles for soul-care. In fact, they believe that by adding the larger bag of psychological marbles to the mix, they will be able to play a better game of marbles. They increasingly rely, however, upon the psychological marbles that are distorted and misshapen by a foreign worldview. Their biblical marbles are eventually marginalized by their integrationist epistemology. With skewed vision, they cannot weed out the bad marbles, much less play an effective game. Powlison asked, "Is the Bible a bag of marbles or the all-sufficient eyeglasses of truth—with lots of illustrative marbles—by which God corrects our sin-tainted vision?[29]

The difference between biblical counseling and Christian psychology is a worldview issue. Biblical counselors believe the counselor needs new glasses. Christian psychologists believe the counselor needs more marbles. When the Bible is the Christian counselor's corrective lens, he has a suffi-cient worldview perspective, with abundant illustrative material, to reinter-pret biblically all human experience for soul-care.

BIBLICAL COUNSELING IN THE BIBLE

Does the Bible justify this counseling worldview? If so, can the biblical counselor trust assertions drawn from research in the natural world? A care-fully reasoned justification exists for not only prioritizing the Bible in one's counseling schema, but also making it the reliable resource for the Christian counselor's etiology of the soul. As such, the Bible provides the diagnostic terminology and remedy, as well as the theoretical framework, from which soul-problems are properly interpreted and resolved. Not only do the noetic effects of sin cause the counselor to wrongly interpret soul-problems, they also encourage the selection of wrong categories for understanding the significance of these soul-problems, beginning with the counselor's view of God and extending to the counselor's view of man.

The Bible, and not psychology, should set the determinative categories for understanding theology and anthropology. For example, Scripture con-tains no hint that man struggles with a "poor view of self" or "low self-esteem." Yet this idea has been the rubric of a considerable amount of Christian pop-psychology. The theoretical source material came, not from the Bible, but from secular psychologists like William James, Erich Fromm, Karen Horney, and Abraham Maslow. In fact, biblical anthropology teaches that man loves himself too much, and if he loved God and others as much as he already loves himself, he would have a better life.[30]

In addition, no justification for personality classification as a major determining factor in interpersonal and marital conflict can be found in Scripture. A psychological etiology of such problems causes Christians to focus on the wrong issues, avoiding the critical matter of the idolatrous heart that needs to change. Classification categories of personality have nothing to do with the Bible, rather they find their inspiration in ancient Greek mythology.[31] Mythology aside, personality in the Bible is fluid and not an intact characteristic. An avid student of the Bible should be able to distinguish psychological claims, both new and ancient, from the authorita-tive criteria of God's truth. Similarly, the Christian counselor should not only refer *to* scriptural truth in counseling, but to reason *from* it.

Furthermore, certification organizations have arisen over the last thirty years to return Christians to Bible-based, not-for-profit, church-sponsored, counseling ministries. Notably, the National Association of Nouthetic Counselors (NANC)[32] is the grandfather of such organizations created to assist the church in developing and maintaining excellence in biblical counseling. The term "nouthetic" is derived from the New Testament word that means, to warn, admonish, or counsel. NANC has been extremely influential in helping churches create counseling ministries built upon a biblically consistent counseling model.

The Psalm 19 Paradigm

The weight that the Bible carries in the counseling process is beautifully illustrated in Psalm 19. It has been called "the Psalm of two books," because the first half presents God revealing Himself in the created domain (general revelation), and the second half presents God revealing Himself through the Word (special revelation). A careful study of the Psalm, however, demonstrates that David did not change topics in the middle of his writing. Psalm 19 is a psalm of one not two books.

General Revelation

The first half of this psalm theologically describes the scope and extent of general revelation (vv. 1–6). Our shepherd/poet introduced the psalm with a riveting display of the glory of God in the heavens by stating, "The heavens are telling of the glory of God" (v. 1). God's glory is painted in brilliant colors across the sky. David asserted that the cosmic design and power of the universe places His resplendent glory on display like an unfurled banner stretching from horizon to horizon. The Hebrew word for "glory" originally carried the more literal connotation of "weight" or "heaviness." The later more extended meaning developed into the concept of "importance" or "glory." As a person's eyes scan the glimmering night sky he is able to understand the weightiness or importance of Almighty God. General revelation elicits breathless awe for the raw intelligence of the omnipotent Creator.

Next, in synonymous parallelism, there is a restatement of the same idea in the second line using different words. David said, "And their expanse is declaring the work of His hand" (v. 1). Each of the main verbs in the first two lines, "telling" and "declaring," use the Hebrew aspect indicating an ongoing action. God's glory is constantly being displayed by the created world around us.

Verse two continues to highlight the ongoing duration of nature's work in demonstrating God's glory for man to see. "Day to day pours forth speech, / And night to night reveals knowledge." "Pours forth" is a verb that means "bubbles forth." Like a bottle of soda that gushes when shaken and released, natural revelation is under pressure to bring to the forefront God's glory.

Without a word being spoken, this is accomplished. The English Standard Version has a superb translation here: "There is no speech, nor are there words, / Whose voice is not heard" (v. 3). The King James Version inserted the word *where*—"*where* their voice is not heard," and thereby confused the meaning. The emphasis of this verse is not the location of the message; it is the language of the message. God is able to get the essential message across without the use of a single verbal utterance. Through non-verbal communication, people from all cultures and all languages have the capacity to understand that Almighty God exists in all of His weighty importance.

The first part of verse four reinforces the message: "Their line has gone out through all the earth, / And their utterances to the end of world." No one can escape this powerful nonverbal message, because it extends to the horizon. People cannot hide from it, and they cannot run from it. Everyone is visually bombarded with God's might and unrivaled creative design.

Then, in emblematic parallelism, David extended the reader's understanding of the role of general revelation with the use of two vivid images: the bridegroom and the strong runner (vv. 4–6).

> In them He has placed a tent for the sun,
> Which is as a bridegroom coming out of his chamber;
> It rejoices as a strong man to run his course.
> Its rising is from one end of the heavens.
> And its circuit to the other end of them;
> And there is nothing hidden from its heat.

The sun is compared to a determined bridegroom stepping from his tent to claim his bride. It has a predetermined course as it comes forth each morning from the veil of darkness with God's glory promising a fresh day. The sun also runs its course from one end of the heavens to the other like a strong man; it does not stop and no one can stop it. So a good runner keeps focused on the goal of finishing the race like the sun is focused on completing the course that the Creator has given it. All of this determination, ordered movement, regularity, and power is abundant evidence of the glory of God.

The description does not end there, because a subsequent verse (6) indicates that no one can escape the influence of God's glory in creation: "And there is nothing hidden from its heat." Still using the analogy of the sun, the psalmist emphasized that everyone can feel the heat of God's glory. Even the limited sensory world of one who is blind, deaf, and mute has the capacity to feel the ebb and flow of warmth from the rhythmic setting and rising of the sun. People with "subaverage intellectual functioning" or those with profound retardation (IQs 39 and below) are significantly impacted with the basic message of the presence of God and His glory. That is the penetration power of this nonverbal message. Clearly, general revelation was intended to put God's power and creative design on display.

At this point a question must be asked: "What does the Bible say is God's intended pedagogic role for general revelation?" One Christian psychological integrationist has said, "All truth is certainly God's truth. The doctrine of General Revelation provides warrant for going beyond the propositional revelation of Scripture into the secular world of scientific study expecting to find true and useable concepts. . . . Again, let me insist that psychology does offer real help to the Christian endeavoring to understand and solve personal problems."[33] While it is certainly true that "all truth is God's truth," it is also true that "all error is the devil's error."[34] So the sentiment "all truth is God's truth" reduces the argument to *reduction ad absurdum* and begs the question. Another Christian psychologist held to a reductionistic view of the Bible by maintaining, "That as God's statutes in scriptures are binding upon His people, His 'statutes' or fixed patterns within the framework of heaven and earth are binding upon the whole of the cosmos."[35] Then he proceeded to suggest that just as the authors of Proverbs appealed to natural phenomena, so the Christian psychologist can do the same in determining psychological "*quasi causal*" laws for life. Not only does this place the psychologist on the same level as the writers of inspired Scripture, but it nullifies the warning of Proverbs 30:5–6 about adding to the unique Word of God. No one questions the many benefits of natural revelation for mankind, including discoveries made through the natural sciences and medical research. Even then, these discoveries may have measured application to the one who believes in the sanctity of life because God created people in His image (for example, abortion and fertility technology). But when the metaphysical bridge into the soul is crossed by an encroaching psychology, what does Scripture identify as the role of general revelation?

According to Psalm 19 the role of general revelation is to impact all men with the supreme glory of God. An ordered Creator with design and might exceeds one's imagination. The apostle Paul understood the role of general revelation and declared, "For since the creation of the world His invisible attributes, His eternal power and divine nature, have been clearly seen, being understood through what has been made, so that they are without excuse" (Rom. 1:20).

A major problem hinders general revelation's role, however, in that it can be totally ignored or even misunderstood. This omnipresent, powerful message can be distorted and censored. Again Paul explained God's anger, "For the wrath of God is revealed from heaven against all ungodliness and unrighteousness of men, who suppress the truth in unrighteousness, because that which is known about God is evident within them; for God made it evident to them" (Rom. 1:18–19). Man's heart can never be neutral about the truth. In his unrighteousness, man is opposed to God and any fundamental knowledge of God. Often the problem with psychology is not its untrustworthiness but man's. Information derived from the natural world is static information that can be twisted and obscured by the deceitful cunningness of the sinful heart.

Special Revelation

Now this is the point of Psalm 19: *Far greater than all general revelation is the glory of God revealed in His Word, because the Word transforms the heart of man.* Ronald Barclay Allen commented on this psalm, "I believe that it is the teaching of this movement of the Psalm that *God reveals His glory more fully in His Word than in all of creation* [author's emphasis]."[36] General revelation fulfills its duty by rendering man without excuse, but it can never yield transforming, authoritative truth for soul-problems because it can be resisted and dismissed. Active and living truth is needed for that—divine, authoritative truth that can convert the soul.

The entire psalm pivots on verse seven which declares, "The law of the LORD is perfect, restoring the soul." "Restoring" is the same word often translated as "converting," "reviving," or "turning back."[37] God's Word is perfect, in the sense that it is ideal or perfectly suited for man; the soul that has been warped and deformed by sin and serious problems can be reshaped by its power. As Hebrews says, "For the word of God is living and active and sharper than any two-edged sword, and piercing as far as the division of soul and spirit, of both joints and marrow, and able to judge the thoughts and intentions of the heart" (Heb. 4:12). This text is not saying God's Word divides the soul from the spirit, but that it divides the soul in parts and also divides the spirit in parts, so much so that it gets down into the thoughts and intentions (or motivations) of the heart. Information from general revelation can never hope to do that. The occasional helpful insights provided through research on things like sleep disorders, visual perception, and organic brain disorders will never approach the power of the Word of God for change. The Word of God is matchless within the jurisdictional domain of the soul.

Using psychology for soul-care is like dressing cancer with Band-Aids. It may temporarily relieve the pain or even mask the symptoms, but it will never penetrate the issues of the heart like God's Word.

Some may argue that the passage is only speaking about unregenerate men, and does not apply to Christians who are being counseled. However, this is not the case. Even though a broader application can be made to the unbeliever, the final eight verses of Psalm 19 (vv. 7–14) describe the sanctifying power of the Word of God in the life of the believer. And if it is true that the Word of God is greater in bringing about the glory of God in man than general revelation, then why would the Christian want to return to the simpler and more fundamental truths of general revelation when he has a far greater life-transforming truth at his disposal?

Notice the effect of the Word in man's life: "restoring the soul," "making wise the simple," "rejoicing the heart," "enlightening the eyes," "enduring forever," and it is "righteous altogether." The first five characteristics are participles, meaning the Word of God refreshes life, grants depth of insight, renders joy to the heart, opens the eyes of understanding, and will never be outdated. Where else can a person go to find counsel like that? They express the ongoing ministry and relevance of the Word of God. The sixth characteristic is a summary statement conveying the idea that the Word of God is capable of producing comprehensive righteousness.

Also notice the adjectives in reference to the Word of God, which is variously described as perfect, sure, right, pure, clean, and true counsel. The synonyms for the Word of God demonstrate how its counsel should be approached. These synonyms include the law of the Lord (Torah), testimony, precepts, commandment, the fear of Yahweh, and the judgments of Yahweh. In other words, God's truth is not optional. It is not a set of His suggestions. If the Word is to have the rightful impact upon the counselee's heart, it must be approached with utmost reverence and not with the cavalier attitudes of many evangelicals. When this is done, the counselee will find its aftertaste sweet (v. 10).

Verses 11 through 14 encompass the final movement of the psalm. The radical impact this Word has had upon the life of David becomes evident. He opened his life to show how he had been transformed by the counsel of God, thereby glorifying God. David pointed out that apart from Scripture not only do people misunderstand the universe of general revelation, but they also misunderstand their own soul-problems. Apart from the written Word, David asked, "Who can discern his errors?" (v. 12). This rhetorical question evoked a strong answer—No one can! David prayed, "Acquit me of hidden faults. / Also keep back Thy servant from presumptuous sins; / Let them not rule over me" (vv. 12–13). Hidden faults are the unknown sins of the soul, while presumptuous sins are the known sins. Presumptuous sins have an enslaving quality to them; they will assume an enslaving domination in the counselee's life (for example, sexual lust, gluttony, drunkenness, or rage). These are the sins done in full knowledge of their sinfulness, and yet they are compulsively committed anyway.

Scripture identifies sin as the chief (not the only) problem of man for counseling. Other contributing factors include both organic problems and sins committed by others. These sins by others, against or around the counselee, have a direct impact upon the counselee (for example, rape, incest, physical abuse, financial irresponsibility, hatred, anger, and jealousy). All counseling matters result from the wickedness of a sin-cursed and demon-infested world (James 3:14–16). But even in cases of unjust suffering, how does the counselee's heart respond?[38] When the Word of God has its way, the counselee walks free from guilt. David announced boldly, "Then I shall be blameless, / And I shall be acquitted of great transgression" (Ps. 19:13).

His final prayer was to be acceptable before God (v. 14). He knew this would be true only if both his actions, "the words of my mouth," and his desires, "the meditation of my heart," were pleasing to God. The Lord was this counselee's "rock and Redeemer."

THE CRITICAL QUESTION

Far greater than all the universe of general revelation is the glory of God revealed in His Word, because it *alone* transforms the heart of man! So the question remains, Why biblical counseling and not psychology? The answer must necessarily be that the Word of God reigns supreme in the jurisdictional domain of the soul where psychology trespasses and seeks to usurp authority. Only the Word of God can effectively instruct believers concerning how to glorify Him.

In keeping with David's sentiments in Psalm 19, Christians have always understood this chief aim of glorifying God and enjoying Him forever. This can only be accomplished through the Word of God. All the psychotherapies and psychologies of man will never sanctify the heart to such high and noble purposes. In fact, the rudimentary core of all psychologies is *self*—living for the welfare and enjoyment of *self*. Most psychological remedies cater to self with messages of loving self more, esteeming self, and pampering self. All psychologies see this as their "chief end," and, tragically, the Christian psychologies have also been dramatically infected with it.

Furthermore, general revelation will never yield absolute, universally authoritative truth on which the counselee can confidently base the welfare of his/her soul. Why? Because that was never its intended purpose. By its very nature, it cannot express a complete picture of God, much less His will for His creatures. On the deficiencies of general revelation John Calvin commented, "It is therefore clear that God has provided the assistance of the Word for the sake of all those to whom he has been pleased to give useful instruction because he foresaw that his likeness imprinted upon the most beautiful form of the universe would be insufficiently effective."[39] Natural revelation is impotent when it comes to changing the soul. As David so poignantly described in Psalm 19, God delivered to man a more powerful revelation that is capable of penetrating the deep recesses of the soul and not only redeeming him but instructing him in righteousness so he could glorify and enjoy Him forever. Every counseling problem hangs on these fundamental facts. The Scriptures are the key to what makes life life! The Lord asks a rhetorical question that needs no answer, "Do not My words do good / To the one walking uprightly?" (Mic. 2:7).

FURTHER READING

Adams, Jay E. *The Christian Counselor's Manual.* Grand Rapids, MI: Zondervan, 1973.

————. *Competent to Counsel.* Grand Rapids, MI: Zondervan, 1970.

Bobgan, Martin and Deidre. *Prophets of Psychoheresy I.* Santa Barbara, CA: EastGate Publishers, 1989.

Ganz, Richard. *Psychobabble.* Wheaton, IL: Crossway, 1993.

MacArthur, John F., and Wayne A. Mack. *Introduction to Biblical Counseling.* Dallas, TX: Word, 1994.

Part II

The Theological Foundations of Biblical Counseling

4

The Godward Focus of Biblical Counseling

Douglas Bookman

By definition, the biblical counselor is one who is persuaded of and allegiant to a Christian worldview, that is, one who functions within a frame of reference that consciously sees all of the realities and relationships of life from a perspective that is biblically coherent and consistent, and thus honors the God of Scriptures. The one element of such a worldview that most dramatically distinguishes it from all pretenders is the commitment to a theocentric perspective on all of life and thought. Thus any model of counseling that is authentically biblical will be framed, designed, and executed in happy submission to the biblical demand that our lives be lived out entirely for the glory of God! In short, biblical counseling is animated by a godward focus.

The temptation today, even within the Christian community, is to do otherwise, to conduct counseling with a primary focus on someone or something other than God. But the biblical counselor must be committed to a preeminently godward focus in counseling. Why? There are three basic reasons: (1) because God demands it; (2) because the natural exaltation of self is destructive; and (3) because the soul-satisfying life God intends for His children can only be found through Jesus' spiritual paradox: deny self and focus on God.

THE MORAL IMPERATIVE

Simply stated, a godward focus must be zealously maintained in biblical counseling because God demands that it be so. In one of the Old Testament's most precise articulations of the covenant-keeping nature of God, YHWH declared through the prophet Isaiah,

> Thus says God the LORD,
> Who created the heavens and stretched them out,
> Who spread out the earth and its offspring,
> Who gives breath to the people on it,

> And spirit to those who walk in it, . . .
> "I am the LORD, that is My name;
> I will not give My glory to another,
> Nor My praise to graven images." (Is. 42:5, 8)

Later in the same section of prophecy, as YHWH foretold the mighty deliverance He would accomplish on behalf of His covenant people, He reiterated this profound reality: "For My own sake, for My own sake, I will act; / For how can My name be profaned? / And My glory I will not give to another" (Is. 48:11).

God, who has made Himself known in Scripture, is jealous for His own glory (Deut. 4:24). He is a sovereign God who demands that people acknowledge Him as God and honor Him as the Creator and Sovereign of all the universe. This moral imperative to honor God is most often communicated in Scripture in contexts relating to God's glory. The Hebrew term for "glory" is *chabod,* which basically means "to be heavy, weighty."[1] Deriving the idea of glory, dignity, or personal worth from the concept of weightiness is typical of Hebrew progression of thought. To the Semitic mind, honor or dignity could not be reduced to a purely ideal quality; rather, those concepts depended for their significance upon the concrete concept of something "weighty in a man which gives him importance."[2] Although the term *chabod* is used with various literal connotations in the Old Testament, the concept most often conveyed by the term is that of a weighty person: one who is honorable, impressive, and worthy of respect.[3] This connotation prevails in more than half the occurrences of the term in the Old Testament.[4]

Thus, the biblical notion of glory involves more than intrinsic dignity or value; it includes the visible representation of that intrinsic value. For example, *chabod* connotes not only a rich man's dignity and standing in his community but the riches that demonstrated his dignity (livestock, silver, and gold in Gen. 13:2; the wealth Jacob carried away from Laban in Gen. 31:1);[5] not only the honor of the priestly office but the distinctive garments worn by the priests to manifest the dignity of their office (Ex. 28:2, 40);[6] not only the unique and infinite splendor and majesty of the person of YHWH, but the ineffable physical glory-cloud that testified of His covenant-keeping nature and sovereign rule in the midst of His people.[7] In sum, the term *chabod* speaks not only of intrinsic dignity and worth but of the external and tangible manifestation of that worth.

Thus when YHWH insists that He "will not give His *glory* to another" (Is. 42:3; 48:11), there is more at stake than the intrinsic worth of His sovereign person. Based on God's use of the term *glory* in those statements, we conclude that His demand is not only that we personally acknowledge His unique dignity and infinite perfection, but that we consciously and publicly parade those majestic realities. Indeed, it is the stewardship of every child of

God not only to embrace the truths that God has revealed concerning Himself but to deliberately and consistently order every aspect of life to display the grace, justice, and faithfulness of God, to whom that child belongs.[8]

To clarify this concept, consider how God publicly maintained His glory (that is, His reputation) in various narratives of the Old Testament. For instance, the drama of deliverance from Egypt, which culminated in the miracle of the Red Sea, was carefully framed by YHWH so that He would "be honored through Pharaoh and all his army, through his chariots and his horsemen" (Ex. 14:17–18).[9] The ten plagues that immediately and causally preceded the Red Sea experience were so ordered and timed by YHWH that the Pharaoh gradually steeled himself to Moses' demands. All of which prepared the way for Pharoah's command—a command as militarily and spiritually stupid as any in history—that his chariot forces pursue the fleeing Israelites across the miraculously dried up Red Sea. When Moses stretched out his hand over the sea and the waters covered the Egyptians, God did indeed get glory upon Egypt. And He answered the arrogant question posed by the Pharaoh some months earlier, "Who is this YHWH that I should obey His voice to let Israel go?" (Ex. 5:2). In effect, by miraculously delivering Israel from Egypt, YHWH confronted the world of that day, and of centuries to come, with the indisputable evidence of His might and His character. (Compare the reaction of Rahab in Joshua 2:9–14 and the flawed remembrance of the Red Sea evinced by the Philistines some four hundred years later in 1 Samuel 4:8.)

Again, when the southern kingdom of Judah was taken captive to Babylon, the name of YHWH was in severe jeopardy of being dishonored. God had covenanted with Israel that if they persevered in rebellion and disobedience He would cause them to be taken captive by a "nation of fierce countenance" (Deut. 28:49–57; see 1 Kin. 8:46). And yet, given the universal superstition of the time that if one nation were defeated by another it was because the gods of the victorious nation were more powerful than those of the vanquished, God's name was in danger of being dishonored if He kept that promise of judgment upon His covenant people. But God intervened to publicly preserve His glory through the man Daniel.

As a young man, Daniel was taken captive by King Nebuchadnezzar in the first stage of Judah's deportation to Babylon (about 605 B.C., see Daniel 1). Later, God enabled Daniel to provide the content and interpretation of the Babylonian monarch's dream, but only after all of the king's pagan soothsayers had confessed their absolute inability to do so (ch. 2). Thus YHWH was publicly honored as Nebuchadnezzar acknowledged the power of the God worshiped by Daniel and his friends (vv. 46–47).

Some decades later, the prophet interpreted another dream for the king. This time King Nebuchadnezzar wrote a decree to be read throughout all the kingdom that told the story of his own madness and thus honored

Daniel's God as "the Most High . . . who lives forever." The king's decree concluded with this encomium of praise to YHWH.

> For His dominion is an everlasting dominion,
> And His kingdom endures from generation to generation.
> And all the inhabitants of the earth are accounted as nothing,
> But He does according to His will in the host of heaven
> And among the inhabitants of earth;
> And no one can ward off His hand,
> Or say to Him, "What hast Thou done?" (Dan. 4:34–35)

Thus did Nebuchadnezzar publicly and universally declare the glory of YHWH.[10]

The historical examples from Scripture could be multiplied, but with these the point is made: when YHWH insists He will not share His glory with another, He wants us to understand not only that He possesses such personal majesty, but also that it is His sovereign will that His majesty be publicly displayed. It is His concern and must be our concern.

Obedience and Fallenness

There are profound implications in this mandate to deliberately and publicly reflect the God whom we serve. It means that the children of God are under scriptural obligation to see themselves as vehicles of God's glory, as mirrors with which the Sovereign of the universe has chosen to reflect His glory, as conduits to display Him before a watching world. It is morally imperative that believers frame their lives, order their priorities, fashion their relationships, and discipline their souls in ways appropriate to this relationship and responsibility.

Of course, the infernal fly in the ointment is the fallenness of mankind. Although it is cosmically appropriate for human creatures to content themselves with playing the moon to the Creator's sun and to be satisfied with the privilege of reflecting YHWH's glory (even though in so doing they are confessing that they have no glory of their own), people are not willing to do so. Indeed, it is the stuff of fallenness to be offended by God's claim that He alone is worthy of honor, and instead to exalt oneself, to thrust oneself onto the throne of one's private universe. The Luciferian rebellion is reiterated moment by moment in the souls of the unredeemed offspring of Adam when they, in effect, intone the most cardinal credo of fallenness:

> I will raise my throne above the stars of God,
> And I will sit on the mount of assembly
> In the recesses of the north.
> I will ascend above the heights of the clouds;
> I will make myself like the Most High.
>   (Is. 14:13–14)[11]

It might be argued, in fact, that this proclivity to exalt self is the essence of sinfulness. As Strong observed,

> Sin, therefore, is not merely a negative thing, or an absence of love to God. It is a fundamental and positive choice or preference of self instead of God, as the object of affection and the supreme end of being. Instead of making God the centre of his life, surrendering himself unconditionally to God and possessing himself only in subordination to God's will, the sinner makes himself the centre of his life, sets himself directly against God, and constitutes his own interest the supreme motive and his own will the supreme rule.[12]

This is the flesh that even in the believer sets its desire against the Spirit (Gal. 5:17); the lofty thing that raises itself up against Christ (2 Cor. 10:5); and the old self that has been corrupted in accordance with the lusts of deceit (Eph. 4:22).

It is in such a moral universe that biblical counselors must minister, indeed must consciously conceive of themselves as ministering. On the one hand, the omnipotent Creator and Sovereign of the universe demands that finite humans honor Him as such, and it is altogether appropriate that He receive that honor. On the other hand, every fallen person, whether unredeemed or redeemed, is possessed of an Adamic nature that longs to be like God, that compels each one of us to usurp the place of honor and dominion that rightly belongs only to God, despite the fact that it is altogether inappropriate that any person receive such honor.

God Alone Is God

By reason of these two factors, biblical counselors must constantly and consciously arm their spirit, inform their instruction, and constrain their counselees with a commitment to glorify God and God alone. Such a commitment will compel us to exult in the truth that God alone is God, and to acknowledge joyfully that every creature of God is under sacred obligation both to resist the temptation to exalt self and to honor God as God!

All of this might be more simply expressed in this short rendering: *God is God, and I am not!* God alone is eternal; He knows the end from the beginning, and thus He is able to comprehend exactly how all things will in fact "work together for good," no matter how distressing some of those things might seem to us (given that we can know only today, and that but haltingly and partially). God alone is sovereign; we can depend on Him to order the affairs of the moral universe so as to silence the great accuser of the brethren and to cause His children to grow in the grace and knowledge of the Lord Jesus Christ. God alone is true altogether; His word is life and light, and thus are we eternally well-advised to cast ourselves entirely upon His promises and to find in His word (and in His word alone) all things that pertain to life and godliness; even though we will be set upon from every quarter by theories and truth-claims that contravene the Word of God and are so seductive as to be alluring almost beyond resistance.

But *God is God, and I am not!* Therefore, God deserves to be honored, worshiped, trusted, feared, and loved as God. Our responsibility and privilege is to glorify Him: to enhance His reputation in the minds of rational creatures and to live our lives and order our days so that all who encounter us will have a higher regard for God than they might have had they never encountered us! But our besetting temptation is to glorify self: to live life as if we were the center of the universe, as if the enhancement of our reputation were a meritorious pursuit, and as if our contentment were the greatest good of the cosmos. That is why every believer must continually be confronted with the demand that God be honored as God. And that is why biblical counseling must be framed by a conscious, undeviating commitment to the glory of God!

SELFISH PREDISPOSITIONS RESULT IN DESTRUCTION

A conscious commitment to a godward focus in biblical counseling is also imperative because destructive consequences are certain to follow when people exalt themselves rather than God. This truth is particularly significant in biblical counseling, because so many who seek our help have, in fact, plunged themselves into just such destruction. They have fulfilled the longing to aggrandize self, and the price to be paid for such spiritual rebellion is the most profound tragedy of the human soul. In short, the temptation to exalt self is at once terribly seductive and certainly destructive.

Jonah: Tempted, Fallen, Restored

The prophet Jonah struggled with the temptation to exalt himself over God, to pursue his own desires rather than obey God's commands, and he lost that struggle. The prophet high-handedly rejected God's Word and became so morally inept that he convinced himself he could run from the presence of God. He discovered in rather dramatic fashion, however, that YHWH was no stranger to Joppa or to the sea-lanes that led to Tarshish. The result of the prophet's rebellion was three days and three nights in the belly of a great fish!

Jonah did come to repentance, of course, and his prayer of contrition and confession is recorded in Jonah 2. In that prayer Jonah called out in distress after he had been cast into "the deep, into the heart of the seas" (v. 3). He bemoaned the fact that because of his own wickedness he found himself in the "great deep" with seaweed wrapped about his head (v. 5). Even as he was "fainting away," as the breath of life was about to slip from him, he "remembered the Lord," fastened his soul's eye upon the temple in which YHWH had placed His name (v. 7), and acknowledged his foolishness and sin. Then God responded by rescuing the prophet from the great fish.

In Jonah's psalm of repentance (vv. 2–9) we find a brief statement that speaks directly to the issue at hand: "They that observe lying vanities forsake their own mercies" (v. 8, KJV). In other words, sin is both seductive and destructive.

Sin: Deceptive and Delicious

In speaking of the seductive nature of sin, Jonah acknowledged that he had "observed lying vanities." The Hebrew verb translated "observe" means "to give themselves up to" or "devote themselves to."[13] It suggests dogged determination or clinging to something in spite of influences to do otherwise.[14] The lying vanity Jonah clung to was "false love for his country, that he would not have his people go into captivity, when God would; would not have Nineveh preserved, the enemy of his country."[15] But the phrase "lying vanities" is more generic, it encompasses "all things which man makes into idols or objects of trust."[16]

> Human devices contrary to the will of God are "lying vanities;" empty, they bring no satisfaction; lying, they promise peace and safety, but bring misery and horrible troubles. So Eve found, so Pharaoh, so Israel when they went after the ways of the heathen. So Jonah himself. So all who forsake the Fountain of living waters and hew out to themselves broken cisterns that can hold no water. Worldly devices to get happiness apart from God are indeed "vanity of vanities."[17]

With regard to the destructive nature of sin, Jonah acknowledged in his prayer that by clinging to empty, self-serving lies he had forsaken his "own mercy"; he had forfeited the goodness and grace that God longed to bestow upon him.

> In God is salvation; out of him is destruction. There is something appalling in the doom which is here described as overtaking those who, when the Saviour may be found, turn their back upon him, in order to seek and to serve other gods. Such are said to "forsake their own mercy." They act against their highest interests; they refuse the richest blessing; they abjure their truest Friend.[18]

Keil developed this same thought with reference to Jonah's warning concerning "forsaking one's own mercy":

> The soul of man cannot be satisfied with husks. For God's servants to follow them is to forsake their own mercy. It is for the prodigal son

to change the father's house for the society of rioters and harlots: "Many sorrows shall be to the wicked: but he that trusteth in the Lord, mercy shall compass him about" (Ps. 32:10). The way of duty is ever the way of safety, peace, and comfort; neglected duty is a sure fore-runner of trouble; an evil conscience can never be the harbinger of sweet content.[19]

The significance, then, of Jonah's confession is simply this: those who stubbornly cling to seductive lies deprive themselves of the mercy and goodness God longs to shower upon them. From the belly of Sheol (Jon. 2:2), Jonah acknowledged the God-dishonoring wickedness and soul-destroying foolishness of his stubbornness and repented.

"Lying Vanities": Empty, Self-Serving Lies

Jonah obeyed a lie. That lie was two-fold: (1) he believed that his desire for the destruction of Nineveh was more worthy than YHWH's desire for the repentance of that city; and (2) he believed that he could actually flee from the "presence of YHWH" (1:3). It is difficult to accept that Jonah actually *believed* that lie; he was, after all, a true prophet of YHWH (2 Kin. 14:25). It defies credulity to suggest that a ministering prophet was persuaded that his desire transcended the command of God in worthiness or importance, or that such a spokesman for God consciously conceived of YHWH as a local deity so bound by space that a person could escape His presence by taking ship. But the issue whether Jonah actually believed the lie and whether he would have consciously affirmed the credibility of its claims is moot; the historical fact, recorded in the Bible, is that he obeyed the lie. Jonah confessed that because of his own desires ("lying vanities": empty and self-serving lies) he rendered himself so spiritually foolish that he behaved as if the lie were true ("they that observe": cling to, embrace, cherish in spite of all influences to the contrary) and thus brought suffering upon himself.

The horrifying spiritual reality of Jonah's experience is this: the power of a lie is not intrinsic in its inherent credibility but in its attractiveness. The pivotal moral issue is not whether people will believe the lie but whether they will obey it! The father of lies learned in the Garden that a lie of almost infinite implausibility ("in the day ye eat . . . ye shall be as gods," Gen. 3:5) will seduce if it is sufficiently tantalizing ("good for food . . . pleasant to the eyes . . . to be desired to make one wise," v. 6). In short, a lie is powerful not because it is deceptive but because it is delicious.[20]

To make the same point from a different perspective, a lie is effective only because of our selfish predisposition, because as fallen creatures we are so bent upon pandering to our own desires that we will render ourselves so spiritually foolish as to obey a lie we would never consciously affirm. But that selfish predisposition is in every case destructive. When people determine to abandon what they know to be the truth in order to embrace a beguiling lie, they forsake God's mercy. That is the testimony of the prophet Jonah.

Anyone who counsels will, by the nature of that ministry, confront people who have obeyed seductive lies, and who have forsaken their own mercy. They have obeyed lies because of their selfish predisposition. In other words, they have rejected a godward focus in favor of a self-ward focus, and the result has been spiritual, emotional, physical, and/or relational destruction. They are living in the middle of Jonah 2:8, but their only hope is found in Jonah 2:9. They have set their eyes upon themselves and have brought havoc into their lives. We must confront them with this wickedness and challenge them to set their eyes upon God, to obey His word, to live their lives for His glory, and in this to confess and experience that "Salvation is of the Lord"!

Lying Vanities in Christian Counseling

The tragedy in the contemporary marketplace is that many models of Christian counseling are based on theories more accurately subsumed under the error of Jonah 2:8 ("lying vanities") than under the truth of Jonah 2:9 ("Salvation is of the Lord!"). Wittingly or not, some counselors have proven themselves to be blind leaders of the blind; they have acquiesced to ear-tickling notions that are sub-biblical and God-dishonoring, notions that only make people more comfortable in their wickedness.

It is distressing to contemplate the catalogue of "lying vanities" that have insinuated themselves into sundry models of "Christian" counseling: models that legitimize a narcissistic preoccupation with self; models that fabricate a dimension to the human psyche that cannot be proven to exist, but the acknowledgment of which has the insidious practical effect of making individuals the victims of forces for which they cannot be held accountable, and thus of denying that people are morally responsible for the way they act, think, or feel; models that validate the notion that finite creatures have a right to be angry with the infinite Judge of the universe (who has, in fact, assured us that He will do right, Gen. 18:25), and that there can be spiritual and therapeutic benefit to expressing such an attitude of rage against God; models that speak of emotional healing and growth in relationships and in maturity while deliberately eschewing any appeal to the Holy Spirit or to the standard graces vouchsafed us by God.

All of these are lies! They are not intellectually compelling to anyone operating within a scriptural worldview, but because they make people comfortable in their sin they are extremely seductive. Furthermore, because it is a fixed reality of the moral universe that all who observe lying vanities will *always* forsake their own mercy, these lies are also destructive.

For both the counselor and the counselee, the means to counter these destructive lies is to make a deliberate and practical commitment to focus on the glory of God. This was the delivering discovery of the prophet Jonah. When he focused on his selfish desires he found himself in a mess, but when he recognized the destructiveness of his selfish predisposition, when he confessed the enslaving character of the lying vanities he had embraced, when he acknowledged that in clinging to those vanities he had forsaken God's goodness and brought destruction upon himself, Jonah found release. Millions have followed his example, people who would happily confess that all the glory and praise for the relief they found belongs to God alone.

THE DYNAMICS OF JESUS' SPIRITUAL PARADOX

Well into His eighteen-month ministry in Galilee, when opposition had increased dramatically and it was apparent that time was short, Jesus called to Himself the twelve men He had authorized as apostles. He empowered them to work miracles as proof of that authorization and then dispatched them to "preach, saying, 'The kingdom of heaven is at hand!' " (Matt. 10:7). Anticipating the difficulties His apostles would encounter, however, the Lord armed them with a promise as enigmatic as it was blessed. It was a paradoxical promise, at once the most rudimentary governing principle of the moral universe as framed by God and the greatest stumbling stone to mortals, who insist on defining that moral universe based on finite perspectives and distorted human values. What was that paradoxical promise? "He who has found his life shall lose it, and he who has lost his life for My sake shall find it" (Matt. 10:39).

On three other occasions recorded in the Gospels, Jesus proclaimed this principle. Some weeks after the Lord had authorized the apostles, He traveled with them to a remote area known as Caesarea-Philippi. There He told them for the first time that He would suffer many things of the Jewish leaders and would die (16:21). The disciples were horrified. Then Jesus followed this unhappy revelation with the warning that they, too, would have to be willing to take up a cross, deny themselves, and follow Him (Matt. 16:24; Mark 8:34; Luke 9:23). As part of that challenge, Jesus said,

> For whoever wishes to save his life shall lose it;
> and whoever loses his life for My sake and the gospel's shall save it.
> (Mark 8:3)

And again, in the midst of His final trip to Jerusalem for the Passover feast, Jesus confronted His antagonists, the Pharisees, with this cryptic warning:

> Whoever seeks to keep his life shall lose it,
> and whoever loses his life shall preserve it.
> (Luke 17:33)

Finally, during the final Passion Week, Jesus addressed "certain Greeks" who had sought Him out. Contemplating His own impending death, Jesus said,

> He who loves his life loses it;
> and he who hates his life in this world shall keep it to life eternal.
> (John 12:25)

On at least four different occasions, while addressing three different audiences, our Lord uttered this hard saying. To finite humans, these are difficult words: paradoxical at best, nonsensical at worst. But they are, in fact, the words of the Savior Himself and they are words that communicate a truth central to His teaching about living successfully.

Losing Life—Finding Life

To understand Christ's promise we need to consider two nuances of the word *life* that are at stake.[21] The warning is that whoever wishes to save his or her life (that is, temporal, material life) will lose it (that is, eternal blessedness). The promise is that whoever is willing to lose life (again, temporal matters) for the sake of the Savior will, in fact, find life (again, eternally significant matters). Indeed, Hort insisted that "this 'paradoxical' saying gets its point from the fact that men call by the name of 'life' that which is not truly life: 'he that wishes to save his 'life' (i.e. life in the narrower sense) will lose his true 'life' (i.e. life in its highest sense)."[22] Morison acknowledged this same distinction; he paraphrased the warning: "In grasping at the shadow he shall infallibly lose the substance."[23]

The statement is paradoxical, then, only because people do not comprehend what constitutes real life. They are fully persuaded that life consists in the things that a person has; Jesus said it does not (Luke 12:15). They live under the delusion that satisfaction lies in accomplishing goals, establishing a reputation, exercising great power, and amassing much wealth; Jesus stated simply that the person who learns to hunger and thirst after righteousness is blessed, because that person will be filled (that is, satisfied, Matt. 5:6). The soulish individuals, who have persuaded themselves that happiness and contentment are to be found in the present world, are compelled by the force of their own abominable logic to set their eyes on this world.

But the dynamic of Jesus' spiritual paradox constrains us to focus on the glory of God rather than upon the gratification of our own desires. The rationale for such a selfless ethic is as uncomplicated to the eye of faith as it is inscrutable to the natural man; it is as compelling to one impelled by the Spirit as it is repugnant to one controlled by the flesh. That rationale is simply this: "Whoever loses his life for My sake and the gospel's sake shall save it!" In other words, the only way to find a fruitful and contented life is to give one's self away to God ("My sake") and to others ("the gospel's sake").

It might be argued that there is egocentrism latent in this ethic, that giving one's life away with the motive of getting it back is only selfishness once removed. But this argument is based on the mistaken notion that God is displeased if people are happy, that God wants them to be miserable, and, thus, that it is morally inappropriate for anyone to long for or strive for happiness. In fact, God is a good and loving God who yearns for His creatures to find the soul-satisfaction He has provided for them. The univocal testimony of Scripture is that God's heart longs for each person to find contentment. Indeed, God so loved the world that He gave His own Son in order to provide such soul-satisfying peace. Wickedness lies not in the desire to find contentment of soul but in the determination to find it at the expense of God's standards and mandates. God takes immeasurable delight in those who determine to obey Him and by means of that obedience to know the peace that transcends human comprehension.

Focusing on God

So we see again the necessity of a focus upon the glory of God in the ministry of counseling. Tragedy will certainly befall people who live each day in an attempt to find satisfaction, for in that very effort they will lose it! When these soul-sick individuals come to us for counseling, we need to encourage them to honor the dynamic of Jesus' spiritual paradox; that is, to redirect their focus, to set their soul's gaze first of all upon God and then upon those about them, and then to order their lives in ways consistent with that focus. Lamentably, the effect of much counseling today is to reinforce the counselee's focus upon self. Exegetical and theological acrobatics are attempted to justify this strategy, but such efforts notwithstanding, this counsel is twice grievous: it is explicitly condemned by the Scriptures, and it is disastrous to the counselee.

How much wiser and God-honoring it is to acknowledge the authority of Jesus' person and the truth of His words, and to prove the life-changing power of the spiritual paradox He gave to us.

> The way of self-crucifixion and sanctification may seem foolishness and waste to the world, just as burying good seed-corn seems waste to the child and the fool. But there never lived the man who did not find that, by sowing to the Spirit, he reaped life everlasting.[24]

In sum, the spirit of the biblical counselor must be like that expressed by the psalmist David: "Be thou exalted, O God above the heavens; let thy glory be above all the earth" (Ps. 57:5, KJV). Indeed, the primary goal of counselor must be to see this same spirit functioning as the controlling attitude in counselee's lives. Only as a person's heart becomes overwhelmed with the desire articulated by the psalmist and is consumed with the prayer,

"Be thou exalted, O God," is that person going to know the peace God longs to give to His children.

The realities of the moral universe demand that I live my life out in every way for His honor rather than for my own; after all, God is God, and I am not! But the deepest need of my soul also constrains me to honor God as God, to submit to His standards and cherish His instruction; only as I thus hunger and thirst after righteousness will I be filled. Indeed, as Tozer has reminded us:

> There is a logic behind God's claim to preeminence. That place is His by every right in earth or heaven. While we take to ourselves the place that is His, the whole course of our lives is out of joint. Nothing will or can restore order till our hearts make the great decision: God shall be exalted above.[25]

5

Counseling and the Sinfulness of Humanity[1]

John MacArthur

No concept is more important to the gurus of modern psychology than self-esteem. According to the self-esteem credo, there are no bad people, only people who think badly of themselves.

For years, educational experts, psychologists, and a growing number of Christian leaders have championed self-esteem as a panacea for all sorts of human miseries. According to the purveyors of this doctrine, if people feel good about themselves, they will behave better, have fewer emotional problems, and achieve more. People with high self-esteem, we are told, are less likely to commit crimes, act immorally, fail academically, or have problems in their relationships with others.

THE BLIND FAITH OF SELF-ESTEEM

Advocates of self-esteem have been remarkably successful in convincing people that self-esteem is the solution to whatever ails anyone. One survey revealed that a majority of people view self-esteem as the single most important motivator for hard work and success. In fact, self-esteem ranked several points higher than a sense of responsibility or fear of failure.[2]

But does self-esteem really work? Does it, for example, promote higher achievement? There is plenty of evidence to suggest it does not. In a recent study, a standardized math test was given to teenagers from six different nations. Besides the math questions, the test asked the youngsters to respond yes or no to the question, "I am good at mathematics." American students scored lowest on the math questions, far behind Korean students, who had the top scores. Ironically, more than three-fourths of the Korean students had answered *no* to the "I am good at math" question. In stark contrast, however, 68 percent of the American students believed their math skills were just fine.[3] Our kids may be failing math, but they obviously feel pretty good about how they are doing.

Morally, our culture is in precisely the same boat. Empirical evidence strongly suggests that society is at an all-time moral low. We might expect people's self-esteem to be suffering as well. But statistics show Americans are feeling better about themselves than ever. In a survey conducted in 1940, 11 percent of women and 20 percent of men agreed with the statement, "I am an important person." In the 1990s, those figures jumped to 66 percent of women and 62 percent of men.[4] Ninety percent of people surveyed in a Gallup Poll say their own sense of self-esteem is robust and healthy.[5] Incredibly, while the moral fabric of society is unraveling, self-esteem is thriving. All the positive thinking about ourselves seems not to be doing anything to elevate the culture or motivate people to live better lives.

Can it really be that low self-esteem is what is wrong with people today? Does anyone seriously believe that making people feel better about themselves has helped the problems of crime, moral decay, divorce, child abuse, juvenile delinquency, drug addiction, and all the other evils that have dragged society down? Could so much still be wrong in our culture if the assumptions of self-esteem theory were true? Do we really imagine that more self-esteem will finally solve society's problems? Is there even a shred of evidence that would support such a belief?

Absolutely none. A report in *Newsweek* suggested that "the case for self-esteem . . . is a matter less of scientific pedagogy than of faith—faith that positive thoughts can make manifest the inherent goodness in any one."[6] In other words, the notion that self-esteem makes people better is simply a matter of blind religious faith. Not only that, it is a religion that is antithetical to Christianity, because it is predicated on the unbiblical presupposition that people are basically good and need to recognize their own goodness.

THE CHURCH AND THE SELF-ESTEEM CULT

Nevertheless, the most persuasive proponents of self-esteem religion have always included clergymen. Norman Vincent Peale's "positive thinking" doctrine, which was popular a generation ago, was simply an early self-esteem model. Peale wrote *The Power of Positive Thinking* in 1952.[7] The book opened with these words: "Believe in yourself! Have faith in your abilities!" In the introduction, Peale called the book a "personal-improvement manual . . . written with the sole objective of helping the reader achieve a happy, satisfying, and worthwhile life."[8] The book was marketed as motivational therapy, not theology. But in Peale's estimation the whole system was merely "applied Christianity; a simple yet scientific system of practical techniques of successful living that works."[9]

Evangelicals, for the most part, were slow to embrace a system that called people to faith in themselves rather than faith in Jesus Christ. Self-esteem as

Norman Vincent Peale outlined it was the offspring of theological liberalism married to neo-orthodoxy.

Time has evidently worn away evangelicals' resistance to such doctrine. Now many of the hottest-selling books in evangelical bookstores promote self-esteem and positive thinking. Even *Newsweek* has commented on the trend. Noting that self-esteem is considered "religiously correct" nowadays, the magazine observed:

> The notion [of self-esteem] may put off anyone old enough to remember when "Christian" as an adjective was often followed by "humility." But American churches, which once did not shrink from calling their congregants wretches, have moved toward a more congenial view of human nature. . . . Chastising sinners is considered counterproductive: it makes them feel worse about themselves.[10]

Psychology and self-esteem theology have fed one another. And as evangelicals become more and more accepting of psychological counseling, they become more and more vulnerable to the dangers posed by self-esteem teaching. As even the *Newsweek* article suggested, those who are concerned primarily with self-esteem are hardly in a position to deal with human transgressions as *sin against God* or to inform people already comfortable in self-love and self-righteousness that they are actually sinners in need of spiritual salvation.

Here one's theology becomes intensely practical. These are questions that must be settled in the heart before the counselor can offer truly biblical counsel: Does God really want all people to feel good about themselves? Or does He first call sinners to recognize the utter helplessness of their own estate? Of course, the answer is obvious to those who let Scripture speak for itself.

UNDERSTANDING THE DOCTRINE OF TOTAL DEPRAVITY

Scripture, of course, teaches from beginning to end that all humanity is *totally depraved*. Paul said unredeemed people are "dead in . . . trespasses and sins" (Eph. 2:1). Apart from salvation, all people walk in worldliness and disobedience (v. 2). We who know and love the Lord once "lived in the lusts of our flesh, indulging the desires of the flesh and of the mind, and were by nature children of wrath, even as the rest" (v. 3). We were "separate from Christ, excluded from the commonwealth of Israel, and strangers to the covenants of promise, having no hope and without God in the world" (v. 12).

In those passages Paul described the state of unbelievers as estrangement from God. It is that they *hate* God, not that they are intimidated by

Him. In fact, Paul said, "There is no fear of God" in the unregenerate person (Rom. 3:18). Before our salvation, we were actually God's enemies (5:8, 10). We were "alienated and hostile in mind, engaged in evil deeds" (Col. 1:21). Sinful passions, inflamed by our hatred of God's law, motivated all our living (Rom. 7:5). We were tainted by sin in every part of our being. We were corrupt, evil, thoroughly sinful.

Theologians refer to this doctrine as *total depravity*. It does not mean that unbelieving sinners are always as bad as they could be (see Luke 6:33; Rom. 2:14). It does not mean that the expression of sinful human nature is always lived out to the fullest. It does not mean that unbelievers are incapable of acts of kindness, benevolence, goodwill, or human altruism. It certainly does not mean that non-Christians cannot appreciate goodness, beauty, honesty, decency, or excellence. It *does* mean that none of this has any merit with God.

Depravity also means that evil has contaminated every aspect of our humanity: our heart, mind, personality, emotions, conscience, motives, and will (see Jer. 17:9; John 8:44). Unredeemed sinners are therefore incapable of doing anything to please God (Is. 64:6). They are incapable of truly loving the God who reveals Himself in Scripture. They are incapable of obedience from the heart, with righteous motives. They are incapable of understanding spiritual truth. They are incapable of genuine faith. And that means they are incapable of pleasing God or truly seeking Him (Heb. 11:1).

Total depravity means sinners have no ability to do spiritual good or to work for their own salvation from sin. They are so completely disinclined to love righteousness, so thoroughly dead in sin, that they are not able to save themselves or even to fit themselves for God's salvation. Unbelieving humanity has no capacity to desire, understand, believe, or apply spiritual truth: "A natural man does not accept the things of the Spirit of God; for they are foolishness to him, and he cannot understand them, because they are spiritually appraised" (1 Cor. 2:14). In spite of all this, people are *proud* of themselves! Lack of self-esteem is not the issue.

Because of Adam's sin, this state of spiritual death called total depravity has passed to all mankind. Another term for this is *original sin.* Scripture explains it this way: "Through one man sin entered into the world, and death through sin, and so death spread to all men, because all sinned (Rom. 5:12). When, as head of the human race, Adam sinned, the whole race was corrupted. "Through the one man's disobedience the many were made sinners" (v. 19). How such a thing could happen has been the subject of much theological discussion for centuries. For our purposes, however, it is sufficient to affirm that Scripture clearly teaches that Adam's sin brought guilt upon the entire race. We were "in Adam" when he sinned, and therefore the guilt of sin and the sentence of death passed upon all of us: "In Adam all die" (1 Cor. 15:22).

We might be tempted to think, *If I'm sinful by birth and never had a morally neutral nature, how can I be held responsible for being a sinner?* But our corrupt nature is precisely why our guilt is such a serious matter. Sin flows from the very soul of our being. It is because of our sinful nature that we commit sinful acts: "For from within, out of the heart of men, proceed the evil thoughts, fornications, thefts, murders, adulteries, deeds of coveting and wickedness, as well as deceit, sensuality, envy, slander, pride and foolishness. All these evil things proceed from within and defile the man" (Mark 7:21–23). We are "by nature children of wrath" (Eph. 2:3). Original sin, including all the corrupt tendencies and sinful passions of the soul, is as deserving of punishment as all our voluntary acts of sin. What is sin, after all, but *anomia*—"lawlessness" (1 John 3:4)? Or as the Westminster Shorter Catechism said, "Sin is any want of conformity to, or transgression of, the law of God" (question 14). Far from being an excuse, original sin itself is at the heart of *why* we are guilty. And original sin itself is sufficient grounds for our condemnation before God.

Moreover, original sin with its resulting depravity is the *reason* we commit voluntary acts of sin. D. Martyn Lloyd-Jones wrote,

> Why is it that man ever chooses to sin? The answer is that man has fallen away from God, and as a result, his whole nature has become perverted and sinful. Man's whole bias is away from God. By nature he hates God and feels that God is opposed to him. His god is himself, his own abilities and powers, his own desires. He objects to the whole idea of God and the demands which God makes upon him. . . . Furthermore, man likes and covets the things which God prohibits, and dislikes the things and the kind of life to which God calls him. These are no mere dogmatic statements. They are facts. . . . They alone explain the moral muddle and the ugliness that characterise life to such an extent today.[11]

Salvation from original sin is only through the cross of Christ: "As through the one man's disobedience [Adam's sin] the many were made sinners, even so through the obedience of the One [Jesus Christ] the many will be made righteous" (Rom. 5:19). We are born in sin (Ps. 51:5), and if we are to become children of God and enter God's kingdom, we must be born again by God's Spirit (John 3:3–8).

In other words, contrary to what most people think—contrary to the presuppositions of self-esteem doctrine—men and women are not naturally good. Just the opposite is true. We are by nature enemies of God, sinners, lovers of ourselves, and in bondage to our own sin. We are blind, deaf, and dead to spiritual matters, unable even to believe apart from God's gracious intervention. Yet we are relentlessly proud! In fact, nothing is more illustrative of human wickedness than the desire for self-esteem. And the first step to a proper self-image is a recognition that these things are true.

That is why Jesus *commended* the tax-gatherer, rather than rebuking him for his low self-esteem, when the man pounded his chest and pleaded, "God, be merciful to me, the sinner!" (Luke 18:13). The man had finally come to the point where he saw himself for what he was, and he was so overcome that his emotion released in acts of self-condemnation. The truth is, his self-image had never been more sound than at that moment. Rid of pride and pretense, he now saw there was nothing he could ever do to earn God's favor. Instead, he pleaded with God for mercy. And therefore he "went down to his house justified," exalted by God because he had humbled himself (v. 14). For the first time ever he was in a position to realize true joy, peace with God, and a new sense of self-worth that is granted by God's grace to those He adopts as His children (Rom. 8:15).

ALL HAVE SINNED AND FALL SHORT

Deep in our hearts, we all know something is desperately wrong with us. Our conscience constantly confronts us with our own sinfulness. Try as we might to blame others or seek psychological explanations for how we feel, we cannot escape reality. We cannot ultimately deny our own consciences. We all feel our guilt, and we all know the horrible truth about who we are on the inside.

We *feel* guilty because we *are* guilty. Only the cross of Christ can answer sin in a way that frees us from our own shame. Psychology might mask some of the pain of our guilt. Self-esteem might sweep it under the rug for a time. Other things, such as seeking comfort in relationships, or blaming our problems on someone else, might make us feel better, but the relief is only superficial. And it is dangerous. In fact, it often intensifies the guilt, because it adds dishonesty and pride to the sin that originally wounded the conscience.

True guilt has only one cause, and that is sin. Until sin is dealt with, the conscience will fight to accuse. And sin, not low self-esteem, is the very thing the gospel is given to conquer. That is why the apostle Paul began his presentation of the gospel to the Romans with a lengthy discourse about sin. Total depravity is the first gospel truth he introduced, and he spent nearly three full chapters on the subject. Romans 1:18–32 demonstrates the guilt of the pagans. Romans 2:1–16 proves the guilt of the moralist, who violates the very standard by which he judges others. And Romans 2:17—3:8 establishes the guilt of the Jews, who had access to all the benefits of divine grace but as a whole rejected God's righteousness nonetheless.

Starting in Romans 1, Paul argued eloquently, citing evidence from nature, history, sound reason, and conscience, to prove the utter sinfulness of all humanity. In verses 9–20 of chapter 3, he summed it all up. Paul reasoned like an attorney giving his final summation. He reviewed his arguments like a prosecutor who has made an ironclad case against all humanity. It is a powerful and compelling presentation, replete with a charge, convincing proof, and the inescapable verdict.

The Charge

"What then? Are we better than they? Not at all; for we have already charged that both Jews and Greeks are all under sin" (Rom. 3:9). Paul's indictment thus began with two questions: What then? or, "Is there any need of further testimony?" and, Are we better than they? or, "Can anyone honestly claim to live above the level of human nature I have been describing?"

"Not at all," he answered. Everyone from the most degenerate, perverted sinner (1:28–32) to the most rigidly legalistic Jew falls into the same category of total depravity. In other words, the entire human race, without exception, is arraigned in the divine courtroom and charged with being "under sin," wholly subjugated to the power of sin. All unredeemed people, Paul said, are subservient to sin, in thrall to it, taken captive to sin's authority.

Paul's Jewish readers would have found this truth every bit as shocking and unbelievable as it must be to those weaned on modern self-esteem doctrine. They believed they were acceptable to God by birth and that only Gentiles were sinners by nature. Jews were, after all, God's chosen people. The idea that all Jews were sinners was contrary to the beliefs of the Pharisees. They taught that only derelicts, beggars, and Gentiles were born in sin (see John 9:34). But Scripture clearly pronounces otherwise. Even David said, "I was brought forth in iniquity, and in sin my mother conceived me" (Ps. 51:5). The apostle John wrote, "The whole world lies in the power of the evil one" (1 John 5:19). Modern humanity, weaned on self-esteem psychology, also finds it shocking to learn that all of us are by nature sinful and unworthy creatures.

The Proof

Paul, continuing his courtroom summation, went on to prove from the Old Testament Scriptures the universality of human depravity:

> As it is written, "There is none righteous, not even one; / There is none who understands, / There is none who seeks for God; / All have turned aside, together they have become useless; / There is none who does good, / There is not even one." / "Their throat is an open grave, / With their tongues they keep deceiving," / "The poison of asps is under their lips"; / "Whose mouth is full of cursing and bitterness"; / "Their feet are swift to shed blood, / Destruction and misery are in their paths, / And the path of peace have they not known" (Rom. 3:10–17).

Notice how Paul underscored the universality of sin. In those few verses, he said "none" or "not even one" six times. No person escapes the accusation. "The Scripture has shut up all men under sin" (Gal. 3:22).

Paul's argument is constructed in three parts. First he showed *how sin corrupts the character:* "There is none righteous . . . / There is none who does good, / There is not even one" (Rom. 3:10–12). Here Paul made six charges. He said that because of their innate depravity, people are universally evil ("none righteous"); spiritually ignorant ("none who understands"), rebellious ("none who seeks for God"), wayward ("all have turned aside"), spiritually useless ("together they have become useless"), and morally corrupt ("there is none who does good").

The verse Paul was quoting is Psalm 14:1: "The fool has said in his heart, 'There is no God.' / They are corrupt, they have committed abominable deeds; / There is no one who does good." The words at the end of Romans 3:12, "not even one," are an editorial comment from Paul, added to make the truth inescapable for someone who might otherwise think of himself as an exception to the rule, as is the common attitude of self-justifying sinners.

Notice, Paul did not suggest that some sinners might be prone to think worse of themselves than they ought to. The very opposite is true: "I say to every man among you not to think more highly of himself than he ought to think" (Rom. 12:3). Undue pride is the typical and expected response of sinners. Self-esteem teaching is the expression of that very pride. Making a savage feel good about himself only increases his deadliness.

Again, the utter depravity Paul was describing certainly does not mean that all people play out the expression of their sin to the ultimate degree. There are certainly some people who are good in a relative sense. They may have characteristics of compassion, generosity, kindness, integrity, decency, thoughtfulness, and so on. But even those characteristics are imperfect and sullied with human sin and weakness. No one—"not even one"—comes close to true righteousness. God's standard, after all, is absolute perfection: "You are to be perfect, as your heavenly Father is perfect" (Matt. 5:48). In other words, no one who falls short of the touchstone of perfection is acceptable to God! What does that do to self-esteem theology? How does one feel good about oneself when God Himself declares us worthy of wrath?

There *is* an answer to the dilemma, of course. God justifies the ungodly by faith (Rom. 4:5). Christ's own perfect righteousness is imputed to our account, so by faith we can stand before God clothed in a perfect righteousness that is not our own (Phil. 3:9). This does not speak of external works that we do. It is a superior righteousness, the totality of Christ's own righteousness, credited to our account. Christ, on our behalf, has already fulfilled the requirement of being as perfect as our heavenly Father is perfect. His virtue is assigned to our account, so God regards us as fully righteous.

But we are jumping ahead of the apostle's carefully arranged evidence. He added a paraphrase also from Psalm 14: "The LORD has looked down from heaven upon the sons of men, / To see if there are any who understand, / Who seek after God" (v. 2; see 53:3). Ignorance and depravity go hand in hand. But people are not sinful and enemies of God because of their spiritual ignorance; rather they are spiritually ignorant because of their sinfulness and their adversarial disposition toward God. They are "darkened in their understanding, excluded from the life of God, because of the ignorance that is in them, *because of the hardness of their heart*" (Eph. 4:18, emphasis added). In other words, because of their hatred of God and their love for their own sin, they reject the witness of God in creation and the testimony of their conscience (Rom. 1:19–20). This hardens the heart and darkens the mind.

The hard heart and darkened mind refuse to seek for God: "There is *none* who seeks for God." That again echoes Psalm 14:2. God invites the seeker and promises that those who seek Him with all their hearts will find Him (Jer. 29:13). Jesus also promised that everyone who seeks Him will find Him (Matt. 7:8). But the sinful heart is inclined away from God and does not seek Him. Without God's gracious, sovereign intervention seeking and drawing sinners to Himself first, no one would seek and be saved. Jesus Himself said, "No one can come to Me, unless the Father who sent Me draws him . . . (John 6:44).

Rather than seeking God, sinners inevitably go their own way. Still using Psalm 14, Paul cited verse 3: "They have all turned aside," or as Romans 3:12 has it, "All have turned aside." This is reminiscent of Isaiah 53:6: "All of us like sheep have gone astray, each of us has turned to his own way." Sinners are naturally wayward. Inherent in human depravity is an inescapable drift away from truth and righteousness. Sinners always lose their way: "There is a way which seems right to a man, but its end is the way of death" (Prov. 14:12).

The taint of sin further renders the sinner "useless" (Rom. 3:12). "Useless" translates a Greek word used to describe spoiled milk or contaminated food to be thrown out. Unredeemed people are unfit for any spiritual good, useless for righteousness, fit only to be thrown into the fire and burned (John 15:6). Their great need is not self-esteem or positive thinking, but redemption from their prideful sin.

In the next few verses Paul described *how sin defiles the conversation:* "Their throat is an open grave, with their tongues they keep deceiving, the poison of asps is under their lips; whose mouth is full of cursing and bitterness" (Rom. 3:13–14). One's true character inevitably becomes apparent in conversation. Scripture is filled with affirmation of this truth:

- "The mouth speaks out of that which fills the heart. The good man out of his good treasure brings forth what is good; and the evil man out of his evil treasure brings forth what is evil" (Matt. 12:34–35).
- "The things that proceed out of the mouth come from the heart" (Matt. 15:18).

- "The mouth of the righteous flows with wisdom, / But the perverted tongue will be cut out. The lips of the righteous bring forth what is acceptable, / But the mouth of the wicked, what is perverted" (Prov. 10:31–32).
- "The tongue of the wise makes knowledge acceptable, / But the mouth of fools spouts folly. . . . The heart of the righteous ponders how to answer, / But the mouth of the wicked pours out evil things" (Prov. 15:2, 28).
- "Your iniquities have made a separation between you and your God, / And your sins have hidden His face from you, so that He does not hear. / For your hands are defiled with blood, / And your fingers with iniquity; / Your lips have spoken falsehood, / Your tongue mutters wickedness" (Is. 59:2–3).
- "They bend their tongue like their bow; / Lies and not truth prevail in the land. . . . / Every neighbor goes about as a slanderer. / And everyone deceives his neighbor, / And does not speak the truth, / They have taught their tongue to speak lies" (Jer. 9:3–5).

Paul chose more passages from the psalms to underscore the point:

- "Poison of a viper is under their lips" (Ps. 140:3).
- "There is nothing reliable in what they say; / Their inward part is destruction itself; / Their throat is an open grave; / They flatter with their tongue" (Ps. 5:9).
- "His mouth is full of curses and deceit and oppression; / Under his tongue is mischief and wickedness" (Ps. 10:7).

Those verses, all written to condemn "the wicked," Paul applied to everyone. He was making the point that human depravity is universal. *All* are wicked. *Everyone* is guilty. *No one* can claim exemption from the charges Paul leveled.

Moreover, he was illustrating how thoroughly sin pervades and permeates every aspect of our humanity. Note how completely sin contaminates the conversation: it defiles the "throat," corrupts the "tongue," poisons the "lips," and pollutes the "mouth." Evil speech, an expression of the wickedness of the heart, thus defiles every organ it touches as it "proceeds out of the mouth," defiling the whole person (Matt. 15:11).

Third, Paul quoted several verses to show *how sin perverts the conduct:* "'Their feet are swift to shed blood, / Destruction and misery are in their paths, / And the path of peace have they not known'" (Rom. 3:15–17). Here Paul was quoting a passage from Isaiah. This is significant, because in these verses Isaiah was excoriating Israel for their sins against Jehovah. This was no denunciation of wicked pagans, but an indictment of religious people who believed in God: "Their feet run to evil, / And they hasten to shed innocent blood; / Their thoughts are thoughts of iniquity; / Devastation and destruction are in their highways. / They do not know the way of peace, / And there is no justice in their tracks; / They have made their paths crooked; / Whoever treads on them does not know peace" (Is. 59:7–8).

The phrase "their feet are swift to shed blood" describes sinful humanity's penchant for murder. Remember, Jesus taught that hatred is the moral equivalent of murder (Matt. 5:21–22). The seed of hatred ripens and matures, and the fruit it bears is the shedding of blood. Sinners are naturally attracted to hatred and its violent offspring. People are "swift" in their advance toward such acts. We see this very clearly in our own society. An article in *Newsweek,* for example, reported that "a 12-year-old boy turn[ed] without a word and [shot] dead a 7-year-old girl because she 'dis'ed' him by standing on his shadow."[12]

In some of our larger cities, as many as two hundred murders will occur in a typical week. Drive-by shootings, drunken brawls, gang violence, family strife, and other crimes all contribute to the body count. If lack of self-esteem is the problem of the human heart, why, we must ask, is the murder rate on the rise so dramatically in a society where self-esteem is also growing? The answer is that low self-esteem is not the problem. On the contrary, pride itself is the very problem that leads to all sin, including hate, hostility, and killing. A love for bloodshed festers in the heart of sinful humanity. Remove the moral restraints from society, and the inevitable result will be an escalation of murder and violence, no matter how good people feel about themselves.

"Destruction and misery" further characterize the tendencies of depraved humanity. Again, no one familiar with the trends of modern society can deny the truth of Scripture on this point. The lid is off, and we can see clearly the true nature of the human heart. What else could explain our culture where people are robbed, beaten, raped, or murdered for no reason other than sheer enjoyment? Wanton destruction is so much a part of society that we have become inured to much of it.

"Gangsta rap," music that glorifies murder, rape, and drug use, now accounts for many of the hottest-selling albums on the record charts. The lyrics of most gangsta rap are indescribably vile. They mix violence, sexual imagery, and unimaginable profanity in a way that is repulsive and purposely offensive. Worse, they openly incite young people to join gangs, kill policemen, rape women, riot, and commit other acts of wanton destruction. Gangsta rap is big business. These recordings are not sold secretly out of the back of some hoodlum's car, but marketed openly in retail stores everywhere, with slick ad campaigns designed by executives in companies like Capitol Records. And the prime target for such products are kids younger than eighteen. A whole generation is being indoctrinated with these vices. Destruction and misery *are* in their path. And woe to those unfortunate enough to cross their path! Several nationally known rap artists have been charged with violent crimes, including murder and gang rape.

Why is it that misery and despair are so characteristic of this modern age, even though humanity has made such remarkable advances in technology, psychology, and medicine? It is because depravity is at the very heart of the human soul. All these problems are so bound up in the human heart that no amount of learning and no measure of self-esteem will ever erase them. As science advances, people only become more sophisticated in their use of evil means. The destruction and misery wrought by human sin does not diminish; it accelerates. The history of the last century, filled with world wars, holocausts, serial killers, escalating crime, and bloody revolutions, is graphic proof of that. Depravity is bound up in the human heart.

In other words, "the path of peace" is unknown to sinful humanity (Rom. 3:17). Though we hear much talk these days of "peace, peace," there is no peace (see Jer. 6:14).

Paul summed up the evidence for human depravity: "There is no fear of God before their eyes" (Rom. 3:18). There he returned to the psalms for a final quotation. Psalm 36:1 says, "Transgression speaks to the ungodly within his heart; / There is no fear of God before his eyes." Human sinfulness is a defect of the human heart itself. Evil commands the heart of man. People's hearts are naturally attuned to wickedness. They have no native fear of God.

Fear of the Lord, of course, is the primary prerequisite to spiritual wisdom (Prov. 9:10). Moses commanded Israel, "You shall fear only the LORD your God; and you shall worship Him, and swear by His name" (Deut. 6:13). In fact, as Moses summed up the responsibilities of the Israelites, this is what he said: "And now, Israel, what does the LORD your God require from you, but to *fear* the LORD your God, to walk in all His ways and love Him, and to serve the LORD your God with all your heart and with all your soul, and to keep the LORD's commandments and His statutes which I am commanding you today for your good?" (Deut. 10:12–13, emphasis added). We in the New Testament era are likewise commanded to "cleanse ourselves from all defilement of flesh and spirit, perfecting holiness in the fear of God" (2 Cor. 7:1). We are to "honor all men; love the brotherhood, *fear God,* honor the king" (1 Pet. 2:17, emphasis added, see Rev. 14:7).

"The fear of the LORD is the instruction for wisdom" (Prov. 15:33). "By the fear of the LORD one keeps away from evil" (16:6). "The fear of the LORD is a fountain of life, / That one may avoid the snares of death" (14:27).

We do not hear much about fearing God these days. Even many Christians seem to feel the language of fear is somehow too harsh or too negative. How much easier it is to speak of God's love and infinite mercy. But longsuffering, kindness, and such attributes are not the truths that are missing from most people's concept of God. The problem is that most people do not think of God as someone to be *feared*. They do not realize that He hates the proud and punishes evildoers. They presume on His grace. They fear what people think more than they care what God thinks. They seek their own pleasure, unmindful of God's displeasure. Their consciences are defiled and in danger of vanishing. "There is no fear of God before their eyes."

The fear of God, by the way, is a concept diametrically opposed to the doctrine of self-esteem. How can we encourage fear of the Lord in people and at the same time be obsessed with boosting their self-esteem? Which is the more biblical pursuit? The Scriptures speak for themselves.

The Verdict

Having presented a convincing case for total depravity, Paul made the verdict clear: "Now we know that what things soever the law saith, it saith to them who are under the law: *that every mouth may be stopped, and all the world may become guilty before God*" (Rom. 3:19, KJV, emphasis added).

Here Paul blasted the assumption of those who believed that merely *having* the law of God somehow made the Jews morally superior to pagan Gentiles. The law carried its own condemnation against those who did not keep it perfectly: "Cursed is he who does not confirm the words of this law by doing them" (Deut. 27:26; see Gal. 3:10). "Whoever keeps the whole law and yet stumbles in one point, he has become guilty of all" (James 2:10). Merely having the law did not make the Jews any better than the rest of humanity.

The Gentiles, on the other hand, were accountable to the law written on their own consciences (Rom. 2:11–15). Both groups are proven in violation of the law they possess. The prosecution rests. There can be no defense. Every mouth must be stopped. The case is closed. Unredeemed humanity is guilty of all charges. There are no grounds for acquittal. The whole world stands guilty before God.

Self-esteem is no solution to human depravity. It aggravates it! The problems of our culture, especially the anguish that wracks individual human hearts, will not be solved by the deception of getting people to think better of themselves. People really *are* sinful to the core. The guilt and shame we all feel as sinners is legitimate, natural, and even appropriate. It has the beneficial purpose of letting us know the depth of our own sinfulness. We dare not whisk it aside for the faulty teachings of humanistic self-esteem.

I recently read an unusually clear-sighted article dealing with the myth of human goodness from a non-Christian perspective. The author, a Jewish social critic, wrote,

> To believe that people are basically good after Auschwitz, the Gulag and the other horrors of our century, is a statement of irrational faith, as irrational as any [fanatical] religious belief. Whenever I meet

people—especially Jews, victims of the most concentrated evil in history—who persist in believing in the essential goodness of people, I know that I have met people for whom evidence is irrelevant. How many evils would human beings have to commit in order to shake a Jew's faith in humanity? How many more innocent people have to be murdered and tortured? How many more women need to be raped?[13]

This article listed five consequences of the people-are-basically-good myth. Notice how they all contribute to the destruction of the conscience:

> The first such consequence is, quite logically, the attribution of all evil to causes outside of people. Since people are basically good, the bad that they do must be caused by some external force. Depending on who is doing the blaming, that outside force could be the social environment, economic circumstances, parents, schools, television violence, handguns, racism, the devil, government cutbacks, or even corrupt politicians (as expressed by this frequently heard foolishness: "How can we expect our children to be honest when the government isn't?").
>
> People are therefore not responsible for the evil they commit. It's not my fault that I mug old women, or that I cheat much of the time—something (chosen from the previous list) made me do it.
>
> A second terrible consequence is the denial of evil. If good is natural, then bad must be unnatural, or "sick." Moral categories have been replaced by psychological ones. There is no longer good and evil, only "normal" and "sick."
>
> Third, neither parents nor schools take the need to teach children goodness seriously—why teach what comes naturally? Only those who recognize that people are not basically good recognize the need to teach goodness.
>
> Fourth, since much of society believes that evil comes from outside of people, it has ceased trying to change people's values and concentrates instead on changing outside forces. People commit crimes? It is not values and character development that we need to be concerned with; we need to change the socioeconomic environment that "produces" rapists and murderers. Irresponsible men impregnate irresponsible women? It is not better values they need, but better sex education and better access to condoms and abortions.
>
> Fifth, and most destructive of all, those who believe that people are basically good conclude that people do not need to feel accountable of their behavior to God and to a religion, only to themselves.[14]

That author, oddly enough, denied human depravity as well as human goodness. He believes people are neither good *nor* bad but choose their way in life. (At the outset of his article, however, he quoted Genesis 8:21: "The intent of man's heart is evil from his youth.") Despite this inconsistency in the author's position, the article shows very clearly the dangers of the myth of human goodness.

The church must safeguard sound doctrine by recovering the doctrine of human depravity. As J. C. Ryle wrote more than a century ago,

> A scriptural view of sin is one of the best antidotes to that vague, dim, misty, hazy kind of theology which is so painfully current in the present age. It is vain to shut our eyes to the fact that there is a vast quantity of so-called Christianity nowadays which you cannot declare positively unsound, but which, nevertheless, is not full measure, good weight and sixteen ounces to the pound. It is a Christianity in which there is undeniably "something about Christ and something about grace and something about faith and something about repentance and something about holiness," but it is not the real "thing as it is" in the Bible. Things are out of place and out of proportion. As old Latimer would have said, it is a kind of "mingle-mangle," and does no good. It neither exercises influence on daily conduct, nor comforts in life, nor gives peace in death; and those who hold it often wake too late to find that they have got nothing solid under their feet. Now I believe that the likeliest way to cure and mend this defective kind of religion is to bring forward more prominently the old scriptural truth about the sinfulness of sin.[15]

You may be asking, on the other hand, *Does God want us to wallow in shame and self-condemnation permanently?* Not at all. God offers freedom from sin and shame through faith in Jesus Christ. If we are willing to acknowledge our sinfulness and seek His grace, He will wonderfully deliver us from our sin and all its effects. "There is therefore now no condemnation for those who are in Christ Jesus. For the law of the Spirit of life in Christ Jesus has set you free from the law of sin and of death" (Rom. 8:1–2). The liberation from sin those verses describe is the only basis on which we can really feel good about ourselves.

6

The Work of the Spirit and Biblical Counseling

John MacArthur

A recent book titled *I'm Dysfunctional, You're Dysfunctional,* by Wendy Kaminer, debunked much of the mystique of modern psychology.[1] The author did not purport to be a Christian. In fact, she described herself as "a skeptical, secular humanist, Jewish, feminist, intellectual lawyer."[2] Yet she wrote as a bitter critic of the marriage of religion and psychology. She noted that religion and psychology have always more or less deemed one another incompatible. Now she sees "not just a truce but a remarkable accommodation."[3] Even from her perspective as an unbeliever, she could see that this accommodation has meant a change in the fundamental message Christians convey to the world. She wrote:

> Religious writers would minimize or dismiss the effect of psychology on religion, fiercely denying that it has made doctrinal changes, but it does seem to have influenced the tone and packaging of religious appeals. . . . Christian codependency books, like those produced by the Minirth-Meier clinic in Texas, are practically indistinguishable from codependency books published by secular writers. . . . Religious writers justify their reliance on psychology by praising it for "catching up" to some eternal truths, but they've also found a way to make the temporal truths of psychology palatable. Religious leaders once condemned psychoanalysis for its moral neutrality. . . . Now popular religious literature equates illness with sin.[4]

Some of the criticism Kaminer leveled against evangelicals is unwarranted or misguided, but in this respect she is right on target: evangelicalism has been infiltrated by a worldly anthropology-psychology-theology that is diametrically opposed to the biblical doctrines of sin and sanctification. As a result of this accommodation, the church has compromised and hopelessly muddled the message it is to proclaim.

Visit your local Christian bookstore and notice the proliferation of books on addiction recovery, emotional therapy, self-esteem, and other psychology-related topics. The language of such books carries a common theme: "look within yourself"; "get in touch with your inner child"; "explore the recesses of your past fears, hurts, and disappointments"; and "find the real answers to your problems within your own heart." Why? Because "the answers lie deep within."

Those books may sport logos from Christian publishers, but that kind of advice is not biblical and is unworthy of being labeled Christian. In fact, it sums up the very worst advice secular psychology offers.

Nowhere does Scripture advise people to seek answers by looking within. In fact, Scripture explicitly teaches us that we are sinners and should distrust our own hearts: "'The heart is more deceitful than all else / And is desperately sick; / Who can understand it? / 'I, the LORD, search the heart, / I test the mind'" (Jer. 17:9–10). Those who look within themselves to find answers are in a hopeless situation. Instead of answers, they get lies.

Psychology cannot solve this dilemma. Virtually all psychotherapy turns people inward, studying feelings, groping for suppressed memories, seeking self-esteem, scrutinizing attitudes, and generally listening to one's own heart. But emotions are hopelessly subjective, and our own hearts are deceitful. Only biblical counseling can offer reliable, authoritative, objective answers. And the objective truth of Scripture is the only tool God uses in the process of sanctification. Jesus Himself prayed, "Sanctify them in the truth; Thy word is truth" (John 17:17).

Unfortunately, psychology and worldly therapies have usurped the role of sanctification in some Christians' thinking. Psychological sanctification has become a substitute for the Spirit-filled life. The notion is abroad within the church that psychotherapy is often a more effective change agent—particularly in dealing with the most difficult cases—than the Holy Spirit who sanctifies.

But can psychotherapy possibly accomplish something that the Holy Spirit cannot? Can an earthly therapist achieve more than a heavenly Comforter? Is behavior modification more helpful than sanctification? Of course not.

THE PARACLETE

To understand the crucial role the Holy Spirit plays in meeting people's inner needs, we must go back to what Jesus taught His disciples when He first promised them He would send the Holy Spirit. It happened on the night Jesus was betrayed. His crucifixion was drawing near, and the disciples were fearful and confused. When Jesus spoke to them about going away, their hearts were troubled (John 14:1–2). In that hour of turmoil, they feared being left alone. But Jesus assured them that they would not be left to fend for themselves. He comforted them with this wonderful promise:

"I will ask the Father, and He will give you another Helper, that He may be with you forever; that is the Spirit of truth, whom the world cannot receive, because it does not behold Him or know Him, but you know Him because He abides with you, and will be in you.

"I will not leave you as orphans; I will come to you. After a little while the world will behold Me no more; but you will behold Me; because I live, you shall live also. In that day you shall know that I am in My Father, and you in Me, and I in you.

"He who has My commandments and keeps them, he it is who loves Me; and he who loves Me shall be loved by My Father, and I will love him, and will disclose Myself to him."

Judas (not Iscariot) said to Him, "Lord, what then has happened that You are going to disclose Yourself to us, and not to the world?"

Jesus answered and said to him, "If anyone loves Me, he will keep My word; and My Father will love him, and We will come to him, and make Our abode with him. He who does not love Me does not keep My words; and the word which you hear is not Mine, but the Father's who sent Me. These things I have spoken to you, while abiding with you. But the Helper, the Holy Spirit, whom the Father will send in My name, He will teach you all things, and bring to your remembrance all that I said to you" (John 14:16–26).

"Helper" in verse 16 is the Greek word *paraklētos,* meaning someone called to another's aid. First John 2:1 applies the same term to Jesus Himself: "If anyone sins, we have an Advocate [*paraklētos*] with the Father, Jesus Christ the righteous." The word is sometimes transliterated into English as "paraclete." It describes a spiritual attendant whose role is to offer assistance, succor, support, relief, advocacy, and guidance—a divine Counselor whose ministry to believers is to offer the very things that so many people vainly seek in therapy!

The promises Jesus made with regard to the Holy Spirit and His ministry are staggering in their scope. Let's look at some of the key elements of this text.

A DIVINE HELPER

The word translated "another" (John 14:16) is a key to understanding the nature of the Holy Spirit. The Greek text carries a precision that is not immediately evident in English. Two Greek words can be translated "another." One is *heteros,* which means "a different one, a different kind" as in, "If that style is not what you want, try another." *Allos* is also translated "another" in English, but it means "another of the same kind," as in, "That cookie was tasty; may I have another?"

Jesus used *allos* to describe the Holy Spirit: "another [*allos*] Helper [of the same kind]." He was promising to send His disciples a Helper exactly like

Himself, a compassionate, loving, divine Paraclete. They had grown dependent on Jesus' ministry to them. He had been their Wonderful Counselor, Teacher, Leader, Friend, and had shown them the Father. But from now on, they would have another Paraclete, One like Jesus, to meet the same needs He had met.

Here, for the first time, Jesus gave the disciples extensive teaching about the Holy Spirit and His role. Note that our Lord spoke of the Spirit as a person, not an influence, not a mystical power, not some ethereal, impersonal, phantom force. The Spirit has all the attributes of personality (mind, Rom. 8:27; emotions, Eph. 4:30; and will, Heb. 2:4) and all the attributes of deity (see Acts 5:3–4). He is another Paraclete of exactly the same essence as Jesus.

There was, however, a significant difference: Jesus was returning to the Father, but the Holy Spirit would "be with you forever" (John 14:16). The Holy Spirit is a constant, sure, trustworthy, divine Paraclete graciously given by Christ to His disciples to be with them forever.

A Guide to Truth

It is noteworthy that Jesus referred to the Holy Spirit as "the Spirit of truth" (v. 17). As God, He is the essence of truth; as a Paraclete, He is the One who guides us into truth. That is why apart from Him, it is impossible for sinful beings to know or understand *any* spiritual truth. Jesus said, "The world cannot receive [Him], because it does not behold Him or know Him" (v. 17). Echoing that truth, Paul wrote, "To us God revealed [things which the world cannot see or understand] through the Spirit. . . . Now we have received, not the spirit of the world, but the Spirit who is from God, that we might know the things freely given to us by God. . . . But a natural man does not accept the things of the Spirit of God; for they are foolishness to him, and he cannot understand them, because they are spiritually appraised" (1 Cor. 2:10, 12, 14).

The unregenerate have no facility for spiritual perception. They cannot comprehend spiritual truth because they are spiritually dead (Eph. 2:1), unable to respond to anything except their own sinful passions. Believers, on the other hand, are actually taught spiritual truth by God Himself (see John 6:45). In fact, much of the Holy Spirit's ministry to believers involves teaching them (John 14:26; 1 Cor. 2:13; 1 John 2:20, 27); guiding them into the truth of Christ (John 16:13–14); and illuminating the truth for them (1 Cor. 2:12).

This promise of a supernatural Teacher had a special application for the eleven disciples. Often, Jesus' teaching was difficult for them to understand immediately. In fact, much of what He told them meant nothing to them until after His resurrection. For example, in John 2:22 we read, "When . . .

He was raised from the dead, His disciples remembered that He said this; and they believed the Scripture, and the word which Jesus had spoken." John 12:16 says, "These things His disciples did not understand at the first; but when Jesus was glorified, then they remembered that these things were written of Him, and that they had done these things to Him." In John 16:12, Jesus said, "I have many more things to say to you, but you cannot bear them now."

After Jesus ascended to heaven, one of the crucial ministries of the Holy Spirit was to bring to the disciples' minds what Jesus had said and to teach them what He meant: "These things I have spoken to you, while abiding with you. But the Helper, the Holy Spirit, whom the Father will send in My name, He will teach you all things, and bring to your remembrance all that I said to you" (14:25–26). That means that the Holy Spirit enabled the disciples to recall the precise words Jesus had spoken to them, so that when they recorded them as Scripture, the words were perfect and error free. This assured that the gospel accounts were recorded infallibly, and that the apostolic teaching was unadulterated.

But this promise of our Lord also reveals the Holy Spirit as a supernatural Teacher who ministers truth to the hearts of those whom He indwells. The Spirit guides us into the truth of God's Word. He teaches us, affirms the truth in our hearts, convicts us of sin, and often brings to mind specific truths and statements of Scripture that are applicable to our lives. As we noted, "Things which eye has not seen and ear has not heard, and which have not entered the heart of man, all that God has prepared for those who love him . . . to us God revealed them *through the Spirit*" (1 Cor. 2:9–10, emphasis added).

As a divinely indwelling teacher, the Spirit of Truth fills a function that no human counselor can even approach. He is constantly there, pointing the way to truth, applying the truth directly to our hearts, prompting us to conform to the truth—in short, sanctifying us in the truth (John 17:17).

THE INDWELLING PRESENCE

Look a little more closely at Jesus' words at the end of John 14:17: "He abides with you, and will be in you." Our Lord was promising that the Holy Spirit would take up permanent, uninterrupted residence within His disciples. It was not only that the Spirit would be *present with* them; the greater truth was that He would be *resident within* them permanently.

This truth of the permanently indwelling Spirit is one of the wonderful new covenant realities. Ezekiel 37:14 foretold it: "I will put My Spirit within you, and you will come to life." In the Old Testament, the Holy Spirit was often present with believers, but He did not indwell them. Moreover, His presence seemed to be conditional; so David prayed, "Do not take Thy Holy Spirit from me" (Ps. 51:11).

In the New Testament era, however, believers have a permanently resident Paraclete, not *with,* but *within.* In fact, the indwelling presence of the Spirit is one of the proofs of salvation: "You are not in the flesh but in the Spirit, if indeed the Spirit of God dwells in you. But if anyone does not have the Spirit of Christ, he does not belong to Him" (Rom. 8:9).

Jesus' promise in John 14 that the Holy Spirit would reside within was not limited to the eleven apostles who were present that night. The Holy Spirit indwells every Christian. In verse 23, Jesus said, "If *anyone* loves Me, he will keep My word; and My Father will love him, and We will come to him, and make Our abode with him" (emphasis added). Paul, writing to the Corinthians, said, "Do you not know that your body is a temple of the Holy Spirit who is in you, whom you have from God, and that you are not your own?" (1 Cor. 6:19). Thus each believer enjoys the permanent, continuing presence of the Holy Spirit living within.

UNION WITH CHRIST

In John 14:18–19, Jesus continued, "I will not leave you as orphans; I will come to you. After a little while the world will behold Me no more; but you will behold Me." Christ knew that within hours He would be crucified. His earthly ministry was coming to an end. But He reassured the disciples that He was not leaving them altogether. They would continue to behold Him.

What does that mean? In what sense would they be able to behold Him? There seem to be two key elements to that promise. First, He was reassuring them by implication that He would rise from the dead. Death would neither conquer Him nor end His ministry in their lives. Second, He promised, "I will come to you" (v. 18). That promise can be interpreted in various ways. Some see it as a reference to the Second Coming. Others view it as a promise that He would appear to them after He rose from the dead. In this context, however, this promise seems linked to the coming of the Holy Spirit to dwell within them. What Jesus seems to be saying is that He would be spiritually present in the disciples through the agency of the indwelling Holy Spirit. Compare this to the subsequent promise He gave just before He ascended: "Lo, I am with you always, even to the end of the age" (Matt. 28:20). In what sense is He "with" His chosen ones? And in what sense would they "behold" Him? The answer seems to be that He would also indwell them through the Holy Spirit.

This doctrine is known as union with Christ. John Murray wrote, "Union with Christ is really the central truth of the whole doctrine of salvation."[5] All believers are joined with Christ by the Holy Spirit in an inseparable union. Scripture sometimes speaks of this union as our being *in Christ* (see 2 Cor.

5:17; Phil. 3:9), and sometimes as Christ's being *in us* (see Rom. 8:10; Gal. 2:20; Col. 1:27). A few passages even merge the twin concepts: "Abide in Me, and I in you" (John 15:4). "By this we know that we abide in Him and He in us, because He has given us of His Spirit" (1 John 4:13).

As that last verse shows, our union with Christ is inextricably linked to the Holy Spirit's indwelling. It is through the Holy Spirit that we become one with Christ, and through the Spirit that Christ lives in our hearts. Those in whom the Spirit abides operate in a different dimension. They are alive to the spiritual realm. They commune with Christ. They move and participate in the life of the Spirit. They have the mind of Christ (1 Cor. 2:16).

Jesus continued His comforting words to the disciples in John 14: "In that day you shall know that I am in My Father, and you in Me, and I in you" (v. 20). Here He was emphasizing our spiritual union with Him and His own union with the Father. It seems evident that on this dreadful night when Jesus was about to be betrayed, the disciples still did not understand the mystery of Christ's relationship to His Father. Much less could they have grasped the concept of their own union with Christ. But Jesus told them that the time would come when they would begin to understand the richness of these realities: "In that day you shall know" (v. 20) seems to refer to the day of Pentecost, when the Holy Spirit came in power. What happened that day demonstrates the power of God's Spirit to teach us, to untangle our confusion, and to empower us for service. Peter suddenly stood up and began preaching with a power, a clarity, and a boldness that were foreign to him. It was as if everything suddenly fell into place spiritually for him. He had the mind of Christ and was immediately transformed from a cowering, confused disciple, into a fearless, forthright apostle. He was united through faith with Christ and filled with the Holy Spirit. He now had access to a power and a confidence that he had never shown before.

THE LOVE OF GOD

There is at least one more important aspect of Jesus' promise to His disciples on that final night. He told them, "He who has My commandments and keeps them, he it is who loves Me; and he who loves Me shall be loved by My Father, and I will love him, and will disclose Myself to him" (John 14:21). There Jesus echoed a statement He had made just a few verses earlier ("If you love Me, you will keep My commandments," v. 15), then expanded that truth into a promise of the Father's love graciously shown to those who follow the Son.

That passage describes the believer's relationship with the Father and the Son. We love Christ, so we keep His commandments. Those who love Christ are loved by the Father, and Christ manifests Himself to them. The Spirit's role is not explicitly stated here, but it is the Spirit within who empowers believers to love and obey Christ: "The love of God has been poured out within our hearts through the Holy Spirit who was given to us" (Rom. 5:5). It is not that God loves us *because* we love the Son. On the contrary, our love for Him is prompted by His grace to us. The apostle John says elsewhere, "We love, because He first loved us" (1 John 4:19).

Thus Christianity involves a supernatural relationship with the Trinity. The Spirit indwells the believer, kindling righteous desires and holy affections, pouring out the love of God in our hearts. The believer thus loves Christ and strives to obey Him. Moreover, both the Father and the Son pledge their love to believers, and Christ continually manifests Himself in that love. The believer, then, is the beneficiary of a loving relationship involving Father, Son, and Holy Spirit.

At this point in Jesus' discourse, Judas, not Judas Iscariot but the disciple who is also called Lebbaeus and Thaddaeus, spoke out: "Lord, what then has happened that You are going to disclose Yourself to us, and not to the world?" (John 14:22). Jesus answered, "If anyone loves Me, he will keep My word; and My Father will love him, and We will come to him, and make Our abode with him" (v. 23).

That answer simply reiterated what the Lord had said in verses 15 and 21. But Jesus continued: "He who does not love Me does not keep My words; and the word which you hear is not Mine, but the Father's who sent Me" (v. 24). The implication is clear: The Lord Jesus will not manifest Himself to those who are disobedient. Those who do not love Christ, who do not want Him, and who refuse to obey His words are cut off from any relationship or fellowship with Him.

Moreover, those who reject the Son reject the Father as well. When they turn from the commandments of Christ, they scorn the Father's Word. They cut themselves off from any of the spiritual benefits of fellowship with God.

That raises a question essential to the issue of biblical counseling. Can the biblical counselor offer meaningful help for non-Christians? If the counselee lacks all the spiritual resources Jesus has described, if the Holy Spirit does not dwell within, and if the person has no fellowship with the Father or the Son, can any amount of counsel ultimately help resolve the problems that brought the individual for help in the first place?

The answer seems obvious. Some superficial problems might be addressed by the application of biblical principles. For example, a husband might be encouraged to live with his wife in an understanding way (1 Pet. 3:7), and the quality of that marriage might improve some. Or a young person struggling with submission to authority might learn the importance of complying with parents and authority figures, and thereby avoid some conflicts. But apart from the regenerating influence of the Holy Spirit, no amount of counseling can resolve the root problems. External conformity even to biblical law cannot undo the effects of sin.

Therefore, the biblical counselor's first priority is to determine whether the counselee is a believer. Those who are not must be shown their need for redemption first of all. That is, in fact, the way Jesus Himself modeled counseling. When Nicodemus came to Him by night, Jesus told him, "You must be born again" (John 3:7).

THE HOLY SPIRIT IN BIBLICAL COUNSELING

The new birth is the Holy Spirit's sovereign work (John 3:8). And every aspect of true spiritual growth in the life of the believer is prompted by the Spirit, using the truth of Scripture (17:17). The counselor who misses that point will experience failure, frustration, and discouragement.

Only the Holy Spirit can work fundamental changes in the human heart. Therefore, the Holy Spirit is the necessary agent in all effective biblical counseling. The counselor, armed with biblical truth, can offer objective guidance and steps for change. But unless the Holy Spirit is working in the heart of the counselee, any apparent change will be illusory, superficial, or temporary, and the same problems or worse ones will soon reappear.

At the outset of this chapter we spoke of the futility of looking within to find answers to our problems. And it is certainly true that those who focus on themselves, their childhood traumas, their wounded feelings, their emotional cravings, or other egocentric sources will never find genuine answers to their troubles.

The true believer, however, does have a Helper who dwells within. He is the Holy Spirit, who applies the objective truth of Scripture in the process of sanctification. Yet even He does not draw our attention inward, or to Himself. Instead, He directs our focus upward, to Christ. Jesus said, "When the Helper comes, whom I will send to you from the Father, that is the Spirit of truth, who proceeds from the Father, *He will bear witness of Me*" (15:26).

Ultimately, it is unto Christ that the counselee's focus must be directed. "Beholding as in a mirror the glory of the Lord, [we] are being transformed into the same image from glory to glory, just as from the Lord, the Spirit" (2 Cor. 3:18). That is the process of sanctification. And it is the ultimate goal of all truly biblical counseling.

7

Spiritual Discipline and the Biblical Counselor

Robert Smith

When we hear that a counselor has been involved in sexual sin with a counselee, we ask, "How did it happen? How could it have been prevented?" Then it is easy to add, "That will never happen to me!"

Perhaps we know a counselor who is excessively overweight and yet does an excellent job of counseling. Again a question comes to mind. "How can this person possibly help counselees develop discipline in their lives when he (or she) is obviously undisciplined?"

Such questions cause us to reflect on a basic necessity in the life of a biblical counselor: spiritual discipline. This is particularly true in light of Paul's warning that those who seek to restore another must be careful not to get caught up in the offender's sin (Gal. 6:1). Biblical counselors must have a growing relationship with the Lord, must be growing both in knowledge of and obedience to the Word of God, and must be aware of their potential to sin.

RELATIONSHIP TO THE LORD

The biblical counselor must, of course, be born again; for how can counselors correctly use the Word of God unless they are indwelt by His Spirit? And how can counselors encourage others to change and grow in their relationship with the Lord unless they are a growing model of the changing power of the gospel themselves? In the discussion that follows, we will describe eight essential elements of spiritual discipline for maintaining a growing relationship with Jesus Christ.

Reading God's Word

To correctly apply the Word of God to counseling situations we must know it and practice it. We must read it and study it in order to apply it to our lives before we can use it effectively in the counseling room. A regular reading program can be a helpful structure to do this. There are many different ways to study the Bible and while one method will be productive for one person, a different method will be more productive for someone else. Counselors who study the Bible for sermon or Sunday school lesson preparation or Bible study instruction will find that the insights gained from that study will naturally spill over into counseling.

Scripture Memorization

Scripture memorization is an essential part of the counselor's relationship with God, as well as a means of increasing personal knowledge of the Word to be used with others. As the counselor applies memorized passages to daily life, he or she is able to help the counselee use them effectively also. The Bible is the Spirit's sword and the counselor must have that sword available and ready to use at a moment's notice, not only in personal practice but also in the counseling sessions.

It is helpful to use a guided program in Scripture memorization. As you memorize Scripture, try to memorize passages rather than individual verses (other than proverbs) in order to avoid using verses out of context. Memorize verses that are useful in your own life and verses that teach doctrines applicable to counseling problems. In his book, *What to Do on Thursday*, Dr. Adams included an excellent list of verses for memorization that are particularly beneficial for counseling.[1]

Prayer

Counselees often have a wrong view of prayer. In order to help them understand prayer, counselors need to have a correct understanding of prayer and to practice prayer.

Why do we need to pray? The Bible gives many reasons, but three are particularly important. First, God commands it (Col. 4:2; 1 Tim. 5:17). Second, Christ modeled the example of prayer for us (Mark 1:35; Luke 6:12). If He, the sinless perfect One prayed, how much more should we pray? Third, since Christ taught us to pray we can assume He wants us to pray. Prayer is an act of obedience and worship of God (Matt. 6:5–9).

Prayer is basically one-way communication with God. We do not expect Him to speak to us in a mystical way in prayer because He has already spoken through His Word. If we want to hear Him, we must "search the Scriptures."

We must also remind ourselves (and frequently our counselees) that God responds to prayer with answers other than an immediate yes. For example, in Acts, Paul's request to go to Rome as a preacher was answered a different way. He went instead as a prisoner, with all expenses paid by the Roman government! Sometimes answers to prayer are delayed. George Mueller prayed for a man all his life and never experienced the answer to his prayer. Years after Mueller's death the man was saved.

In order to establish a habit of prayer it is helpful to schedule a time to pray. When you pray, use your time efficiently by praying from a prayer list. Some items on the list may be prioritized for daily prayer and others will be scheduled for weekly prayer. Praying every day for a need is not as important as praying regularly. And recognize that a long prayer time has no merit simply because it is long. On some days, when crises, and other responsibilities take over your schedule, your structured prayer time may be reduced to praying on the run. But on other days you can return to your schedule of regular prayer.

The ministry of counseling is impossible without the Spirit's guidance in understanding the Word. Counselors must seek His help in prayer to understand and rightly utilize the sword of truth in dealing with counselees' problems. In gathering data we need the Spirit's help to correctly piece it all together. And we must continually depend on the Holy Spirit to help with counselees' problems. Change will occur in counselees' lives in proportion to their understanding of the biblical principles that apply to their situation. And although wise counsel from a counselor may produce external change, it will not be permanent change. Only the Spirit can give the necessary insight and motivation for permanent change. So counselors must pray that the Spirit will work in their counselees' lives and must pray that their own lives will be examples of obedience to biblical principles and constant growth in the knowledge of the Word of God.

Here are two observations on prayer by Jay Adams:

> Prayer is a resource that Satan doesn't possess and the flesh knows nothing of it. Yet it is yours—a powerful asset which the Lord warns you not to neglect. Of course faithful prayer is difficult, as the disciples discovered and as we all know. And right here many battles are lost. People who know the Word, whose minds are fixed on the right goals and who want to win the war within, nevertheless fail because they do not pray.
>
> It is important to have the Spirit's aid in praying as well as in the battle itself. . . . If God provides for all aspects of the battle, including the very prayer with which you call on Him for provision, then make no mistake—there is no excuse for failure. You cannot even plead that you do not know how to pray![2]

Relationship with a Local Church

Maintaining a relationship with a local body of believers is an essential part of the counselor's relationship with the Lord. This relationship is mandated in the Bible. Of approximately 110 references to the church in the New Testament over 90 refer to the local church. In the New Testament, believers quickly united with the local assembly (Acts 2:41, 47). Thus if we attempt to minister apart from the local church we are ignoring God's view and purpose of the church.

There are many benefits for the counselor who maintains a relationship with a local church. One of the benefits is the preaching of the Word. This is where the counselor is fed apart from personal study. No believer can be in the Word too much to need the preaching of the Word. An irregular relationship with a local church will only diminish the counselor's spiritual growth and, thus, his or her counseling ministry. Another benefit of maintaining close ties with a local church is that this provides accountability— accountability for discipline, repentance, and restoration. A counselor who is a member of a local church accepts this protection and declares submission to biblical principles in all aspects of life.

Submission to the authority of other church leaders is particularly important for counselors. In this way they model submission to the Word of God and to imperfect leadership for counselees who must also be encouraged to submit to authority that is not perfect. Those who refuse to submit to local church leadership miss all the blessings God promises in biblical submission and have no answer to those in similar situations who come to them for counsel.

Worship

Worship is mandated for the believer and thus must be an important part of the counselor's life. Worship is not an experience or a warm feeling, it is a cognitive awe and reverence of the Holy God that focuses on Him. Without worship it is easy to minimize sin and to fail in spiritual growth that would please God. Worship makes us aware of our own spiritual needs.

The church is the biblical place for corporate worship. The music, the order of service, and all that is done should focus toward the sermon, which is designed to help the listeners accomplish the ultimate act of worship: daily obedience to God.

Worship includes praise and thanksgiving for what the Lord is doing both in the counselor's life and in the lives of counselees. Praise and thanksgiving can help to prevent discouragement when dealing with difficult problems. Such problems then become an opportunity to praise God for what He has done and can do.

Theological Correctness

Since the basis of nearly every counseling problem is a doctrinal problem, a correct understanding of theology is essential for the biblical counselor. This does not mean that we can find the answers to counseling problems in a theology textbook. The Bible is our textbook, and if we understand the Bible correctly we will adhere to a correct theology.

It is particularly important in biblical counseling for the counselor to understand the correct theology of sin. So many counseling problems are a direct result of sin, yet, frequently, counselees minimize sin. They do not understand the doctrine of sin, how bad sin is, how pervasive it is, what God thinks about it, or what they must do about it. Theological correctness is necessary in other counseling situations also. For example, when a husband does not love his wife as he should, he does not understand the doctrine of Christ: His love for the Church, His demonstrations of that love, and His driving desire to obey the Father. In all counseling problems involving a conflict with another person, there is evidence of failure in that person's relationship with God.

Theological correctness is also essential to understanding biblical counseling as opposed to other forms and philosophies of counseling. Some so-called Christian counseling attempts to manipulate others—even God—using the Bible or claims that the Bible is insufficient and that modern counselors must add their wisdom to the Bible. A correct understanding of the theology of the Bible helps sort out these issues.

Goal of Christ-Likeness

Romans 8:28–29 teaches that the goal of all believers is to become more like Christ. All that happens in a person's life is divinely orchestrated to help that person become more like God's Son (2 Cor. 3:18). Certainly this must be a priority goal in the counselor's life.

Stewardship

Believers are stewards of all that God has entrusted to them. There is nothing we have that God has not given to us and entrusted us to use for His glory. This includes spouse, children, abilities, possessions, and ministry. In entrusting them to us, He expects us to use them faithfully for His glory (1 Pet. 4:10).

RELATIONSHIP TO OTHERS

As commendable and necessary as it is, a growing relationship with the Lord is not enough to qualify one as a biblical counselor. A genuine spiritual love for people is also a prime prerequisite.

Evangelizing Others

A biblical counselor must evangelize, because God's Word commands it (Matt. 28:19–20; Mark 16:15; Acts 1:8). But beyond this, without evangelism there is no need for counseling, since the nonbeliever cannot be counseled biblically. Adams correctly stated that we can only do precounseling of nonbelievers to prepare them for salvation through the counseling relationship.[3] Thus, the counselor must be able to show people, from the Bible, how they can obtain the gift of eternal life. A counselor who is not grieved about the eternal destiny of lost souls is missing the primary focus of Christ's life and of all ministry.

Success in evangelism is not measured by results, but by the careful and accurate presentation of the gospel. This includes all the facets that lead up to being able to present the gospel. One who is building bridges of relationships to others is off to a good start in evangelism even though no gospel presentation has been made. Being all things to all men to enhance the presentation of the gospel is essential and part of the success (1 Cor. 9:19–23). However, it is also true that if one works only on bridge building and never carries the message over the bridge (perhaps because of personal failure, such as fear or neglect), then this is not success either.

Evangelism is particularly important for biblical counseling because unless the counselee experiences (or has experienced) saving faith, there cannot be much further progress in the counseling process. The counselor may use the Bible to help people improve their situations, but must always tell unsaved counselees that they will never achieve all the success God desires because they do not have the help of the indwelling Spirit. They will settle for far less than the Spirit's goals since they cannot understand His Word (2 Cor. 4:4). Success in such instances might be defined as an improvement in the circumstances, but could not be considered as change for the glory of God. In the process of solving daily problems, the counselor must not overlook the greater problem of the counselee's eternal destiny.

Discipling Others

Biblical counseling is simply an extension of discipling. There is no sharp distinction between the two. Discipling might be described as teaching basic Christian principles to a believer, whereas counseling is using those principles to deal with specific situations in a person's life. The most productive counseling grows out of the ministry of discipling a person after salvation, of teaching that individual the basic principles of living the Christian life. Biblical counselors who want to see lives change must be aggressive disciplers.

Serving Others

Jesus did not come to this earth to be served, but to serve (Matt. 20:28). If the One who created came to serve those who were created, how much more should those who were created be willing to serve. The ministry of counseling must not focus on generating an income, but on serving. Service to others is essential in establishing integrity and authenticity in biblical counseling. The counselor must be a servant in the home, in the church, even in positions of leadership.

Dealing with Criticism

One of the best means to handle criticism successfully is to approach it as a learning situation. Become a student of your critic, especially when you believe you are innocent of the criticism. Although the natural response when we believe we are innocent is to defend ourselves or try to make the accuser see that we are innocent, it is better to learn how the critic reached the conclusion. We need to ask what the accuser observed that caused him or her to make the accusation. The answers to that question can inform us how we look or sound to others with whom we communicate. We may have been totally innocent in our thoughts and motives, but inadvertently communicated something different.

For example, you may be accused of being angry with a counselee. As you reflect on the previous counseling session, you may not remember any anger or distress with the person during the discussion. But when you ask what made the person think you were angry, you learn that as you were talking you were scowling, you appeared restless, and your voice became somewhat firmer than usual. The counselee interpreted these nonverbal responses as demonstrations of anger. Although you were not angry, you can understand why the counselee felt that you were angry, and you can determine to take more care to monitor your voice and facial expressions in the future.

When you are challenged, do not run but determine to learn from the conflict. Your best defense is to ask the critic to defend the criticism as you attempt to learn from it. Proverbs 29:1 warns about ignoring reproof and in 2 Samuel 16:5–13, David saw his critic Shimei as being directed by God for his benefit. We need to remind ourselves that God is in control of our critics and could have prevented the criticism if He thought that was best. When He allows it, it is for our benefit and the benefit of our critic. By observing how we learn rather than defend, the critic sees a biblical response.

The best defense of innocence is to allow the facts to prove it, and the only facts are those that can be observed. We can ask a challenger for the facts behind an inferred conclusion and ask how the conclusion is legitimate, at the same time reminding the person that conclusions about *attitudes* based on those facts are only inferences and cannot be treated as facts. By showing we are not afraid to have our innocence carefully examined, we produce the best defense of our innocence, even when the accusation threatens our integrity. First Peter 2:12 and 3:16 teach that a godly character is the best defense against false accusation. If you have nothing to hide or to be ashamed of, let the quality of your character be closely examined. Your godly character will prove your innocence.

PERSONAL RELATIONSHIPS

Marriage

The Bible teaches that marriage is a picture of the love of Christ for His bride, the church, and the submission of that bride to her Lord (Eph.

5:22–33). The biblical counselor's marriage must be an example of this relationship. If counselors do not apply biblical principles to make their marriages successful, they will not be in a position to help counselees with their marriages. We cannot expect other couples to build a biblical marriage if we have not built one ourselves.

A spouse's companionship is God's provision to help prevent wrong relationships with counselees. God has ordained that our needs for intimacy be met only through the marriage relationship and through a relationship with His Son. Although no marriage is completely free of problems, the counselor's marriage must be an example of how sin-cursed people live in biblical harmony with one another, even in difficult times. Counselors must first successfully minister in their homes if they are effectively to demonstrate Christian principles for living to counselees.

Family

The counselor's first ministry is to his or her spouse and family. We cannot help other parents with their children if we are not spending time properly training and disciplining our own children. We must bring them up in the nurture and admonition of the Lord (Eph. 6:4). The time we spend with our children should include fun times (doing what they want) as well as times of direct spiritual teaching.

RELATIONSHIP TO SELF

Galatians 6:1 warns restorers (counselors) to be aware of their own lives. They must be growing in their relationships to Christ. Counselors should be characterized as people who are growing and changing. No counselor is perfect, for perfection is impossible, but we are to be growing more like Jesus Christ who is perfect. Here are four important concepts to consider in relationship to self.

Potential for Sin

Counselors must take a realistic view of themselves and their potential for sin. This is part of the warning in Galatians 6:1, for though we are regenerated, we still live under the curse of sin. This means that we are capable of committing the same sin as nonbelievers. To believe anything else is not only theologically erroneous but is naive and potentially dangerous. Keeping this fact in mind, we must take great precautions to make it very hard to sin (Matt. 5:28–30).

For example, if your sexual relationship with your spouse is not all you hope for, be alert to your potential to be tempted in this area. Work on serving and ministering to your spouse and thank God for the good qualities in her or him. When you see failure, recognize that God is using this to make you more like Christ. When you are tempted to think of a sexual relationship with a fictional person or a real person, recognize such thoughts as sin and immediately replace them with biblical thoughts. If you find yourself attracted to a counselee, recognize that such thinking and feeling is violating your marriage covenant. Then take every precaution necessary to remove yourself from tempting situations with that counselee.

Response to Sin

A counselor who sins must do just what counselees do: repent and change by developing a specific plan to change. It is extremely important not to form a habit of becoming comfortable with sin. No matter how small or big, sin must stop. As counselors who study the Word of God, we need to be alert to the Spirit's teaching about sin that applies to our lives.

When we are confronted with sin in our lives, we cannot ignore it. If we are guilty we must repent and change. If we are innocent, we must consider why God would allow us to be accused of the sin. Perhaps we need to be more consistent in adhering to protective guidelines to prevent that sin in our lives.

Personal Discipline

In 1 Corinthians 3:17 believers are commanded not to defile their body, which is the temple of the Holy Spirit. This admonition would include the injunction to take proper care of the body. Taking proper care of our bodies includes getting sufficient sleep, exercising daily, and disciplining ourselves to maintain a balanced weight.

Sleep. Most people need between seven and eight hours of sleep each night. Very few people can function well on less than this on a regular basis, and very few of those who think they can, actually do. Counselors should not let busy schedules keep them from getting adequate sleep. Sufficient rest is as important as all the other physical aspects of the body. Without adequate rest, fatigue makes it difficult to concentrate, especially when studying or listening to a counselee.

Exercise. Taking proper care of our bodies also includes adequate physical exercise. Numerous medical studies have confirmed the necessity of exercise for maintaining good health as well as the long-range benefits of exercise to mental and physical health. Not only does it keep our bodies functioning well, but exercise helps to reduce stress and thus lessens the risk for illness. Counselors need to develop a daily habit of exercise and at least some physical exertion. It will clear the mind and provide extra energy.

Weight. Maintaining a balanced weight level is also an important health factor. For many counselors who have desk jobs that do not require much physical exercise, this requires extra measures of self-discipline and determination, not only in choosing a balanced low-fat diet but in burning excess calories through exercise. Keeping our weight under control is a necessity, for how can a counselor insist that a counselee be disciplined in various areas of his or her life when the counselor is not disciplined in the very basic areas of diet and weight control?

TOTAL LIFE VIEW

A biblical counselor must see all of life from God's perspective. No event in the counselor's life or the counselee's life is isolated from God; He has total and complete control of everything. Nothing in this world is out of control. The Scriptures teach that every facet of life is under His control and He is using it for His glory and our benefit (Rom. 8:28–29). We can rest assured that "God never pursues His glory at the expense of the good of His people, nor does He ever seek our good at the expense of His glory. He has designed His eternal purpose so that His glory and our good are inextricably bound together."[4]

Part III

The Practice of Biblical Counseling

8

Developing a Helping Relationship with Counselees

Wayne A. Mack

Biblical counseling is about solving people's problems. It is about discovering the causes of their problems and then applying biblical principles to those causes. Sometimes, even well-intentioned counselors err by counseling without cultivating the key element of *involvement*.[1]

Consider the approach of this counselor described in *The Christian Counselor's Casebook* by Jay Adams:

> Clara comes to you stating that she has filed for divorce on the grounds of mental and bodily cruelty.
>
> Clara returns for the third session. "I tried to get him here but he had *other* things to do," she begins. "You know what his other things are, of course. I told you all of them."
>
> "I don't want to hear such charges behind Marty's back," you respond. "This continuing hostility toward him, even though you told him you forgave him, seems to indicate that you made little or no attempt to bury the issue and start afresh. I don't think that you understand forgiveness. You . . ."
>
> "Forgive him! You know there is a limit. After he has beat me, and his drinking away our money maybe, but when I came home and found him in my bed with that woman, I can never bury that! He is just an immature, immoral, animalistic pig," she declares.
>
> You tell her that it will be necessary for her to change her language about her husband and that you are here to help but not to salve her self-righteous attitude and listen to her ever-increasing charges against her husband.
>
> "Why are you siding with him? I'm the one that belongs to this church!" She breaks into tears.[2]

Why did that session deteriorate into near hopelessness before it had hardly begun? Although most of what the counselor said was probably true, the session turned sour because the counselor took, what I call, the auto mechanic approach to counseling.

When someone leaves a car for repair, the mechanic pulls out the shop manual, puts the car through various diagnostic tests, then repairs the problem according to the manual. Some counselors, I fear, treat people this way. They are interested only in finding out what the problem is and what the book says to do about it. Then they immediately try to fix the problem with little regard to their relationship with the counselee.[3]

This approach to counseling is faulty because it regards the counselee as a mechanism, while the biblical counselor is trying to help a whole *person*. This is not to say, of course, that the person should be emphasized to the extent that his or her problems are disregarded. A genuine care and concern for the individual will compel us to deal with the person and the problems. The point is, counselors cannot allow themselves to become exclusively *problem-oriented*. Rather, they need to be *person-oriented;* then the treatment of problems that flows from that emphasis will be set in the proper context.

The counselor in Clara's case failed because he was too problem-oriented in his approach. Apparently, he had done little to establish involvement with his counselee. He had not endeavored to develop a facilitative relationship that would assure her of his concern. He could have taken time to listen to her and sympathize with the pain she was experiencing, but, instead, he jumped right in and addressed her sin.[4] Almost immediately, Clara viewed him as an enemy or opponent rather than an ally. And as long as she viewed her counselor this way, his counsel would mean little to her. His words might be truthful and appropriate to her situation, but she would reject them.

Proverbs 27 says, "Faithful are the wounds of a *friend*" (v. 6) and "A man's counsel is sweet to his *friend*" (v. 9, emphasis added). We are most receptive to counsel from those we know are with us and for us. They can speak to us frankly about our faults, and though we may be annoyed temporarily, we soon realize that they are only trying to help us because they are concerned for us. On the other hand, if someone whom we perceive as a stranger or an enemy criticizes us, we tend to react defensively and with suspicion about their motives.

In counseling, as in any other relationship, we must remember that *our impact and influence in people's lives is usually related to their perception of us.* That is why involvement is so important to the counseling process. Usually, the counseling process is truly effective only when an acceptable level of involvement has been established.[5]

With that in mind, let us consider three ways that counselors can develop involvement with counselees. The facilitative relationship must be built on the foundations of *compassion, respect,* and *sincerity.*

INVOLVEMENT THROUGH COMPASSION

Involvement is established when people know that we sincerely care for them.

Two Impressive Examples of Compassion

Jesus. Undoubtedly, the greatest counselor of all times was our Lord Jesus Christ. Isaiah the prophet told us, "His name shall be called Wonderful Counselor" (9:6) and that upon Him would rest "the spirit of wisdom and understanding, / The spirit of counsel and strength" (11:2). One of the keys to Jesus' success as a counselor was His intense compassion for men and women, which is apparent throughout the gospel accounts of His life and ministry.

The book of Matthew tells us that "seeing the multitudes, He felt compassion for them, because they were distressed and downcast like sheep without a shepherd" (Matt. 9:36). Jesus suffered with the needy multitudes. He felt for them and cared for them. His compassion permeated all of his attempts to meet their needs (Matt. 9:35, 37–38). Far from being a cold-hearted, auto mechanic type counselor who merely attacked problems and treated people like statistics, Jesus was motivated by compassion for them.

Mark 3:1–5 says that when Jesus noticed a man with a withered arm in the synagogue, He became angry and grieved at the Pharisees for their lack of sensitivity toward the man. Jesus showed compassion for the man by healing him of his malady.

A rich young ruler came to Jesus seeking eternal life, but left without it because he loved his riches too much to give them up. Mark 10:21 says that "looking at him, Jesus felt a love for him." Even when Jesus had to tell people what they did not want to hear, He did so with compassion.

One day Jesus was walking with His disciples when a funeral procession passed nearby (Luke 7:11–15). The only child of a widow had died, and Christ stopped to comfort her: "And when the Lord saw her, He felt compassion for her, and said to her, 'Do not weep.'" Then He proceeded to raise her boy from the dead.

Jesus' compassion caused Him to shed tears of sorrow and grief. Luke 19:41 records that Jesus wept over Jerusalem as He predicted the judgment of God that would soon fall upon it. In John 11:33–35, when Jesus saw Mary's grief over the death of Lazarus, "He was deeply moved in spirit, and was troubled," and He wept. Mary and all the others Jesus interacted with throughout His ministry knew how much He cared for them. That is one of the qualities that made Him the Wonderful Counselor. He did not just observe problems and dispense platitudes; He epitomized the compassion that every counselor needs.

Paul. Another compassionate counselor was the apostle Paul. Many people think of Paul only as a staunch defender of the faith and a brilliant theologian. They fail to realize that he also was a compassionate man who cared deeply for people. In Acts 20:31 he reminded the Ephesian elders, "Night and day for a period of three years I did not cease to admonish each one with tears." The Greek word translated "admonish" (*noutheteō*) can also be translated "counsel," and it most often means "to correct or to warn." Even when Paul rebuked them for their sin, his tears communicated a genuine, caring, and loving heart.

Paul's great love for his fellow Jews is also shown in Romans 9:1–3. There he said, "I am telling the truth in Christ, I am not lying, my conscience bearing me witness in the Holy Spirit, that I have great sorrow and unceasing grief in my heart. For I could wish that I myself were accursed, separated from Christ for the sake of my brethren, my kinsmen according to the flesh." Paul was willing to burn in hell if that would save other Jews! Surely you and I have a long way to go before we match that kind of compassion.

In 2 Corinthians 2:4, Paul referred to a strong letter of admonishment he had previously written to that church: "For out of much affliction and anguish of heart I wrote to you with many tears; not that you should be made sorrowful, but that you might know the love which I have especially for you." Later he spoke of the "daily pressure" of concern he feels for all the churches and then said, "Who is weak without my being weak? Who is led into sin without my intense concern?" (2 Cor. 11:28–29). Paul identified with the problems and weaknesses of his "counselees" to the extent that it seemed he experienced them himself.

The Thessalonian church received an especially moving expression of Paul's love for them: "We proved to be gentle among you, as a nursing mother tenderly cares for her own children. Having thus a fond affection for you, we were well-pleased to impart to you not only the gospel of God but also our own lives, because you had become very dear to us" (1 Thess. 2:7–8).

Paul cared for people, and people knew that he cared. His heart was "opened wide" to them (2 Cor. 6:11). That is why he could be so straightforward in addressing their faults without alienating them. If we are to be effective counselors, we must have this same kind of compassion.

How to Develop Genuine Compassion

Perhaps you are questioning whether you have the kind of compassion Jesus and Paul had, or perhaps you are wondering how to develop such compassion. Fortunately, the Bible does not merely give us these examples, it tells us how we can emulate them. The following suggestions about developing compassion toward others are taken from Scripture.

Think about how you would feel if you were in the counselee's position. Many passages that refer to Jesus' compassion state first that he "saw" the people or He "looked upon" them. For instance, Matthew 9:36 says, "*Seeing* the multitudes, He felt compassion for them" (emphasis added).

And the account of the mourning widow states, "When the Lord *saw* her, He felt compassion for her" (Luke 7:13).[6] These verses indicate that Jesus looked thoughtfully at others who were experiencing difficulty; He put Himself in their place and intentionally tried to feel what they were feeling. His compassion for them arose from this empathy. Hebrews 4:15 says that even now in heaven He is "touched with the feeling of our infirmities" (KJV).

Consider again the case of Clara. She quickly concluded that her counselor was not sympathetic with her. All she sensed from him was condemnation. He needed to listen to her complaints and concerns before he tried to understand how she felt. Before responding, he could have asked himself, "What would it be like for me to come home to a wife who was wasting all of our money on alcohol? What would it be like to have a wife calling me names, scratching me, and throwing things at me? What would it be like to have a wife who didn't care about what I thought or what I said? What would it be like for me to come home and find my wife in my bed with another man? How would I feel? What emotions would I be experiencing?"

This is where the counseling process must start. And although the sin problems must be addressed and solved, in most cases, effective counseling cannot occur until the counselor has shown the counselee the compassion of Christ by identifying with his or her struggles.

Think of the counselee as a family member. Paul said in 1 Timothy 5:1–2, "Do not sharply rebuke an older man, but rather appeal to him as a father, to the younger men as brothers, the older women as mothers, and the younger women as sisters." When I counsel, I deliberately try to imagine how I would treat one of my close relatives. I ask myself, "How would I talk to them? How would I proceed if this were my mother or my father or my brother or my sister sitting across the desk from me?" In reality, our counselees *are* our spiritual brothers and sisters, and our heavenly Father demands that they be treated as such.

Think about your own sinfulness. Galatians 6:1 instructs and cautions counselors: "Brethren, even if a man is caught in any trespass, you who are spiritual, restore such a one in a spirit of gentleness; *each one looking to yourself, lest you too be tempted*" (emphasis added). When we become aware of sin in the counselee's life, we must always remember that we are not immune to sin ourselves; we can fall into it just as easily as anyone else. No one has done anything that we could not do, but for the grace of God. If we keep this in mind we will avoid becoming self-righteous or condescending toward those who sin. Instead, we will reach out to them in compassion just as Jesus did to the adulterous woman (John 8:1–11).

Think about practical ways to show compassion. In reality, compassion is not so much an emotion as it is a choice of the will. Even if we do not feel like being kind to someone, we can still be kind (see Luke 6:27–28). Often, feelings of love for others follow the decision to act in a way that pleases and benefits them. Use the following questions to help you determine whether you are demonstrating genuine compassion toward your counselees:

- Have you told your counselees that you care for them? (Phil. 1:8).
- Have you prayed for them and with them? (Col. 4:12–13).
- Have you rejoiced and grieved with them? (Rom. 12:15).
- Have you dealt with them gently and tenderly? (Matt. 12:20).
- Have you been tactful with them? (Prov. 15:23).
- Have you spoken graciously to them? (Col. 4:6).
- Have you continued to love and accept them even when they have rejected your counsel? (Mark 10:21).
- Have you defended them against those who mistreat and accuse them? (Matt. 12:1–7).
- Have you forgiven them for any wrong they have done to you? (Matt. 18:21–22).
- Have you been willing to meet their physical needs if necessary? (1 John 3:17).

INVOLVEMENT THROUGH RESPECT

Not only do people need to know that we care for them, they also need to know that we respect them. Webster defines respect as "deferential regard" and "considering another worthy of honor." The Bible lauds this quality repeatedly. Romans 12:10 says that we are to "give preference to one another in honor"; Philippians 2:3 commands, "With humility of mind let each of you regard one another as more important than himself"; and 1 Peter 2:17 tells us to "honor all men."

To return once more to the example of Clara, the counselor failed her miserably in this regard. His conversation with her communicated only disrespect, which undoubtedly was a major reason their relationship deteriorated.

In cases when a counselee shows little respect for the counselor, it may be because the counselor has shown little respect for the counselee. It is a matter of reaping what the counselor has sown. So when those we are trying to help fail to look to us for guidance (as we think they should), the first question we need to ask ourselves is, "Have I honored them as God commands me to?"[7]

How to Show Respect to a Counselee

There are several ways the counselor can show respect that will help establish involvement with the counselee:

Use proper verbal communication. We can show respect both in the way we talk to our counselees and in the way we talk about them. In 2 Timothy 2:24–25 Paul said, "The Lord's bond-servant must not be quarrelsome, but be kind to all, able to teach, patient when wronged, with gentleness correcting those who are in opposition, if perhaps God may grant them repentance leading to the knowledge of the truth." Rude or harsh speech is never condoned in Scripture, even when one is speaking the truth (see Eph. 4:15). Proverbs 16 says that "sweetness of speech increases persuasiveness" (v. 21) and "Pleasant words are a honeycomb, / Sweet to the soul and healing to the bones" (v. 24). So the method of verbal communication is important in showing respect to a counselee.

Use proper nonverbal communication. Showing respect involves what we say with our mouths and what we do with the rest of our bodies. Leviticus 19:32 says, "Rise in the presence of the aged, show respect for the elderly" (NIV). In the Old Testament, etiquette required that a young person stand when an older person entered the room. It was a nonverbal way of saying, "I honor you; I respect you." Such nonverbal communication is as important to God today as it was then because it reveals what we think of others.

The acronym S-O-L-V-E-R is a useful device for remembering several nonverbal ways to show respect for a counselee:

S—squared shoulders. Face counselees in a way that indicates you are alert and giving them all your attention.

O—open stance. Relax your arms, hands, and shoulders as if to say, "I am here to receive whatever you want to communicate. You have access to me."

L—lean forward slightly. This shows interest in what the person is saying to you.

V—vocal quality. Maintain a volume and intensity in your speech that is neither abrasive nor hard to hear. Always let your voice reflect tenderness and compassion, rather than anger and irritation.

E—eye contact. Look at people, especially when they are speaking. Do not stare at them so that they are uncomfortable, but show your interest in what they are saying by giving them your rapt attention.

R—relational posture. Coordinate all your body, head, and facial movements in a way that is most conducive to the comfort of the counselee. Your posture should not be stiff and robotic, but neither should it be so totally relaxed that the person thinks you are about to go to sleep.[8]

In all of these forms of nonverbal communication, maintain a balance so the counselee does not perceive you as either uptight or indifferent; both perceptions can build a wall between the two of you that will interfere with the counseling process.

Take the counselee's problems seriously. Never minimize the problems presented by your counselees. You may think, "This is so trivial. Why are they making a big deal out of it?" But while it may seem trivial to you, it is extremely important to them, or they would not be discussing it with you. When you take their problems seriously, you communicate respect. On the other hand, if you make light of their problems you will alienate them from the beginning and will remove any hope they had that you could help them.

Trust your counselees. First Corinthians 13:7 says that love "believes all things." Applied to counseling, this means that we should believe what our counselees tell us, until the facts prove otherwise. We should also believe that they have entered counseling because they want to please God more. Presumptive suspicion is a worldly attitude, not a Christian one (Phil. 2:3).

Note what one psychology textbook says about Gestalt therapist Fritz Perls:

> Perls . . . expresses his skepticism about those who seek therapy and indicates that not very many people really want to invest themselves in the hard work involved in changing. As he points out, "Anybody who goes to a therapist has something up his sleeve. I would say roughly ninety percent don't go to a therapist to be cured, but to be more adequate in their neurosis. If they are power mad, they want to get more power. . . . If they are ridiculers, they want to have a sharper wit to ridicule, and so on."[9]

As believers, we cannot approach counseling with such a cynical attitude. Although at times people will come to us with insincere motives, we should not allow ourselves to think they are insincere without good reason.

Express confidence in the counselee. The Corinthian church had more problems than any church Paul wrote to, yet he told them, "I rejoice that in everything I have confidence in you" (2 Cor. 7:16). No matter how many weaknesses our counselees have, if they are believers we need to convey the attitude that we are confident they will respond well to counseling and will grow through it.

Scripture states that "God . . . is at work in [us believers], both to will and to work for His good pleasure" (Phil. 2:13), and Jesus said, "My sheep hear My voice, . . . and they follow Me" (John 10:27). So we should have an attitude of confidence that believers will respond positively to the directives of our Lord. And we should communicate this confidence to our counselees. The apostle Paul followed this practice with people. He counseled believers about serious problems in their circumstances and in their lives, yet with only one exception (the letter to the Galatian church), his teaching, reproof, correction, and admonition were accompanied with expressions of confidence and respect.

Welcome the counselee's input. We can show respect for our counselees by asking them to evaluate the sessions and suggest improvements. We can say to them, "God has brought us together, and He not only wants to use me in your life, He also wants to use you in my life." This also means that we must receive any negative input without becoming defensive or irritated. We can view criticism or complaints as an opportunity to model the godly responses we want counselees to develop in their lives.

Maintain confidentiality. A final way to show respect to counselees is to guard their reputations as much as possible without disobeying God. Unfortunately, confidentiality is not always possible (or desirable) in light of Jesus' commands. In Matthew 18:16–17 He says that if a brother is sinning and proves unwilling to listen to private rebuke, we should "take one or two more with you, so that by the mouth of two or three witnesses every fact may be confirmed. And if he refuses to listen to them, tell it to the church." Jay Adams added these comments to those verses:

> The implication of this biblical requirement to seek additional help in order to reclaim an offender is that Christians must never promise absolute confidentiality to any person. Frequently it is the practice of Bible-believing Christians to give assurances of absolute confidentiality, never realizing that they are following a policy that originated in the Middle Ages and that is unbiblical. . . .
>
> Is it right, then, to refuse any confidentiality at all? No, confidentiality is assumed in the gradual widening of the sphere of concern to other persons set forth in Matthew 18:15ff. As you read the words of our Lord in that passage, you get the impression that it is only reluctantly, when all else fails, that more and more persons may be called in. The ideal seems to be to keep the matter as narrow as possible. . . .
>
> What then does one say when asked to keep a matter in confidence? We ought to say, "I am glad to keep confidence in the way that the Bible instructs me. That means, of course, I shall never involve others unless God requires me to do so." In other words, we must not promise *absolute* confidentiality, but rather, confidentiality that is consistent with biblical requirements.[10]

Biblical confidentiality is essential in building a relationship of trust between counselor and counselee.

Involvement Through Sincerity

The kind of relationship we want to develop with our counselees can exist only when they know that we are genuine and honest. Paul described his ministry as "not walking in craftiness . . . but by the manifestation of truth commending ourselves to every man's conscience in the sight of God"

(2 Cor. 4:2). Commentator Philip E. Hughes wrote concerning that verse, "So far from being marked by subterfuge, self-interest, and deceit, however, Paul's ministry was one in which the truth was manifested, openly displayed, outspokenly proclaimed (cf. 3:12f.), in such a manner that none could gainsay the genuineness and sincerity of his motives."[11]

We must be like Paul in our counseling, having no hidden agendas or disguised motives, but openly revealing the truth about who we are (and even what we are thinking) to those we seek to help.[12] Only then will they be able to trust us through the process.

How can we be sincere and honest in our counseling? Scripture indicates the following methods:

Be honest about your qualifications. It is easy for counselors to misrepresent their credentials to counselees in an attempt to gain respect and confidence. But while this motive may be legitimate, the method is not. Even the great counselor Paul, who had every right to throw around his title of apostle, more often referred to himself as merely "a servant of Christ" (see for example, Rom. 1:1; Phil. 1:1; Titus 1:1). We should follow his humble example and represent ourselves in a similar way to our counselees. Certainly we must never exaggerate or otherwise deceive them about our qualifications. A relationship of trust will be highly unlikely if they find out we have lied to them!

Be honest about your own weaknesses. Being open about personal problems and struggles is an effective way for counselors to demonstrate sincerity to counselees. Paul told the Corinthians, "When I came to you, brethren, I did not come with superiority of speech or of wisdom, . . . I was with you in weakness and in fear and in much trembling" (1 Cor. 2:1–3). He did not present himself as somebody who always had it all together. He was honest about his weaknesses and fears. When he wrote to the Corinthians again, he told them that during a time of affliction he and Timothy had been "burdened excessively, beyond our strength, so that we despaired even of life" (2 Cor. 1:8).

This was the man who said in 1 Corinthians 10:13 that God would never allow us to be tempted beyond what we are able to bear. Yet he admitted that there was a time when he was so burdened he did not think he could take it anymore. This is one of the reasons Paul was such a great counselor: he was able to proclaim the truth firmly without leaving people under the impression that he was perfect or unable to relate to their failings (see Rom. 7:14–25).

Of course we need to be careful that our self-disclosure is not inappropriate in nature or in duration (we do not want to make our counselees think that we need counseling more than they do!), nor should we spend an inordinate amount of time talking about our problems when counselees come to receive help for theirs. But an appropriate openness shows sincerity, which helps to establish involvement. Whatever we do, we must never pretend to be something we are not.

Be honest about your goals and agenda. Generally speaking, it is advisable and fitting to let counselees know from the beginning what we are trying to do and how we intend to do it. We need to be honest about our counseling methods and standards. We need to make it clear that God and His Word are our source of authority. We must let them know that we approach counseling this way because we are convinced that God's way of describing problems, identifying their causes, and solving them is superior to any other way.

Occasionally, people come to me wanting their problems to be labeled, interpreted, and solved psychologically. My frequent response to this request is something like this: "I want to serve and help you and I am firmly convinced that the best way to do that is God's way. I am resolutely committed to the Scriptures as my sole authority because I believe God knows far better than anyone else what our problems are, why we have them, and what to do about them. So because I am a Christian who is convinced that God's way of understanding and dealing with problems is far superior to any other way and because I want to give you the best help available, my method will be based on the Scripture. If you want a different approach, you will have to secure another counselor. For the Lord's sake and for yours, I cannot approach counseling in any other way." Over the years, as I have responded to people in this way, most of them have appreciated my honesty and have stayed for help. From the very start, counselees know I will be honest with them and this enhances our relationship.

We must never be like many non-Christian therapists, who hide their true intentions and play games with people in order to get them to change. Jay Haley is one such therapist:

> A third tactic [of Haley's counseling approach] is the encouraging of usual behavior. In this case resistance to the advice can only result in change. For instance, asking a domineering woman to take charge of the family will often highlight her interaction and result in her wanting to recede more into the background. What is important in Haley's approach is the question of control. If the therapist tells the domineering woman to lead, she is no longer leading but following the instructions of the therapist. . . . Like the Zen Master the therapist induces change in the client by the use of paradox.[13]

Any type of reverse psychology like this is unacceptable for the biblical counselor. It only creates barriers to the desired involvement with the counselee.

Be honest about your limitations as a counselor. When we make mistakes or have difficulty knowing how to proceed in a particular case, we should admit it. Paul told the Galatians that he was "perplexed" about them (Gal. 4:20; see 2 Cor. 4:8), and in 2 Corinthians 12:20 he wrote, "I'm afraid that when I come again my God will humiliate me before you." Now that is being honest! Paul knew and admitted that he was fallible as a minister, an admission that revealed his sincerity and enabled people to trust him.

What role does establishing a facilitative relationship with a counselee play in the counseling process? Scripture underscores its significance by exhortation and example, and what Scripture teaches, counseling experience illustrates. Here, for example, is one counselee's evaluation of some of the factors she considered most helpful in her counseling experience:

> For me the content of the counseling in many ways was secondary. Often it was who the counselor was that laid the foundation for whether I could trust, accept, and do what was presented during counseling.
>
> It was a big step for me to be under the tutelage of a male. My relationships with both men and women had been so bad that I didn't trust anyone, although it was worse with men than with women. A counselor needs to be trustworthy. For me some of the hardest things in my life did not hit the table until long after I knew my counselor. Much of that was simply because I needed to know that no matter what was happening, he could be trusted. I had many experiences with people who didn't believe me when I told them certain things were happening in my life. I assumed that most people were like that, and feared that they all were. So I did not easily trust anyone. Time was needed and I needed to see that this counselor believed in me. I needed to see that he trusted me. I don't mean to suggest that he never had the right to question the validity of my situation (in fact he did), but I simply needed to see that I was going to be trusted, accepted, and believed in.
>
> On one occasion I walked out on the counselor and slipped back down the slide, yet he was patient with me. He hurt with me and even in the midst of my own failings, I sensed the respect from him that helped me start climbing the ladder again. My counselor's credibility was built over the long haul—he continued to love when I did not love and tried to run.
>
> One counselor I've had seemed to have the answers too available on his cuff. At times he responded too quickly and gave the impression of having a canned approach. I left feeling that he didn't sense the difficulty that existed and the time needed for rebuilding. Whereas my counselor seemed much more sensitive to my own hurts, and although he didn't hesitate to confront me with hard truths, he did it in ways that I knew without a doubt that he loved and cared for me and my growth in Christ.
>
> One other element I needed and looked for was whether or not I was accepted. Even when things would seem to go from bad to worse,

did he still accept me? This didn't mean that he condoned everything I had done or still did. It didn't mean that he never rebuked or reproved me or called on me to repent, but it did mean that he did it in a loving and gracious way so that I knew he was my friend and not my enemy. It also meant that my counselor affirmed me when possible—he commended and complimented as well as challenged.

As this letter illustrates, those who come for counsel are often scrutinizing the counselor to see if he or she is someone who can be trusted. Only if the counselor proves to be trustworthy, can a helping relationship be established that will make the counseling process a mutually profitable experience.

Though God sometimes chooses to accomplish His work through unlikely ways and unlikely people, the Bible emphasizes (and the counselee's letter illustrates) that God usually changes lives in a situation where a relationship of concern and trust exists between the helper and the one who needs help. As biblical counselors, we must do all we can to wrap the content of our counseling in a package of compassion, respect, and honesty.

9

Instilling Hope in the Counselee

Wayne A. Mack

Biblical change cannot take place without hope, especially in the difficult situations we face as counselors. People who have had life-shattering experiences like divorce, a death of a loved one, or a loss of a job need hope. People who have faced the same problem for a long time need hope. People who have sincerely tried to solve their problems and failed need hope. People who have compounded their initial problems with other unbiblical responses need hope. People whose problems have been wrongly described need hope, and people whose hopes have been dashed repeatedly need hope. If we want to help any of these people, we must make sure that inspiration and hope are operative elements in our counseling.

The Biblical Emphasis on Hope

The role of hope in the process of sanctification should never be underestimated. Consider what Scripture says about its many contributions to that process:

- Hope produces joy that remains, even through the most difficult trials (Prov. 10:28; Rom. 5:2–3; 12:12; 1 Thess. 4:13).
- Hope produces perseverance (Rom. 8:24–25).
- Hope produces confidence (2 Cor. 3:12; Phil. 1:20).
- Hope produces effective ministry (2 Cor. 4:8–18).
- Hope produces greater faith and love (Col. 1:4–5).
- Hope produces consistency (1 Thess. 1:3).
- Hope produces increased energy and enthusiasm (1 Tim. 4:10).
- Hope produces stability (Heb. 6:19).
- Hope produces a more intimate relationship with God (Heb. 7:19).
- Hope produces personal purity (1 John 3:3).

Since the Bible places such emphasis on the role of hope in spiritual growth, it must be a strong emphasis in our counseling as well.

Most counselors, both Christian and non-Christian, realize that people with problems need hope. Unfortunately, however, the hope that many counselors provide is a false hope that rests on an unbiblical foundation and will inevitably crumble (Prov. 10:28; 11:7). It is important to understand the difference between this false hope and the true hope that the Bible describes.

Characteristics of False Hope

False hope is based on human ideas of what is pleasurable and desirable. Many people think that their problems will disappear if they can just get what they want, and sometimes counselors encourage them in that error by promising or intimating that their desires will be satisfied. This is a serious mistake, because God never promises us that we will get everything we want, nor does He even tell us that getting what we want will make us happy. Often what we want is *not* what is best for us, and a name-it-and-claim-it approach to our desires only compounds our problems. When a certain lady came for counseling concerning severe financial difficulties, her counselor discovered that her problems resulted from this kind of thinking. She had visited a car dealership, walked around a Lincoln Town Car seven times, laid hands on it, and "claimed" it from the Lord. God did not provide the money to pay for it, of course, and now she was in dire straits financially.

This is an extreme example, but many people cling to similar false hopes. They think, "If I could just get married, my problems would be solved" or, "If I could get a better job, I would be nicer to live with." Unfortunately, the objects of their desire are physical rather than spiritual and temporal rather than heavenly. Because God has not promised them freedom from tribulation in this world (John 16:33; see James 1:2–4), they become disillusioned when they do not get what they want.

False hope is based on a denial of reality. I once counseled a young man who wanted to make his living as a musician. Some of his friends encouraged him in this pursuit because they did not want to hurt him. But, in reality, he did not have any musical ability. He thought he did, but he did not. So, as a counselor I needed to point him in another direction rather than perpetuate a false hope.

I also remember a young lady whose husband left her and whose well-meaning friends continually told her they were sure he would come back. When she asked me about this in counseling, I had to say repeatedly, "I don't know. What I do know is that God can use this in your life to make you a greater woman of God, and if that happens you have benefited from the situation. I wish I could tell you for sure that your husband is going to come back, but I cannot do that."

"All my friends tell me my husband will come back," she said to me once, "and every time I come here, instead of encouraging me, you discourage me." I then asked her why she kept coming back to me for counseling, and she replied that it was because she knew I would tell her the truth. Deep inside she knew that her friends were bending reality in an attempt to comfort her, and that provided no true comfort.

False hope is based on mystical or magical thinking. Sometimes Christians place their hope in fanciful ideas that have no biblical substance. For example, some people's approach to daily devotions is "a verse a day keeps the devil away." They read their Bible every morning as a magical rite to ward off trouble. If they happen to miss their devotions one time, they suffer throughout the day in fear.

Certainly we should begin the day with God by having devotions in the morning, but we must recognize that there is no mystical power in that activity. In fact, Bible reading (and even memorization) only benefits us when we understand and apply the Scriptures to our lives. Only the person who "looks intently" at the Word and is an "effectual doer" of the Word will be blessed in what he or she does (James 1:25).

False hope is based on an unbiblical view of prayer. One of the questions on the personal inventory sheets[1] we use in counseling is "What have you done about your problem?" Under that question, counselees will sometimes write that they have prayed about it and nothing else. When we talk with them further, we find that they believe prayer is all God requires them to do. One such man, who was having constant problems with sexual sin, was angry at God because God had not taken away his problems in response to his prayer.

This can be called the "quarterback approach" to spirituality; we pass the ball or hand it off to God (by praying) and expect Him to run it across the goal line without any help from us. But such an approach only creates a false hope, because God never promised that we could reach the goal of godliness without strenuous personal effort (1 Tim. 4:7b). We need His divine strength to succeed (John 15:5), and that is where prayer comes in, but prayer alone will seldom solve our problems.

In Matthew 6:11 Jesus said that we should pray, "Give us this day our daily bread." But in 2 Thessalonians 3:10 Paul says, "If any one will not work, neither let him eat." These two commands are not contrary, for while we are to pray that God will provide the things we need to live, we must not expect them to fall from heaven. We need to work for them with the strength God gives us. So even the hope we place in prayer can be false if we hope that prayer alone will take care of everything.

False hope is based on an improper interpretation of Scripture. Many Christians suffer from the errors of eisogesis, the practice of reading personal meaning into a text rather than drawing the author's true meaning out of it (exegesis). Another way to describe this practice is "lucky dipping" or seeking guidance and hope by reading random verses in Scripture and assigning meaning to them regardless of their context.[2] This approach leads to a misunderstanding of what the Bible actually teaches and to disillusionment when the supposed promises do not come true.

A woman who had gotten involved in an extramarital affair came to me for counseling, and I found that one of the causes leading to her sin was a false hope based on misinterpreted Scripture. Several years before, her father had threatened to leave her mother and she found refuge from her fears by reading Matthew 18:19, "If two of you agree on earth about anything that they may ask, it shall be done for them by My Father who is in heaven." This woman found a Christian friend who agreed with her that her father should stay with her mother, and they prayed and expected God to keep them together. Her hopes were dashed, however, because her father left her mother anyway. In the woman's mind God had failed to keep His Word, and her faith was severely damaged. Doubt and bitterness toward God grew in her heart until finally she broke her marriage vows and got involved with another man.

Unfortunately, her hope was based on a misinterpretation of Scripture. Matthew 18:19 is part of a passage discussing church discipline (vv. 15–20) and has no direct application to prayer.[3] God never had promised her that He would keep her father and mother together simply because she and her friend agreed together in prayer. Showing her that her hope had been false and that God had not been unfaithful to His Word was an important step in bringing her back to holiness.

As counselors, we need to challenge the hopes that people hold when we are concerned that they might be false. When we do, however, we need to realize that the response we receive may be rather unpleasant. While true hope usually holds firm even when someone challenges it, those who hold a false hope tend to get upset when their hope is called into question. An example of this phenomenon is the story of Micaiah the prophet in 2 Chronicles 18. He prophesied against King Ahab's confidence that Israel could conquer the Arameans (a hope that had been bolstered by four hundred men who claimed to be prophets), so Ahab had him thrown into prison (vv. 16–19, 26). Micaiah suffered only because he had the courage and concern to challenge the king's false hope.

Micaiah was right, by the way. The Israelites were routed and Ahab died in the battle. We must be careful not to provide false hope as a temporary comfort, and we must be willing to examine and challenge the basis of our counselees' hopes. We must not allow them to build hope on an unbiblical foundation that will topple when the storms come (see Luke 6:47–49).

Characteristics of True Hope

Now that we understand some characteristics of false hope, we can contrast these with what the Bible says about true hope.

True hope is a biblically based expectation of good. In other words, it is biblical hope, an expectation based on the promises of God. Romans 4:18 says about Abraham, "In hope against hope he believed, in order that he might become a father of many nations, according to that which had been spoken, 'So shall your descendants be.'" His hope was grounded on the promises given to him by God (see 2 Pet. 1:4).

Notice also that his hope was a *believing* hope, not a mere speculation. Today we often use the word *hope* to refer to something that may or may not happen. We say, "I hope my friend comes to visit tomorrow." But the biblical meaning of the word *hope* is different. It is more like "I know my friend is coming over tomorrow, and I can't wait to see him." That is why I say true hope is an *expectation*. It is based on the promises of an Almighty God, and there is no doubt that it will be rewarded. Consider this definition of biblical hope from *The New International Dictionary of New Testament Theology:*

> The hope of faith, . . . is a concrete personal expectation. Despite the "not yet" of the realization of salvation, it looks forward confidently though not without tension. However, Yawheh, for whom it waits, is not like us men. Since he knows, promises, and brings to pass what the future holds for his people, hope attains unparalleled assurance in the realm of revelation. Despite everything which at present runs counter to the promise, the one who hopes trusts God for his faithfulness' sake not to disappoint the hope he has awakened through his word (Isa. 8:17; Mic. 7:7; Ps. 42:5).[4]

True hope is the result of true salvation. In Scripture hope is always tied to the new birth by the Holy Spirit and personal faith in Christ. Consider these verses:

> Blessed be the God and Father of our Lord Jesus Christ, who according to His great mercy has caused us to be born again to a living hope (1 Pet. 1:3).
> Since we heard of your faith in Christ Jesus and the love which you have for all the saints; because of the hope laid up for you in heaven, of which you previously heard in the word of truth, the gospel (Col. 1:4–5).
> Of this church I was made a minister according to the stewardship from God bestowed on me for your benefit, that I might fully carry out the preaching of the word of God, that is, the mystery which has been

hidden from the past ages and generations; . . . which is Christ in you, the hope of glory (Col. 1:25–27).

Paul, an apostle of Christ Jesus according to the commandment of God our Savior, and of Christ Jesus, who is our hope (1 Tim. 1:1).

Those last two passages clearly say that Christ Himself is our hope. His person is the sum and substance of it. So how can someone have true hope if they do not love and trust in Jesus Christ? It simply is not possible, and we have to remember as counselors that we cannot affirm the hopes of anyone who has not been born again by the Spirit of God.

True hope is holistic in focus. By holistic we mean that true hope does not merely focus on the *part* (an individual life) but also the *whole* (God's plan for the universe). It finds encouragement in the eternal as well as the temporal and in the intangible as well as the tangible. Instead of being concerned only with what happens in one's life, true hope is concerned with what happens in the lives of others and whether God receives glory in the events that transpire.

The apostle Paul was a tremendous example of a man whose hope was holistic in focus. Read these verses carefully and consider what they reveal about his attitude:

Now I want you to know, brethren, that my circumstances have turned out for the greater progress of the gospel, so that my imprisonment in the cause of Christ has become well known throughout the whole praetorian guard and to everyone else, and that most of the brethren, trusting in the Lord because of my imprisonment, have far more courage to speak the word of God without fear (Phil. 1:12–14).

For I know that this [more bad circumstances] shall turn out for my deliverance through your prayers and the provision of the Spirit of Jesus Christ, according to my earnest expectation and hope, that I shall not be put to shame in anything, but that with all boldness, Christ shall even now, as always, be exalted in my body, whether by life or by death (Phil. 1:19–20).

But even if I am being poured out as a drink offering upon the sacrifice and service of your faith, I rejoice and share my joy with you all (Phil. 2:17).

Remember Jesus Christ, risen from the dead, descendant of David, according to my gospel, for which I suffer hardship even to imprisonment as a criminal; but the word of God is not imprisoned. For this reason I endure all things for the sake of those who are chosen, that they also may obtain the salvation which is in Christ Jesus and with it eternal glory (2 Tim. 2:8–10).

Paul's hope did not rest simply on what happened to him personally. He saw himself as a part of a great and glorious movement of God, through which people were being brought to Jesus Christ and the church was being edified. He placed his hope in the kingdom purposes of God in this world. So if furthering God's plan involved suffering on Paul's part, that was all right with him. His hope did not waver when he faced imprisonment, slander, and even death because he was more concerned with God's glory than with his personal comfort. What happened to him was of little importance compared to the bigger picture.[5]

Joseph and Job are two Old Testament illustrations of the holistic aspect of true hope. Joseph's hope remained solid even when he was sold into slavery, lied about, and thrown into prison, and the reason it did is revealed in his famous statement in Genesis 50:20. There he told his treacherous brothers, "As for you, you meant evil against me, but God meant it for good in order to bring about this present result, to preserve many people alive." And even though Job lost everything he had and never knew the greater purposes God had in mind for his suffering, he said, "Though He slay me, / I will hope in Him" (Job 13:15) and, "As for me, I know that my Redeemer lives, / And at the last He will take His stand on the earth" (19:25).

The Christian's cup in this world is never half empty. It is always half full. Christians are never in a no-win situation, but always in a *no-lose* situation, because even though we may not understand God's reasons for whatever happens to us, we can know that He is accomplishing a grand divine plan that will ultimately glorify Him and benefit us.[6] "The steps of a man are established by the LORD" (Ps. 37:23); "God causes all things to work together for good to those who love God, to those who are called according to His purpose" (Rom. 8:28); and He "works all things after the counsel of His will" (Eph. 1:11). True hope focuses on the glorious plans of a God who says, "My purpose will be established, and I will accomplish all My good pleasure" (Is. 46:10). Therefore, this hope is never shaken, even through unpleasant circumstances.

True hope is realistic. Romans 8:28 says that all things work together for good, but it does not say that all things *are* good. Even though true hope expects good to eventually come from trials, it does not try to deny the reality of sin and suffering, or the pain they cause.[7] True hope does not preclude tears and grief, nor does it rest on an illegitimate perception of personal capabilities. Notice in Romans 4:19 that Abraham "contemplated his own body, now as good as dead since he was about a hundred years old, and the deadness of Sarah's womb." Then verses 20–21 say, "*Yet,* with respect to the promise of God, he did not waver in unbelief, but grew strong in faith, giving glory to God, and being fully assured that what He had promised, He was able also to perform" (emphasis added). Abraham's hope was not based on an unrealistic view of his own capabilities (or Sarah's) but, rather, on God's ability to do what was humanly impossible. Likewise, true hope for us is not created by denying or twisting reality but by accurately considering it and basing our hope in God's power.

True hope must be renewed daily. God does not inject people with a huge dose of hope that will last for years. Our hope corresponds with the gradual work of sanctification that God is doing in our lives, so it cannot be sustained unless we allow that work to continue every day. In 2 Corinthians 4:16 Paul said that he did not lose hope because "though our outer man is decaying, yet our inner man is being renewed day by day." Only as Paul saw the work of renewal going on in his life each day could he have true hope. So we, too, must maintain a consistent relationship with God so that our hope will remain.

True hope is inseparable from a diligent and accurate study of God's Word. Psalm 119:49 says, "Remember the word to Thy servant, / In which Thou hast made me hope," and Psalm 130:5 says, "I wait for the LORD, my soul does wait, / And in His word do I hope." Scripture is the means by which God gives hope. Remember the experience of the two disciples on the Emmaus Road in Luke 24? They were walking along together, despondently discussing the murder of Christ and how their hopes had been crushed by that event. But after the risen Jesus (unrecognized by them) came alongside and "was explaining the Scriptures" to them, they said, "Were not our hearts burning within us while He was speaking to us?" (v. 32).

Their heaviness was lifted and their hope renewed by an increased understanding of the Word of God. The same thing happens to believers today who faithfully read and study the Bible, and without that diligent pursuit there can be no true hope.

True hope is a matter of the will. Hope is a choice, just as hopelessness is a choice. We can choose either to have hope or not to have hope. First Peter 1:13 says, "Fix your hope completely on the grace to be brought to you at the revelation of Jesus Christ." That is a command from God; therefore, we must have the ability (with the help of the Holy Spirit) to choose and to do what it says. God does not give us commands that we cannot keep, contrary to the implication made in the following article, published recently. The article claimed that the idea of helplessness was an important contribution of psychology to the church, and then said this:

> "There is an implication in all of [our critics'] writings that people are able to choose what is right," says [psychologist] Henry Cloud. "There is a total denial of the fact that we are sold into slavery." Psychotherapists constantly indict the evangelical church for failing to grasp people's helplessness. They suggest Evangelicals—especially those from a fundamentalist background—have deified willpower, as though a sinking person can pull himself up by his own bootstraps.[8]

This is a caricature of what biblical counselors believe, because choosing what is right through the power of the Holy Spirit is far different from pulling oneself up by one's own bootstraps (see John 15:5). Also, that emphasis on helplessness only produces an enslaving *hopelessness*. What hope do we have if we are unable to choose what is right?[9] Contrary to the claims in that article, the Bible does say we have the ability to choose what is right (1 Cor. 10:13; Phil. 2:12; 4:13), which also applies to our responsibility to hope.

There are times when we need to choose to place our hope in God and in His Word by turning to His resources and focusing our minds on His promises. We need to choose to view our circumstances from a hope-filled perspective rather than a hopeless one.

True hope is based on knowledge. Romans 5:2–3 says, "We exult in hope of the glory of God. And not only this, but we also exult in our tribulations, knowing that tribulation brings about perseverance." James 1:2–3 says, "Consider it all joy, my brethren, when you encounter various trials, knowing that the testing of your faith produces endurance." Paul and James said that true hope is based on what we know, not on *how we feel*. If the latter were the case, we could never have hope during painful trials! The more truth we understand from God's Word, the more hopeful we will be even in the worst circumstances. But if we base our hope on feelings, it will crumble.

HOW TO INSPIRE HOPE

Now that we have learned how to distinguish between true and false hope, let us consider how we can help to produce true hope in the people we counsel.

Help People to Grow in Their Relationship with Christ

Because Jesus Christ Himself is our hope (1 Tim. 1:1), an intimate relationship with Him is essential to true hope. Therefore, we need to do everything we can to insure that our counselees have this relationship. In some cases this may require evangelism. Those counselees who are avowedly non-Christians must be told that there is no true hope for them until they are born again by the Spirit of God (John 3:3, 36).[10] And sometimes even professing Christians need to be taught about the nature of true salvation before they can have hope.

If we are doubtful whether a counselee has entered into a genuine relationship with Christ, then we need to ask questions along those lines and challenge the person in that area. One such case would be someone who seems to have a *historical* relationship with God rather than a *personal* one. When asked if they are Christians, these people will often say, "Yes, I accepted Jesus as my Savior when I was four" or, "Yes, I believe Jesus died on the cross for me." However, they do not say anything pertaining to a present, vital relationship with God. They do not talk about how they are obeying Him each day or how close they have grown to Him.[11]

Another situation in which professing Christians may need to be challenged about their salvation is when the trials they face begin to destroy their faith. People who do not have a true relationship with Christ may coast along fine until pressures come. Then the weakness of their faith and the invalidity of their profession is revealed (Luke 6:46–49).[12]

Not only do we need to help people begin a relationship with Christ but we must also provide hope to true Christians by helping them strengthen their relationship with Jesus Christ. Many Christians lack hope simply because they lack maturity in their interaction with Christ and His Word.

An illustration of this is a woman who came to me some time ago for counseling. She was having problems with an intense, debilitating, and irrational fear. She heard voices and saw things that made her think Satan and demons were harassing her. Paralyzed by this fear, she did not want to leave the house, go to church, or be involved in other normal activities. She was able to sleep at night only if she wore a certain leather coat and vinyl hat. Her husband, who accompanied her to the counseling session, had not experienced any of the alleged phenomena.

Her problems made me think of Daniel 11:32: "The people who know their God will display strength." This verse says that a deep personal relationship with God gives us strength and delivers us from fear (see 1 John 4:18), which raised a question in my mind about her relationship with God. So I asked both the husband and wife to read sections from the book of Mark every day as a homework assignment and to write down what they learned about Jesus as a person. And I told them, "I don't want you just to record historical facts, but I want you to interact with the material and let Jesus reveal Himself to you through your reading."

This is what the husband wrote about Mark 2:

> The most telling verse of this chapter to me is verse 17. It is not the healthy who need a doctor but the sick. I have not come to call the righteous but sinners. Isaiah 53:6 says all we like sheep have gone astray, each of us has turned to his own way and the Lord has laid on Him the iniquity of us all. For me there is reassurance for forgiveness. I am a sinner. We all are. Christ came for us all, not because of our righteousness but because of our sins. If I were really righteous I wouldn't need Christ, but I'm not, I'm simply sinful. I need Him. The most revealing aspect of God's immense love is shown here. It's as if He said I know that you are sinful but I love you so much that a part of Me, My Son, will live among you. He'll die for you. So great is My power that I'll raise Him from the dead. Believe in Me and by believing in Him and you will have

eternal life. If God loves me so much in spite of my sin, how can I doubt? How can I not enjoy the fruits of life that He would have me sample? The inner peace that He gives, the flowers in the spring, the green grass, the sun and the rain, life with Christ really is fantastic. Lord, help me to share this gift with others.

That paragraph intimated that this man had a real and personal relationship with Christ. Now consider his wife's notes on the same passage:

In Capernaum Jesus forgave a paralytic. When his sins were forgiven Jesus told the man to pick up his bed and walk home, which he did and the scribes were amazed. After Jesus talked to a large crowd of people, He went to Levi's house. Here Jesus and the disciples ate and drank with the tax collectors and the scribes wondered why Jesus would do that. He said that those who were sick needed a physician and that He came so that sinners might repent. I believe that Jesus felt the people in Levi's house needed him. Another name for Levi is Matthew and he became one of Jesus' disciples. John and the Pharisees wanted to know why the disciples did not fast as they did. They were told that the Jewish fast was a practice or ritual and the disciples did not fast for they felt it would take the joy from their faith. But he said there would be a time when the disciples would have to fast.

It was apparent to me from those notes that her relationship with Christ needed to be strengthened, because to her He was more a historical figure than a friend. So for a number of weeks I focused on helping her know Him better. As she came to know Christ in a deeper and fuller way, I observed dramatic changes in this woman. Gradually, her fears began to disappear and her confidence grew as her relationship with the Lord developed. Where there had been fear, there was hope, because she had come to know the One who gives hope.

Teach People to Think Biblically

Both false hope and a lack of hope spring from an ignorance or misunderstanding of God's truth. If we understood the Scriptures perfectly and all our thoughts were in line with it, we would never suffer from either of these maladies. So if we want our counselees to have hope, we must help them to think biblically about various aspects of their lives.

Think biblically[13] *about the specific situation.* I once counseled a man who was in despair because he was unable to sleep at night. In the course of our counseling, we looked at several passages in Scripture that pertain to sleep.[14] Like many people, he did not know that the Bible speaks to this problem, and I discerned his hope growing as we studied a number of passages that referred to sleep. We need to show people that the Word of God speaks specifically about their problem, rather than merely quoting abstract passages that have general applications. Knowing that God gives specific instruction for our personal situation is a tremendous source of hope.

Think biblically about God's character. We can provide hope for counselees by enlarging or correcting their concepts of God. People often lack hope simply because they have erroneous concepts of God. They may view Him as a cruel disciplinarian and, therefore, lack hope because they think they will never be pleasing to Him as long as they struggle with sin. On the other hand, they may view Him as an all-forgiving "nice guy," and they lack hope because they let sin run rampant in their lives. Whatever the errors may be in a counselee's concept of God, that person will benefit and gain hope by learning to think biblically about Him.

Think biblically about the possibilities for good. Sometimes people lack hope because they see only the negative side of their circumstances and fail to recognize the potential for good that exists in every situation. They only see the problems and the pain; they do not see what God wants to accomplish through the situation. We need to help them realize that when God pushes us out of our comfort zone, He does so for the purpose of our growth and development. James 1:2 says, "Consider it all joy, my brethren, when you encounter various kinds of trials." Why does James say to consider trials to be joy? Because he is a masochist? No, he says that because we can know "that the testing of [our] faith produces endurance" (vv. 3–4). As Jerry Bridges wrote,

> Paul and James both say that we should rejoice in our trials because of their beneficial results. It is not the adversity considered in itself that is to be the ground of our joy. Rather, it is the expectation of the results, the development of our character, that should cause us to rejoice in adversity. God does not ask us to rejoice because we have lost our job, or a loved one has been stricken with cancer, or a child has been born with an incurable birth defect. But he does tell us to rejoice because we believe He is in control of those circumstances and is at work through them for our ultimate good.[15]

When people understand and believe that even the darkest cloud has a silver lining, they are inspired to have a tremendous hope that will sustain them through any difficulty.

Think biblically about the divine resources. We can provide hope for people by helping them to understand and appropriate the resources God has given them. People lose hope because they do not think they have the ability to handle whatever they are facing. But God's Word says that "in all these things we overwhelmingly conquer through Him who loved us" (Rom. 8:37), and that "God is able to make all grace abound to you, that always having all sufficiency in everything, you may have an abundance for every good deed" (2 Cor. 9:8). As Christians realize that they can do all things through Christ who strengthens them (Phil. 4:13), they will have a blessed confidence in the face of any struggle.[16]

Think biblically about the nature and cause of the problem. During the years that I have been involved in counseling, I have encountered many people who have lost hope because they have adopted an unbiblical psychological diagnosis of their problem. In some instances, this has occurred because someone else has given them the diagnosis. On other occasions they have read something, seen a television program, listened to a radio program, or taken a psychology course and decided they are suffering from a particular kind of psychological problem. They fail to realize that what is called a diagnosis is only a descriptive identification that someone has decided to use as a label for certain kinds of observable human behavior or experience. And while the descriptive word or phrase may sound intelligent and meaningful, it does not describe the cause or nature of the problem.

This is clear when we compare how diseases are diagnosed with how psychological problems are usually diagnosed. In medical science, if a patient has certain symptoms, the physician may suspect a certain disease. But before giving a definitive diagnosis, various scientific tests are performed (blood tests, x-rays, etc.) to confirm or negate the diagnosis. Then on the basis of scientific evidence, the physician can say either the patient has or does not have a certain disease. This diagnosis is not based solely on symptoms but on demonstrable proof or evidence concerning both the cause and nature of the problem.

Contrary to what many people seem to think, this is not the case in secular psychology. In psychology it is assumed that because a person has certain feelings, behaves and thinks in certain ways, or has certain symptoms for a prescribed period of time, that person has a certain psychological problem, even though the cause of the problem has not been proven, and in most cases cannot be proven by scientific methods. Without demonstrable evidence derived from hard facts about the cause and nature of a person's problems, it is deduced that certain symptoms indicate a specified psychological malady. This unproven (and in most cases unprovable) decision is then offered and frequently accepted as an indisputable and unquestionable diagnosis.

Unfortunately, when people believe that the nature of their problem is psychological, rather than spiritual, several things can happen: (1) in their attempt to resolve their difficulties, they bypass Christ and the Bible and look primarily (sometimes exclusively) to drugs or the ideas and concepts of secularistic psychology for solutions; (2) they begin to think of Christ as a cosmic psychologist whose primary purpose for coming was to fix their psychological problems, help build their self-esteem, deliver them from codependency, or meet their ego needs; (3) they lose hope and descend into despair because many of these psychological labels carry with them the idea of fixedness (this is what I am and it cannot be changed); or (4) they become discouraged because these unbiblical labels subtly or overtly encourage people to think that the primary solution to their difficulties is humanistic in nature. They must do it on their own (they can and must change themselves) or others, preferably experts, must do it for them.

So, many people try to change by relying on their own efforts or the help of others, and they fail. They come to realize that neither they nor any other human being can provide the power to break the slavery of sinful ways of thinking, feeling, and acting and enable them to think, feel, and live differently. When problems are viewed as primarily psychological in nature, we encounter people whose hope is dissipated, people who doubt that change can ever happen.

On the other hand, hopefulness blossoms when people begin to realize that their problems are basically spiritual: they are somehow linked to sin. Indeed, acknowledging that personal and interpersonal problems are related to sin[17] is truly good news, because then there is plenty of hope. Why? Because the primary reason Christ came into the world was to deliver us from the penalty and ruling power of sin (and, eventually, from the presence and possibility of sin). The clear Bible message is this: (1) Jesus is "the Lamb of God who takes away the sin of the world" (John 1:29); (2) "[This] is a trustworthy statement, deserving full acceptance, that Christ Jesus came into the world to save sinners" (1 Tim. 1:15); (3) "You shall call His name Jesus, for it is He who will save His people from their sins" (Matt. 1:21); and (4) He "gave Himself for us that He might redeem us from every lawless deed and purify for Himself a people for His own possession, zealous for good deeds" (Titus 2:14).

The good news of the Bible is not that Christ Jesus came into the world to be a cosmic psychologist, to cure all our psychological ills, but that He came into the world to provide deliverance from the penalty and ruling power of sin (Rom. 6:1–23). The good news is this: there is hope for full deliverance from the penalty of sin and substantial deliverance from the ruling power of sin and its effects.

This biblical perspective of our basic problem comes loaded with hope for people who are struggling with unbiblical patterns of thinking, desiring, feeling, and living. This perspective is freeing, liberating, and encouraging; it is biblical, and it is true! It tells people that though their personal and interpersonal problems are serious and intense, there is hope for change because Christ Jesus came into the world to provide deliverance from condemnation and corruption, from guilt and pollution, and from the penalty and reigning power of sin in their lives. It tells people that in Christ Jesus they have all the resources they need to escape the corruption in the world and to live godly, fruitful lives characterized by moral excellence, knowledge, self-control, perseverance, brotherly kindness, and Christian love (2 Pet. 1:3–8).

Think biblically about what they say. Language is a tool God has chosen to use in communicating with us. Words are important to Him. If we are doing biblical counseling, we need to help our counselees think and talk biblically about their problems. To do this we need to use biblical terms, rather than psychological terms, to describe people's problems. Psychological terms tend to direct the counselee's thinking away from Christ and His Word, whereas the use of biblical words such as sin, fear, anger, worry, lying, lust, bitterness, coveting, envy, and jealousy direct thinking toward the Scriptures.

Counselors also need to be aware of the unbiblical language counselees may use to describe their difficulties. Here are three examples of the hope-diminishing language a counselee may use:

1. *"I can't."* These two words usually mean one of three things: "I won't"; "I don't understand my resources in Christ"; or "I don't know how to do what the Bible tells me to do". When someone repeatedly says "I can't," the counselor needs to explore precisely what the person means by those words and then follow up with the appropriate biblical response.

   For example, if "I can't" signifies overt rebellion against God, the counselee needs to understand and acknowledge that rebellion. The counselor will want to use appropriate motivational strategies to help the counselee choose obedience to Christ. If a counselee is a Christian and the "I can't" means the person does not think he or she is able to obey biblical directives, the counselor will need to remind the individual of the resources that are available in Christ and will need to explain how to use those resources. Still further, if the "I can't" of a believer indicates a lack of practical know-how or skills to put biblical directives into practice, the counselor will want to help that person gain the skill to put God's instructions into practice.

2. *"My wife makes me mad."* This is a false and hopeless statement. It is false because the wife did not cause the sinful anger; the husband chose to be angry in response to her actions. Such a statement implies that the husband is a victim of the wife's actions and that he cannot help himself. According to the Bible, this is false. The husband needs to understand and believe that if he is a Christian, with God's help he can learn to respond correctly in spite of his wife's provocation.

3. *"I've tried everything, and it hasn't worked."* When people believe they have exhausted every alternative without success, the inevitable consequence is a sense of hopelessness. So we must question whether they have, in fact, tried everything and suggest to them some things they have not tried. It is likely that people who say they have tried everything have only done what was convenient to them. It may also be that they have an unbiblical understanding of or expectations about the results of doing things God's way. Then too, they may have unrealistic and unbiblical ideas of timing; they may be looking for a "quick, easy fix", expecting immediate results. Or they may have been doing the right thing for the wrong reasons: not because it was right or because God wanted them to but primarily because they wanted to be released from hardship and difficulty.

When we hear counselees make these types of statements we need to help them discern the reasons behind their unbiblical language and provide hope for them by correcting their misconceptions.

Provide Godly Examples for Counselees

Another way we can inspire our counselees is to demonstrate hope through our own lives and the lives of others.

Our own example of hope. Many people who seek counsel need to see hope modeled before they can experience it themselves, and what better person to model hope for them than the counselor? The counselor's biblically based attitude of hope will inspire hopefulness in the counselee. From the beginning we must show them that even if their situation is extremely difficult, we believe that God "is able to do exceeding abundantly beyond all that we ask or think" and that "with man this is impossible but with God all things are possible" (Eph. 3:20; Matt. 19:26). We should commend people for their willingness to seek counsel, be liberal with sincere praise, and encourage them with Paul's words: "I am confident of this very thing, that He who began a good work in you will perfect it until the day of Christ Jesus" (Phil. 1:6).

The example of hope in others. We can give people hope by showing them how others faced similar situations and handled them successfully. They need to know that they are not alone and that they are not the first person to experience such trials (1 Cor. 10:13). It can help counselees to read specific examples in Scripture of Christians who endured similar circumstances (and worse), or to talk to others who have experienced such situations. God can use the hope they see in the lives of others who have suffered to strengthen their own hope.

Romans 15:4 explains how God produces an attitude of hopefulness: "Whatever was written in earlier times was written for our instruction, that through perseverance and the encouragement of the Scriptures we might have hope."

The people Paul was writing to certainly experienced difficult circumstances. Paul was asking them to refocus and reorient patterns of thinking and behaving that were based on centuries of teaching and tradition. It was a costly form of self-denial. With good reason, Paul recognized that some of these people were discouraged. He knew that they would never have the desire or ability to make the necessary changes without hope. Thus, he wrote this verse to build up their hope.

Note carefully the three things this verse tells us about how hope is generated. First, it reminds us that Scripture must always play a central role in developing hope. "Whatever is written" refers, of course, to what was written in the Scripture. Hope comes through the encouragement of the Scriptures. Second, this verse indicates that the Scriptures promote perseverance and encourage a hopeful attitude through the example of others who have faced similar circumstances and have overcome them. Verse three calls attention to the example of Christ. Hope is developed as we realize that others, even Christ the Son of God, experienced hardship, denied Himself, and responded in the way that God asks us to respond. And third, the text suggests that the Scriptures generate hope by removing the surprise element from what is happening. That is, while things may be out of *our* control, they are definitely *not* out of God's control. In fact, what happens to us is exactly what God has said will happen. When properly understood through the Scriptures, we begin to realize that things are happening just as the Scriptures indicated they would. This builds hope, because it helps us to realize that God is in charge, that things are not happening by accident, that what is happening has meaning and purpose, and that God is present to sustain and support us in the midst of our difficulties.

Yes, hope is a powerful change agent. With hope people are inspired to do positive things, but without it they will flounder and fail. Mark it down and note it well: when people are not changing through our counseling efforts, perhaps they do not have hope, a solidly based biblical hope. We must never underestimate the importance of hope in the counseling process. For while we recognize that God is the ultimate hope giver (who provides hope through His Son, by His Spirit, and in His Word), at the same time, we realize that He also uses men and women to inspire and encourage the hopeless to find their hope in Him.

10

Taking Counselee Inventory: Collecting Data

Wayne A. Mack

When Eli saw Hannah's lips moving but heard no sound, he assumed she was drunk and condemned her without so much as smelling her breath (1 Sam. 1:12–14)! In reality, her problem was far different than he had interpreted it to be: she was praying for a child. Job suffered a similar misunderstanding. His counselors, who never asked questions or gathered information, assumed they knew his problem from the very start. Even when Job tried to correct their misconceptions with pertinent facts, they stubbornly stuck to their theories. They could not interpret Job's problem accurately, because they never gained enough information about it. And because of that, their counsel to him only made his situation worse and added to his distress.

We must be careful that we do not make this mistake in our counseling. If we attempt to interpret people's problems before we gather adequate data, we will only add to their difficulty rather than relieve it. James 1:19 says, "Be quick to hear, slow to speak," and nowhere is that command more important than in counseling.

In Proverbs 18:15 we read that "the mind of the prudent acquires knowledge / And the ear of the wise seeks knowledge." The wise person seeks and acquires knowledge, not assumptions, speculations, or imaginations. And knowledge has to do with facts. The verse suggests that getting those facts will require the use of our minds (in planning) and the use of our ears (in listening). Accurate biblical counseling must include an organized method of gaining information that incorporates substantial times of listening to the counselee. It is particularly helpful in the initial stages of counseling to encourage the counselee to do much of the talking.[1]

Here is a counseling case that illustrates the importance of taking inventory of the counselee.

> Violet is now 54 years old. She is a Christian, lives with her son and his wife, and for many years has complained of depression. She does little or nothing else, but does still attend church regularly. Yet every week she comes home more upset and gets more depressed than before.

In this first session she has admitted to bitterness and resentment that she connects vaguely with church attendance. She claims to be lonely, says she daydreams, and on her Personal Data Inventory hints at an undisclosed problem: ". . . And, there is a difficulty that I could mention only to God." Initial inquiries about this matter are met with hesitance, reluctance to speak, evasion, and embarrassment.[2]

Sometimes counselees will quickly reveal much of what you need to know. In fact, the greatest challenge with these counselees may be to convince them to listen. But most are more like Violet. She is holding something back, and the counselor cannot help her without addressing the difficulty that she "could mention only to God." To be effective, the counselor must first gather enough information to adequately understand the person and the problems.

With people like Violet, that may be easier said than done. They may feel embarrassed about their problems and be reluctant to share them with anyone. They may also be concerned that the counselor will look down on them, ridicule them, or betray their confidence. Perhaps all of this has happened to them before, and they are worried that it will happen again if they reveal too much. Like the city of Jerusalem, these people have built a wall around themselves. But do you remember the twelve gates of Jerusalem? The walls people build around their lives also have gates, and it is our job as counselors to find a way into the "city" through those gates. If we come to one gate and find it closed, we must try another until we find an open gate and gain access into the real thoughts, hopes, and fears of the counselee.[3]

THE KINDS OF DATA TO GATHER

What information do we need to be able to help people with their problems? We need to gather data in at least six areas: physical state, resources, emotions, actions, concepts, and historical background.

Physical Data

Physical problems can both contribute to and proceed from spiritual problems. The success of our counsel will sometimes be dependent upon understanding a particular aspect of someone's health. In 2 Corinthians 4:16, Paul implied that when "our outer man is decaying," our inner man tends to lose heart. There is a close connection between the two. The inner man can affect the outer man and vice versa. Thus, we must be aware of any physical problems of our counselees if we desire to solve the inward problems they face.

In the following paragraphs we will discuss five aspects of our physical lives that can influence our spiritual health:

1. *Sleep.* Irregular sleep patterns can be caused by spiritual problems (such as anxiety, laziness, or guilt) or they can contribute to spiritual problems. Dr. Bob Smith wrote this about sleep loss:

> From the sleep studies conducted it has been learned that the average individual needs approximately seven to eight hours sleep per night. In most cases, those who regularly require amounts in excess of this need to be explored for the possibility of depression. . . .
>
> "Scientists do not yet understand what lies behind our basic requirement for sleep, but this much they have made clear: Sleep is one of the most essential needs of man, and we sacrifice it at considerable peril to our bodies and minds.
>
> "Few of us would seriously consider going very long without food, yet hunger is hardly as serious as protracted sleep loss. A man can survive starvation for over three weeks. But deprive him of sleep for that time and he will disintegrate and become psychotic. . . .
>
> "Today's man-on-the-move is like the wreckless gambler who loses his shirt and then plays on with borrowed money. The sleepless American—feeling the angry pinch of fatigue and the erosion of his well-being—begins living in the red, using the 'pep' offered by well-advertised drugs that propel the body and mind onward with energies that are not really there."
>
> All the while, however, there lurks a day of reckoning, "when symptoms can no longer be denied: agonizing fatigue, irritability, lapses in attention, withdrawal, fading judgment, erratic behavior, and even a weakening of ethical standards."[4]

That is why we need to find out how much sleep our counselees are getting. And we may find that some of their problems will lessen immediately once they begin to practice regular sleep habits.

2. *Diet.* The old saying, "You are what you eat," is partly true. We need to be aware of what our counselees eat, because nutritional imbalance can affect behavior. For example, stimulants such as sugar and caffeine can affect people in a pronounced way.[5] If you are dealing with a person who is nervous and hyperactive all the time, you will want to find out the quantity of stimulants they are consuming. Other individuals experience allergic reactions to dietary agents and so forth. In short, we must not ignore the diet factor.

3. *Exercise.* In counseling, it may be necessary to address the amount of physical activity people are involved in. Ecclesiastes 5:12 says, "The sleep of the working man is pleasant," and that verse was written in a day when most people earned their living by the sweat of their brow. Today in our culture, demanding physical labor is less common; most of our occupations call for the use of the mind more than the body. So for many of us the

exercise we need to stay healthy must be a planned event in our free time, and that can often be overlooked to our detriment.

A lack of exercise can actually produce or heighten anxiety. The daily stress we face causes our bodies to produce chemicals (like adrenalin) that provide energy and even tighten up our muscles. Physical activity is one way God has designed for this everyday tension to be released, and without that activity our bodies can be affected negatively, and our moods may suffer as well. Gathering information about a person's activity level—how much exercise he or she gets—can be a significant factor in counseling people who struggle with anxiety or other ungodly emotions. Frequently, I have found that a homework assignment requiring regular exercise significantly helps counselees to relax.[6]

4. *Illness.* Sickness can sometimes be caused by personal sin (Ps. 32:3–4; 38:3; Prov. 14:30; 1 Cor. 11:30).[7] But sickness that is not caused by personal sin can also be an important factor in the struggles and temptations our counselees face. For instance, viral infection, hepatitis, mononucleosis, diabetes, and hypothyroidism are all associated with depression. In many cases, when Christians suffer from those conditions their depression symptoms may simply be a consequence of the exhaustion and discomfort caused by the malady. So we must not assume that in every case depression is a direct result of personal sin. It may be relieved or eliminated simply by the correct diagnosis and treatment of a medical problem.

5. *Medication.* Various medications, both prescription and over-the-counter, cause side effects that are harmful to one degree or another. These drugs can contribute to ongoing problems, especially if the individual is not aware of the possibility of side effects. Some cases of mild depression, for example, may be solved simply by finding out what medication the person has been taking and whether it might be causing side effects that are contributing to the depression. A counselor must learn to gather pertinent data and look for possible connections between problematic experiences and medication.[8]

A useful tool for this process is *The Physician's Desk Reference*. This book, available through bookstores and some doctors' offices, contains a listing of all medicines on the market and describes the physiological dynamics of the drug, indications for use, possible adverse reactions, potentially dangerous side effects, and other accompanying symptoms it may cause.[9] Although it is not our place as biblical counselors to prescribe drugs or remove counselees from drug regimens, we can put ourselves in a better position to address some problems by learning what medicine a counselee has taken.[10]

Resources

A second area of data concerns the resources that the counselee has at his or her disposal. What resources does that person have that can aid in the counseling process, and what lack of resources might hinder the process?

The most important resources, of course, are the spiritual ones, so we must first find out if a counselee possesses these resources. In other words, is he or she a Christian? If not, the person has no spiritual resources to work with.[11] Thus, early in the counseling process it is important to ask questions pertaining to a person's spiritual condition. In some cases, when a counselee professes to be a Christian it may be necessary to question that person further to establish the validity of that profession.[12] When we are fairly certain that a counselee is born again we need to discover the extent of his or her Christian growth, because a person with greater spiritual maturity will find it easier to make use of available resources in Christ than a person who is a new Christian.

Counselors also need to gather information about other kinds of resources that can affect the spiritual dimension: intellectual, educational, experiential, and social.[13] Any one or all of these can be an important piece in the puzzle of an individual's problems.

Emotions

Emotions are like smoke detectors. One night as I was relaxing in the family room, my children were trying to cook something on the stove in the basement. Apparently, some cooking oil spilled over the side of the pan and caught fire, igniting the top of the stove and sending flames high into the air. The smoke detector blared a high-pitched warning and I was able to throw a blanket over the flame and smother it before it did any major damage.

Emotions are like that smoke detector: they are not the primary problem but are warnings of the primary problem. Imagine if I had silenced the smoke detector with a hammer and gone back to relax in my chair. The house would have burned down! I had to take care of the source problem, the fire. Likewise, some people (and, unfortunately, some counselors) seek to eliminate negative emotions such as depression, anxiety, fear, or rage by attacking the emotions themselves through medication or behavior therapy. But they fail to address and eliminate the "fires" in the basement of their lives, the underlying problems that disturb their emotions.

The smoke detector analogy illustrates another truth about emotions: they should never be ignored. What if I had responded to the smoke alarm by slipping in some ear plugs? I would have lost more than my house! Likewise, counselors must recognize the significance of emotions. God has given them to us as outward indicators of what is happening in our hearts, and they are often inextricably linked to the problems we face.

Through the power of the Holy Spirit, Christians have the ability to control their emotions and do what God wants them to do regardless of how they feel (1 Cor. 10:13). On the other hand, emotions are powerful enough to make it much harder to do what is right. Consider the first murder in Genesis 4:1–8, for instance. Most likely it would never have happened if Cain had not become "very angry" (v. 5). His anger was the result of sinful pride and could have been eliminated through repentance, but without repentance his anger provided the impetus for the most heinous of crimes. That is why we must ask questions about how our counselees feel and be sensitive to the effects those emotions have on their lives.

Actions

A fourth area to consider in gathering data is actions. We need to consider what our counselees do and what they do not do.[14] The Bible makes a close connection between our actions and other aspects of our lives. Actions have a profound effect on our spiritual, emotional, and physical health. Again consider Cain, who was not only angry but also depressed. God said to him, "Why has your countenance fallen? If you do well, will not your countenance be lifted up? And if you do not do well, sin is crouching at the door" (vv. 6–7). Cain sinned by bringing an inappropriate sacrifice to the Lord (v. 3), and the rest of the chapter indicates a direct correlation between that action and every part of his life. One disobedient action affected his relationship to God, produced various negative emotions, and led to further sinful action against his brother.

Time and again the Bible emphasizes the importance of our actions:

- "How blessed is the man who does not walk in the counsel of the wicked, / Nor stand in the path of sinners, / Nor sit in the seat of scoffers! / But his delight is in the law of the LORD, / And in His law he meditates day and night. / And he will be like a tree firmly planted by streams of water, / Which yields its fruit in its season, / And its leaf does not wither; / And in whatever he does, he prospers" (Ps. 1:1–3).
- "Who is the man who desires life, / And loves length of days that he may see good? / Keep your tongue from evil, / And your lips from speaking deceit. / Depart from evil, and do good; / Seek peace, and pursue it" (Ps. 34:12–14).
- "Why do you call Me, 'Lord, Lord,' and do not do what I say? Everyone who comes to Me, and hears My words, and acts upon them, I will show you whom he is like: he is like a man building a house, who dug deep and laid a foundation upon the rock; and when a flood rose, the torrent burst against that house and could not shake it, because it had been well built. But the one who has heard, and has not acted accordingly, is like a man who built a house upon the ground without any foundation; and the torrent burst against it and immediately it collapsed, and the ruin of that house was great" (Luke 6:46–49).

- "Blessed are those who hear the word of God, and observe it" (Luke 11:28).
- "One who looks intently at the perfect law, the law of liberty, and abides by it, not having become a forgetful hearer but an effectual doer, this man shall be blessed in what he does" (James 1:25).

God's commands are not merely demands, they are invitations—invitations to fullness of life. They are not merely obligations, they are opportunities. They are not merely precepts, they are promises. "I set before you the way of life and the way of death," God says (Jer. 21:8; see Deut. 30:15, 19). The way of life requires obedience to the commands in His Word, and the way of death is assured by disobedience to them. Counselors who take God's commands seriously must realize the relationship between obedience to God and all aspects of life and must gather data about a counselee's actions to see if they are in line with the Word of God.

Concepts

We must also gather data about the counselee's concepts. *Concepts* refers to what Hebrews 4:12 describes as "the thoughts and intentions of the heart." This includes personal convictions, attitudes, expectations, desires, and values. It includes what or whom people are trusting, fearing, listening to, and depending on; what or whom they are serving in life (Matt. 6:24); what or who their functional gods are; and what or who controls them and calls the shots in their lives. As important as actions and emotions are, in a sense they are secondary to the conceptual area of life because what we think and desire (our thoughts and intentions) ultimately determines how we act and feel.

Here are several passages that reinforce this truth:

Mark 7:18-23. After listing numerous sins of action, such as "fornications, thefts, murders, adulteries, deeds of coveting and wickedness" (vv. 21–22), Jesus said, "All these evil things proceed from within and defile the man." His intention was to teach the Jews that sin is an inner problem, one that runs much deeper than surface behavior. It is a heart problem. And the term *heart* in Scripture is often used interchangeably with the word *mind* (see Gen. 6:15; Heb. 4:12). They both refer to the inner part of us that influences how we will act. This dimension of life must be addressed if lasting change is to take place.

Romans 12:1-2. In this passage Paul exhorted the Romans how to respond to the doctrinal truth he shared with them in Romans 1—11. These two verses serve as a good summary of the entire process of spiritual growth that makes up the Christian life: We are to be "transformed by the renewing of our mind, that we may prove what the will of God is, that which is good and acceptable and perfect." If we want to see lives transformed we must understand what is going on in people's minds and focus on that as we seek to help them change.

Galatians 5:16-21. Verses 19 through 21 of this passage list some of the more common actions and emotions that constitute "the deeds of the flesh." Ungodly actions and reactions such as immorality, strife, enmities, disputes, dissensions, drunkenness, carousing, jealousy, and outbursts of anger are included in this extensive, though not exhaustive, catalog of behavioral and emotional sins. Verse 16, which refers to "the desires of the flesh," takes us behind outward behaviors to a deeper level and gives us another important perspective for understanding people and their problems. Understanding people not only requires an understanding of their deeds, it involves a knowledge of the *desires* that motivate their deeds. According to Paul, ungodly desires are the engine that drives ungodly deeds. The ungodly actions and feelings of people are related to and rooted in their ungodly, idolatrous thoughts and desires.

Ephesians 4:22-24. This is another well-known passage that summarizes the process of spiritual growth. In verse 22 Paul said to "lay aside the old self," and in verse 24 he said to "put on the new self." But the key to that process of change is in verse 23: "Be renewed in the spirit of your mind." We cannot eliminate unbiblical practices and cultivate biblical practices until our minds are being renewed.[15]

Few truths are more essential to biblical counseling. Many counselors wonder why they see only temporary change in the lives of counselees, who, they observe with frustration, return to the same sins shortly afterward. In most cases, the reason is that the minds or hearts of those counselees have not been renewed. They experienced mere behavioral change because of the influence of someone who manipulated them through psychological tricks or pressured them week after week to conform. But when that external pressure is gone, their unrenewed minds quickly revert back to plotting the sins that their bodies are more than willing to carry out.

If we want to practice true biblical counseling, we must gain as much information as we can about our counselees' thoughts and desires so we can correct their misconceptions and help them to have "the mind of Christ" concerning their problems (see 1 Cor. 2:16).

Historical Data

Securing historical data about counselees and their problems is another important part of taking inventory. Historical data refers to information about people's present and past life-context: the external circumstances in their lives, the influences or pressures they have experienced or are experiencing, how they have been sinned against, their frustrations and hardships, their failures, temptations, temporal blessings, successes, comforts, wealth, etc.[16]

Some counselors, who have an unhealthy preoccupation with the past, believe that everything in a counselee's present life is somehow connected to the past. As a result they tend to transfer responsibility from the counselee to those who mistreated him or her long ago. But this is a dangerous tendency that must be avoided.[17] Yet we cannot allow ourselves to ignore the past, because what has happened in the past does affect our counselees, especially if it involves patterns of sin or has somehow provided them with an excuse to blame others for their problems.[18]

I once talked with a young man who could not get along with his boss, although there were no apparent or objective reasons for the conflict. It was only when I started asking him about his previous work experience that I obtained a clue to the problem. When I asked him about each of his former jobs and how he perceived previous bosses, he responded negatively about every one of them. Then I asked him about his relationship with his father while growing up and discovered that he had extensive problems with his father. This indicated to me that, most likely, this man had never learned how to respond to authority, an insight that provided direction for questions and counsel from that point on.

In that case, it was primarily the man's own sin in the past that was contributing to his current problems. In other instances, the sins of others in the past can contribute to a counselee's problems. When people have been abused, mistreated, or neglected, they are usually tempted to blame the abuser for their problems and to respond negatively to anyone who reminds them of that person. The biblical counselor does not approach such situations by ignoring what occurred in the past, but listens attentively to their history, identifies with the pain they have experienced, then lovingly and patiently deals with their sinful responses and seeks to refocus their attention on their resources in Christ and His way of dealing with their past.[19]

In addition to taking historical inventory of people's lives, biblical counselors will also want to gather current data. What is presently occurring in their lives is equally important to what occurred in the past. Biblical counselors should never excuse or justify ungodly behavior in themselves or others because of past or present circumstances. God's Word is unequivocal about that.[20] Nevertheless, giving accurate, appropriate, and sensitive biblical counsel will require some understanding of the present context in which people live and respond. We must understand how people are being sinned against as well as how they are responding sinfully.[21]

Counsel given without the acquisition of life-context information may be irrelevant, inappropriate, clinical, sterile, and even hurtful. Without pertinent historical and current facts, biblical counselors may make the same mistakes that Job's counselors made and actually add to the distress of counselees. To use the words of Job, they may be guilty of tormenting, insulting, crushing, and wronging people, the very people they are trying to help (see Job 19:1–3). In their attempt to do good, they may actually do evil (see Rom. 14:16).

To avoid these mistakes, biblical counselors must observe what is being done to people, what is going on around them, as well as what that person is doing, feeling, and desiring. They will want to acquire and process information about marriage and family situations, living conditions, relationships, church involvement, occupation or school situations, finances, and any other pressures, problems, joys, or successes that are relevant to the lives of their counselees.

How to Gather Data

We have discussed the importance of gathering data and how this is significant to the process of accurate biblical counseling. Now we need to consider methods for gathering the data. The primary methods we will discuss are: (1) using personal data inventory forms, (2) asking good questions, and (3) observing halo data.

Using Personal Data Inventory Forms

A helpful sample of a personal data inventory form (PDIF) is provided in the appendix of this book. This form can be a useful tool in the initial stages of counseling for the following reasons:

1. Requiring that counselees complete a PDIF indicates a counselor's concern for thoroughness.
2. The form provides constant access to basic information that the counselor may forget or neglect to cover during the counseling sessions.
3. The information helps to prepare the counselor for the counseling sessions. It will often reveal the initial direction the counseling should take.
4. Completing the form helps counselees think about the issues that will be discussed.
5. Discussing information from the form with the counselee can provide a natural and appropriate entry point into the counseling session.

Even when a counselor is working with someone familiar, it is wise to use the PDIF. Invariably, the form provides new and significant information.

Asking Appropriate Questions

In addition to the PDIF, the amount of data the counselor gathers will depend largely on the quantity and quality of questions he or she asks. While compassion and concern for the counselee should determine quantity, the following guidelines can help to develop quality questions.

1. *Appropriate questions are thoughtful and gracious.* If questions are not asked in an appropriate manner the counselor's efforts to gather data will be in vain. The Bible says, "Let your speech always be with grace, seasoned, as it were, with salt" (Col. 4:6). We need to ask questions in a way that sets our counselees at ease and does not put them on edge. One way to do this is to explain to them initially that you will be asking questions and gathering information in order to help them.

Another way to ensure a gracious manner is to ask questions using an advance-and-retreat method. That is, when the counselor senses the counselee becoming apprehensive or uncomfortable with a line of questioning, he or she backs off that issue temporarily and explores another. Perhaps later in the session or in another session the counselor will return to that issue.

2. *Appropriate questions are relevant.* All questions should relate to issues the counselor is seeking to address; they should not serve merely to satisfy curiosity. Like the young widows mentioned in 1 Timothy 5:13, counselors can sometimes become "gossips and busybodies" when they become privy to information they do not necessarily need to know. Irrelevant questions can also send people down rabbit trails in the discussion and distract them from the real issues at hand. So to keep counselees focused and to save precious time always ask questions that are relevant to the problems of the counselee.[22]

3. *Appropriate questions produce facts.* The following case illustrates the kinds of questions that do *not* produce significant information:

> Bruce and Maggie appear with their daughter, Karen. The pastor is surprised; he expected only the parents.
> Counselor: "Why are you here, Karen?" (Shrug of shoulders)
> Maggie: "I asked her to come. She and I can't get along and it is wrecking our home."
> Counselor: "Do you see a problem between you and Mom?"
> Karen: "Um, yes."
> Counselor: "Would you say there's animosity between you and Mom?"
> Karen: (Hesitating, then) "Much!"
> Counselor: "Why is there this problem with Mom?"
> Karen: "I don't know."
> Counselor: "Do you have this problem with anyone else?"
> Karen: "No."
> Counselor: "Karen, you know you are to honor your mother. It is sin not to. Do you see this as sin?"
> Karen: "Yes."

> Counselor: "Why haven't you made a move to right this situation?"
> Karen: "I don't know how."[23]

The counselor in that situation gathered embarrassingly little data in the conversation because he failed to ask questions that produce facts.

First, notice that he asked several questions that began with the word *why*. Instead, he should have made an effort to ask more *what* questions. Generally, *what* questions produce much more information than *why* questions, which will often receive only the answer that Karen gave twice, "I don't know." Counselors will see better results in data gathering by asking questions like these: What is your problem? What is happening? What do you mean? What have you done about it? What has helped? What has made it worse? What do you think about it?

Other helpful questions start with the word *how:* How do you feel? How have you acted? How have you reacted? How have you tried to resolve it? How long have you had the problem? How often have you had it? How can I be of help?"[24]

Another problem with the counselor's questions to Karen was that the rest of his questions were closed-ended, which means they could be answered sufficiently with a yes or no.[25] Rather, he should have asked more open-ended questions, so that the counselee could not answer with a yes or no, but would have to provide further information. Following are some examples of these two types of questions:

Closed: Do you want to get married?
Open: What are your thoughts on marriage?
Closed: Do you love your husband?
Open: How would you describe your attitude toward your husband?
Closed: Are you satisfied with your job?
Open: What do you like or dislike about your job?
Closed: Do you get along with your parents?
Open: What kind of relationship do you have with your parents?

We need to be conscious of the kinds of questions we ask in counseling; we need to choose them carefully so that they will provide the most information possible. Here are some examples of useful questions to ask in each of the six categories of data.

Physical
Generally speaking, how would you describe your present and past physical health?

Tell me about your sleep patterns.

What is involved in the work you do?

If you could change four things about your work, what would you change?

Give me a description of what you do in a typical day in your life.

Resources

Tell me about the most important persons in your life, and why they are so important to you.

Share with me the relationships in your life that give you the most joy; the most sadness or heartache.

When you have a problem, what do you usually do?

Tell me about the persons in your life with whom you feel comfortable sharing your private thoughts and feelings.

Tell me about your relationship with God: how it began, how it has developed, how important it is, where God fits into the total picture of your life or the picture of what is happening to you now, what you are doing to strengthen your relationship with God.

Describe what your church means to you.

When you have had problems in the past, what has helped you most in resolving them?

What are some of your greatest resources, strengths; greatest deficiencies/weaknesses?

What are your Bible reading and prayer practices?

Emotions

What are some emotions that you frequently experience?

How do others see you emotionally?

If you were able to change anything about yourself emotionally, what would you want to change?

Give me a few examples of times when you were extremely . . . (angry, happy, sad).

How do you feel about what is happening in your life right now?

If I had tape-recorded what you have just said and played it back to you, what emotions would you hear?

Actions

As you look back over your life, what are some of the things you have done that were worthwhile?

What are some of the things you wish you could undo?

As you look at your life right now, what are some of the things you think you are doing that are right? that are wrong?

Tell me some of the ways you see yourself growing as a Christian.

Tell me some of the ways you could improve as a Christian; in your relationship with Christ; as a testimony for Christ.

Tell me how you have helped other people; been a hindrance to other people.

When you think of the Ten Commandments, which ones do you have the greatest problem with?

Concepts

What do you see as your most pressing problem?*[26]

Do you have any idea why the problem has become so severe?*

What do you think about the way you have been handling the problem?*

What does all of this tell you about yourself?*

Do you have any idea why criticism is so hard for you to handle?*

If I had a tape recorder and could record your thoughts at this moment, what would I hear?*

What happens inside your head when I give you a suggestion about handling a problem?*

What do/did you want, desire, seek, aim for, pursue, hope for?*

What are your goals, expectations, or intentions?*

Where do you look for security, meaning, happiness, fulfillment, joy, or comfort?*

What do you fear most? What do you tend to avoid?*

What would make you happy?*

What brings out the worst or best in you?*

What or who rules or controls you in the nitty-gritty of life? To what or whom do you listen?*

In what or whom do you place your functional trust? What drives you? In what or whom do you set your hope?*

When you are pressured or tense, where do you turn? Where do you find relief? How do you escape?*

Historical

When did you first begin to experience this problem?

Tell me what was happening in your life when. . . .

Tell me about your relationship with the Lord over the years: the high points and low points.

As you look back over your life, what are the happiest and saddest experiences you have ever had?

Tell me about some of the most positive influences in your life; the most negative influences in your life.

Tell me about your marriage, your family, your church, your work, etc.

If you could change anything about circumstances in your life, what would you change?

What is going on in your life that brings you the most pleasure? the most pain or distress?

What external pressures are you presently experiencing?

OBSERVING HALO DATA

Counselors can also learn about counselees through *halo data,* or information that is communicated in nonverbal ways. This includes both nonverbal behavior and paralinguistic communication.

1. *Nonverbal behavior.* Genesis 3:8 says that "the man and his wife hid themselves from the presence of the LORD God among the trees of the garden." Adam and Eve had never fled from God before, and this action revealed something important about what they were feeling. They did not have to say one word for us to know that they were experiencing the guilt and fear of sin. Likewise in counseling we can learn much from the actions of our counselees during the sessions.

Sometimes their faces will exhibit expressions that clearly reveal anger, sorrow, or other emotions. Sometimes they will move the chairs closer to the desk or farther away from it when they enter the room. Sometimes couples will move their chairs away from each other. Sometimes families will arrange themselves in a way that shows who is getting along and who is not, or which child is favored by the parents. Counselees may squeeze their chair handles or look at the floor every time the counselor mentions a particular issue. Some counselees will be late to the sessions every time. All these things (and many more) can reveal information that will be useful to help counselees change.

2. *Paralinguistic communication.* This type of halo data has to do primarily with the manner in which our counselees speak, not in what they say, but in *how* they say it. Does their tone of voice communicate hope, or does it communicate hopelessness? Does it communicate anxiety or peace? Anger or forgiveness? Love or hate? Interest or indifference? And does their voice portray them as rude, inconsiderate, or manipulative, or does it give other negative impressions that could be contributing to their interpersonal struggles? Paralinguistic communication also involves what counselees are willing to talk about and what they refuse to talk about. Sometimes the issues they hesitate to talk about are the very issues at the source of their problems.

Both types of halo data are especially important to notice in regard to how counselees relate to their counselors, because they probably treat others the same way they treat the counselor, and others probably perceive them in the same way that the counselor does. Never underestimate the importance of this kind of observation; it can provide as much information as merely concentrating on what the counselees say.[27]

CONCLUSION

Some other ways to gather data effectively include assigning homework specifically designed for this purpose,[28] talking with others who have a relationship with the counselee, and taking accurate notes for review as counseling proceeds.[29]

The importance of becoming skillful in taking inventory can hardly be overestimated. To a large degree, all other elements of the biblical counseling process depend on it. How we effectively build involvement with our counselees and inspire hope in them will be determined and directed by what we learn about them and their problems.

Understanding and counseling people biblically is a challenging and rewarding responsibility. But sloppiness or neglect in gathering data can undermine the whole process. That is why biblical counselors need to develop expertise in this endeavor. We need to work carefully and prayerfully at improving our inventory-taking skills as though our effectiveness as a counselor depended on it, because from a human point of view, it does!

11

Interpreting Counselee Data

Wayne A. Mack

In the last chapter we discussed the process of gathering data. Now we turn to the challenge of using that data. No matter how much information we obtain about our counselees, it is of no value unless we use it to draw conclusions about what is happening in their lives. We must not only interpret that data ourselves, but in many cases must also help our counselees to reinterpret it, because they may already have drawn wrong conclusions about their situations.

The process of biblical counseling we discuss in the following chapters depends upon an accurate interpretation of the counselee's problems. If the counselor's interpretation is wrong, the instruction, inducement, and implementation will be wrong as well. An accurate understanding of the meaning of the collected data provides strategic direction for the entire counseling process.

THE DEFINITION OF INTERPRETING DATA

What do we mean by interpreting data? This process involves two basic elements: accurately analyzing or conceptualizing the data and explaining it to the counselee. In other words, one aspect of interpretation involves what goes on in our minds as counselors. We must analyze the data gathered during the inventory phase so that we can understand it from a biblical viewpoint. And we must decide what should be done about the problems according to Scripture.

The second facet of interpretation involves what we say to our counselees about their problems. Our interpretation of the situation is not complete until we interpret it *for them.* We must explain our analysis and conceptions to the counselee in such a way that he or she understands the real nature and causes of the difficulties from a biblical perspective. In many instances, progress is not made in counseling simply because the counselor did not identify the problem correctly, or did not explain it adequately so the counselee could agree with the interpretation and follow the counsel. In such a situation, two different interpretations of the problem exist, the counselor's and the counselee's, and these work against each other.

So when we discuss interpretation of data we must consider not only how the counselor should think about the problems but also how the counselor should communicate those conclusions to the counselee.

THE PROCESS OF INTERPRETING DATA

The biblical counselor can best achieve the goal of accurate analysis and clear explanation by following these four steps: (1) gather adequate data, (2) interpret the data, (3) formulate a working interpretation of the data, and (4) test the validity of the interpretation.

As these steps are explained throughout this chapter, you may think, "This process is going to take a tremendous amount of time and effort!" Yes, it will take much time and effort. People are complex, and a simplistic approach to helping them almost always fails. We are not like Jesus, who knew immediately the thoughts of people when He walked the earth. We certainly cannot take one look at someone and tell that person what he or she needs. In most cases, we will not even be able to talk to people once and tell them what they need. The process of interpretation can be somewhat lengthy and extensive. And although with experience a counselor is able to reach conclusions in less time, we must never get to a point where we are not willing to think long and hard about each person's problems.

Before we begin discussing the steps in the process of interpretation, consider the following case study, which will serve as an illustration throughout the rest of this chapter:

> "Feelings of inferiority have made me sick physically and generally impotent as a person," says Gus. "I've tried to do as you said, but I just can't." At a previous session you asked Gus to seek the forgiveness of his father for several admitted offenses against him. Gus is now in his fourth session and the one assignment that has been given for the past two weeks still remains uncompleted. "You 'can't,' really means you 'won't,' doesn't it?" is your reply. "No, I just can't do anything," he responds. "I'm not a quitter or anything, but I can't do that. I want to; I know I should and if I had more ego strength, I might be able to do so."[1]

First, consider this case from Gus's perspective. How is he interpreting the problem? He believes that he does not have the ability to complete the homework assignment or otherwise overcome his problems. He sees himself as a victim who does not bear responsibility for his actions. He cites "feelings of inferiority" and a lack of "ego strength" as the cause of his impotency to do what is right.

We can see that Gus's counselor needs to interpret the problem biblically and communicate that interpretation to Gus. As we discuss this process in the following pages, we will provide some suggestions for interpreting Gus's situation in a way that will be helpful to him and glorifying to God.

Gather Adequate Data

The first step in the interpretation process is to make sure we have gathered enough data. Let's apply each category we discussed in chapter 10 to Gus's situation.

Physical. What does Gus mean when he says he is sick physically? When did this illness begin? How much sleep is he getting? Has he been to a doctor to see if there is anything wrong organically? What does he mean by the word *impotent?*[2]

Resources. Is Gus a Christian? Has he been taught from the Scriptures concerning his sufficiency in Christ? What kind of relationship does he have with other family members?[3] Does he have godly friends who can encourage him and help him? Are his friends part of the problem or the solution? Does he lack social skills? Is he comparing his abilities and skills to others and thus concluding that he is inferior? How is he involved in church? Does he have a pastor or other shepherds who would be able and willing to help him?

Emotions. Is Gus excitable or indifferent? Does he harbor bitterness, resentment, or anger? Is he fearful? Is he angry with his father or afraid of him? Is he fretting about his problems? What does he mean by "feelings of inferiority"? Does he understand the biblical purpose and role of emotions? What role do emotions or feelings play in Gus's life, in his decision making, in what he does and does not do, and in how he views and interprets himself and situations? How much confidence does he put in the accuracy and validity of his feelings?

Actions. Has Gus attempted anything the counselor or (more important) God is asking him to do? If so, what happened? What other things has he not done or is he not doing because he lacks "ego strength"? What would he like to do if he had more "ego strength"? He said that he is "not a quitter." What are some of the things he has stuck with and carried through to completion? In what ways is he not living biblically or failing to fulfill his biblical responsibilities? What is he currently achieving in any area of his life?[4]

Concepts. How does Gus define the term *ego strength?* How does he believe he should go about getting more of that? What does he think it takes for a person to be successful? What is his view of the nature of the Christian life? What are his expectations? Who is he seeking to please and serve? How does he think God would describe his problem? Would God say feelings of inferiority have made him impotent and generally sick as a person?[5] What does he think would satisfy him? Does he understand what the Bible says about true success? What are his functional gods at this point in his life? To what voices is he listening? What are his cravings? What are his ruling desires? Who is Gus worshiping? On whom is he depending for the resources to live the Christian life and do what God wants him to do?

History. How long has Gus had these "feelings of inferiority," and is there some event in his life connected with them? Is there one particular event through which he is seeing his entire life? How has his perceived lack of ego strength affected his life through the years? Is the problem with his father due to a series of things that have happened? When did those things develop? What is his job history? Are there other authority figures he has had problems with at his job; at school? When he was required to do difficult things in the past, how did he respond? What escapes has Gus previously used to evade responsibility?

Interpret the Data

This second step is the most difficult aspect of the process of interpretation because it involves thinking through the meaning and implications of the inventory data. After asking the counselee numerous questions, the counselor needs to answer some questions. The following questions are helpful for this part of the interpretive process.

What biblical category best describes the person I am counseling? We need to avoid the dangers of stereotyping or overgeneralizing when we evaluate people, but we must also realize that the Bible does speak of various categories into which people fit to one degree or another.

Is this person saved or unsaved? Every person falls into one of these two categories, and as we discussed in chapter 10,[6] those who are saved have resources available that unbelievers do not. So we must consider what the data suggests about whether the counselee is a true believer. What does the data suggest about the person's relationship with Christ? Is it genuine and growing? Does the person spend time with the Lord in consistent prayer and Bible study? Is there any indication that this person's relationship with God is merely historical, meaning that the individual clings to a past decision for assurance without evidence of God's current work in his or her life? Do the convictions belong to that person, or are they borrowed from parents or friends? Your approach to the other phases of counseling, particularly instruction and inducement, will depend heavily on your interpretation in this area.

Is this person spiritually mature or immature? A second way of evaluating counselees is to assess whether they are spiritually mature or immature. Hebrews 5:11–14 mentions these two categories:

> "Concerning him [Melchizedek] we have much to say, and it is
> hard to explain, since you have become dull of hearing. For though by

this time you ought to be teachers, you have need for someone to teach you the elementary principles of the oracles of God, and you have come to need milk and not solid food. For everyone who partakes only of milk is not accustomed to the word of righteousness, for he is a babe. But solid food is for the mature, who because of practice have their senses trained to discern good and evil."

This passage teaches that spiritual maturity is more than what someone knows. It is what they put into practice. Mature Christians are able to discern between good and evil because they have practiced consistent godliness. On the other hand, immature Christians are described as those who have been taught many truths but have not practiced them sufficiently. By that definition even people who have been saved for many years may be immature. Their heads may be filled with scriptural facts and information; they may be able to recite verses and creeds forward and backward; they may even be skilled in discussing theology, but they are not mature because they have not lived out those truths.

Evaluating whether your counselees are mature or immature will determine to some extent the depth of the instruction you can give them, whether it should be "solid food" or merely "milk."[7] It will also help you to know how much you should focus on instruction, because if the person you are dealing with is a mature Christian, he or she will primarily need encouragement and support. Mature Christians with problems often know what needs to be done; counseling becomes simply a matter of helping them to do what they already know is right. Immature Christians, on the other hand, often require extensive instruction before they are ready to take the steps necessary to solve their problems.

Is this person unruly, fainthearted, or weak? In 1 Thessalonians 5:14, the apostle Paul provided a third way of evaluating counselees. He mentioned three categories of people and the general approach we should take in dealing with each of them: "And we urge you, brethren, admonish the unruly, encourage the fainthearted, help the weak, be patient with all men."

The first type of person mentioned is the "unruly." In the original Greek this word (*ataktos*) means to be out of step, to be defiant and rebellious. It speaks of people who are disrespectful, self-willed, and stubborn. They are obviously set against doing what God wants them to do. Paul said to "admonish" these people (that is, warn them). He also said in Titus 3:10 that we should reject a factious person after a first and second admonition. If these people do not respond to our warning and merely want to argue, then we would be wasting our time to continue counseling them. And Proverbs 26:4 says, "Do not answer a fool according to his folly, / Lest you also be like him."[8] We do not want to allow such people to influence us in a negative way by drawing us into useless arguments or other unprofitable discussion. Therefore, we must simply warn them that the path they are choosing can end only in judgment from God, and that we are available to help them when they are open to counsel.

The second category of people mentioned in this passage are the "fainthearted." That Greek word, *oligopsuchos,* literally means "small-souled." It refers to people whose souls have shriveled up. They have become discouraged, weary, or despondent. Their problems do not stem from rebellion or obstinacy but from a feeling of defeat and a lack of ambition. Instead of warning them or otherwise confronting them, Paul says that we should encourage them.

I believe it is significant that Paul did not say, "Admonish the faint-hearted." Faintheartedness is not necessarily sin; people can end up in that category simply because of difficult trials and disappointments that cause them to struggle with discouragement. Gus may be in that situation. And because of that possibility, his counselor should have been more hesitant about rebuking him before the problem had been adequately interpreted. Sometimes I fear that we biblical counselors are too quick to label discouragement a sin and call for repentance from people when we should first show them compassion and provide encouragement.

The third group of people mentioned in 1 Thessalonians 5:14 are the "weak." The Greek word translated "weak" (*asthenēs*) means "without strength" and is used most often to describe those who are physically limited. It is also used in a general sense to describe people who are simply deficient in some way.[9] Their deficiency may be a lack of education, opportunities, or finances, or perhaps a physical problem. These people sometimes find it harder to do what is right because of their "weaknesses." According to Paul, they need more than encouragement: they actually need someone to come alongside and help them to do what they need to do.

The Greek verb for "help" (*antechomai*) can also be translated "support" or "hold to" (see Matt. 6:24). Some people have never had anybody be faithful and committed to them. They are accustomed to being criticized, neglected, and deserted in their time of need. They have never heard anyone say, "I am committed to you. I am going to be your friend through thick and thin, and I am not going to give up on you." They need to sense that someone sincerely loves them and is willing to support them regardless of their deficiencies.

What biblical language best describes the problems this person is experiencing? The Bible not only contains categories of people, it also labels various kinds of behavior. So we need to identify the terms the Bible uses to describe each problem we face in counseling. This will help us in finding the scriptural insight we need about the causes of the problem and the solutions; it will also help us to think in biblical terminology throughout the process. So ask yourself, "What biblical words, labels, or categories could be used to describe the various problems this person is experiencing?"

For example, in Gus's case it is apparent that he has a problem with "confidence in the flesh" (see Phil. 3:3). He believes that the solution to his problems is to gain more "ego strength." But the Scripture says a believer can do all things *through Christ who strengthens us* (Phil. 4:13, emphasis added), and Paul wrote in 2 Corinthians 12:9–11 that God's power operates in our weakness. The Bible teaches that we are only in a position to experience God's power and strength when we understand how weak we are, because that is when we abandon hope in our own resources and rely entirely on God. Our confidence should never be in our own strength, but in His. So Gus is looking in the wrong place when he places his confidence in the flesh. He needs to learn to place His confidence in the Lord.

What insights does the Bible provide about the proximate causes of such problems? The Bible speaks directly to the reasons behind what people do. When we are dealing with a specific problem in counseling, we need to find out if Scripture gives some clues to its cause. There may be examples of people who were in similar situations and experienced similar problems, or there may be direct references to the behavior and its causes. Here are some examples of both to consider.

- *Conflict*
  James 4:1–2 teaches that people who cause fights do so because they are selfish. They become dissatisfied and angry because they want their own way and are not getting it. They view others as merely helps or hindrances in accomplishing what they desire, so they misuse others to get what they want.
- *Instability*
  According to James 1:8, one of the causes of instability is "double-mindedness." That term describes a person who is not truly submitted to the lordship of Jesus Christ. He is "trying to serve two masters" in the sense that he claims to follow Christ, but something else takes priority over Him (see Matt. 6:24). This split focus results in an unstable life.
- *Lying*
  In Genesis 18:1–15, Abraham lied because he was ruled by fear, and many counselees who struggle with lying have the same root problem. They are controlled by fear of being hurt, fear of rejection, fear of failing, fear of losing the respect of people, etc. But merely telling those people to stop lying is a superficial and ineffective way of dealing with their problem. In such cases, we need to address the controlling fear they are experiencing before their problem can be solved.
- *Confusion*
  If we are working with a counselee who seems confused or disorganized, one of the possibilities is the person is committing the sins of jealousy or selfish ambition. James 3:16 says that where those sins

exist, "there is *disorder* and every evil thing" (emphasis added). Dealing with a counselee's confusion or lack of organization may not be sufficient; we may have to go deeper and address issues of the heart before we can help that person.

- *Fear*

First John 4:18 says, "There is no fear in love; but perfect love casts out fear, because fear involves punishment, and the one who fears is not perfected in love." When people struggle with inordinate fears, it may be because they lack an understanding of God's love or (even more often) they lack love for others. Fear is often caused by selfishness. We experience it when we focus on ourselves rather than on serving the Lord and ministering to others. But fear disappears when we become more concerned about the good of others than about what happens to us.[10]

- *Insecurity*

When people exhibit behavior that we would call insecurity (or even paranoia), we often tend to think that is because they have been mistreated by others or because they lack self-confidence.[11] But Proverbs 28:1 provides an interesting insight into that behavior. It says, "The wicked flee when no one is pursuing, / But the righteous are bold as a lion." Some who exhibit insecurity do so simply because they have been involved in sin and bear guilt from it. Those who make a practice of deceit, for example, will often be extremely guarded and hesitant in their speech, because they have to be careful not to contradict lies they have told. However, those who always speak the truth will generally be more confident and secure in talking to others, because they do not have to worry about being found out

- *Bizarre Behavior*

Scripture contains numerous examples of bizarre behavior that lend insight into why some people act the way they do. For instance, in 1 Samuel 21:10–15 David deliberately feigned insanity to deceive others. Some people today do so for the same reason. They do not want to be held responsible for their actions, and they know that if they act in a bizarre manner, others will expect much less of them. They may have found that they are cared for and catered to when they act that way. (In my counseling experience I have had many people who exhibited bizarre behavior tell me later that they did so intentionally to get attention. In some cases, they have practiced this kind of behavior so often that it has become a habit pattern that is basically an unplanned, automatic, reflex reaction. It has become a way of life.)[12]

Another scriptural example of bizarre behavior is king Nebuchadnezzar of Babylon who was transformed into a raving lunatic and acted more like an animal than a man (Dan. 4:28–33). This oc-curred as part of God's judgment upon him because of his pride.[13] And notice that the solution to his bizarre behavior was a divinely granted repentance (vv. 34–37).

- *Worry or Anxiety*

  When we encounter people who claim they have so much going on in their lives that they cannot cope with it all, we can remind ourselves of Martha in Luke 10:38–42 and ask if their situation might be similar to hers. Martha interpreted her problem as having too much work to do, but Jesus pointed out that her problem was that her priorities were not right. She should have been worshiping Him rather than worrying about temporal things and judging her sister.

- *Judgmentalism*

  Third John 9–10 mentions an extremely critical and schismatic man named Diotrephes. And in those verses John tells us the root cause of Diotrephes' behavior, saying that "he loves to be first" or to have the preeminence. This man's pride needed to be dealt with before he would stop creating factions in the church.

As you can see from these examples, the Bible provides a wealth of insight into why people do what they do. The biblical counselor must be committed to searching God's Word continually for help in interpreting the causes of a counselee's problems.

What does the data suggest about the relationship of the various problems to each other? When dealing with several problems in a particular case, we need to ask questions like, "Which came first, the chicken or the egg?" Suppose you are counseling a person who is experiencing anxiety and also having difficulty sleeping at night. Is the anxiety making it difficult for the person to sleep, or is the lack of sleep influencing the anxiety? We all know that when we lose sleep it is much harder to handle problems than when we are well rested. When we are tired, our problems seem gigantic. On the other hand, failure to handle stress biblically can also cause sleep loss. Is one the root and the other the fruit? Is one the cause and the other the result? These questions are important to determine the structure and emphasis of our counseling.

Also, we need to notice if there are certain patterns running through a particular case. Does a lack of self-control, an improper response to author-ity, or some other single problem keep recurring in the person's life? It may be that a common denominator will turn out to be a key to every other aspect of the situation.

What hindrances to biblical change exist in the counselee's life? First, we must find out whether he or she has a proper understanding of biblical change. I have found that many people really do not understand how change comes about from a biblical perspective. They are expecting God to zap them (usually in response to prayer) and supernaturally take their problem away or eliminate their desire to do wrong. Unfortunately, they do not understand what the Bible has to say about the role of self-discipline in sanctification, and they need to be taught this before true change can take place.[14]

Biblical change can also be hindered when the cart is put before the horse. In Gus's case, he has not been able to ask forgiveness from his father at the counselor's direction, probably because he harbors bitterness against his father. This internal issue must be dealt with before he will be able to reconcile the relationship.

Here are some other questions that can help ascertain what hindrances need to be cleared away in counselees' lives:

- Does the data indicate why they have not been able to resolve the difficulties on their own?
- How do they view the problem? What is their understanding of the problem?
- Have they failed to change because they do not want to, or because they do not know how?
- What factors in their environment may be exacerbating the problem?[15]
- What erroneous ideas are contributing to the problems?
- What rewards are they receiving for their behavior? In other words, do they perceive the results of their behavior to be beneficial in some way, or are others encouraging it in some way?

What does the data indicate about the person's expectations and desires for the counseling process? We need to find out why our counselees are coming to us for counseling. Sometimes a husband really does not want to be there, but his wife has laid down an ultimatum. Or maybe their pastor has insisted, but they are determined not to change just to prove the pastor wrong. We also need to know if our counselees are looking for a quick fix or are expecting a long process with numerous meetings. Have they come to achieve change, or are they simply looking for sympathy?

What does the data indicate about any possible organic or physiological factors?[16] It is important to learn whether our counselees have seen a physician, and, if so, what conclusions the doctor reached. In some cases people have genuine medical problems (such as irregular thyroid function, diabetes, or a tumor) that negatively affect their thought patterns and behavior. In these cases the counselor must work with the physician to correct the physical problem and must counsel the person about the biblical response to sickness and suffering.

Counselors are also likely to encounter people who think their problem is physical when there is no proof that this is the case. They go to one or more physicians and have multiple tests, yet no documentable organic cause for their problem is discovered. Although the possibility of an organic cause can still exist, it is likely that the problem is not physiological. Even when a physician does diagnose a medical problem, we must not necessarily assume that the diagnosis is accurate, because some diagnoses are based strictly on the report of symptoms by the patient, symptoms that can be the result of wrong thinking and behavior rather than the result of an organic cause. For instance, I have counseled people whose problems were rooted in personal sin, but because of the guilt of that sin, they were experiencing such symptoms as multiple aches and pains and even hallucinations.[17]

What does the data indicate about the person's motive for wanting to change? If a wife wants to change simply because she wants her husband to change and make her life easier, then she has a wrong motive. If someone wants to change simply to win the approval or acceptance of other people, then this motive is wrong. Lasting change will not be produced unless the counselee's motive is to please and glorify God (see 1 Cor. 10:31; 2 Cor. 5:9).

Have I ever experienced a similar situation or similar problem? As a counselor, you should ask yourself how your own experiences can help you to interpret what is happening in each of your cases. Recalling how you felt may help you to empathize with your counselees, and objectively considering the dynamics of your experience may provide insight into the causes of their problems. You can ask yourself, "When I am in a situation similar to this person's, what am I tempted to do? How am I tempted to respond? What am I tempted to think? How do I feel or how am I tempted to feel? What do I want, desire, crave, or demand in a situation like this? What do I think about doing as a possible way of escape? To whom or to what do I turn? On what or on whom do I depend for deliverance?"

Have I counseled someone previously with similar problems? Sometimes a previous counseling experience can help to interpret a current case. However, we must exercise caution when using personal experience or the experience of others to make judgments about the nature of another counselee's problems. Two cases that appear similar may actually be quite different. Since Scripture indicates that none of us fully understands what another person is experiencing (see Prov. 14:13, 19), we must be careful not to assume that two people have the same underlying causes for similar problems. Nevertheless, since Scripture also tells us that "no temptation has overtaken you but such as is common to man" (1 Cor. 10:13), we would be foolish to ignore the possibility of some commonalities.

Formulate a Working Interpretation

After we have thought through the data by asking pertinent questions about it, the third step of the interpretation process is to use our answers to the questions to draw tentative conclusions about the case. They must be tentative conclusions because they have not yet been tested; nevertheless, it is still important to develop them. The counseling process will continue indefinitely unless we begin at some time to identify possible problems and solutions.

Determine Possible Reasons for the Problem. In light of the data you have analyzed and your knowledge of Scripture, identify possible explanations for the counselee's problems. In Gus's case, for example, there are several possibilities: perhaps Gus does not understand biblical change and is waiting for God to zap him with the desire and power to obey, perhaps he is too proud to admit his sin and ask his father for forgiveness; or perhaps he is fearful of embarrassment or rejection and thus is concerned more for his own feelings than for his father's good.

Gus's counselor should weigh each of these possibilities (and others) and then decide the further direction of counseling (particularly the instruction) on the basis of which possibility best fits the data. The counselor would then need to test the validity of that interpretation, but before we discuss that step, there is another issue that must be addressed if we are to have any hope of formulating a helpful interpretation.

Consider the Counselee's Heart. As the counselor reflects on the questions and their answers, a primary purpose should be to identify what is going on in the counselee's heart. According to the Word of God, sinful behavior is merely an outward indication of problems in the heart. A survey of some of Scripture's teaching about the heart will show us how important this is.

- "The LORD is near to the brokenhearted, / And saves those who are crushed in spirit" (Ps. 34:18).
- "Create in me a clean heart, O God, / And renew a steadfast spirit within me. . . . The sacrifices of God are a broken spirit; / A broken and a contrite heart, O God, Thou wilt not despise" (Ps. 51:10, 17).
- "Thy word I have treasured in my heart, / That I may not sin against Thee" (Ps. 119:11).
- "Watch over your heart with all diligence, / For from it flow the springs of life" (Prov. 4:23).
- "As in water face reflects face, / So the heart of man reflects man" (Prov. 27:19).[18]
- "The heart is more deceitful than all else / And is desperately sick; / Who can understand it? / I, the LORD, search the heart, / I test the mind, / Even to give to each man according to his ways" (Jer. 17:9–10).
- "For from within, out of the heart of men, proceed the evil thoughts, fornications, thefts, murders, adulteries, deeds of coveting and wickedness, as well as deceit, sensuality, envy, slander, pride and foolishness. All these evil things proceed from within and defile the man" (Mark 7:21–23).[19]

Two additional passages, one in the Old Testament and one in the New, deserve special comment because of what they reveal about the importance of the heart.

In Ezekiel 13 and 14 God spoke sternly to the elders of Israel about the judgment He was going to bring upon them. He warned them that judgment was coming and told them that it was coming in part because of their evil conduct, but primarily because of what was happening in their hearts. Four times in chapter 14 the Lord referred to the fact that they had set up "idols in their hearts" (vv. 3–5, 7). These people outwardly claimed to be devoted to Jehovah, but in their hearts they were worshiping, serving, fearing, and depending on other gods. So it is with us when we act in unbiblical ways. The primary problem is not our behavior; our hearts have turned from worshiping, serving, fearing, and depending on the true God.

In 1 Corinthians 10:6–7 Paul recounted the events of another time that judgment fell on the Israelites and said that "these things happened as examples for us, that we should not *crave* evil things, as they also *craved*" (emphasis added). Then he exhorted his readers, "Do not be idolaters, as some of them were." Following those statements about desires and idolatry, Paul described the sinful behavior of the people—their immorality and their grumbling. I do not believe it is an accident that Paul referred to their idolatrous cravings before he spoke of their sinful activity. He knew that the Israelites' problem was not merely a behavioral one; it was a heart problem that manifested itself in their behavior.[20]

Because biblical counselors recognize the preeminent place of the heart in the process of understanding and helping people, they will be concerned primarily about what people are thinking, worshiping, trusting, and seeking to please.[21] They will seek to identify the desires or pursuits that have become idols in the life of the counselee. In many instances, identifying and casting down these functional gods will be a significant factor for promoting biblical, God honoring change.[22]

Test the Validity of Your Interpretation

This fourth and final step of the interpretation process is necessary because our initial conclusions should be tentative. We must always recognize that, as human beings, we are finite and fallen, and therefore may misinterpret the situation. Even if we are relatively confident that we have an informed biblical understanding of the nature and causes of someone's problems, our conclusions should still be tested and validated. The following steps can help the counselor to validate interpretive conclusions.

1. Review mental and written notes to confirm that information acquired provides a factual basis for the conclusions. Prayerfully think through the data again to make sure you are not reading into it your

own assumptions or opinions. Do not "shoot from the hip." Let the facts lead you to your interpretations (see Prov. 18:2, 13, 15).

2. Consider the possibility that there may be other ways of interpreting or understanding what is happening in the person's life. Ask yourself, "Could there be other alternatives? Am I missing something? Is there another explanation?"

3. Solicit additional information, knowing that more information may lead to a different perspective. Continue to gather data in the counseling sessions. Have your counselees keep journals (for example, have the counselee describe each occurrence of a certain behavior during the week). Carefully analyze these journals looking for patterns, themes, and other information that may validate or invalidate your interpretation. Secure additional data from other knowledgeable parties. Invite them to a counseling session, have them fill out specialized inventory forms, call them on the telephone, or visit them.[23]

4. Without mentioning names or identifying details (normally), discuss the case with other experienced biblical counselors and ask for their viewpoint and suggestions. What flaws do they see in your interpretation? Do they think you may be overlooking some things? Do they agree that the facts support your conclusions?

5. Lovingly, gently, and prudently explain your interpretation to the counselee and ask for feedback that would either confirm, invalidate, or provide an alternative to your interpretation. My practice is to present my tentative conclusions carefully and prayerfully to the counselee along with an explanation of supporting facts about my conclusions acquired from counseling and biblical insights. Sometimes I share this with my counselees in a straightforward way and then ask for their response to my interpretation. Other times I present the facts to them, highlighting themes and patterns and the biblical insights or examples that may apply, and ask them what they think those facts may indicate about the nature and causes of their problems. I decide which of these approaches to take based on my observations of the spiritual, emotional, and physical condition of the counselees, their personalities, their learning style, and the strength or weakness of my relationship with them.

When you test the validity of your interpretation in these ways, you may find that it fails the test, but do not be discouraged. You have eliminated a possibility and are closer to the right conclusion. You do need to rethink the data, however, and perhaps spend time determining where your interpretation was off the track. You will probably need to gather more data at this point.

If your interpretation tests positive but the counselee does not agree with it, then your job is to provide instruction lovingly so that he or she can learn to think biblically about the situation. (We will discuss biblical instruction extensively in the next chapter.)

CONCLUSION

Interpreting counselee data is both a science and an art. It is a science in that it deals with facts—facts from the Scripture and facts about counselees and their world—that require much research, investigation, and analysis. In this chapter, we have provided numerous suggestions for achieving this scientific aspect of interpretation.

But we must also realize that interpretation is an art as well. One does not become a good artist by merely possessing an aptitude for art, or even by learning the mechanics of artistic procedure. One becomes a good artist by practicing what is learned. So it is in the discipline of biblical counseling. Becoming an effective counselor involves not only spiritual giftedness and knowledge of the science of interpreting data but a continual practice of those principles until they become second nature. After you study the information in this chapter, you will want to continually put that information into practice as you seek to understand the Scriptures and the people God wants you to help. That is how you will become highly skilled in both the science and the art of biblically interpreting counselee data.

12

Providing Instruction through Biblical Counseling

Wayne A. Mack

Two mistaken ideas about counseling instruction are prevalent. One is the idea that counseling is all instruction; that is, if someone has a particular problem, all we need to do is find the Bible verses that apply to it and give the person a sermon on the subject. Hopefully we have countered that idea sufficiently in the previous chapters by showing the importance of other aspects of the counseling process, such as involvement and inventory.

A second mistaken idea is that counseling involves little or no instruction. Those who hold to this idea believe that people know the answers to their problems and that counselors should simply ask questions, listen, and otherwise provide support for them. In other words, they believe that if we build a strong relationship with our counselees, they will find their own solutions and work out their problems without having us tell them what to do.

But this approach to counseling is unbiblical, for Scripture makes clear that instruction plays a necessary part in every person's spiritual growth and that it is indispensable in the process of solving problems.[1] So if we want to help people change, we must be skilled in biblical counseling instruction, and we must make it an important part of our counseling.

THE NATURE OF COUNSELING INSTRUCTION

Since instruction is a vital part of biblical counseling, we need to know what kind of instruction is necessary. In order to be pleasing to God and helpful to our counselees, our instruction must meet three basic requirements: (1) it must be biblically based, (2) it must be biblically accurate, and (3) it must be biblically appropriate.

Instruction Should Be Biblically Based

When we say that our instruction should be based on the Bible, we mean that all the information we impart to our counselees to help them change should proceed from Scripture. It should be based on the Bible *alone,* and never on mere human ideas or observations. Why? Because the Bible is a practical, comprehensive, trustworthy, and thoroughly adequate source of truth, whereas human knowledge is unable to address effectively the problems that we face in life.

The Bible is practical. The Bible is not simply a theological treatise expounding upon esoteric doctrinal subjects. It is a lamp to our feet and a light to our path (Ps. 119:105). It was given to teach us how to live each day in a way that pleases God, and it was given to help us solve our problems. As Henry Ward Beecher said, "The Bible is God's chart for you to steer by, to keep you from the bottom of the sea, and to show you where the harbor is, and how to reach it without running on rocks and bars."[2]

The Bible is comprehensive. Scripture should be the sum and substance of our counseling instruction, because it deals with *all* the issues of life that are necessary for us to understand. Second Peter 1:3 says, "His divine power has granted to us everything pertaining to life and godliness, through the true knowledge of Him who called us by His own glory and excellence." The knowledge Peter spoke of is limited to the realities described in Scripture; thus he is saying that *everything* we need to know to live successfully is found within the pages of God's Word.[3] Some people react incredulously to that statement, but that is what the Bible says. Second Peter 1:3 is either true or it is not, and if it is not true, then the whole Bible could be called into question.

But we know that 2 Peter 1:3 is true. Scripture contains all the information necessary to "life and godliness," and in-depth study of its contents is rewarded with insights into even the most complicated human experiences. What happens all too often in counseling, however, is that the counselor assumes that the Scripture does not speak to the particular problem of a counselee, and therefore, the counselor abandons the Word prematurely and seeks input from the ideas of men. If such counselors would proceed on the assumption that 2 Peter 1:3 is true, they would see complex problems as a challenge to deepen their understanding of theology and grow in their knowledge of how it applies to specific situations.

I have spent my life trying to help people, and I have never encountered a case in which an application of scriptural principles was not relevant, sufficient, and superior to anything the world has to offer. This is not to say we should simply throw Bible verses across the desk at our counselees, but it does mean that the only goal of our instruction should be to communicate *biblical* truth that relates to their problems. The truth of 2 Peter 1:3 certainly indicates that any secular psychological research or theory is unnecessary (at best) in the process of helping people change spiritually (just as insights gleaned from pagan religions would be).

The Bible is trustworthy. A third reason our instruction should be based solely on the Bible is that it is the only book that deals with the practical problems of life in an absolutely reliable and trustworthy fashion. When we instruct our counselees from Scripture, we can know without question that, if applied, it will change their lives for the better. No other source of information and insight can inspire that kind of confidence.

Consider what the psalmists said about the biblical counselor's textbook:

- "The judgments of the LORD are true; they are righteous altogether" (Ps. 19:9).
- "Forever, O LORD, / Thy word is settled in heaven" (Ps. 119:89).
- "I esteem right all Thy precepts concerning everything . . ." (Ps. 119:128).
- "The sum of Thy word is truth, / And every one of Thy righteous ordinances is everlasting" (Ps. 119:160).

Jesus echoed the psalmists when he declared, "Thy word is truth" (John 17:17). These and similar verses teach us that everything the Bible says is true. But they also yield a biblical epistemology that casts suspicion on any claims about human nature or spiritual truth that are not taught by Scripture.[4] According to that epistemology, we as humans cannot discover absolute truth apart from the special revelation of God.[5] An observation made or opinion developed without referencing God's Word may be true, but we cannot be certain that it is true because we are finite and fallen creatures. Let's consider this concept further.

1. *The Finiteness of Man.* One reason we cannot know anything absolutely apart from God's revelation is that we are finite. Our knowledge is necessarily limited because there is only so much we can observe and only so much we can understand. And unless we know everything, we cannot know anything for sure about the ultimate issues of life and its meaning (on our own), because we always may discover something new that will disprove what we know.

This idea is illustrated by the familiar story of four blind men who were walking along and bumped into an elephant. One of them hit the leg of the elephant and concluded that it was the base of a large tree. The second encountered the trunk and thought it was a fire hose. The third walked into the tail and thought it was a rope. And the fourth slammed into the side of the elephant and decided that it was a wall. They had all bumped into the same object, but because of the limitations on their observation each thought it was something different. And we can reach conclusions just as faulty when we rely on our own observations and insights without referring to God's Word, because like those blind men we can comprehend only part of the whole. God, on the other hand, is infinite in His knowledge and understanding. As Isaiah 40:14 asks rhetorically, "With whom did He consult and who gave Him understanding? / And who taught Him in the path of justice and taught Him knowledge, / And informed Him of the way of understanding?" There is no limitation to the wisdom of God. He says, "I am God, and there is no other; / I am God, and there is no one like Me, / Declaring the end from the beginning / And from ancient times things which have not been done" (46:9–10).

God knows the end from the beginning. He knows the past, the present, and the future. He understands every part of us and every part of our world perfectly. And He has been pleased to reveal His truth to us in His Word. That is why we must instruct our counselees from that sufficient repository of truth and never forsake it for the severely limited ideas of man.[6]

2. *The Fallenness of Man.* Another reason we cannot know anything absolutely apart from divine revelation is that we are fallen creatures. The Bible teaches that our minds have been adversely affected by sin to the point that even if we observe something accurately, we are likely to interpret it wrongly. Our sinful minds tend to distort truth, and the only way we can think rightly is to allow the Holy Spirit to renew our minds (Rom. 1:18–32; 12:2; Eph. 4:23). This is achieved only by learning to look at life through the lens of Scripture.

Because of our finiteness and our fallenness, then, we are unable to ascertain truth unless God has revealed it to us. We have no standard by which we can evaluate whether something is true or false except the Word of God. Thus while we can be confident that whatever we share with our counselees from the Word of God is true, we should have a healthy skepticism about any theory or insight that does not proceed from Scripture.[7] If it is not taught by the Word of God, it may be error.

The Bible is adequate. Our counseling instruction should be based on the Bible alone because "all Scripture is inspired by God and profitable for teaching, for reproof, for correction, for training in righteousness; that the man of God may be adequate, equipped for every good work" (2 Tim. 3:16–17). Those verses clearly say that we have everything we need in the Word of God to make us adequate or *complete* (another translation for the Greek word). We do not need to be more than adequate, and we cannot add anything to completeness. As J. C. Ryle wrote,

> The man who has the Bible, and the Holy Spirit in his heart, has everything which is absolutely needful to make him spiritually wise. . . . He has the well of truth open before him, and what can he want more? Yes! though he be shut up alone in a prison, or cast on a desert island, . . .

if he has but the Bible, he has got the infallible guide, and wants no other.[8]

If we truly believe those inspirational words, we will never be tempted to think that we need to study human theories outside of Scripture in order to be able to provide helpful instruction for our counselees. Instead, we will cling to the only infallible guide for that endeavor, the Bible. It is practical, comprehensive, trustworthy, and adequate.[9] Make it your goal to study it zealously, meditate on it deeply, and communicate it accurately. And never sell it short by assuming it does not speak to a particular issue; never forsake it for "cisterns that can hold no water" (Jer. 2:13). If we are faithful to God's Word, He will be faithful to us by empowering our ministry and producing fruit in the lives of our counselees.

Instruction Should Be Biblically Accurate

Not only should our instruction be biblically based, but it should also be biblically accurate. If we do not take care to understand the Word of God accurately, we may end up giving instruction that sounds biblical but, in reality, is not. Paul told us in 2 Timothy 2:15, "Be diligent to present yourself approved to God as a workman who does not need to be ashamed, handling accurately the word of truth." The verse implies that we can inaccurately or wrongly handle the Word of God, and to avoid doing that we must be "diligent." It takes hard work to accurately interpret the Scriptures and instruct others from them.[10]

Here are some suggestions to help guard against misusing the Scriptures and to ensure that our instruction is indeed accurate.

Know the meaning of biblical words. Some words in Scripture are not used in common, ordinary language today, and others that are used commonly have a different meaning than they do in the Bible. We need to take care not to read our understanding of a particular word into a text and assume that is what the Bible means.

For example, when we use the word *hope*, it means something very different from the biblical word. When a girl has a hope chest, she is longing for things that may or may not happen in the future. And we say, "I hope it doesn't rain today," when the clouds indicate that it is likely to do so. There is much uncertainty in our use of the word hope. But this is not so in Scripture. There the word hope speaks of a confident anticipation of an event that *will* most certainly come to pass.[11]

Two biblical words we seldom use in our everyday speech are *justify* and *justification.* I cannot remember the last time I heard somebody use either of those words other than in a theological discussion. Many people, therefore, have no idea what those words mean. If they have heard the word *justify,* it has probably been used in the sense of, "He was trying to justify himself" (meaning that he was making an excuse), and that is not what Scripture means when it talks about justification.

Sanctification, repentance, propitiation, regeneration, meekness, and even *wisdom* are all examples of important biblical words that are not commonly used and thus are often misunderstood. An effective biblical counselor must be able to explain the meaning of such words to counselees to help them understand what they read in Scripture. A comprehensive Bible dictionary or Vine's *An Expository Dictionary of New Testament Words* are useful tools for this purpose. The latter book, and its Old Testament counterpart, provide meanings of words in the original Greek and Hebrew languages.[12]

Determine the meaning of a verse (passage) within its context. Instructing someone with verses taken out of the proper context can be as damaging as adding to the Scriptures. Although the idea the counselor is trying to communicate may be true, careless techniques of interpretation can set a bad example for counselees.

Proverbs 23:7 is an example of a verse that is frequently lifted out of its context for counseling purposes.[13] In the King James Version that verse says, "As a man thinks in his heart, so is he." Commonly, this is limited to mean that our thought life determines who we are, or that whatever we think about we will become. Thus, many Christian books (even many on counseling) will emphasize the importance of one's thoughts by referring to this verse.

It is certainly true that thoughts are important and that they do influence our character greatly, but that is not all that Proverbs 23:7 is saying. Look at the verse in its full context: "Do not eat the bread of a selfish man, / Or desire his delicacies; / *For as he thinks within himself, so he is.* / He says to you, 'Eat and drink!' / But his heart is not with you. / You will vomit up the morsel you have eaten, / And waste your compliments" (Prov. 23:6–8, emphasis added). The helpful insight for counseling from that verse is more complete than the one commonly perceived. It reveals that sometimes a person's actions are really not the same as that person's thoughts. People may think one way and behave another for the purposes of deception and manipulation. So if we want to know the truth about someone's character, we cannot judge merely on the basis of actions; we would also have to find out what that person is thinking.

If I want to instruct my counselees about the importance of their thought lives, I take them to Romans 12:2 or 2 Corinthians 10:5, because those verses, in their contexts, are discussing that issue. I am as concerned about teaching a correct method of interpreting the Scriptures as I am about teaching specific biblical truth. And if I use the Scriptures loosely by making them say whatever I want them to say or limit their intent, I am teaching my counselees an illegitimate method of Bible interpretation. The Bible is

God's book, and we must be careful to represent each part of it with the meaning God intended for that part. Also, every text of Scripture has only one intended meaning. It may have many applications, but it has only one meaning. Therefore, we need to discover the one meaning of the text before we apply it in the lives of our counselees.[14]

Interpret every passage in harmony with the rest of Scripture. Not only is the immediate context surrounding a phrase or verse important, but the larger context of the whole Bible is also crucial in understanding the meaning of a particular passage. Scripture never contradicts itself, so if we find something in one passage of Scripture that seems to be out of accord with what other passages have to say about that subject, it is likely that our understanding of the differing passage is wrong.

For example, in 1 Corinthians 15:29 Paul spoke of those who were "baptized for the dead." Based on that verse the Mormon Church encourages people to be baptized for the dead. The problem with this interpretation (besides the fact that 1 Cor. 15:29 is an obscure and difficult passage) is that the rest of the Word of God says a lot about baptism without ever mentioning baptism by proxy. And other theological considerations negate the possibility that Paul could be teaching this Mormon practice (see Luke 16:26; Heb. 9:27).

Another example is the husband I once counseled who thought he had absolute authority over his wife. He told me that he believed his wife was obligated to do whatever he told her, even if what he told her to do was sinful.

"Do you mean that if you were to tell your wife to shoot somebody, she would be obligated to do it?" I asked him.

"Well, I would never do that," he answered. "But yes, if I told her to do it, then she would have to do it."

"On what do you base that?" I asked.

"I base that on Ephesians 5 where it says that the wives are to submit to their husbands in everything," was his reply. "And everything means everything."

However, other passages in Scripture make it clear that Paul did not mean "everything without exception" in that passage. "Everything you can do without sinning against God" is closer to his meaning. The only absolute authority in a Christian's life is the Lord; a husband's authority is secondary and is derived from the Lord Himself. So if a husband tells his wife to sin against God, she will have to respond to him as the apostles did when they told the Jewish authorities, "We must obey God rather than men" (Acts 5:29).[15]

If that husband had understood the Reformation principle of *analogia scriptura* (Scripture interprets Scripture), he would not have erred so grievously in his theology on that issue. Likewise, counselors must take care to instruct people accurately by comparing each passage with the rest of God's revelation.

Biblical instruction must be Christocentric and evangelical in emphasis. Counseling instruction should always be focused on Christ and the glorious truth of His gospel. Charles Spurgeon used to say that every text in the Word of God is like the roads in England. He said if you followed the roads in England far enough, eventually they would all bring you to London. And if you follow every text in Scripture far enough, it will eventually lead you to Jesus Christ. Martin Luther said that the Bible is the royal chariot in which Jesus rides, and the swaddling clothes in which He is wrapped. He also said, "Faith is, as it were, the center of a circle. If anybody strays from the center, it is impossible for him to have the circle around him, and he must blunder. The center is Christ."[16]

Christ is the Word (John 1:1), and He is the central focus of the Word. Therefore, our counseling instruction is not biblical unless it exalts Jesus Christ. It is not enough for us to espouse certain principles and regulations for living, because that would be pure behaviorism. If our counseling is truly biblical, people should not come away from it saying merely, "The Bible is a wonderful book"; they should also come away saying, "What a wonderful Savior we have." We should labor in all of our instruction to point our counselees to Jesus Christ, and we will be successful in this if we can help them to behold "the Lamb of God who takes away the sin of the world!" (v. 29).

Use instruction that is action-oriented. Our instruction will not be biblically accurate unless its purpose is to produce godly actions. It is not enough merely to provide information or to communicate facts to our counselees. Our goal is not to encourage them to learn Scripture so they can win theological arguments. We want the truth we teach them to change their lives and make them more like Christ.

In Colossians 1:9 Paul said, "We have not ceased to pray for you and to ask that you may be filled with the knowledge of His will in all spiritual wisdom and understanding." Why did he ask that they would be instructed about God's will? Verse 10 says, "So that you may walk in a manner worthy of the Lord, to please Him in all respects, bearing fruit in every good work." And when Jesus gave the Great Commission, He told us not merely to pass on information about Him to others but to be "teaching them to observe all that I commanded you" (Matt. 28:20).

Our goal in giving instruction should be the same as that of Paul and Jesus. If it does not challenge our counselees to godly action, it is not truly biblical. Biblical counselors would do well to follow the advice Martyn Lloyd-Jones gave to preachers:

> Having isolated your doctrine in this way and, having got it quite
> clear in your own mind, you then proceed to consider the relevance of

this particular doctrine to the people who are listening to you. The question of relevance must never be forgotten. . . . You are not an antiquary lecturing on ancient history or on ancient civilisations, or something like that. The preacher [and counselor] is a man who is speaking to people who are alive today and confronted by the problems of life; and therefore you have to show that this is not some academic or theoretical matter which may be of interest to people who take up that particular hobby, as others take up crossword puzzles or something of that type. You are to show that this message is vitally important for them, and that they must listen with the whole of their being, because this really is going to help them to live."[17]

Emphasize both the positive and negative dimensions of biblical change. Biblical change is always a two-factor process: it involves both "putting off" and "putting on" (Eph. 4:22–32). For our instruction to be biblically accurate, we must not merely tell people what they should not do but also what they *should* do, and vice versa. We need to help them replace old, sinful habits with godly ones. Because biblical counselors see the necessity of addressing sin in the lives of counselees, they can focus too much on the negative aspect of "putting off." They tell counselees, "Don't do this," or "Stop doing that," but, unfortunately, this leaves a vacuum in counselees' lives because they do not know the positive counterpart: what they should do. On the other hand, we would be equally wrong in some cases to simply exhort our counselees to do good. It may often be necessary to find out what sins are keeping them from doing what is right before we can instruct them in that regard (see Heb. 12:1). We must consistently strive to balance the positive and negative aspects of instruction.

Distinguish between divine directives and human suggestions. Our counsel will not be biblically accurate if we confuse God's principles with our own ideas. Yet we can fall into this temptation easily in trying to help people. For instance, some pastors have misrepresented Hebrews 10:25 in a sincere attempt to get people to come to church more often. While the verse simply says that it is wrong to be "forsaking our own assembling together, as is the habit of some," pastors quote it to encourage their members to be in church not only Sunday morning, but also Sunday night, Wednesday night, and every other time there is a service.

True, every Christian needs to be involved in the services of the church, and I believe we need to be there as often as we possibly can. I also believe that in some counseling cases we need to encourage people to attend every service because that will help meet their particular spiritual needs. But we cannot conclude that anyone who does not come to every service is unspiritual and disobedient to God. That would be a human idea added to Scripture, because Hebrews 10:25 does not say, "Go to every service." It simply says, "Do not forsake the assembling." We can fulfill that command without being at every service, and in some cases it is best for the individual not to attend every service. For instance, a woman who has an unsaved husband may find that he objects to her being out on Sunday or Wednesday evenings, and it may be God's will for her to be at home ministering to him on those nights (see 1 Pet. 3:1–6).

Another example of confusing divine directives with human suggestions would be a counselor who quotes Ephesians 5:16 ("making the most of your time, because the days are evil") and tells counselees that they need to schedule every hour each week by filling out a block diagram. This type of procedure may be helpful to a particular counselee, but the counselor should not require it of every person or otherwise imply that God requires every one to adhere to a time schedule. On the contrary, the counselor should be careful to communicate that the schedule is the counselor's suggestion; it is not a divine imperative. The counselor may explain that this is one possible application of the truth of Ephesians 5:16, but that the verse itself is teaching only that we should use our time wisely.

We need to understand the distinction between God's truth and man's ideas, and we also need to be careful not to read any application of a text into the meaning of the text itself. Both are important steps toward ensuring the biblical accuracy of counseling instruction.

Instruction Should Be Biblically Appropriate

Counseling instruction should not only be biblically based and biblically accurate, but it should also be appropriate for each particular counselee in both content and method.

The content of instruction should be appropriate. I have seen some counselors prepare beforehand what they are going to say to a counselee, and then proceed to share that instruction without confirming that it is relevant to the person's needs. This is a waste of time, because even though the counsel may have been biblical and accurate, it did not contribute to the process of change in that particular case. In order to avoid this error, we must be aware of pertinent aspects of each counselee's situation and use that information to tailor the instruction accordingly.

First, our instruction should be appropriate to the counselees' *immediate concerns.* Although we may feel that they need a certain instruction (which they are not aware of and are not asking for), it is best to instruct them initially about the issues they have raised, and then build a bridge to the crucial issues we believe need to be addressed. Begin where they are and lead them to where they ought to be.

We also need to consider our counselees' *emotional conditions.* We may need to determine what instruction they can handle emotionally at a particular point in counseling. For instance, someone who is upset emotionally is usually not ready to hear strong rebuke nor to respond to it properly. (That was true in the case of Clara in chapter 8.) In such cases, we should seek first to bring the counselee to a point of emotional stability before we confront that individual more directly.

Biblically appropriate instruction also takes into account the *spiritual maturity* of counselees. Hebrews 5:12–14 makes clear that some Christians are immature and can receive only spiritual "milk," but others are mature and can handle "solid food." And just as a math teacher cannot take a student from number counting to calculus in one giant step, so we cannot expect a counselee who is used to spiritual baby food to manage a filet mignon. With those who are not spiritually mature, we need to build up to deep truths gradually and gently.

Finally, in order for our instruction to be appropriate we must be aware of our counselees' *receptivity to counsel*. Jesus said, "Do not give what is holy to dogs, and do not throw your pearls before swine, lest they trample them under their feet, and turn and tear you to pieces" (Matt. 7:6). There may be times when you are presenting truth to your counselees and you discern that they are resistant to it. At that point it is prudent to back off from that particular line of instruction rather than beating them over the head with it or ending up in fruitless debate (see Titus 3:9–10). If you discuss another issue with them for a while, perhaps God will open their hearts in the previous area and you can return to it later in that session or in another.

The method of instruction should be appropriate. Counseling instruction needs to fit the counseling situation, particularly in the method of communicating that instruction. Jesus, the master counselor and teacher, used many different methods of instruction (see Matt. 5:1–2; 16:13–20; 21:19–21), as did the apostles (see Luke 1:3–4; Acts 20:31). Biblical counselors have many methods of communication at their disposal, methods that are consistent with the biblical model of those great teachers. Some of the instruction will be done in the counseling session and some can be done outside of the session through various types of homework.[18] The following list presents a variety of ways to communicate the truth of Scripture to counselees:

lecture:	Counselor gives instruction from the Scriptures about a particular issue in the session.
observation:	Counselees observe counselor or someone else who is a good model in the areas where they struggle.
experience:	Counselees learn by doing.[19]
research:	Counselees complete study assignments on topics that are relevant to their problems.

discussion: Counselees talk openly about the issue with the counselor and other knowledgeable people.

questions: Counselor uses the Socratic method to lead counselees to a conclusion through their own responses.

assignments: Counselees read assigned books or listen to/watch tapes/CDs/DVDs and write down what they learned. This can be done during the counseling session or as homework.

evaluation: Counselees evaluate and assess a statement, idea, or practice.

self-disclosure: Counselor relates personal experiences relevant to counselees' problems.

illustration: Counselor uses examples to help counselees understand a truth or to challenge them to think more deeply about it.

role-playing: Counselor acts out instances of interaction between people to demonstrate examples of effective communication and the consequences of poor communication.

interviews: Counselees are encouraged to ask questions of people who are knowledgeable in a particular area or who have otherwise excelled in it.

Using a wide variety of instructional methods is helpful because people learn in many different ways, and some people learn better in one way than another. For instance, some learn better listening to tapes/CDs than they would reading a book; others learn far more through observation than they would in either of those ways. The counselor should try to identify the method or methods of instruction that seem to be most beneficial for each counselee.[20]

How to Develop a Knowledge of Scripture

The Bible is God's fully furnished medicine cabinet; it contains the remedy for all the spiritual problems we face in life. But just as no one medicine will cure all of our physical problems, so no one passage in the Word of God will cure all of our spiritual problems. A good physician or pharmacist has to know which medicine to use for each health problem, and biblical counselors must know what portions of the Word of God to apply to each counselee's problem. Therefore, in order to be effective, a biblical counselor must have a thorough knowledge of the Scriptures.

While there are numerous ways a counselor can develop a knowledge of Scripture even while involved in counseling, we suggest these three: (1) develop a topical work list, (2) produce a personalized chain-referenced Bible, and (3) utilize training resources.

Develop a Topical Work List

Over the years, I have accumulated a wealth of valuable information in a simple notebook. I started this project by writing the names of specific problems or issues that I wanted to understand at the top of blank sheets of notebook paper. As I encountered new problems in counseling, I added more pages to the notebook. Then as I read and studied the Word of God, or listened to others teach and learned something that applied to one or more of those problems, I wrote that biblical reference or insight on the appropriate page. After many years of compiling these notes, I now have at least one page of biblical information about almost any problem that I encounter in counseling. This topical work list has proven to be both a tremendous stimulus for learning, as well as a helpful resource for instruction.[21]

Produce a Personalized Chain-Referenced Bible

When you complete a topical study of a particular issue in Scripture, make a prioritized list of the appropriate verses beginning with the verse you want to refer to first when you deal with that particular issue. Find that verse in your Bible and in the margin next to it write verse number two and so on. With this system you can walk through the pertinent passages on a particular issue any time you need to.

For example, suppose you are trying to help someone who is having trouble sleeping, and you want to instruct them initially by showing them what Scripture says about sleep. If you have created a counselor's chain reference for that subject, you can open your Bible to the first verse about sleep. (It would be helpful to have an index of "first verses," perhaps in the front of your Bible.) After you read that first verse and discuss it, you can then turn to the reference of the second verse and do the same with that passage. Using this chain-referenced system you can work your way through strategic Bible verses on the subject of sleep.

Utilize Training Resources

Your knowledge of Scripture and how to use it in counseling can grow by learning from others. Helpful resources include organizations that are devoted to biblical counseling, such as The Master's College and Seminary, the National Association of Nouthetic Counselors, and the Christian Counseling and Educational Foundation.[22] These organizations offer training seminars and conferences each year, and NANC and the Christian Counseling and Educational Foundation publish periodicals about biblical counseling.[23]

Books about biblical counseling are another valuable resource. Also, check local libraries for commentaries, systematic theologies, and other reference works. Audio tapes/CDs and video tapes/DVDs can also provide beneficial information for the counselor and some can serve as homework for counselees.[24]

CONCLUSION

Let me share two final suggestions concerning instruction in counseling. First, the biblical counselor should be extremely hesitant to give instruction on biblical issues that he or she has not studied. If we do not know about something, we should never act as though we do. What we should say in that instance is, "I am not sure what the Bible teaches about that subject, but I will do some research on it and share with you what I discover next week." Do not be embarrassed if you are not sure about a particular issue. Seek help from books and other counselors and take the opportunity to learn and grow in that area.

The second suggestion is that the counselor should practice team counsel whenever possible. Of course this is not always possible because of the lack of counselors and the prevalence of problems, but it is certainly a good idea. One of my former students wrote this note after I had sat in on a counseling session with him. I think it states well the benefit of team counseling.

> I found it very helpful when you interacted with us toward the end of the session. It first showed me how you deal with this kind of situation and it also helped the counselee to understand the concept much more clearly after you had explained it to him in your way. This made me really think about team counseling. I can imagine that in many difficult cases team counseling could be of great help. I think that as an observer you often see things that the one involved in counseling misses. I sometimes think that I still miss too much data because I'm too concentrated on my interaction with the counselee. I think that one of the hardest parts in counseling is to interact well with the counselee at the moment and still be able to conceptualize what's going on in the whole counseling process.

If you can team up with another biblical counselor or conduct a training program in which the students are able to participate in sessions, you will find that a second person's input can be most helpful to the process of instruction. We need to challenge ourselves to communicate biblical truth clearly and consistently. Above all, we must always remember that "the goal of our instruction is love from a pure heart and a good conscience and a sincere faith" (1 Tim. 1:5).

13

Biblical Counseling and Inducement

Wayne A. Mack

Change does not occur by chance but by choice. Many people talk about wanting to solve their problems and change for the better, but only some are willing to make the commitment necessary to accomplish those things. Proverbs 14:23 says, "In all labor there is profit, / But mere talk leads only to poverty." Biblical counseling must take people beyond talk to action, and an essential part of that process is *inducement.*

Defining Inducement

In biblical counseling the term inducement means to motivate counselees to make biblical decisions conducive to change. This motivation includes the following processes:

1. *Help counselees to accept personal responsibility for their desires and motivations, thoughts, attitudes, feelings, words, and actions.* Counselees need to stop blaming circumstances and people for their problems; they need to realize that through the resources available in Christ they can change.

2. *Bring counselees to the realization that biblical change involves personal choice.* People will never change until they decide they want to change. In fact, the reason people fail to change, when God has provided the resources for change, is often because they have decided to remain in a defeated state. When they say "I can't," they really mean "I won't."

3. *Promote a concern about heart sins as well as behavioral sins.* Godly, biblical change in behavior must always begin with a change in the heart. God calls us to rend our hearts not merely our garments; to purify our hearts as well as to cleanse our hands; and to honor and seek Him with our hearts not only our lips. He wants us to repent about heart sins (thoughts, attitudes, desires, motives, intentions) and not just be sorry for unbiblical actions or reactions. Nothing less than heart repentance and heart change will please God and produce change that is genuine and lasting.[1]

4. *Secure a commitment from counselees to put off the desires, thoughts, and actions that hinder biblical change and to replace them with ones that promote biblical change.* To a great degree, counseling is truly successful only when this goal is achieved.

All that we have discussed in the last five chapters finds its culmination in the goal of encouraging counselees to commit themselves to biblical thoughts and behavior in every area of their lives. In counseling, we may have been faithful in implementing all the previously described principles, yet inducement may still prove difficult. Hopefully, this chapter will serve as a guide for the biblical counselor as he or she seeks to overcome such difficulties and secure a godly commitment from the counselee.

Defining Commitment

What is the biblical commitment we are seeking from our counselees? A biblical commitment will include at least six factors. These are described below under the acronym A-C-C-E-P-T.

   A —*Acknowledge personal responsibility for thoughts and actions.* Counselees will not be able to change as long as they excuse, blame, rationalize, or defend their sinful behavior. We must help them to understand that regardless of their circumstances, if they are Christians, they can respond biblically through the power of the Holy Spirit.

   C —*Choose to look at circumstances in the past and present from a biblical point of view.* Human wisdom and feelings often hinder people from looking at things the way God wants them to. They need to interpret their circumstances through the lens of Scripture rather than through their own opinions and emotions.

   C —*Commit to eliminate whatever hinders biblical change.* Romans 13:14 says, "Put on the Lord Jesus Christ, and make no provision for the flesh in regard to its lusts." If a counselee has a problem with lust, that person must commit to destroy seductive materials, to stop watching television programs or movies with sexual content, and to avoid places that encourage temptation. A counselee must be willing to remove any obstruction to biblical change.

   E —*Exert energy toward the goal.* Change is not an automatic overnight occurrence; it is hard work. The counselee will not make progress if there is no willingness to put effort into changing.

   P —*Persevere in obedience.* Some people are ready to quit after two or three weeks if they do not see substantial progress. Therefore, counselees need to be reminded of the truth of Hebrews 10:36: "You have need of endurance, so that when you have done the will of God, you may receive what was promised." Change takes time, so counselees need to know that the counselor will meet with them for at least six or seven weeks before evaluating their progress.

T—Trust God for the strength and resources to change. Paul says in Philippians 2:12–13, "Work out your salvation with fear and trembling; for it is God who is at work in you, both to will and to work for His good pleasure." It is true, people who want to make biblical changes in their lives must work, but they must work trusting in Christ to provide the strength and resources necessary to make those changes. Without Him, living the Christian life and making godly changes is not only difficult, it is impossible. But when we look away from ourselves and trust Him, He enables us to do the impossible. He enables us to put off the old self, which is corrupt through deceitful desires, and to put on the new self, which is being renewed in true righteousness and holiness. As counselees commit themselves to obey Christ completely, they can be confident that the mighty power of God will accomplish His work of change in their lives.[2]

Sometimes a mere explanation of the essence of biblical commitment is not enough in counseling. If a counselor has reason to doubt a person's understanding of commitment and dedication to it, it can be helpful to ask that person to write out his or her commitment. Then, if necessary, help the person to modify that commitment according to biblical criteria. The counselor can also use the written commitment as a tool for accountability if the counselee begins to waver. It can serve as a reminder of what was promised to the Lord.

HOW TO MOTIVATE COUNSELEES TOWARD COMMITMENT

Biblical counselors should make use of every legitimate means to motivate counselees to make a decisive commitment to obey the Lord. The Scripture provides much insight into how we can do this in a manner that pleases God.

Two Approaches to Motivation

A man-centered approach. People can be motivated through their control points, the things that are most important to them. They can be manipulated to act a certain way when they believe their satisfaction in strategic areas is guaranteed by those actions. That is why advertisers spend enormous amounts of time and money studying the control points; they want to find out what compels people to buy products. Not surprisingly, commercials are designed to promise the consumer that the product will fulfill his or her desires. Why are scantily clad women used to advertise everything from beer to automobiles? Because sexual fulfillment is a control point for many people. The products and the seductive women basically have no relation to one another, but the latter appeals to a control point and thus increases sales.

The desire for money is another control point for many people. So advertisements for Toyota appealed to that desire by asking the question, "What will you do with all the money you save?" The company sold thousands of cars on the basis of saving money instead of focusing on the virtue of the car itself.

Other people desire acceptance or approval. So businesses make promises like, "If you brush with this toothpaste, girls will come knocking at your door!" or "WARNING—This perfume causes boys to flock around you."

What is the effect of this type of man-centered motivation? Although it often induces the action desired, the emphasis is on personal satisfaction. Therefore, it encourages people to be concerned primarily with their own desires and with the visible, tangible, earthly things they think will satisfy them. Biblical counselors should never motivate people in a way that encourages this kind of idolatry (see 1 John 2:15–17). Man-centered motivation may induce a particular behavior, but the motives behind that action will be sinful and thus will make even the behavior unacceptable to God.

A God-centered approach. Biblical counselors want to take a God-centered approach in motivating people. Romans 11:36 says, "For from Him and through Him and to Him are all things. To Him be the glory forever." True change takes place when people make choices primarily for the purpose of bringing glory to God rather than seeking to meet their own needs. The focus of God-centered motivation is primarily on the immaterial not the material, the invisible rather than the visible, the eternal rather than the temporal (Matt. 6:33; 2 Cor. 4:18; Col. 3:1).

Paul's Method of Motivation

Many Scriptures teach us how to apply biblical principles of inducement, but none more clearly and thoroughly than Romans 6:1–14.[3] The apostle Paul's goal in that passage was to bring about a commitment to change in his readers (vv. 1–2). It will be helpful for us to see just how he pursued that goal.

1. *Paul motivated his readers through indicative statements about their position in Christ.*[4] In verses 3–10 he taught that believers are free to change through identification with the Lord Jesus Christ. He said that we have been united with Christ in His death, burial, and resurrection; therefore, we have "died to sin" and risen to "live with Him." Being dead to sin means that sin no longer reigns in our lives; the dominating power of sin has been shattered. Verse 7 says, "He who has died has been *freed* from sin." And

living with Christ refers to the new power that is available in a new life in Christ. Through this power the believer is able to conquer any temptation or sin of the flesh (see Rom. 8:37).[5]

Paul understood that in order to change, Christians need to be aware of their position in Christ and the resources available through Him. The tendency is to see oneself as a helpless victim under the powerful control of sin. But as biblical counselors, we can say to Christians (on the authority of God's Word) that they have the ability to overcome any sinful pattern of thought or behavior. This ability comes only from the Holy Spirit (Gal. 5:16) as a result of our union with Christ. It is on that basis alone that we can call for commitment from people to obey God in their thoughts and actions, as Paul did in Romans 6:11–14.

2. *Paul motivated his readers through imperative demands to live out their position in Christ.* Verse 11 says, "Even so consider yourselves to be dead to sin, but alive to God in Christ Jesus." Though we may not feel dead to sin, God said that we are dead to sin, and we must accept that by faith. The Greek word translated "consider" is an accounting term that means "to record something as fact." Paul commanded his readers to think rightly about themselves and their actions in light of the truth he has taught them about their union with Christ. Then he went beyond thoughts and called for a commitment regarding actions: "Therefore do not let sin reign in your mortal body that you should obey its lusts, and do not go on presenting the members of your body to sin as instruments of unrighteousness; but present yourselves to God as those alive from the dead, and your members as instruments of righteousness to God" (vv. 12–13).

As John MacArthur said,

> The key word is *yield,* or present (v. 13), which obviously has to do with the will. Because of the incomprehensible truths about his relationship to God that the believer knows with his mind and feels deeply committed to in his heart, he is therefore able to exercise his will successfully against sin and, by God's power, prevent its reign in his mortal body.
>
> In this present life, sin will always be a powerful force for the Christian to reckon with. But it is no longer master, no longer lord, and it can and must be resisted. Sin is personified by Paul as a dethroned but still powerful monarch who is determined to reign in the believer's life just as he did before salvation. The apostle's admonition to believers, therefore, is for them to not let sin reign, because it now has no right to reign. It now has no power to control a believer unless a believer chooses to obey its lusts.[6]

Paul concluded his call to commitment in verse 14 by reiterating the believer's position in Christ: "For sin shall not be master over you, for you are not under law, but under grace." He never wants to let his readers forget that only by the grace of God can they keep their commitments to Him.

Divine Motivation for Moses

Chapters 3 and 4 of Exodus contain another helpful example of biblical, God-centered inducement. In this passage, God convinced Moses to commit to something that Moses did not want to do, namely, lead the people of Israel out of Egypt. How did God motivate Moses? Notice that God did not focus on Moses' control points—fleshly desires or sinful pride—but, rather, on Himself and His own glory.

One way God motivated Moses was through His *promises* (see 3:8, 12, 17–18). When people understand the character of God—His faithfulness, honesty, and absolute holiness—they discover that His promises are towers of strength in which they can take refuge. I have seen God use His promises in people's lives as an encouragement when all other counseling efforts seemed futile. We need to explain God's promises to people and apply those promises in a practical and relevant way.

God also motivated Moses by giving him *concrete and attainable goals* (see 4:15–17). He told Moses exactly what He wanted him to accomplish; He did not overload Moses with unattainable goals. Often, counselees are not motivated simply because the goals presented to them are unclear or are intimidating. They are not sure what they are being asked to do, and they are not sure whether they can accomplish it.

God also gave Moses *specific instructions* about how to accomplish those goals (see 3:14–22). Counseling falls short if people do not know how to achieve the things we challenge them to do.

Moses was motivated when God showed him *evidences of divine power* (see 4:1–8). When Moses threw his staff to the ground, God turned it into a snake. When Moses picked it up by the tail, it became a staff again. Then God told Moses to put his hand in his bosom, and it became leprous like snow. Sometimes, counselors must remind people of the mighty power of God. A vision of God's great power from the Scriptures or personal experience is sometimes all that is needed to motivate a counselee to action.

God also motivated Moses by *redirecting his focus* (see 4:10–12). Moses used his own inadequacy as an excuse for not doing what he had been called to do, but God redirected his outlook from human inadequacy to divine sufficiency. God affirmed to Moses the divine ability to overcome any human deficiency. When Moses said he could not speak very well, God responded that He was the One who made mouths and He was able to empower them.

Moses was also motivated by a *description of God's character and plan* (see 3:15–18). God not only reminded Moses of who He was but also assured Moses of His divine presence and help. In addition, God provided *someone to help* Moses in his task; He sent Aaron to speak for Moses (4:14–16). After God's repeated motivational efforts, Moses responded in obedience and committed himself to leading the Exodus from Egypt. Biblical counselors can also make use of effective principles of motivation, emulating (as necessary) God's persistence in applying them.[7]

Other Biblical Principles of Motivation

Outlined below are numerous principles of motivation that are found throughout Scripture. Biblical counselors are encouraged to use these principles to help their counselees make scriptural commitments.

a. Share your perception of what is happening in the situation (Gal. 2:11–14; Col. 2:9; 1 John 1:7).

b. Provide biblical information designed to eliminate specific reasons for resistance (Matt. 28:18–20).

c. Remind the counselee who God is (Prov. 8:13; Is. 6:1–8; Heb. 11:24–26).

d. Help counselees reflect on who they are in Christ (Ps. 90:3–6; 100:3; Is. 2:22; 40:12–17; Jer. 10:23).

e. Talk about the love and grace of Christ (2 Cor. 5:14; 8:7–9; 1 John 3:1–4; 4:9–11).

f. Expound the greatness of our resources in Christ (Rom. 8:34; 2 Cor. 9:8; 10:4–5; Eph. 1:3; Phil. 2:1).

g. Share the promises of God (Is. 41:10; Matt. 6:33; 28:20; Heb. 13:5–6; 2 Pet. 1:3–4).

h. Confirm the consequences of obedience (Ps. 1:1–3; 37:5–6; Prov. 3:5–6; Luke 11:28; John 13:17; Gal. 6:7–8; Eph. 6:1–3; 1 Tim. 4:7; James 1:25).

i. Give specific instructions about what the counselee should do and how he or she should do it (Matt. 5:21–26; Phil. 4:6–9).

j. Show the reasonableness of obedience (Is. 1:18; Rom. 12:1).

k. Challenge and exhort counselees to choose to obey (Rom. 6:11–13, 19–20; 1 Tim. 5:21; 6:13–14, 17).

l. Teach counselees about God's benevolent desires and concerns for them (Ps. 100:4–5; 136; Jer. 29:11; Rom. 8:28; Eph. 2:4).

m. Point out the consequences of disobedience (Prov. 5:22–23; 6:32–33; 7:22–23; 13:15; 16:5, 18; 29:1; Gal. 6:7–8).

n. Express astonishment at resistance (Is. 1:2–9; Gal. 1:6; 3:1).

o. Recall the counselee's previous interest in obedience (2 Cor. 9:1–2; Gal. 3:1–5; Phil. 1:4–7; 2:12).

p. Show how God is affected by disobedience (Ps. 66:18; Eph. 4:30).

q. Express personal concern and love for the counselee (Phil. 1:3–8; 2:17; 4:1; 1 Thess. 2:8, 19; 3:1).

r. Liken inappropriate actions to those of unsaved people (Luke 6:27–38; 1 Cor. 5:1; Eph. 4:17).
s. Give information about proper values and priorities (Prov. 15:16–17).
t. Demonstrate how resistance may affect others (Prov. 15:25, 27; 19:13; 27:11; 1 Cor. 5:6–7).
u. Warn about the Father's discipline (1 Cor. 11:27–28; Heb. 12:4–14).
v. Explain the Bible's teaching about church discipline (Matt. 18:15–17; 1 Cor. 5:1–13; 2 Thess. 3:10–15; Titus 3:9–11).
w. Call attention to that day when the counselee will stand in the presence of God (Matt. 16:26; Rom. 13:11–14; 14:10, 12; Heb. 9:26; 1 John 2:18).

Dealing with Resistance to Commitment

The amount of change a counselee experiences is directly proportional to his or her level of commitment. If the counselor identifies the problem accurately and gives proper biblical instruction, yet sees little or no progress, this often indicates a resistance to commitment. In such cases, biblical counselors must be equipped to recognize and overcome the resistance.

Recognizing Resistance

Two kinds of resistance are encountered in the counseling process: overt and covert. The rich young ruler serves as an example of overt resistance. In Mark 10:17–26, Jesus told him to do something and he simply was unwilling to do it. Sometimes I have asked people to commit themselves to their marriage, and they have refused. Others have been openly unwilling to forgive someone. This type of overt resistance is painfully obvious.

The most frequent kind of resistance, however, is covert resistance in which the counselee gives outward assent to commitment but is not willing to follow through with it. The story told by Jesus in Matthew 21:28–30 illustrates this kind of resistance:

> "But what do you think? A man had two sons, and he came to the first and said, 'Son, go work today in the vineyard.' And he answered and said, 'I will, sir'; and he did not go. And he came to the second and said the same thing. But he answered and said, 'I will not'; yet he afterward regretted it and went. Which of the two did the will of his father?"

The disciples answered, "The latter," and Jesus told them they were right. The first son, unfortunately, typifies many counselees. Initially they seem excited about solving their problems biblically, but eventually they prove resistant to the commitment necessary to change. The following symptoms of covert resistance will help the counselor identify when a counselee is not willing to make a commitment.

Absenteeism. A person who frequently cancels appointments, particularly for questionable reasons, may be avoiding confrontation. If this is a repeated pattern, the counselee may be unwilling to change. Chronic tardiness can also be a sign that the counselee is avoiding pertinent issues.

Failure to do homework. A second symptom of covert resistance is failure to complete homework assignments. A pattern of incomplete or sloppy homework may indicate that the counselee prefers talking to working.

Distancing. In instances of distancing, the counselee keeps the counselor at arm's length. When asked about his or her life, the counselee is unwilling to reveal detailed information. This reticence may indicate a lack of desire to change. Unfortunately, counselors cannot help people who shut them out of their lives.

Threats. Some counselees make threats. In subtle ways they communicate, "If you are not careful, I will not come back." They may even make physical threats. For instance, a man once told me, "There is no telling what I might do if I get angry." When he proceeded to tell me some of the things anyway, it was obvious he was warning me to be careful in dealing with him.

Intimidation. Some counselees may become antagonistic, others withdrawn, or even tearful when the counselor addresses a particular issue. In these instances it can be tempting to avoid discussing those areas, since it can be difficult to confront the emotions or behavior of the counselee.[8] However, the reason for the counselee's sensitivity needs to be discovered so the counselor will not be intimidated and drawn off track by emotional reactions.

Manipulation. There are various ways counselees may attempt to manipulate a counselor. They may cry, or they may flatter the counselor. Whatever the tactic used, these are attempts to sidetrack the discussion. If the counselor's pride is susceptible to this type of manipulation, the sessions can turn into a buddy-buddy time where no profitable counseling takes place.

Stories designed only to elicit sympathy, irrelevant arguments, and repeated descriptions of trivial occurrences are other ways that counselees may try to manipulate the counselor and avoid sensitive issues. This is extremely harmful, because by maneuvering the sessions away from the biblical answers to their problems, they actually multiply their pain. It is important for the biblical counselor to identify and eliminate manipulation, because as long as it dominates the counseling session the counselor will never be able to address the issues that are foundational to change.

When we recognize any of these symptoms of resistance to commitment, we can point them out to our counselees and ask them to explain their resistance in light of the verbal commitments they have made or the desires for change they have expressed. Hopefully, they will realize how they are hindering the Holy Spirit's work and their resistance to commitment will cease.

Recognizing the Reasons for Resistance

In order to overcome resistance it is necessary to understand why the resistance is taking place and to address the foundational issues of the problem. Following are some possible causes of resistance.

An unregenerate heart. In Acts 7:51, Stephen told his accusers, "You men who are stiff-necked and uncircumcised in heart and ears are always resisting the Holy Spirit." The people he addressed were unsaved and therefore could not be motivated to change biblically. As 1 Corinthians 2:14 says, "A natural man does not accept the things of the Spirit of God; for they are foolishness to him, and he cannot understand them, because they are spiritually appraised." In order to induce commitment from people who are unregenerate, the counselor must become an evangelist, because those persons first need to commit themselves to the Lordship of Christ.

Repeated failure. If a counselee has tried to solve a problem repeatedly, the counselor may have to deal with severe discouragement. The key to overcoming discouragement is providing biblical hope.[9] The counselor needs to encourage the person that biblical counseling has something better to offer than the advice they received elsewhere.

Fear. Many times counselees are resistant to commitment because they are afraid. I once worked with a lady whose husband had recently committed adultery. He had also had an affair eleven years earlier. Since he had acknowledged sin and asked for forgiveness after the first affair, the woman had difficulty believing the sincerity of this present acknowledgement of sin and recommitment to faithfulness. Now she wanted a guarantee that he would not do it again. She was afraid to put herself back in the same situation she had experienced earlier. Her real problem was fear, and she needed help from the Scriptures to overcome it.

Pride. Counselees may find it difficult to ask forgiveness from those they have sinned against, an act that requires great humility. This difficulty is heightened if those others have sinned against them as well. Also, those who need to make a public confession may find pride holding them back from this commitment.

Ignorance. Unbiblical ideas about the Christian life can be another reason for resistance. For example, some people believe in complete passivity in the Christian life. They believe they are supposed to "let go and let God." I once read a pamphlet telling of a woman who claimed that when Satan knocked at her door, she would send Jesus to answer it. Such a concept removes all personal responsibility, and, in essence, makes Jesus responsible for human failures. Paul wrote in Philippians 4:13, "I can do all things through Him who strengthens me." In that verse the balance of Christian living is evident. Believers cannot have victory apart from Christ's power; yet victory does not come without effort. In fact, Paul taught that victory comes as a result of diligent effort, but effort exerted only through the strength Christ provides through the Holy Spirit.[10]

Other people go astray because they misunderstand the relationship between obedience and feelings. They argue that obedience apart from feelings is legalism. Of course, seeking to earn or maintain salvation through human works is legalism, but obedience motivated by Jesus' love, His sacrificial death, and His gracious forgiveness is simply evangelical obedience. By obeying the Lord in spite of how we feel, we acknowledge that the Lord is more important than our feelings. We need to remember that feelings are the caboose that follows the engine of obedience. If we desire, think, and do what is right regardless of how we feel, our emotions will eventually come into line as a result of our decision to obey.

Though some might object that such obedience is hypocritical, it is not, because hypocrisy is feigned obedience, not obedience without feelings. Jesus condemned the hypocrisy of the Pharisees because they sought the praise of people instead of God (see Matt. 6:1–6, 16–18). Hypocrites have wrong motives behind their actions. In contrast, obeying God in spite of how one feels displays virtuous motives.[11]

Unbelief. People who doubt the sufficiency and power of the Word of God to effect change in their lives are, in reality, doubting God. They may be unwilling to make a commitment because they are not convinced that God is able to do what He says He will do. That unbelief, if not confronted and dealt with, will cause them to turn their backs on their only hope for change.

Bitterness. Bitterness and resentment may also trigger resistance. Some see bitterness as a means of getting even with others. So they refuse to talk with them, ask their forgiveness, or take other steps toward reconciliation. However, until these individuals are willing to accept God's providential purpose for what happened (Rom. 8:28) and are ready to forgive those who offended them (Ps. 86:5), the process of biblical change will be hampered.

Improper commitments. Counselees may resist committing themselves to obey God's Word because they have already committed themselves to sinful patterns or fleshly pursuits and are unwilling to break with them. As Jesus said, "No one can serve two masters; for either he will hate the one and love the other, or he will hold to one and despise the other" (Matt. 6:24). Charles Spurgeon said about that verse: "This is often misunderstood. Some read it, 'No man can serve *two* masters.' Yes he can; he can serve three or four. The way to read it is this: 'No man can serve two *masters.*' He can serve two, but they cannot both be his master."[12]

Other reasons for resisting commitment can include shifting the blame, making excuses, or failing to take sin seriously. As biblical counselors, we need to identify the causes of resistance and deal with them before we can expect to secure a biblical commitment from our counselees.

Motivation Through Church Discipline

What if we apply all of the principles discussed above and still are not able to induce a counselee to change? One more biblical method of motivation remains for people who continue to resist change over an extended period of time and who prove unwilling to make the commitments required of them by Scripture. Matthew 18:15–18 teaches that method by providing guidelines for formal church discipline:

> "If your brother sins, go and reprove him in private; if he listens to you, you have won your brother. But if he does not listen to you, take one or two more with you, so that by the mouth of two or three witnesses every fact may be confirmed. And if he refuses to listen to them, tell it to the church; and if he refuses to listen even to the church, let him be to you as a Gentile and a tax-gatherer. Truly I say to you, whatever you shall bind on earth shall be bound in heaven; and whatever you loose on earth shall be loosed in heaven."

The biblical counselor may initially become involved at either the first or second step of that process.[13] If those steps are carried out and yet they fail to effect change, then the counselor must see that the remainder of Jesus' commands are obeyed as well.

When a counselee continues to sin after repeated confrontation, Jesus admonished us to "tell it to the church."[14] At this point the individual is to be publicly rebuked, as 2 Thessalonians 3:14 and 1 Timothy 5:20 affirm. The local church body should be exhorted to withhold fellowship from that person and to call him or her to repentance. In speaking about the sinning person Paul said, "Do not regard him as an enemy, but admonish [or warn] him as a brother" (2 Thess. 3:15). The goal of discipline is not to punish but to promote restoration and reconciliation. And in some cases, church discipline is absolutely necessary in order for this to happen. The Puritan pastor Richard Baxter wrote,

> In the case of public offenses, and even of those of a more private nature, when the offender remains impenitent, he must be reproved before all, and again invited to repentance. This is not the less of our duty, because we have made so little conscience of the practice of it. It is not only Christ's command to tell the church, but Paul's to 'rebuke before all;' and the Church did constantly practice it, till selfishness and

formality caused them to be remiss in this and other duties. There is no room, to doubt whether this be our duty, and as little is there any ground to doubt whether we have been unfaithful as to the performance of it. Many of us, who would be ashamed to omit preaching or praying half so much, have little considered what we are doing, while living in the willful neglect of this duty, and other parts of discipline, so long as we have done. We little think how we have drawn the guilt of swearing, and drunkenness, and fornication, and other crimes upon our own heads, by neglecting to use the means which God has appointed for the cure of them.[15]

The final step of the process of church discipline is to treat individuals who continue to resist as unbelievers, since they evidence a lack of submission to the lordship of Christ. Although we cannot judge their hearts, we can judge their fruit. And the church must act on that judgment to preserve the purity of the body of Christ (see 1 Corinthians 5—6). This final step does not happen overnight; the process may take months to be carried out fully and correctly. But if repeated attempts to secure a godly commitment fail, there remains no option but to put the sinning person out of the church. Yet even at this point in the process, the goal should still be repentance and restoration (1 Cor. 5:5; 1 Tim. 1:20). This "delivering to Satan" (that is, removing the sinner from the fellowship and protection of the church and placing that person in Satan's realm) is simply the best way to help people who continue to reject counsel and resist biblical commitment. Richard Baxter also wrote,

> Much prudence, I confess, is to be exercised in such proceedings, lest we do more hurt than good; but it must be such Christian prudence as ordereth duties, and suiteth them to their ends, not such carnal prudence as shall enervate or exclude them. In performing this duty, we should deal humbly, even when we deal most sharply, and make it appear that it is not from any ill will, nor any lordly disposition, nor from revenge for any injury, but a necessary duty which we cannot conscientiously neglect.[16]

Some might see the process Jesus taught in Matthew 18 as cruel and unloving, but in reality it is an act of kindness. God blesses those who obey His Word (James 1:25), so we need to use whatever means God has provided to help people experience that blessing. And church discipline is one of God's methods for motivating people to change.

The goal of biblical counseling is to help counselees become more like Jesus Christ, a process that necessarily involves commitment. Each counselee must *decide* to take definitive steps to "walk as He walked" (1 John 2:6). Some of them will say that they want to change and grow, but may not be sure they want to make the necessary commitment. These individuals are at an important crossroads, and through the grace of God and the biblical principles discussed in this chapter we must try to induce them to follow the Lord.

14

Implementing Biblical Instruction

Wayne A. Mack

A final key element of the counseling procedure is implementation: the process of actualizing biblical instruction and making it permanent in the lives of counselees. Biblical counseling seeks to promote holiness or *biblical change* as a life-style. It endeavors to foster the implementation and integration of biblical principles into people's lives so they will become *consistently Christ-centered and Christlike in every area of life including their desires, thoughts, attitudes, feelings and behavior.*

This implementation process involves three major components: (1) The counselor plans specific strategies to help the counselee act on pertinent biblical directives (the counselor must not only clarify what to do but how to do it); (2) the counselee practices those strategies in the nitty-gritty of life; and (3) the counselee perseveres in applying biblical principles until godly patterns of thinking, feeling, and living have been integrated in that person's life and he or she has become integrated into the life of the church.

PLANNING STRATEGIES OF IMPLEMENTATION

Romans 12:17 says that we should "respect what is right in the sight of all men." The Greek word translated "respect" literally means "to plan ahead of time." So the verse speaks of advance planning for right behavior. This is necessary to make biblical instruction relevant and applicable.

Off With the Old

The first aspect of planning is to identify factors that hinder biblical change and to take steps to eliminate them. Romans 13:14 tells us to "make no provision for the flesh in regard to its lusts." The things that stir up the lusts of the flesh must be identified and eliminated. This may require that counselees break off undesirable associations with other people. The apostle Paul warned us, "Do not be deceived: 'Bad company corrupts good morals'" (1 Cor. 15:33).

The book of Proverbs also repeatedly warns of the dangers of wrong associations:

- "He who walks with wise men will be wise, / But the companion of fools will suffer harm" (13:20).
- "He who goes about as a slanderer reveals secrets, / Therefore do not associate with a gossip" (20:19).
- "Do not associate with a man given to anger; / Or go with a hot-tempered man, / Lest you learn his ways, / And find a snare for yourself" (22:24–25).
- "Do not be with heavy drinkers of wine, / Or with gluttonous eaters of meat; / For the heavy drinker and the glutton will come to poverty, / And drowsiness will clothe a man with rags" (23:20–21).

According to those verses, individuals who associate with wicked people often end up just like them. Biblical counselors, therefore, need to advise their counselees to break off any relationships with people who encourage them to do evil, if it is biblically legitimate to do so. This does not mean someone should file for divorce if his or her spouse is ungodly. But it may apply to roommates, friends, or coworkers who are bad influences. In some cases it may be necessary to move or change jobs in order to "make no provision for the flesh."

Counselees also need to avoid places that create unique sources of temptation for them. For example, one young lady who struggled with lesbianism discovered that she had difficulty with temptation when she was in dressing rooms in department stores. I asked her to keep a journal of where she was most tempted, and then encouraged her to avoid those places until she became strong enough to overcome the temptation. Similarly, a man struggling with homosexuality may be tempted if he goes to a gym or health club. He may need to avoid those places until he is strong enough to withstand the temptation.

Not only should our counselees avoid people and places that may lead to temptation but they must also deal with any practices that contribute to their problems. Whatever triggers the counselee's sin, whether daydreaming, fantasizing, watching certain movies or television programs, or listening to certain kinds of music, must be eliminated. Those who balk at doing this may not sincerely want to change, because God makes clear to us in His Word that it is often necessary to take drastic measures to eliminate sin in our lives. Jesus' admonition graphically illustrates that God expects believers to treat temptation seriously:

> "If your right eye makes you stumble, tear it out, and throw it from you; for it is better for you that one of the parts of your body perish,

than for your whole body to be thrown into hell. And if your right hand makes you stumble, cut it off, and throw it from you; for it is better for you that one of the parts of your body perish, than for your whole body to go into hell" (Matt. 5:29–30).

The great preacher Martyn Lloyd-Jones explained that passage clearly and echoed the necessity of removing hindrances to biblical change:

> Our Lord was anxious to teach at one and the same time the real and horrible nature of sin, the terrible danger in which sin involves us, and the importance of dealing with sin and getting rid of it. So He deliberately puts it in this way. He talks about the precious things, the eye and the hand, and He singles out in particular the right eye and the right hand. Why? At that time people held the view that the right eye and hand were more important than the left. It is not difficult to see why they believed that. We all know the importance of the right hand and the similar relative importance of the right eye. Now our Lord takes up that common, popular belief, and what He says in effect is this: 'If the most precious thing you have, in a sense, is the cause of sin, get rid of it.' Sin is as important as that in life; and its importance can be put in that way. . . . He is saying that, however valuable a thing may be to you in and of itself, if it is going to trap you and cause you to stumble, get rid of it, throw it away. Such is His way of emphasizing the importance of holiness, and the terrible danger which confronts us as the result of sin.
> *We must never "feed the flesh."* "Make no provision for the flesh," says Paul, "to fulfill the lusts thereof." There is a fire within you; never bring any oil anywhere near it, because if you do there will be a flame, and there will be trouble. . . . We must avoid everything that tends to tarnish and hinder our holiness. "Abstain from all appearance of evil," which means, "avoid every form of evil." It does not matter what form it takes. Anything that I know does me harm, anything that arouses, and disturbs, and shakes my composure, no matter what it is, I must avoid it. I must "keep under my body," I must "mortify my members." That is what it means; and we must be strictly honest with ourselves.[1]

To avoid temptation, counselees must shun whatever stimulates evil thoughts. One young lady who came to me for help with depression had previously been involved in an affair with a married man. I discovered that she still had letters, photos, and gifts that he had given her. She also listened to the kinds of music that they had enjoyed together. In order to eliminate all reminders of her sin, she destroyed the letters and threw away the photos and gifts. She also stopped listening to that music. These steps were crucial in helping her put off ungodly desires for an illegitimate relationship (a major factor in her depression dynamic) and put on a godly life-style.[2]

Similarly, after being confronted with the truth of Romans 13:14 the young lady who had been involved in lesbianism wrote a letter to her former lover. In that letter she confessed her part in their sinful relationship. Admitting she had failed to love the other woman as God expected her to, she asked for forgiveness. Since her life was now committed to obeying Jesus Christ, she made it clear that their relationship was over. To reinforce that point to her former lover (who continued to harass her), she threatened legal action if the woman continued to pursue the relationship.[3] Finally, she pleaded with the other woman to consider her ways and turn in repentance to God. By writing that letter, the counselee burned the bridges to her past sin and eliminated that source of temptation from her life.[4]

On with the New

The planning process involves not only eliminating sin but also cultivating godly thinking and behavior. Romans 13:14 not only says "make no provision for the flesh" but also commands us to "put on the Lord Jesus Christ." Indeed, the latter is the prerequisite for the former. Thus biblical counselors must help their counselees to develop a specific plan to put on the Lord Jesus Christ. That plan should involve at least the following elements.

Involvement in a local church. Since the church is described as Christ's body, putting on the Lord Jesus Christ means getting involved in a local church (Col. 1:18, 24). We need to exhort our counselees to become vitally, not just casually, involved in a church where Christ can meet their needs in a special way.[5]

Godly associations. While the wrong kind of associations lead to sin, the right ones stimulate godliness. Paul told Timothy to "pursue righteousness, faith, love and peace, with those who call on the Lord from a pure heart" (2 Tim. 2:22). The godly virtues Paul mentioned are stimulated by associating with others who seek after them. Christians are to "stimulate one another to love and good deeds" (Heb. 10:24). The way to become wise, according to Proverbs 13:20, is to walk with wise men. Counselees need to develop relationships with other Christians who are mature in the faith, because we become like those with whom we associate.

Meaningful devotions. Since Jesus is revealed in the Scriptures, it is impossible to put on the Lord Jesus Christ without studying the Word of God.[6] This requires more than a mechanical or academic reading of the Bible. We may need to teach counselees how to study the Bible profitably and how to pray effectively. This might include guidance for Bible memorization and meditation. As someone aptly remarked, "Either sin will keep you from God's Word, or God's Word will keep you from sin."

Accountability. Sometimes during counseling, and many times after the counseling is over, it is helpful for counselees to establish a relationship of accountability with someone who will inquire how they are doing from week to week. This can be an important aspect of the implementation and integration process.[7] Just the assurance that someone else knows what they are struggling with and will ask questions about those struggles can provide the impetus to resist temptation and do the right thing. From my counseling experience, I have found that counselees who resist accountability usually do not successfully implement and integrate biblical change, whereas those who welcome it do.

Proper diet, rest, sleep, and exercise. Even seemingly mundane matters such as diet and sleep are important in our counselees' planning. It is much easier to resist evil when a person is not tired or sick. As 1 Timothy 4:8 implies, bodily discipline is important. We are to eat and drink to the glory of God, which implies that inappropriate eating (including neglect) and drinking dishonors God.[8] Adequate rest and sleep are also God's will for us: "The sleep of a working man is pleasant"; "He gives to His beloved sleep"; "My son, let them (godly teachings and commandments) not depart from your sight . . . then . . . when you lie down, your sleep will be sweet."[9] On occasion, Jesus denied himself sleep and food for special purposes, but there is no indication that He did this as a general rule. Rather, there is every indication that He recognized the importance of attending to the God-given physical needs of proper sleep and food. When we encourage people to put on the Lord Jesus Christ we need to help them be responsible in diet, exercise, rest, and sleep. People who are careless about these physical needs are not only disobeying God, they are also putting themselves in an unnecessary place of temptation.

Service for others. Jesus taught that when we serve other Christians we serve Him (see Matt. 25:40), and that unselfish service is a key to personal relationships (20:20–28). Our Lord Jesus Christ, who came not to be served but to serve, exhorts us to follow His example.[10] Furthermore, His Word tells us that He has given spiritual gifts (divinely bestowed abilities for ministry in the church) to His people, and that these spiritual gifts are to be used for the benefit of other believers.[11] Putting on the Lord Jesus Christ, therefore, includes following Christ's example in becoming a servant to other people. It involves accepting the teaching of the Bible about spiritual gifts, and discovering, developing, and deploying those gifts in service to others. Thus the implementation/integration aspect of our counseling should include some discussion of each counselee's spiritual gifts and a practical plan for using them in the body.

A wise use of time. Ephesians 5:16 commands us to make the most of our time because the days are evil. In other words, our time is valuable and can be wasted or used wisely; it can be used for constructive purposes or destructive purposes, in godly ways or ungodly ways. It can be invested in ways that will honor God or dishonor God, in ways that will build lives up or tear lives down. Many people have careless attitudes about the use of time, but this was never true of the Lord Jesus Christ. He could say of the way He used time, as well as of everything else in His life, "I always do the things that are pleasing to Him [the Father]."[12] Putting on the Lord Jesus Christ means we will follow His example in the constructive use of time. We need to help counselees develop a time schedule, not only so they will have time for the important things, but also so they will not have time for sinful pursuits.[13]

All of these suggestions can be adapted to particular situations and applied effectively in counseling. For example, a counselor might ask a wife to write down specific ways she can show respect and love for her husband. To follow up on the plan she would report to the counselor each week about what she did and what the results were. Without a plan she might not do those things, or she would not be aware of their effects on the relationship and the blessing they can bring.

Prepare for Temptation

Planning also involves deciding how to handle temptation before it comes. Proverbs 22:3 says, "The prudent sees the evil and hides himself." Temptation is easier to face if we have decided in advance how to respond to it.

A woman whose husband was abusive and had a violent temper came to see me for counseling. In our planning session I asked her to think through those situations of temptation she was likely to face and to plan a biblical response to each. She listed over a dozen situations that could be troublesome. Among them were when her husband yelled at her for doing something he did not like (for example, when she spent money that was not in the budget), when he criticized how she handled their children, when he became angry when she put something away where he could not find it, and when he made derogatory remarks about her cooking. I then asked her to develop and record a biblical plan describing how God wanted her to respond when she encountered each of those situations. This type of detailed, advance planning can help counselees resist temptation successfully.

A plan for biblical response to temptation might include the following items: (1) recognize and acknowledge in the earliest stages of temptation that you are being tempted; (2) quickly ask God for His help to resist;[14] (3) if possible, remove yourself immediately from the source of temptation; (4) identify the unbiblical desire that would be served by yielding to the temptation;[15] (5) quote and meditate on appropriate Scripture; (6) remind yourself of God's presence, power, and promises;[16] (7) reflect on the purpose of Christ's death;[17] (8) mentally and verbally make a commitment to do the godly thing; (9) get busy with a mind-engaging, godly activity; (10) call a godly friend and ask for help; (11) repeat key aspects of this temptation plan until the power of the temptation is reduced.

The planning phase of the implementation process should also include strategies for dealing with failure. Since change is usually a process rather than an event, people often experience setbacks in their efforts to become more godly. Yet this frequently takes people by surprise, and because they have come to counseling with unrealistic expectations (that progress will be swift, easy, and continuous), they become discouraged by the struggles and failures. When this happens, they tend to think that no progress has been made, that counseling is useless, and that they have not, cannot, and will not ever change.

At this point it is critical for the success of the counseling to develop a recovery plan (a what-to-do-with-failure plan). Counselees must know that while failure is serious and was not unavoidable, it does not mean all that they have judged it to mean. Lapses there may be, but the lapse (a failure, a temporary defeat or setback) does not have to turn into a relapse (a total defeat, a complete return to former ungodliness, a thorough domination by and yielding to sinful patterns). God's people may fall, but by His grace and power they can and will get up, learn from the experience, go on, and triumph over their sinful patterns of life.[18] Recovery from failure and transformation out of the control of indwelling sin(s) is possible if people develop and follow biblical strategies for handling lapses.

A recovery plan could include the following steps: (1) call unbiblical desires, thoughts, feelings, and actions what God does—sin; (2) take full responsibility for the sin; (3) confess the sin, both to God and to any others who were hurt;[19] (4) ask God for help in not doing it again; (5) remind yourself what Christ has done and is doing for you; (6) reflect on the resources available to believers in Christ; (7) meditate on God's promises of forgiveness and deliverance from the power of sin; (8) accurately evaluate the changes that have already occurred and the progress that has been made; (9) learn from failure by briefly examining what you did that you should not have done and what you did not do that you should have done; (10) make restitution where necessary; (11) purpose to put the past behind you in a biblical way and to resume your efforts to change in a godly manner.[20]

Planning is the necessary first step to implementation. By determining how they will handle both success and failure, our counselees will greatly increase their chances for biblical change.

PUTTING BIBLICAL CHANGE INTO PRACTICE

Planning is an important first step in effecting biblical change, but planning alone will accomplish nothing. For a plan to be effective, it must be put into practice. A key to doing that is to understand the importance of habits.

Habits are learned ways of living. A habit is created when something is done repeatedly until it becomes a pattern. Habits may be actions, attitudes, or patterns of thinking that have become so ingrained they are second nature. Hebrews 5:14, for example, speaks of people who "because of practice have their senses trained to discern good and evil," and 2 Peter 2:14 says that false teachers have "a heart trained in greed."

As that first verse indicates, habits are not necessarily evil. In fact, they are a gift from God, because if it were not for habits, we would continually have to relearn everything. For example, we go through a long process to learn how to walk, but once learned, walking is so habitual that we rarely think about it. Likewise, we seldom have to think about what to do when we get up in the morning. We just go through our morning ritual of getting out of bed, getting dressed, and getting ready for the day. These things have become habits that scarcely require a thought. If we had to think through these steps each morning, it would be noon before we got out of the bedroom!

We must remember, too, that habits can be unlearned as well as learned. First Corinthians 6:9–11 describes people whose lives had been characterized by adultery, immorality, homosexuality, thievery, greed, drunkenness, and slander. Paul said to these Corinthians, "Such were some of you; but you were washed, but you were sanctified, but you were justified in the name of the Lord Jesus Christ, and in the Spirit of our God" (v. 11). Those sinful habits had characterized their lives as unbelievers, but they had changed. Our counselees, too, can change patterns of thinking, attitudes, practices, or responses if they are willing. Through consistent practice unbiblical habits can be unlearned, and biblical habits can be learned or strengthened.

Paul wrote, "I have learned to be content in whatever circumstances I am" (Phil. 4:11). Contentment did not come naturally to Paul. He wrote earlier that the Law had convicted him of coveting (Rom. 7:7–8), which is an expression of discontent. But this discontented man was later able to proclaim, "I have learned to be content." Contentment does not come naturally to us either; it must be learned. We either train ourselves to be content, as did Paul, or we train ourselves to be discontent.

We can help our counselees to avoid frustration and discouragement by helping them to understand that change is a gradual process requiring practice. And we can help them through the change process by assigning homework that facilitates practice, not just homework that teaches principles but homework that requires application of those principles.

In the Word of God, learning is never a mere academic exercise but is always dependent upon practical responses in a person's life. The psalmist said, "It is good for me that I was afflicted, / That I may learn Thy statutes" (Ps. 119:71). While he understood God's statutes intellectually, he learned them practically by experiencing affliction. True biblical learning always comes through obedience. Therefore, biblical counselors must help people to practice principles for living from the Word of God.

The following assignment, which I gave to the woman with the abusive husband, is an example of homework that facilitates practice. I asked her to go over her plans the first thing each morning. This reminded her how she planned to handle specific situations. She also prayed for about fifteen minutes, asking God to help her put her plans into action. Each day at noon she went over her plans and her journal to see where she had succeeded and failed. She then thanked God for her successes, and asked Him for His help throughout the afternoon. When she failed, she asked God to forgive her and then asked Him for help in changing in that area. Early in the evening, she reviewed the events of the afternoon, and then did the same for the evening before she went to bed. Each day she repeated this pattern and recorded everything in a journal for discussion in the counseling session at the end of the week.

Specific homework assignments like this help counselees to practice the biblical truths they are learning. We should never let our counselees merely make a mental or verbal commitment to change; instead, we should give them the opportunity to live out their commitment and make concrete changes in their lives. As they do this over time, new habit patterns will form, and the old sinful ones will begin to disappear.[21]

Persevering in Biblical Change

The third aspect of implementation is perseverance. As the writer of Hebrews said, our counselees "have need of endurance" (10:36), because biblical change following salvation is a process; it is seldom an instantaneous event. "We all," said Paul in 2 Corinthians 3:18, ". . . are being transformed into the same image from glory to glory." In another place, Paul wrote that we are "being renewed to a true knowledge according to the image of the One who created [us]" (Col. 3:10). Some people learn and change more quickly than others, but it takes time for everyone to learn new habit patterns. Counselors should be aware of this and encourage counselees to persevere while they are involved in the change process.

Biblical change also requires daily practice. According to Jesus, we must deny ourselves, take up our cross, and follow Him on a daily basis.[22] Yesterday's practice will not do for today. Every day is, in a sense, a new day in our relationship with Christ and in the process of changing into His image. Coasting or relying on the past successes and victories is not a luxury believers can afford.

The Puritan Thomas Boston wrote, "Sin is fastened in our souls by nature, as with bands of iron and brass. Converting grace looses it at the root, but it must be loosed more and more, by the daily practice of mortification. 'For if ye live after the flesh, ye shall die; but if ye, through the Spirit, do mortify the deeds of the body, ye shall live'" (Rom. 8:13, KJV).[23]

Athletes can be in the best physical shape possible, but if they stop working out they will quickly lose the benefits of all their exercise. The same is true spiritually. If counselees do not persevere in practicing godliness on a daily basis, they will soon be back to where they started. Second Peter 2:20–22 warns that those who turn back to sin will be worse off than they were at the beginning. Some people begin well, and their movement toward godly living provides them with some freedom from their pain. But so often that pain served as a primary motivator, so when the pain is relieved, they quit practicing what is right. Before long they end up in the same mess they were in before. This time, however, they may feel hopeless, and decide that the counsel they received and the commitment they made did not work.

The problem in many such cases is caused not by the counsel or the commitment but by a lack of perseverance. That is why biblical counselors need to emphasize that change requires daily practice. The apostle Paul echoed this truth when he wrote to the Corinthians, "I die *daily*" (1 Cor. 15:31, emphasis added). In explaining the meaning of this verse, Thomas Boston wrote,

> We should as it were habituate ourselves to dying, and be frequently making an essay of dying. . . . Ask yourselves what you would do, if you were just to expire; and do the same. A Christian should be frequently making his testament. When you go to a duty, do it as if it were the last you were ever to do on earth. When you awake in the morning, do as if you were to have the grave for your next bed; and when you lie down at night, so compose yourselves as if you were never to awaken again.[24]

When significant change has occurred in a counselee's life I usually lengthen the period of time between counseling sessions. This allows me to monitor the progress of counselees and at the same time decreases counselor dependency. It also develops counselee initiative and responsibility, and encourages the continuance of implementation. Instead of seeing counselees every week, I may see them every two weeks, and then when they have done well with a two-week arrangement, I may schedule them for what I think will be a final checkup session in four to six weeks. At that session we review what has happened in their lives, particularly in reference to their original problems. I will ask them to list the specific ways they have made progress since counseling began.[25] Then we use that list as an opportunity to emphasize the importance of perseverance and the need to continue developing godly patterns in specific areas of their lives. I warn them that if they cease to implement the biblical principles we have discussed, they will revert to what they were previously or even worse.[26] If it is evident that they have continued to implement the biblical principles and strategies presented during the previous counseling, we terminate formal counseling with praise to God for the changes that have occurred and encouragement to persevere.

CONCLUSION

Establishing involvement with counselees; inspiring them to have biblical hope; taking a thorough inventory; making a reliable, biblical interpretation of counselees and their problems; instructing them in an accurate and appropriately biblical way; and inducing them to decisive commitment to biblical obedience: each is a vital dimension of biblical counseling. However, biblical counselors know that skillfully and faithfully fulfilling these elements is not all there is to biblical counseling. They know that each of these functions is a means to an end.

And what is that end? It is the ultimate goal stated at the beginning of this chapter. Biblical counselors want to promote *biblical change as a lifestyle;* they want to foster the implementation and integration of biblical principles into the lives of people so that they will become *consistently Christ-centered and Christlike in every area of life including desires, thoughts, attitudes, feelings, and behavior.*

That is what biblical counseling is all about. Biblical counseling is not primarily about making people happy or successful or fulfilled; it is not mainly about eliminating the emotional distress, the pain and hurts that people experience. Of course biblical counselors are concerned about these things, and, in fact, all of these desirable things and many more will happen in the fullest sense through biblical counseling. They are not, however, the main concern of biblical counselors; rather they are the byproducts of accomplishing the real purpose of biblical counseling, which is to promote holiness and biblical living as a life-style and thereby to help people be transformed into the image of Christ in every aspect of life.

Part IV

The Ministry of Biblical Counseling

15

Preaching and Biblical Counseling

John MacArthur

The rise in psychotherapy and the decline of biblical counseling in the church has paralleled a decline in biblical preaching. The psychology epidemic began infecting evangelical pulpits several years ago, and its effect on preaching has been disastrous.

Sermons in many evangelical churches contain no exposition of Scripture whatsoever. Biblical content has been replaced by illustrations, stories, allegories, and psychological discourses. Issues such as human relationships, depression, and behavior are dealt with from a psychological, rather than biblical, perspective. Psychological notions such as self-love and self-esteem have even driven the concepts of repentance and the sinfulness of humanity right out of the pulpit.

Some preachers seem to view psychotherapy with an awe that approaches reverence. The authorities they cite are not Scripture but eminent psychologists and behavioral experts. Psychology has laid siege to the pulpit, and biblical preaching is in serious decline.

This has set up a chain of events that only perpetuates the problems that drive people to therapy. By failing to offer biblical answers to people's problems, many preachers have actually given people the idea that Scripture offers no answers to the issues that trouble them. Then by offering psychology as a substitute, they have fed the widespread misconception that psychology's answers are more reliable, more helpful, and more sophisticated than "mere" biblical counsel.

The answer to such thinking is a renewed emphasis on the sufficiency of Scripture, starting in the pulpit. Scripture offers sufficient help for all the deepest needs of the human heart. When the preacher is confident of that truth, the counseling ministry will inevitably reflect the same faith in Scripture's sufficiency. And when the Word of God is preached with conviction, it begins to address the very problems that people often seek counseling for. The Word of God *always* accomplishes its intended purposes: "So shall My word be which goes forth from My mouth; / It shall not return to

Me empty, / Without accomplishing what I desire, / And without succeeding in the matter for which I sent it" (Is. 55:11). "The word of God is living and active and sharper than any two-edged sword, and piercing as far as the division of soul and spirit, of both joints and marrow, and able to judge the thoughts and intentions of the heart" (Heb. 4:12).

OUR SUFFICIENCY IS OF GOD

Since Scripture itself claims to be a sufficient resource for meeting emotional and spiritual needs, I suggest that those who are saying it is not are in serious error. Since the Word of God teaches that all Christians possess ample spiritual means for genuine victory, should it not be patently clear that modern psychology offers no spiritual benefit that the church lacks?

Second Corinthians 3:5 sums up the matter of our spiritual sufficiency: "Not that we are adequate in ourselves to consider anything as coming from ourselves, but *our adequacy is from God*" (emphasis added). The King James Version states, "Our sufficiency is of God."

Expanding on that great truth later in the same epistle, Paul wrote, "God is able to make all grace abound to you, that always having all sufficiency in everything, you may have an abundance for every good deed" (9:8). The "alls" and "everys" of that verse underscore its utter comprehensiveness. In other words, there is nothing for which we are not sufficient through the provision of God's grace. If God is to glorify Himself through us, He must provide the necessary resources.

And He does. Peter wrote, "His divine power has granted to us *everything pertaining to life and godliness,* through the true knowledge of Him who called us by His own glory and excellence" (2 Pet. 1:3, emphasis added).

Scripture clearly warns us not to look beyond the resources God has so abundantly provided. Paul cautioned the Colossians, "See to it that no one takes you captive through philosophy and empty deception, according to the tradition of men, according to the elementary principles of the world, rather than according to Christ. For in Him all the fullness of Deity dwells in bodily form, and in Him you have been made complete" (Col. 2:8–10). In another epistle he added, "He who did not spare His own Son, but delivered Him up for us all, how will He not also with Him freely give us all things?" (Rom. 8:32). What more does the Christian need? Certainly not the philosophizing and empty deception of a spiritually destitute system of behaviorism.

The resources that belong to every believer include many rich spiritual benefits: the fruit of the Spirit, the fellowship of other believers, the assurance of hope, and the eternal, abundant life Jesus promised (John 10:10). But all those realities are described for us and supplied to us through God's

Word. So the sufficiency of the Bible itself is the overriding issue every preacher must come to grips with.

THE WORD OF GOD IS LIVING AND POWERFUL

Jesus prayed for His disciples, "Sanctify them in the truth; Thy word is truth" (John 17:17). That is as clear and comprehensive a statement as any in all Scripture that sanctification in its fullest sense is accomplished by God's Word.

Paul wrote that the Spirit of God revealed God's truth to us not in the words that human wisdom teaches but in words the Holy Spirit teaches (1 Cor. 2:13). And because we have the Word of God through the Holy Spirit, we can judge, appraise, evaluate *all things* (v. 15). Why? Because through the Scriptures and the Spirit we have been given the mind of Christ (v. 16).

In Mark 12:24 Jesus affirmed that to know the Scriptures is to experience the power of God. As we noted above, God's Word is living and powerful. It reveals the deepest part of a person's inner soul, "piercing as far as the division of soul and spirit, of both joints and marrow, and able to judge the thoughts and intentions of the heart" (Heb. 4:12). Scripture cuts to the very depth of the deepest part of a person's being so that "all things are open and laid bare" (v. 13). In other words, the Word can do what no psychotherapy can do: it opens the soul.

John added, "The anointing which you received from Him abides in you, and you have no need for anyone to teach you; but as His anointing teaches you about all things, and is true and is not a lie, and just as it has taught you, you abide in Him" (1 John 2:27). That does not mean we have no need for pastors or Bible teachers; God has graciously supplied them for the edification of the church (Eph. 4:11–12). The apostle John was talking about teachers of human wisdom. We who have the Holy Spirit living in us have the ability to comprehend eternal truth (1 Cor. 2:15–16). When it comes to spiritual truth, we have no need of human instruction.

THE LAW OF THE LORD IS PERFECT

No passage in all the Old Testament deals with biblical sufficiency as succinctly as Psalm 19. (Psalm 119 covers the subject in more depth, but to cover it thoroughly would require more space than the limits of this brief chapter allow.) In Psalm 19:7–14 we have a brief, potent statement of the utter sufficiency of God's Word. In my view, this passage is definitive in showing why psychology is incompatible with biblical counseling.

The theme of the psalm is the revelation of God. The first six verses deal with *natural revelation,* that is, God's revelation of Himself as seen in creation (also described in Romans chapter 1). Verses 7 to 9 describe *special revelation,* or God's revelation of Himself in His Word. It is these verses we want to consider most carefully:

- The law of the LORD is perfect, restoring the soul;
- The testimony of the LORD is sure, making wise the simple.
- The precepts of the LORD are right, rejoicing the heart;
- The commandment of the LORD is pure, enlightening the eyes.
- The fear of the LORD is clean, enduring forever;
- The judgments of the LORD are true; they are righteous altogether.

First of all, the structure of the passage needs to be noted.

- There are six statements. Each contains three elements.
- There are six titles for Scripture. It is called *law* and *testimony* in verse 7. It is called *precepts* and *commandment* in verse 8. It is called *fear* and *judgments* in verse 9. Those are all titles for Scripture.
- There are six characteristics of Scripture, again two in each verse. It is *perfect,* it is *sure,* it is *right,* it is *clear,* it is *clean,* and it is *true.*
- There are six benefits of Scripture. It *restores the soul,* it *makes wise the simple,* it *rejoices the heart,* it *enlightens the eyes,* it *endures forever,* and it is *righteous altogether.*
- There are six occurrences of the covenant name of YHWH translated in the phrase "of the LORD." And thus six times we are reminded that the source of special revelation is from God, in six statements about the Word of God.

These verses show the utter comprehensiveness of biblical sufficiency; they are God's own witness and testimony to the total adequacy of His Word for all spiritual needs. As we look at each of these six statements, note how sweeping is the claim God makes about the utter sufficiency of His Word to meet every spiritual need.

The law of the LORD is perfect, restoring the soul. The first title for Scripture in these verses is "law," or *torah,* a favorite biblical word for Scripture. This word identifies the Scriptures as divine instruction. It refers to the fact that Scripture is God teaching truth to humanity. It has in view divine instruction relative to creed, character, and conduct. It pictures Scripture as a complete manual laying out God's law for our lives. In other words, the Bible is the law of the Lord for human living. As such, it is perfect. Here the psalmist is setting Scripture in contrast to the imperfect, flawed reasonings and instructions of mankind.

I once spent an afternoon looking up the Hebrew word translated "perfect" in my lexicons and following it through all the Old Testament to try to get a feel for what it meant. After several hours, I came to the conclusion that what this word really means is "perfect." It speaks of perfection in every sense of the word—not merely something that is perfect as opposed to imperfect, but also something that is perfect as opposed to incomplete. The word could also be translated accurately as "comprehensive." It speaks of something so complete as to cover comprehensively all aspects of a matter. In other words, the Word of God lacks nothing. It is flawless, comprehensive, and completely sufficient.

The law of the Lord—this divine instruction that is utterly comprehensive—has the effect of restoring the soul, converting the soul, reviving the soul, and refreshing the soul. All of those could be apt translations of that Hebrew verb. "Soul" here is the Hebrew word *nephesh,* a Hebrew noun familiar to any Old Testament student. *Nephesh* is translated with at least twenty-one English words throughout the Old Testament: "life," "person," "self," and "heart" are some samples. It speaks of the inner person.

Here, then, is the sense of this first statement: Scripture, which is divine instruction, is so comprehensive that it can totally transform the inner person. That is a monumental claim. It means Scripture is utterly sufficient for conversion, transformation, restoration, and spiritual birth and growth to perfection. The statement is made without any equivocation and without any caveats.

The testimony of the LORD is sure, making wise the simple. The word "testimony" in this phrase speaks of Scripture as divine witness. It is God's own witness to Himself. It is His personal testimony about who He is. And it is "sure"; meaning it is unmistakable, trustworthy, unwavering, reliable. Scripture is more certain than anything else. It provides a foundation that will not move and on which a person may build a life and an eternal destiny without hesitation. And this sure Word, this sure testimony from God about Himself, makes simple people wise.

The Hebrew word translated "simple" in this verse comes from a root that describes an open door. The Old Testament saints viewed a simple-minded person as having an open door in the intellect. Did you ever hear somebody say, "I'm open-minded"? An Old Testament Jew would say, "Close it." In their way of thinking, a simpleton was someone who was literally open-minded—unable to keep anything in or out. The same Hebrew term is used often in the Proverbs to identify the naive person, the undiscerning, nondiscriminating, inexperienced, and uninformed fool. According to the psalmist, then, Scripture—the sure, reliable, trustworthy, unwavering testimony from God about Himself—comes to the one who is simple and makes that one wise.

Note carefully, the wisdom spoken of here is not intellectual data to be stored in the brain. The Hebrew concept of wisdom has more to do with the way one lives. In the Old Testament, wisdom is defined as the ability to make right choices in daily conduct or to live on earth with a heavenly understanding. The word *wise* really means "skilled in all aspects of holy living." The biggest fool of all is the one who knows the truth but does not live according to it.

Thus this couplet means that Scripture is so sure and reliable and trustworthy and unwavering that it takes the simpleminded, undiscerning, uninformed, ignorant person and makes that person skilled in all aspects of holy living. Therein is the sanctifying power of the Word.

The precepts of the LORD are right, rejoicing the heart. This third statement about Scripture speaks of God's Word as divine principles. In other words, the Word of God is a divine set of guidelines for living. And these principles are *right.* The intent of the Hebrew word here is that God's precepts lay out a right path. We are not left to wander around in a fog of human opinion. We have a true Word that lays out a true path that can be followed. And what is the product of that? "Rejoicing the heart." The life of true joy comes from walking according to divine principles. People who go the way of the world, away from the Word, find no joy. Those who live according to the path outlined in Scripture find complete and full joy.

And so this phrase is saying that God's Word lays down right principles that make a sure path on which all who walk will find fullness of joy. You can begin to see how these descriptions of Scripture dovetail, answering every need of the human heart.

The commandment of the LORD is pure, enlightening the eyes. The word "commandment" in this phrase pictures Scripture as the divine mandate. That is to say, the Word of God is authoritative, binding, and non-optional. The Bible is not a book of suggestions from God. It contains divine commands, nonnegotiables. These demands, the psalmist said, are "pure," meaning, simply, "clear." The divine commandments are lucid, easy to see, and they give clear direction. The point is that Scripture enlightens our eyes to the dark things in life.

New Christians who have lived many years in darkness will understand the import of this phrase. You have probably noticed that whenever relatively new Christians speak of the change wrought in their lives, they frequently underscore this truth. When a person is born again, many dark things become clear. That is because the Word of God enlightens the eyes. So much becomes clear. The confusing things of life become understandable.

And so the Word of God is sufficient for salvation, total transformation of the inner person, the source of skill in all matters of holy living, the path to joy, and the source of a clear understanding of things.

The fear of the LORD is clean, enduring forever. The noun used here is *fear,* but because of the parallelism, we know it refers to Scripture. Why is Scripture spoken of as fear? Because the Bible is the manual on worship. It teaches us how to fear God, how to reverence Him. Since the habit of the human soul is to worship, we need instruction about Whom to worship and how to worship Him properly.

As a manual on worship, the Bible is "clean," that is, without evil, without corruption, and without error. The Hebrew word is *tahor,* meaning "without impurity, defilement, filthiness, or imperfection." The psalmist was saying that Scripture is unsullied by sin. A parallel verse is Psalm 12:6: "The words of the LORD are pure words; / As silver tried in a furnace on the earth, refined seven times." There is no impurity in it. It is hallowed; it is holy. It is separated from sin.

The point is that the Word of God will lead us into purity. You will never find in Scripture any misrepresentation of God, man, Satan, angels, or demons. You will never find any misstatement of what is right or wrong. Everything here is absolutely clean and unsullied. Here is a perfect resource for us.

And note that this "fear of the LORD" endures forever. It is permanently and eternally relevant. It does not need updating. It does not need editing. It does not need to be polished or refined. Any person living at any time in human history, in any culture, in any climate, will find the Bible completely applicable. The same basic principles of the Word of God apply equally to a myriad of different peoples and situations with the same powerful effect.

The judgments of the LORD are true; they are righteous altogether. The word *judgments* looks at Scripture as divine verdicts. This phrase views God as the judge of all the earth and the Scriptures as His pronouncement from the divine bench. These judgments, according to the psalmist, are true. There is a wealth of import in that simple adjective.

Where do we go to find salvation? Where do we go to find the skill of living in daily life? Where do we go to find an overcoming joy through all the trials of life? Where do we go to get light on the dark things of life? Where do we go for a permanent resource that never changes? Where do we go for truth?

There is only one answer: God's Word, the Bible. Nowhere else can we find that which can totally transform the whole person, make wise, bring joy, enlighten the eyes, be permanently relevant, and produce comprehensive righteousness.

Is it any wonder verse 10 says what it says? "They are more desirable than gold, yes, than much fine gold; / Sweeter also than honey and the drippings of the honeycomb." Is there anything as sweet? Is there anything as precious? "Moreover, by them Thy servant is warned; / In keeping them there is great reward. / Who can discern his errors? Acquit me of hidden faults. / Also keep back Thy servant from presumptuous sins; / Let them not rule over me; / Then I shall be blameless, / And I shall be acquitted of great transgression" (vv. 11–13).

Here the psalmist summed up what God is saying to us about His Word:

Scripture is our greatest possession, more precious than gold. It is the greatest pleasure, sweeter than honey. It is the greatest protection, warning us from error. It offers the greatest promise: an eternal reward. It is the greatest purifier, keeping us from sin. And so in verse 14 the psalmist's response is predictable: "Let the words of my mouth and the meditation of my heart / Be acceptable in Thy sight, / O LORD, my rock and my Redeemer."

The psalmist seems to have in mind Joshua 1:8: "This book of the law shall not depart from your mouth, but you shall meditate on it day and night, so that you may be careful to do according to all that is written in it; for then you will make your way prosperous, and then you will have success." What kind of meditation and what kind of words are acceptable? Scripture, according to Joshua 1:8. It is the only resource that is all-sufficient, guaranteeing success to the one whose mind is fixed and meditating on its immense richness. Psalm 1:1–3 echoes the same thought: "How blessed is the man who does not walk in the counsel of the wicked, / Nor stand in the path of sinners, / Nor sit in the seat of scoffers! / But his delight is in the law of the LORD, / And in His law he meditates day and night. / And he will be like a tree firmly planted by streams of water, / Which yields its fruit in its season, / And its leaf does not wither; / And in whatever he does, he prospers."

PREACH THE WORD

Those passages preclude the possibility that the people of God can find essential spiritual truth in any other resource besides God's Word.

Second Timothy 3:16–17 settles the question of biblical sufficiency for the Christian. These verses are often thought of as an affirmation of inspiration, and they certainly are that. But notice how clearly and definitively they affirm the sufficiency of Scripture as well: "All Scripture is inspired by God and profitable for teaching, for reproof, for correction, for training in righteousness; *that the man of God may be adequate, equipped for every good work*" (emphasis added).

The preacher's task is to proclaim the all-sufficient Word of God, and nothing else. Paul wrote this to Timothy:

> I solemnly charge you in the presence of God and of Christ Jesus, who is to judge the living and the dead, and by His appearing and His kingdom: *preach the word;* be ready in season and out of season; reprove, rebuke, exhort, with great patience and instruction. For the time will come when they will not endure sound doctrine; but wanting to have their ears tickled, they will accumulate for themselves teachers in accordance to their own desires; and will turn away their ears from the truth, and will turn aside to myths" (2 Tim. 4:1–4, emphasis added).

Notice, Paul recognized that Scripture would not always be popular. He readily conceded that the time would come when people would turn away, seeking to have their ears tickled (or "needs met") by preachers who were willing to cater to selfish desires, offering an alternative message besides biblical truth. Yet Paul reminded Timothy that preaching the Word of God is the only reliable guide for teaching, reproving, rebuking, or exhorting people according to the will of God. Moreover, it is the only legitimate message for any preacher called by God. And so Paul solemnly charged Timothy to keep preaching the Word.

The preaching of the Word is, I am convinced, the necessary foundation on which an effective ministry of counseling must be built. Even the strongest biblical counseling is undermined if it is accompanied by weak or ambiguous preaching. On the other hand, clear and powerful preaching often succeeds in touching hearts resistant to wise counsel.

In contrast, preaching that is devoid of a clear biblical message can have little or no positive effect. Preachers who fill their sermons with psychology while minimizing biblical content will find more of their people struggling with chronic emotional and spiritual disabilities, and desperately seeking answers in all the wrong places. That is precisely the state of affairs in much of the contemporary evangelical church.

It is my conviction that the crisis and the controversy in church counseling today would soon fade away if preachers obeyed this simple directive from the apostle Paul: "Preach the word." Preachers would be pointing their people to the only source of real help for their spiritual problems. People's confidence in the sufficiency of Scripture would be restored. The Word of God would be unleashed to accomplish its intended purpose. And the whole church would be revolutionized.

16

Spirit-Giftedness and Biblical Counseling

John MacArthur

We live in the age of the expert. The spirit of self-sufficiency that enabled our pioneer ancestors to settle the frontier has all but disappeared from our culture. People look increasingly to experts and professionals to help them do, or do for them, what they once did for themselves. The effect is not always positive.

Parenting, for example, was once based on common-sense wisdom handed down from generation to generation. In our day, however, various gurus specializing in child rearing have flooded the market with new, often contradictory, theories that debunk most of the old wisdom handed down to us from previous generations. The results have been disastrous for both the family and society.

Unfortunately, the church has not escaped this onslaught of expert mentality. Ministries such as visiting the sick and evangelizing the lost are often handed over to paid professionals. Specialists are now deemed necessary to advise church leaders on everything from demographics, to church growth strategies, to administrative policies, to how to stage an entertaining Sunday service.

Nowhere has the veneration of "experts" had a more insidious impact than in the area of counseling. More and more voices from within the church are touting the notion that counseling is an activity best left to skilled professionals, specifically trained psychotherapists. Psychologist O. Hobart Mowrer, although not an evangelical, noted the trend and asked pointedly, "Has Evangelical religion sold its birthright for a mess of psychological pottage?"[1] To our shame, the answer in many cases is yes. Incredibly, many churches that affirm the inerrancy and sufficiency of Scripture are nonetheless quick to shuffle their hurting members off to the psychological and psychiatric "experts," often even non-Christian counselors utterly blind to the things of God (1 Cor. 2:14).

The psalmist who penned Psalm 1 would never have understood that practice. He noted the folly of seeking counsel from ungodly sources. He wrote, "How blessed is the man who does not walk in the counsel of the wicked, / Nor stand in the path of sinners, nor sit in the seat of scoffers!" (Ps. 1:1). He understood clearly what the church seems to have forgotten. True happiness comes not from following the futile speculations of humanistic psychology but from living out biblical principles. Listen to his description of the individual blessed by God:

> His delight is in the law of the LORD, / And in His law he meditates day and night. / And he will be like a tree firmly planted by streams of water, / Which yields its fruit in its season, / And its leaf does not wither; / And in whatever he does, he prospers (Ps. 1:2–3).

COUNSELING: A FUNCTION OF FELLOWSHIP

Ephesians 4:15–16 gives a prescription for the spiritual health of Christ's body:

> Speaking the truth in love, we are to grow up in all aspects into Him, who is the head, even Christ, from whom the whole body, being fitted and held together by that which every joint supplies, according to the proper working of each individual part, causes the growth of the body for the building up of itself in love.

As the members of the body minister to each other, speaking the truth in love, the church is built up. The strengthening of each member results in a collective growing up to the fullness of the stature of Christ. Thus the entire body is matured as the members minister to each other according to their giftedness.

Counseling is an important means through which the members of the body are supposed to minister to each other. When the body is functioning correctly, the unruly are admonished, the fainthearted encouraged, and the weak helped (1 Thess. 5:14). The notion that counseling is the exclusive domain of those who have been initiated into the esoteric secrets of modern psychological theory is utterly at odds with the scriptural concept of life in the body. The Bible presents counseling, like all other aspects of ministry, as a function of fellowship that takes place naturally when the body is healthy. Study the biblical passages pertaining to church life and fellowship, and this clear truth will emerge: all believers are *expected* to counsel one another. Every Christian is commanded to share in the ministry of exhorting, admonishing, and encouraging others in the flock. Our duty to counsel is even heightened, not diminished, when we see a brother or sister struggling with serious difficulties and sin. We cited some of the key passages on this matter at the beginning of chapter 1. Let's examine one of them a little more closely:

> Brethren, even if a man is caught in any trespass, you who are spiritual, restore such a one in a spirit of gentleness; each one looking to yourself, lest you too be tempted. Bear one another's burdens, and thus fulfill the law of Christ. For if anyone thinks he is something when he is nothing, he deceives himself. But let each one examine his own work, and then he will have reason for boasting in regard to himself alone, and not in regard to another. For each one shall bear his own load. And let the one who is taught the word share all good things with him who teaches (Gal. 6:1–6).

In that passage, Paul outlined a three-step process for restoring sinning members of the body to spiritual health: pick them up, hold them up, and build them up.

Before someone who has fallen into sin can get back in the Christian race, that person must first be picked up. Those caught in sin's vicious grasp need help as much as they need rebuke. Counseling, therefore, involves helping people get back on their feet spiritually through confession of sin and repentance. That responsibility clearly lies with members of the congregation, not hired professionals, and certainly not with secular counselors. Only fellow believers, through the use of their spiritual gifts, are truly able to help those who stumble. The spiritually strong, wrote Paul, "ought to bear the weaknesses of those without strength and not just please [themselves]" (Rom. 15:1).

Not only are those who are spiritually strong supposed to pick up those who fall; they must also help hold them up after the weaker brethren are back on their feet. Those who have just confessed and turned from their sin are extremely vulnerable to further temptation. Satan launches his most savage attacks after a spiritual victory. "Burdens" in Galatians 6:2 refers to the temptations to fall back into the very sins from which a believer has just been delivered. There is no more crushing burden than a persistent, oppressive temptation. Those delivered from the grasp of a stubborn sin often need further encouragement, counsel, and, above all, prayer.

Finally, after picking up and holding up sinning believers, the spiritually strong must build them up. "The one who is taught the word" and "him who teaches" are to "share all" the "good things" of the Word with each other (v. 6). Note that the same command applies to the teacher and the taught one. Thus all believers—leaders, disciples, weak, and strong—are responsible for sharing the good things of the Word. This is the essence of biblical counseling.

If, as this passage affirms, all believers are responsible to counsel one another, then all must be gifted to some extent to do that. The apostle Paul confirms that truth in Romans 15:14: "Concerning you, my brethren, I myself also am convinced that you yourselves are full of goodness, filled with all knowledge, and *able also to admonish one another*" (emphasis added).

Equipped with Spiritual Gifts

In what way are believers equipped to admonish and counsel one another? They are equipped through the spiritual gifts that are imparted to each member of the body. The primary purpose of spiritual gifts is ministry in the church itself: "There are varieties of ministries, and the same Lord. And there are varieties of effects, but the same God who works all things in all persons. But to each one is given the manifestation of the Spirit *for the common good*" (1 Cor. 12:5–7, emphasis added). Nearly all the spiritual gifts delineated in the New Testament have usefulness in the counseling ministry.

It is important that we understand that the spiritual gifts described in Scripture are not detached entities given in identical measure or stamped according to a singular pattern. Every believer has a distinctive spiritual gift: "To *each one* is given the manifestation of the Spirit for the common good" (v. 7, emphasis added). Each gift is thoroughly unique, designed by God's grace for each individual in particular: "There are varieties of gifts, but the same Spirit" (v. 4). "We have gifts that differ according to the grace given to us" (Rom. 12:6). Spiritual gifts are offered in infinite variety, each with a different design, like snowflakes. The gifts listed in the New Testament (for example, Rom. 12:4–8; 1 Cor. 12:4–10) are simply categories. An individual's spiritual gift should comprise several features of the various abilities named as gifts in these passages. In other words, someone whose primary gift is teaching will probably also be gifted to some degree in wisdom, discernment, or mercy. That person's gift is a singular blend of abilities and characteristics that enable him or her to minister according to God's calling.

Let's examine some of the main kinds of gifts enumerated in Scripture.

Prophecy

Prophecy is commonly associated with foretelling the future. The Greek word *prophēteuō,* however, simply means "to speak forth," or "proclaim." It refers to the public proclamation of Scripture. In biblical times, of course, the work of a prophet often involved the reception and proclamation of new revelation. But the title *prophet* actually refers to anyone whose gift is declaring truth with authority, or preaching. Thus a prophet, particularly in this present age, is simply a proclaimer of biblical truth, not someone who receives revelation directly from God. The great Reformer John Calvin understood the gift of prophecy in that light. He wrote, "I prefer, however, to follow those who understand the word in a wider sense to mean the peculiar gift of revelation by which a man performs the office of interpreter with skill and dexterity in expounding the will of God."[2]

The apostle Peter said much the same thing when he exhorted those with the gift of prophecy in these words: "Whoever speaks, let him speak, as it were, the utterances of God" (1 Pet. 4:11).

Perhaps the clearest statement of how the gift of prophecy functions comes in 1 Corinthians 14:3–4: "One who prophesies speaks to men for edification and exhortation and consolation. . . . One who prophesies edifies the church." The gift of prophecy can be employed to edify believers, call them to obey God's Word, and encourage them in time of need: edify, exhort, and console. What are those but aspects of biblical counseling? Thus the prophet is equipped to counsel simply by virtue of this gifting.

The importance of the gift of prophecy can be seen in Paul's emphasis on it in 1 Corinthians 14. There the apostle contrasted it with the gift of languages, demonstrating the superiority of prophecy. He exhorted the Corinthians to "pursue love, yet desire earnestly spiritual gifts, but especially that you may prophesy" (v. 1).

And in a sense, the preacher fulfills an important element of the counselor's task with every sermon. Acts 15:32 gives an example of the gift of prophecy in action. After delivering the letter from the Jerusalem Council to the church at Antioch, "Judas and Silas, also being prophets themselves, encouraged and strengthened the brethren with a lengthy message." They spent time strengthening the believers there by proclaiming to them the truths of the Word of God. Their prophetic preaching ministry itself had the same effect as good counsel.

One of Paul's final exhortations to his protégé Timothy stresses the importance of proclaiming the Word:

> I solemnly charge you in the presence of God and of Christ Jesus, who is to judge the living and the dead, and by His appearing and His kingdom: preach the word; be ready in season and out of season; *reprove, rebuke, exhort, with great patience and instruction.* For the time will come when they will not endure sound doctrine; but wanting to have their ears tickled, they will accumulate for themselves teachers in accordance to their own desires; and will turn away their ears from the truth, and will turn aside to myths. But you, be sober in all things, endure hardship, do the work of an evangelist, fulfill your ministry (2 Tim. 4:1–5, emphasis added).

In other words, preachers of the Word ought to exercise their gifts exactly like wise counselors: reproving, rebuking, and exhorting with all patience and careful instruction.

Preaching and counseling that is truly biblical will be applied to the heart by the Holy Spirit and will produce spiritual growth. After all, God's Word is "profitable for teaching, for reproof, for correction, for training in righteousness" (3:16). A pastor who faithfully exercises his prophetic office is acting as counselor for the whole congregation. By equipping them and instructing them, the pastor facilitates their giftedness and furnishes them with what they need to counsel one another effectively. Strong biblical preaching is thus inextricably linked to effective biblical counseling in the church. The counseling ministry begins with the pulpit and extends from there to every level of ministry in the church.

Teaching

Closely associated with prophecy is the gift of teaching. Indeed, biblical preaching must include a strong element of teaching as well. Unlike preaching, teaching is carried out on all levels of the church, not just from the pulpit. Those who teach Sunday school classes, lead Bible studies, or disciple others all exercise the gift of teaching.

The Greek word *didaskō* ("I teach") includes the idea of systematic training or instruction. The gift of teaching is the ability to lead others to a deeper understanding of Scripture.

An emphasis on teaching marked our Lord's ministry. At the conclusion of the Sermon on the Mount, "the multitudes were amazed at His teaching; for He was teaching them as one having authority, and not as their scribes" (Matt. 7:28–29). Matthew 4:23; 9:35; Mark 2:13; 6:6; Luke 13:22; 20:1, along with many other passages, describe the centrality of teaching in Jesus' ministry.

A strong emphasis on teaching also characterized the apostles' ministry. Acts 2:42 describes the early church as "continually devoting themselves to the apostles' teaching" (also see 5:42). Acts 15:35 records that "Paul and Barnabas stayed in Antioch, teaching and preaching, with many others also, the word of the Lord." From Acts 18:11 we learn that Paul "settled [in Corinth] a year and six months, teaching the word of God among them." "I did not shrink," Paul testified to the Ephesian elders, "from declaring to you anything that was profitable, and teaching you publicly and from house to house" (20:20). In his letter to the Colossians, the great apostle summed up his ministry in these words: "We proclaim Him, admonishing every man and teaching every man with all wisdom, that we may present every man complete in Christ" (Col. 1:28).

The gift of teaching is a prerequisite for being an elder (1 Tim. 3:2; Titus 1:9). Not all elders are called to proclaim the Word publicly; however, all must be able to teach the Word systematically to those over whom they have oversight. It is that qualification that sets elders apart from deacons. Teaching the Word is a primary way elders exercise oversight of their flock (see 1 Tim. 4:6, 11, 13, 16; 5:17; 2 Tim. 2:15, 24; Titus 2:1). Through the teaching of the Word, elders guard the congregation from doctrinal and practical errors. They also teach principles for godly living.

What marks an effective teacher? First, the teacher must live consistently with biblical teaching. Paul admonished Timothy, "In speech, conduct, love, faith and purity, show yourself an example of those who believe" (1 Tim.

4:12). The godly Puritan Richard Baxter wrote, "He that means as he speaks will surely do as he speaks."[3]

Second, the teacher must be "constantly nourished on the words of the faith and of . . . sound doctrine" (1 Tim. 4:6). The greater the depths of doctrinal knowledge, the more effective will be the teaching. "He must not be himself a babe in knowledge," wrote Richard Baxter, "that will teach men all those mysterious things which must be known in order to salvation."[4] Like Timothy, the teacher must "be diligent to present [himself] approved to God as a workman who does not need to be ashamed, handling accurately the word of truth" (2 Tim. 2:15).

Third, such knowledge should produce humility, not pride. Those whose teaching is marked by an arrogant attitude contradict with their lives the very truths they teach. Paul described to Timothy the proper attitude for those who teach:

> And the Lord's bond-servant must not be quarrelsome, but be kind to all, able to teach, patient when wronged, with gentleness correcting those who are in opposition, if perhaps God may grant them repentance leading to the knowledge of the truth (vv. 24–25).

Finally, a skilled teacher will be characterized by purity of heart and holiness of life. Paul's exhortations to Timothy to "discipline yourself for the purpose of godliness" (1 Tim. 4:7), and "pursue righteousness, godliness, faith, love, perseverance and gentleness" (6:11) should be taken to heart by all who would teach God's Word.

The importance of teaching in counseling cannot be overstated. Counseling is essentially a process of teaching. The wise counselor must be able to listen carefully, then apply the Word of God accurately to whatever problems arise in the counseling session. Counselees will never live out principles they do not know. Teaching biblical principles, therefore, is at the heart of the biblical counseling process. Adams wrote, "Nouthetic confrontation must be scriptural confrontation. Nouthetic confrontation is, in short, confrontation with the principles and practices of the Scriptures."[5] In contrast to the Rogerian "client-centered" nondirective methodology embraced by many today, the goal of biblical counseling is to change sinful patterns of thinking and living. This is done through the power of Scripture.

> The Bible is the only unchanging touchstone to measure thinking, feeling, and behaving. The Word of God abounds with guidance and direction for living. Therefore, the methodology of biblical counseling relies on the Word of God rather than the wisdom of men. . . . Therefore, biblical counselors will seek to help their counselees live in submission to God's love, His Word, and His enabling.[6]

Those who are gifted to teach, then, are specially gifted for this aspect of counseling.

Exhortation

While prophecy proclaims biblical truth, and teaching systematizes it, exhortation demands a proper response to it. Romans 12:8 lists exhortation as one of the gifts of the Spirit. The Greek word is *paraklēsis,* also used in such passages as Acts 20:2; 1 Corinthians 14:3; 1 Timothy 4:13; and Hebrews 13:22. It means "to exhort," "to encourage," "to advise," or "to confront." Its relationship to the counseling ministry should be obvious.

To exhort is to challenge fellow believers to act consistently with God's will. As already noted, biblical counseling involves admonishing the unruly, encouraging the fainthearted, and helping the weak (1 Thess. 5:14). Through the gift of exhortation, counselors encourage sinning Christians to forsake their sin and practice righteousness, they comfort those devastated by trouble or sorrow, and they strengthen the faith of those who are discouraged and weak. Those particularly gifted in exhortation are invaluable counselors, often the backbone of a local church's counseling ministry.

Wisdom

The gift of wisdom, referred to in 1 Corinthians 12:8, is the ability to understand how the truths of Scripture apply to the practical issues of daily living. *Sophia* ("wisdom") is used frequently in the New Testament to describe the ability to discern and conform to God's will (see Matt. 11:19; 13:54; James 1:5; 3:13, 17). As such, some degree of wisdom is essential for all biblical counselors. Obviously, it would do little good to teach counselees biblical principles and exhort them to follow those principles without showing them specifically how to do that. Wise counsel is what the counselee needs (see Prov. 1:5; 12:15; 19:20), and the gift of wisdom enables the counselor to provide it.

Knowledge

Foundational to preaching, teaching, and counseling is knowledge. The gift of knowledge is the God-given ability to understand the mysteries of God's revealed Word, those truths unknowable apart from God's revelation (see Rom. 16:25; Eph. 3:3; Col. 1:26; 2:2; 4:3). It also entails skill in presenting that knowledge so others can understand it. The gift of knowledge is not merely the ability to accumulate and collate facts but a spiritual ability to see biblical and doctrinal truth in a coherent and meaningful way.

Without some degree of spiritual knowledge, counselors have little to offer except the foolish and futile speculations of worldly wisdom. God's view of such counsel may be seen in His condemnation of Job's counselors.

The gift of knowledge enables counselors to give the wise counsel from God's Word that alone offers hope to their counselees.

Administration

Mentioned in Romans 12:8 ("he who leads") and 1 Corinthians 12:28 ("administrations"), this is the gift of leadership. *Proistēmi,* the term used in Romans 12:8, means "to lead," "to manage," "to be in charge," or "to oversee," while *kubernēsis* (1 Cor. 12:28) means "to steer or pilot a ship." The gift of leadership, or administration, is the Spirit-given ability to organize, oversee, and motivate others to accomplish a task.

Since many counselees, especially those suffering from depression, lead unstructured lives, the gift of administration is a useful one for a counselor. To help counselees order their lives to glorify God is an important aspect of biblical counseling.

Mercy

Those with this gift have a special love for and sensitivity to those in misery, whether from poverty, physical illness, or the ravages of sin. The Lord Jesus Christ is the supreme example of One who showed mercy. In Luke 4:18, Jesus said,

> The Spirit of the Lord is upon Me, / Because He anointed Me to preach the gospel to the poor. / He has sent Me to proclaim release to the captives, / And recovery of sight to the blind, / To set free those who are downtrodden.

Without the spiritual gift of mercy, counseling is often cold and clinical. Many people struggling with emotional upset, reeling from some disaster of life, or seeking relief from depression need to be able to share the burden with someone whose gift is mercy. Such people are often actually set back by psychoanalysis, which only prompts them to be introspective, self-focused, or obsessed with their feelings. What they really need is relief from the burden and a lightening of the load (see Matt. 11:28–29). Fellow believers with the gift of mercy are best equipped to help with such burden bearing.

MINISTRY IN THE BODY

Healthy churches breed relationships that are conducive to spiritual growth and emotional health, because as Christians minister with their gifts to one another, much of the work of counseling takes place in the natural interaction of fellowship. As is evident in this brief list of key spiritual gifts, the express purpose of our giftedness is to help meet the needs that drive most people to seek counseling.

All ministry in the body of Christ thus incorporates features of counseling. Both formal and informal counseling should always be taking place in the local church at every level of ministry and fellowship. Gifted members naturally minister to one another by admonishing, encouraging, strengthening, and teaching—all forms of counseling. When these functions are moved out of the fellowship and into remote clinics, the whole life of the body is disrupted.

Unfortunately, in the stampede to integrate psychology into the church, gifted believers have often been discouraged from counseling fellow Christians according to Scripture. As a result, spiritual gifts have fallen into a severe state of neglect. People who should be admonishing, correcting, encouraging, and showing mercy are instead referring people to professional therapists. Many Christians have accepted the notion that tolerance and deference are the only acceptable attitudes we ought to communicate to struggling people. The unavoidable consequence is that many believers have unnecessarily stunted their own spiritual gifts.

I am convinced that a healthy emphasis on the ministry of spiritual gifts would alleviate much of the need for formal counseling. People would minister to one another more effectively as a natural result of everyday fellowship. And as gifted believers gained skill in employing their gifts, a whole new generation of spiritually capable counselors would arise from within the church.

If that does not happen, the church is doomed. The boom in counseling clinics is not producing healthier Christians. On the contrary, it is producing a generation of believers who are utterly dependent on therapy and unable to enjoy life in the body of Christ as it was meant to be. Professional psychologists are no substitute for spiritually gifted people. Moreover, the counsel psychology offers cannot replace biblical wisdom and divine power.

Each Christian is gifted uniquely by God to help meet the needs of fellow believers in the body. If we can recover that simple truth and live it out with new enthusiasm in our fellowships, we can restore health to the body and at the same time fill even the deepest needs of the most troubled lives.

17

Biblical Counseling and the Local Church

William W. Goode

Almost every week someone asks me how to start a counseling ministry in a local church, a question that, to me, illustrates a widespread misunderstanding of the true nature of counseling. For too long biblical counseling has been seen as an optional ministry in the church. Along with radio programs and homes for unwed mothers, it has been relegated to a growing heap of "frivolous" ministries, the ones we hope to get around to some day.

However, biblical counseling is not an option, a point on which Scripture never equivocates. Our Lord commanded believers to love one another, and to consider counseling an optional ministry is to withhold biblical love at the time it is needed most in the believer's life: when he or she is in trouble. As the apostle Paul commanded the Galatian believers, we must be about the business of restoring rather than ignoring such Christians.

The greatest threat to the process of discipleship is the believer who is overtaken by sin. The man or woman with a continual pattern of sin needs help to change and to reestablish a pattern of growth. Thus Paul addressed all church members, not just the pastors and elders, when he said, "We urge you brethren, admonish the unruly, encourage the fainthearted, help the weak, be patient with all men" (1 Thess. 5:14). On another occasion, Paul reminded the believers in Rome of their responsibility to counsel and encourage each other, assuring them that they were "able also to admonish one another" (Rom. 15:14).

Believers will never become like Christ if they are not winning the battle against sin in their lives and investing themselves in the lives of others. And there can be no discipling if there is no plan to help the disciple who gets into trouble. Restoring and encouraging cannot be separated from loving, as we see in the life of our Savior.

COUNSELING: AN INTEGRAL PART OF THE CHURCH

Counseling must never be thought of as a weekly hour of magic, or an independent ministry conducted aside from the church. Preaching, teaching, evangelism, discipleship, and counseling are all integral parts that make up effective, biblical ministry. The local church is the instrument Christ ordained to help believers grow into His likeness. It is the only organization—or better, organism—He promised to build, sustain, and use. Counseling is an essential part of the local church's ministry as it disciples and helps believers mature in Christ's image. Paul had this goal in mind when he wrote: "We proclaim Him, admonishing every man and teaching every man with all wisdom that we may present every man complete in Christ" (Col. 1:28).

The Pastor's Involvement and Leadership in Counseling

Counseling is the responsibility of each believer and its only rightful arena is the church. These truths carry a strong implication: the pastor's involvement and leadership is crucial.

In Ephesians 4, the purpose of the pastor-teacher and the church is described as "the equipping of the saints for the work of service to the building up of the body of Christ . . . to the measure of the stature which belongs to the fullness of Christ" (4:12–13). This includes a plan for believers who are tossed about by bad doctrine and deceitful philosophies. And so many of the problems we encounter in counseling are doctrinal problems based on an inadequate view of God, sin, or self. God wants these problems solved, and He has raised up pastor-teachers to equip the saints to do just that.

In the next few verses, it is as if Paul anticipated that some would doubt believers could be trusted with this job. So he described the wonder of the spiritual gifts God has provided, assuring us that "the whole body, being fitted and held together by that which every joint supplies, according to the proper working of each individual part, causes the growth of the body for the building up of itself in love" (v. 16). In other words, all believers should be using their gifts, talents, and abilities to meet the needs of others. As Colossians 1:28 reiterates, the saints are equipped to use their gifts through preaching, counseling, and teaching.

It goes without saying that the pastor's involvement must be more than a token once-a-week venture. Paul reminded the Ephesian elders of his ministry to them, of his selfless sacrifice, and his bold, nouthetic confrontation (counsel) night and day as he ministered with tears. Paul dared not abandon his God-ordained duty. When he saw fellow believers in trouble, he did not hide; he counseled them day and night. Jesus said the hireling flees when the wolf comes, but the shepherd cares for the sheep when they are in trouble. This is the picture we see of Paul in Acts 20:31, a true shepherd actively involved in ministry whenever he was needed.

Yet a word of caution is necessary. Yes, the pastor needs to be involved in counseling, but it must be a balanced involvement. If the pastor pursues counseling to the neglect of his sermon preparation and study, his preaching will no doubt suffer, causing more counseling problems rather than strengthening the saints and furthering the maturation process.

In addition, if a pastor allows counseling to take the place of caring for his family, his health, or his own spiritual needs, he will not only be unprepared to counsel when the time comes, but his overall ministry will suffer dire consequences. Counseling is important, but it can only be effective when counselors understand correct spiritual priorities.

THE CHURCH—INCOMPLETE WITHOUT COUNSELING

Counseling and the Pastor's Effectiveness

When a pastor neglects the ministry of counseling others, crucial areas of his ministry suffer. For example, his preaching is dramatically affected. Paul said the weapons of our warfare are not carnal but spiritual, empowered by God to tear down the mental strongholds and arguments that have been raised against God. But when a pastor is not involved in the lives of his people, he loses touch with their difficulties and the thought processes and habits that lead to problems. Thus he is not prepared to provide the spiritual weapons they need to overcome those problems.

To illustrate, let's imagine a noncounseling pastor who preaches about drunkenness. Yet the people listening in the pews get drunk regularly for any number of reasons. They may succumb to peer pressure because they want to please people rather than God, or perhaps they are not able to communicate with their spouse, so they hide from their problems by drinking. It is possible that they worship possessions and material success, so they will do anything, including drinking with clients, to get what they want. They may drink to drown their guilt, or for the sheer pleasure of the drinker's high. The reason they drink may even be something as simple as gross irresponsibility. These are all reasons for drinking: reasons a pastor who does not counsel is likely to miss, but reasons he will readily realize if he is involved in counseling those in his congregation. Unless the issues of sin are seriously and properly dealt with, the preaching from the pulpit is merely a Band-Aid solution. Jesus said that what defiles a person is not what goes into the body, but what comes out of the heart; that is what drives the person to sin and that is what he or she must deal with (Matt. 15:17).

The apostle Paul spent a great deal of time counseling people. As he wrote to believers he would pause and state, "You will say to me. . . ." He cut to the heart of the matter because he knew the people he counseled intimately and was able to anticipate their response. He also knew God's Word and always appealed to it for the answers to their problems. Paul understood the fuzzy, confused thinking caused by sin, so he taught clear and specific principles for Christian living. Neither Christ nor Paul coddled those they were helping. They said, "Do this" and "Do not do that," because both knew well those they counseled and saw clearly the walls of excuses they hid behind. They preached with a mind to tear down those barriers.

The pastor who counsels, preaches not merely to inform but to bring about change, which is precisely what growth and progressive sanctification is all about. A pastor who is true to the Word must come to grips with the church's one mission to believers: to facilitate growth in Christ. The pastor's job is not to thrill his congregation, nor should his goal be to stimulate emotions or intellect; his job is to preach God's Word for the purpose of change.

The pastor who counsels will long to be used of God, to preach and teach the Word, to show forth the worthiness of His Holy Son, and to lead His people in growth. Why? Because he sees the results of a hard heart that refuses to deal with problems biblically: the shattered lives, the ruined marriages, the soured relationships, and the stunted spiritual growth. He understands the inextricable link between the failure to understand and apply God's Word and failure in the Christian life. With burning conviction, growth and change become the goal of his preaching.

One of the most tragic reasons pastors do not counsel people and help them understand progressive sanctification is because the pastors themselves do not understand the doctrine. These pastors easily get caught up in the fuzzy, meaningless jargon of pop Christianity. They encourage people to read the Bible for the sake of reading it, to pray for God to pour out a mystical zap to cure all their ills, or to pray for revival, all without a clear understanding of how God works in lives and how He changes hearts. Unfortunately, they are likely to be more a part of the problem than the solution.

That is why the pastor who desires to counsel biblically must become saturated with the truths of progressive sanctification and must come to terms with the sufficiency of Scripture. He must realize that when used correctly, God's Word can identify sinful thought processes and habits and replace them with biblical ones. If he is not counseling from the Word of God alone, he will often fail to differentiate between special revelation and human opinion, theory, or general advice.

Counseling and Evangelism

Biblical counseling can also benefit the local church in evangelism. While many evangelistic tools are effective and worthy of attention, it is important to notice that the scriptural model always began by addressing the challenges, sins, or trials that a person was facing. Thus the biblical counselor who follows Scripture will not simply dispense the Word but will endeavor to listen and ask questions, and then will present the gospel of Jesus Christ.

Over the years, this method of counseling has been a highly effective tool for evangelism in our church. There are many fine couples in our church today whose marriages were once broken, or who were living together before marriage. Yet through counseling they trusted Christ, resolved their problems, and are now effective, productive disciples. Others, who initially came to our church with deep depression and difficulties, not only found the answers they needed through biblical counseling but have become effective evangelists and counselors themselves to both believers and nonbelievers.

THE CHURCH—ESSENTIAL TO COUNSELING

While counseling is a necessary part of the local church, we must remember that it is only one part. An hour of counseling once a week for the hurting people in the church is not God's complete plan for their spiritual growth; it is only part of the plan. In God's blueprint for ministry, counseling is meant to be a synchronized part of the whole.

Indeed, the most effective use of counseling is when it is part of the local church. Counselees need the help of all church ministries: they need the pulpit ministry to teach and motivate growth and change, the love of the collective membership to assist and encourage, the fellowship of the church body for interaction and relationships, the authority of the body for church discipline, and the example of leaders who are growing and changing. Above all, counselees need the decisiveness of a church committed to following biblical principles in practical areas such as communication, finances, and dealing with problems. There is nothing quite as compelling to a counselee as a church committed to leading by example.

DEVELOPING A BIBLICAL COUNSELING MINISTRY IN THE LOCAL CHURCH

Before we discuss the nuts and bolts of developing a counseling ministry in the church, let me make a rather bold statement: I believe there are only two ways to begin a counseling ministry. One way, unfortunately the pattern that is most often followed, is superficial and ultimately leads only to greater problems. It involves a counseling ministry that is developed hastily where the counselee is given direction from the Scriptures in the counseling center, but the same principles are not modeled in the church that is sponsoring the center. In these counseling situations, where progressive sanctification is not the biblical method of growth and church leaders are not committed to the Bible as the only sufficient standard of authority for daily decision, the counselee will be confused.

The other way, a biblical alternative, is actually rather uncomplicated. It begins through careful efforts that mold church leaders—pastors, elders, deacons, teachers, staff, and lay leaders—into a pattern of growth that people who seek counsel can follow. It requires a church ministry that is built upon the biblical concept of progressive sanctification, which produces a God-centered model for growth and change.

Now the obvious question is: "How does one develop a biblical counseling program that is a *natural* part of the church's ministry, a program that moves beyond the superficial remedies adopted by the world and so many churches?" There are several steps to consider in developing such a counseling ministry.

Leaders Must Be Dedicated

If a church is going to strive for spiritual growth and make earnest, spiritual change a priority, the pastor's life must exemplify that same kind of growth and change. If the Word is not effecting change in the pastor's life, he will have trouble teaching it with conviction and inspiring confidence in its sufficiency, and rightly so!

The pastor must also develop a relationship of mutual concern and loving encouragement with other leaders in the church. He must be willing to receive admonition as quickly and with as much grace as he administers it. His conviction that iron does indeed sharpen iron must be far more than mere lip service; he must believe it and rigorously and openly practice it. His relationship with those who serve with him must be marked by sincere encouragement and, if necessary, firm confrontation.

If a church is to grow spiritually, the pastor and leaders must be growing spiritually. The leadership team is the model the counselee will invariably look to as an example of Christian living. That is why a pastor does well to follow God's qualifications for a counselor when he selects teachers and leaders for the church (see Rom. 15:24). He must look for believers who are growing in their knowledge of the Scripture and who are applying it consistently to their lives.

The choices and decisions the pastor and church leaders make are also critical to the development of a biblical counseling ministry. For example, if the pastor admonishes counselees in the congregation to follow biblical principles, he and his leadership team must demonstrate obedience to those same principles. If he counsels a couple on the wise use of their finances, his decisions with regard to church finances must model wise stewardship. If he teaches a counselee about biblical principles of communication, his own communication within the church must be a positive example for that person.

Leaders Must Understand and Observe Progressive Sanctification

All biblical counseling and change must be accomplished through progressive sanctification, God's sole plan for spiritual growth. This truth must be clarified in the church through an articulate, written doctrinal statement. In addition, it must be taught clearly, because it is a truth that so often is poorly understood by counselees. In fact, it is often a major part of their problem. Many people are confused about how a believer grows and realizes positive change. They want spiritual growth and development on their own terms, easily and quickly. Some come for counseling expecting an instant solution from heaven, even though the apostle Paul, when teaching about spiritual growth, spoke not of mysterious, emotional experiences but of hard work. The growth process requires action. That is why Paul spoke of racing, wrestling, and fighting. In 1 Corinthians 9:27, he wrote, "I buffet my body and make it my slave," hardly the words of a man who expected spiritual growth to come through a heavenly zap!

Still others, confused about progressive sanctification, turn to morbid introspection and unwittingly take their eyes off of Christ. This is not to say that people who are confused about sanctification have wandered from that path on their own. Countless books, seminars, and lectures have passed along quasibiblical (sometimes antibiblical) advice that has only served to create more problems. Advice like "Feel good about yourself," "Turn it all over to Jesus," "Read the Bible seven minutes a day," and "Talk to the dead to heal your memories" has created an environment hostile to biblical solutions. That is why a church's counseling ministry will only be biblical and successful if the church is committed to the Scripture's patterns for growth, and if it instills that same commitment in those who come for counseling.

Leaders Must Have a Clear Sense of Direction

Before a church begins a counseling ministry, it must establish a clear purpose for its program. Lloyd Jonas, of the National Association of Nouthetic Counselors, emphasized that "in starting a counseling ministry there must not be anyone either higher up or close by in the chain of command who is not completely sold on nouthetic counseling" (presidential address, NANC conference, 1987).

All staff members must be equipped theologically to counsel others; they must demonstrate both the desire and the ability to counsel; and, ultimately, they must be willing to exert the time needed to train other lay counselors. When training counselors initially it can be helpful to use a counseling program that is approved by the National Association of Nouthetic Counselors. This will ensure that the church's trainees are taught counseling properly, both by observing counseling firsthand and by examining case-study situations.

Leaders Must Be Learners

All biblical counselors must be learners. Without a thirst for God, an appreciation for His Word, and a hunger to know it more deeply, counselors are not likely to have an interest in continuing their counseling education. They must constantly remind themselves that God said, "My thoughts are not your thoughts, neither are your ways My ways" (Is. 55:8). A firm grasp of that concept compels the counselor to further study and development. The counselor who feels adequate for the job and satisfied in his or her understanding of God's truth is likely to be, of all people, the most ill suited for the task.

Counselors must never forget the noetic effect of sin that demands continual nourishment from God's Word. The apostle Paul, a talented and industrious church planter, never boasted of reaching a great spiritual plateau but was ever pressing on. With an attitude of awe and a sound hermeneutical approach, the biblical counselor must regularly study the Word and desire to learn from others who study it.

Leaders Should Be Trained Within a Biblical Church Ministry

Just as church members need to be trained in evangelism, so they need to be trained in counseling. In what context should that training take place? This question is the watershed for the whole issue of counseling. For the biblical counselor, the training ground must be the local church. While some training takes place in counseling classes, most of the training of the biblical counselor comes through normal, active involvement in the church. If we believe the Word of God can bring genuine change, solutions, healing, and growth, then counselor preparation must focus more on the biblical responsibilities of pastoring and less on counseling as a separate, parachurch skill.

In our church, although we offer several classes on biblical counseling, our laypeople receive most of their training by simply becoming active participants in worship, ministry, and fellowship, all natural parts of every believer's life in the body. The believer who clearly understands the spiritual-growth process of progressive sanctification and understands the heavenly resources that are at the believer's disposal is a long way down the path of not only realizing that growth but also of helping others along the way. The heart of biblical counseling is not the form but the substance: God's Word.

The mainstay of our training program for deacons, their wives, and church laymen consists of an eleven-week course. Trainees meet for eight hours each Monday, and in the process of the three-month period, receive forty hours of lecture and twenty-two hours of counseling observation. We also require that trainees complete extensive reading assignments, often between one thousand and two thousand pages. We also occasionally offer short courses, consisting of two one-hour evening sessions combined with a pared-down schedule of counseling observation.

SOME HELPFUL DO'S AND DON'TS

- The church should clarify that its counseling ministry is based on biblical counseling principles.

- For legal protection, we feel it is wise to have nonmembers sign the following statement: "I understand that the counsel I receive will be according to the counselor's interpretation of the Bible." As a word of caution, this statement has not been tested in court. We are simply committed to being honest with our counselees about what they can expect from our counselors. In addition, we insist that each staff member who counsels nonmembers must successfully complete NANC certification.

- The church should not sacrifice the needs of its members to meet the counseling needs of those outside the church. God's plan for change is not based on one isolated hour each week. It is most effective when carried out within the context of a church's full range of biblical ministries. When counselors must choose between counseling someone from within the church—a church that teaches, encourages, and cares for its members biblically—and someone who does not benefit from that setting, they must make the choice that demonstrates the best stewardship of their time and love. Inevitably, there will be a need to make exceptions, but a basic principle to remember is that counselees need the ministry of the entire church.

CONCLUSION

A counseling ministry in a church can have profound, far-reaching effects in the lives of its congregation. In our church, each pastor counsels. As they interact with Scripture in the counseling setting, their understanding of the Word and its practical value deepens, and that, in turn, enters into their teaching from the pulpit. As a result, the members of our church have learned many of the biblical principles that are applied in counseling. Thus, a ministry of counseling provides practical, relevant help based on sound principles from God's Word that enables believers to be adequately equipped unto every good work (2 Tim. 3:17).

18

Resources for Biblical Counseling

Dennis M. Swanson and Wayne A. Mack

Effective counselors must have a core library of materials at their disposal both for personal enrichment and to provide tools to help counselees. In this chapter we present a sampling of materials that are indispensable for biblical counseling. The materials are divided into seven categories: (1) basic resources for biblical counselors, (2) theological resources for biblical counselors, (3) other resources for biblical counselors, (4) resources for counselees, (5) audio and video resources, (6) periodicals, and (7) training opportunities. Some of the more significant titles also have brief annotations.

In a resource chapter of this scope we are indebted to the contributors for their input, particularly David Powlison of the Christian Counseling and Education Foundation and John Street, Chairman of the Department of Biblical Counseling at The Master's College.

Basic Resources for Biblical Counselors

Adams, Jay. *Competent to Counsel*. Grand Rapids: Zondervan, 1970.

This book launched nouthetic counseling with a polemic against psychotherapy and a call to view counseling as an aspect of ministry that aims at sanctification and, hence, is dependent on the Holy Spirit and the Word of God. Psychiatry has attempted to usurp and limit the pastor's roll in counseling and define the problems of life in secular terms, providing non-biblical answers to biblical issues.

————. *Godliness Through Discipline*. Phillipsburg, NJ: Presbyterian and Reformed, 1972.

————. *The Christian Counselor's Manual*. Grand Rapids: Zondervan, 1973.

This sequel and companion volume to *Competent to Counsel* is an instruction manual providing information not only on the philosophy of counseling but ample instruction on counseling methods. This book is a treasure trove that informs the would-be counselor and deals with criticisms of nouthetic or biblical counseling.

_____. *The Christian Counselor's Casebook.* Grand Rapids: Zondervan, 1974.

_____. *Ready to Restore: The Layman's Guide to Christian Counseling.* Phillipsburg, NJ: Presbyterian and Reformed, 1981.

This is an introductory textbook in nouthetic counseling. Accessible and compact, it covers both conceptual and methodological matters. It is designed for both individual study and for a class or Bible study group.

_____. *Solving Marriage Problems: Biblical Solutions for Christian Counselors.* Phillipsburg, NJ: Presbyterian and Reformed, 1983.

_____. *The Biblical View of Self-Esteem, Self-Love, and Self-Image.* Eugene, OR: Harvest House, 1986.

_____. *A Call to Discernment: Distinguishing Truth from Error in Today's Church.* Eugene, OR: Harvest House, 1987.

_____. *A Thirst for Wholeness.* Wheaton: Victor Books, 1988.

_____. *The Grand Demonstration: A Biblical Study of the So-Called Problem of Evil.* Santa Barbara, CA: EastGate Publishers, 1991.

Bobick, Michael W. *From Slavery to Sonship: A Biblical Psychology for Pastoral Counseling.* Sun Valley, CA: Grace Books International, 1989.

Broger, John C. *Self-Confrontation: A Manual for In-Depth Discipleship.* Rancho Mirage, CA: Biblical Counseling Foundation, [1978] 1991.

These twenty-four weekly lessons are intended to move a person through the change process personally as a foundation for becoming a counselor (Matt. 7:1–5). The book can be used for Sunday school and other classes or personal study, and is an important resource.

_____. *Instructor's Guide for the Self-Confrontation Course.* Rancho Mirage, CA: Biblical Counseling Foundation, [1978] 1992.

Bulkley, Ed. *Why Christians Can't Trust Psychology.* Eugene, OR: Harvest House, 1994.

This book is written to demonstrate the fallacies of an integrationist approach to counseling. Bulkley addresses some of the major myths of psychology and presents a positive biblical approach to counseling people.

Kruis, John G. *Quick Scripture Reference for Counseling.* Grand Rapids: Baker, 1988.

Lloyd-Jones, D. Martyn. *Spiritual Depression: Its Causes and Cure.* Grand Rapids: Eeerdmans, 1965.

MacArthur, John. *Our Sufficiency in Christ*. Dallas: Word, 1991.

This is an excellent presentation of the believer's sufficiency in Jesus Christ and the resources of the Holy Spirit and the Word of God. It demonstrates the seductive, yet insufficient offerings of psychology, pragmatism, and mysticism as a basis for Christian living.

_____. *The MacArthur Topical Bible*. Nashville, TN: Thomas Nelson, 1999.

More expansive than the work by Kruis, this topical reference has over 20,000 Bible topics and subtopics and over 100,000 references. This is a must have reference tool for pastors, Bible teachers and counselors.

_____. *The MacArthur Study Bible*. Nashville, TN: Word. 1997.

One of the most detailed study Bibles available today. Presents notations on all of the key and difficult passages in the Bible, along with helpful charts, explanations, and outlines.

_____, and Richard L. Mayhue. *Think Biblically: Recovering a Christian Worldview*. Wheaton, IL: Crossway Books, 2003.

This work contains chapters contributed by faculty members of The Master's College and presents a biblically framed Christian worldview covering all of the academic disciplines.

Mack, Wayne A. *Homework Manual for Biblical Living, Volume 1: Personal and Interpersonal Problems*. Cherry Hill, NJ: Presbyterian and Reformed, 1979.

_____. *Homework Manual for Biblical Living, Volume 2: Family and Marital Problems*. Phillipsburg, NJ: Presbyterian and Reformed, 1980.

_____. *Preparing for Marriage God's Way, Counselor/Teacher's Guide*. Tulsa, OK: Virgil W. Hensley, 1986 ; Sun Valley, CA: Grace Book Shack, 1993.

Payne, Franklin E. *What Every Christian Should Know About the AIDS Epidemic*. Augusta, GA: Covenant Books, 1991.

_____. *Biblical Healing for Modern Medicine*. Augusta, GA: Covenant Books, 1993.

The author is a medical doctor and director of *Covenant Enterprises*. Specializing in medical ethics from a biblical perspective, these are invaluable works dealing with medical considerations that counselors will face.

Playfair, William L. *The Useful Lie*. Wheaton: Crossway Books, 1991.

The author, a medical doctor, demonstrates how the "recovery industry" has created the "disease model" for personal problems. The disease model eliminates personal responsibility for the sins of drug and alcohol abuse and shifts blame elsewhere, trapping people in a unending cycle of therapy groups and counseling. This work documents the origination, background, and goals of the recovery industry and its "useful lie."

Powlison, David. *Seeing with New Eyes: Counseling and the Human Condition Through the Lens of Scripture*. Phillipsburg, NJ: Presbyterian and Reformed, 2003.

Welch, Edward T. *Counselor's Guide to the Brain and its Disorders: Knowing the Difference Between Disease and Sin*. Grand Rapids: Zondervan, 1991.

———. *Addictions: A Banquet in the Grave, Finding Hope in the Power of the Gospel*. Phillipsburg, NJ: Presbyterian and Reformed, 2001.

BASIC THEOLOGICAL RESOURCES FOR BIBLICAL COUNSELORS

The following list presents some of the works that explain the theological foundations of biblical counseling. Most of the titles cited here are well known and there are many others that could be listed. Some works, while not exclusively related to counseling, touch on important issues the biblical counselor will deal with. These works are invaluable study tools not only for pastors but for all who are involved in biblical counseling.

Biblical counselors must be, first of all, students of the Bible. Correct biblical, systematic, and pastoral theology must flow from the text of Scripture. It is impossible to do proper biblical counseling without a solid theological foundation. The practice of counseling must be based on the application of biblical concepts derived from the thorough exegesis of Scripture.

Adams, Jay E. *A Theology of Christian Counseling*. Grand Rapids: Zondervan, 1979.

Berkhof, Louis. *Systematic Theology*. Grand Rapids: Eerdmans, 1959.

Charnock, Stephen. *The Existence and Attributes of God*. Minneapolis, MN: Klock and Klock, 1977.
    Written in 1797, this classic work remains immensely valuable today.

Erickson, Millard J. *Christian Theology* (second edition). Grand Rapids: Baker Books, 1998.

Feinberg, John S. *No One Like Him: The Doctrine of God*. Wheaton, IL: Crossway Books, 2001.
    This is perhaps the best and most thorough work to appear on the doctrine of God in recent years. It contains a thorough and biblical presentation of the person and nature of God.

_____. *Deceived by God: A Journey Through Suffering*. Wheaton, IL: Crossway Books, 1997.

_____, and Paul S. Feinberg. *Ethics for a Brave New World*. Wheaton, IL: Crossway Books, 1993.

Grudem, Wayne A. *Systematic Theology: An Introduction to Biblical Doctrine*. Grand Rapids: Zondervan, 1994.

In many respects one of the best and most readable systematic theologies published in recent years. The Master's College and Seminary would not ascribe to the author's position on covenantalism, noncessationism, and historic premillennialism, but the overall value of this work is significant.

Hodge, A. A. *Outlines of Theology*. Grand Rapids: Eerdmans, 1949.

Hodge, Charles. *Systematic Theology* 3 vols. Grand Rapids: Eerdmans, 1946.

These three volumes are available in different formats, but the full unabridged volumes are by far the best to have. Hodge has been called "the theologian" of the great Princeton tradition. His presentation of the doctrines of sin, salvation, God, the Scriptures, and sanctification are must reading.

Hoekema, Anthony A. *Created in God's Image*. Grand Rapids: Eerdmans, 1986.

In this important work, Hoekema presents a clear, biblical explanation of man as created in God's image. He discusses sin, the fall, total depravity, and common grace. One chapter discusses the issue of sovereignty versus free will and the ability to choose.

MacArthur, John. *The Gospel According to Jesus*. Grand Rapids: Zondervan, 1994.

This is the seminal book on the "lordship salvation" controversy. MacArthur presents the issues and the biblical teaching regarding repentance, saving faith, and sanctification.

_____. *Faith Works: The Gospel According to the Apostles*. Dallas: Word, 1993.

This volume continues the discussion of *The Gospel According to Jesus*. In this book MacArthur clearly explains saving faith as understood both biblically and in the tradition of the history of orthodox Christian doctrine.

_____. *Ashamed of the Gospel: When the Church Becomes Like the World*. Wheaton, IL: Crossway, 1993.

In this work MacArthur effectively develops a comparison between the modern church in America and the "Downgrade" controversy that

Charles H. Spurgeon fought in the late nineteenth century. Although the book does not deal specifically with counseling, it provides valuable insights on integration and compromise in the church today.

————. *Found, God's Will.* Wheaton, IL: Victor Books, 1978.

————. *Anxiety Attacked.* Wheaton, IL: Victor Books, 1993.

————. *Whose Money is it Anyway?* Nashville, TN: Word, 2000.

One of the leading counseling issues that will be faced is the mismanagement of personal and family finances. This is an excellent tool to put in counselees' hands. It is a clear and detailed biblical exposition of the subject of money, wealth and possessions.

————. *Biblical Parenting.* Nashville, TN: Word, 2000.

————. *Battle for the Beginning.* Nashville, TN: Word, 2001.

A clear exposition of Genesis 1—3 detailing the creation account. Discusses the absolute importance of a Biblical view of creation and how non- and sub-biblical views affect every aspect of society and life.

————. *Safe in the Arms of God: Truth from Heaven About the Death of a Child.* Nashville, TN: Thomas Nelson, 2003.

This is a must have resource for any pastor or counselor dealing with parents facing the death of a child. Presents the clear biblical teaching on the subject.

Mayhue, Richard L. *The Healing Promise.* Great Britain: Christian Focus, 1997.

————. *How to Interpret the Bible for Yourself.* Great Britain: Christian Focus, 2001.

————. *Practicing Proverbs: Wise Living for Foolish Times.* Great Britain: Christian Focus, 2003.

Owen, John. *Temptation and Sin.* Grand Rapids: Zondervan, 1958.

Piper, John and Wayne Grudem, eds. *Recovering Biblical Manhood and Womanhood: A Response to Evangelical Feminism.* Wheaton: Crossway Books, 1990.

This is a comprehensive work on the entire subject of the biblical roles of men and women, in the church, in the family, and in life. The writers present a thorough exegetical discussion of the biblical teaching on men and women including: headship, submission, motherhood, ministry, and men and women in the image of God. As the world seeks to eliminate the male-female distinctions, this book is a vital resource for the counselor.

Smith, F. Lagard. *Sodom's Second Coming: What You Need to Know about the Deadly Homosexual Assault.* Eugene, OR: Harvest House, 1993.

A pointed and well-documented presentation on the homosexual agenda in America. The author is a law professor at Pepperdine University and a graduate of Yale.

Wells, David F. *No Place for Truth or Whatever Happened to Evangelical Theology?* Grand Rapids: Eerdmans, 1993.

Perhaps one of the most important books to be released in recent times. Wells chronicles not only the de-emphasis of truth in evangelical theology but the intolerance of it in much of modern evangelicalism.

OTHER RESOURCES FOR BIBLICAL COUNSELORS

The works listed in this section are designed to give the counselor a guide to the available literature dealing with more specific topics related to counseling. This list is by no means exhaustive and the literature in this field continues to grow.

Adams, Jay. *The Big Umbrella and Other Essays and Addresses on Christian Counseling.* Phillipsburg, NJ: Presbyterian and Reformed, 1972.

_____. *Lectures on Counseling.* Grand Rapids: Zondervan, 1975.

_____. *What About Nouthetic Counseling?* Grand Rapids: Baker, 1976.

_____. *Change Them? . . . Into What?: Counseling in America Today.* Laverock, PA: Christian Counseling and Educational Foundation, 1977.

_____. *Matters of Concern to Christian Counselors: A Potpourri of Principles and Practices.* Phillipsburg, NJ: Presbyterian and Reformed, 1977.

_____. *The Power of Error: Demonstrated in an Actual Counseling Case.* Phillipsburg, NJ: Presbyterian and Reformed, 1978.

_____. *Update on Christian Counseling.* vol. 1. Phillipsburg, NJ: Presbyterian and Reformed, 1979.

Continues a series that began with *Matters of Concern to Christian Counselors.*

_____. *Update on Christian Counseling.* vol. 2. Phillipsburg, NJ: Presbyterian and Reformed, 1981.

_____. *Marriage, Divorce, and Remarriage in the Bible.* Grand Rapids: Zondervan, 1980.

_____. *The Language of Counseling.* Grand Rapids: Zondervan, 1981.

_____. *Insight and Creativity in Christian Counseling: An Antidote to Rigid and Mechanical Approaches.* Grand Rapids: Zondervan, 1982.

_____. *Handbook of Church Discipline.* Grand Rapids: Zondervan, 1986.

_____. *How to Help People Change: The Four-Step Biblical Process.* Grand Rapids: Zondervan, 1986.

_____. *Sibling Rivalry in the Household of God.* Denver, CO: Accent Books, 1988.

_____. *From Forgiven to Forgiving: Discover the Path to Biblical Forgiveness.* Wheaton: Victor Books, 1989.

Ennis, Pat and Lisa Tatlock. *Becoming a Woman Who Pleases God.* Chicago, IL: Moody Publishers, 2003.

_____. *Designing a Lifestyle That Pleases God.* Chicago, IL: Moody Publishers, 2004.

Eyrich, Howard A. *Three to Get Ready: A Christian Premarital Counselor's Manual.* Phillipsburg, PA: Presbyterian and Reformed, 1978.

Payne, Franklin E. *Biblical and Medical Ethics.* Milford, MO: Mott Media, 1985.

_____. *Making Biblical Decisions: Birth Control, Artificial Reproduction and Genetic Engineering.* Escondido, CA: Hosanna Book House, 1989.

Scott, Stuart. *The Exemplary Husband.* Bemidji, MN: Focus Publishing, 2000.

RESOURCES FOR COUNSELEES

Adams, Jay. *Christ and Your Problems.* Nutley, NJ: Presbyterian and Reformed, 1971 (pamphlet).

_____. *Christian Living in the Home.* Phillipsburg, NJ: Presbyterian and Reformed, 1972.

_____. *How to Overcome Evil.* Nutley, NJ: Presbyterian and Reformed, 1977.

_____. *What Do You Do When Anger Gets the Upper Hand?* Phillipsburg, NJ: Presbyterian and Reformed, 1975 (pamphlet).

_____. *What Do You Do When Fear Overcomes You?* Phillipsburg, NJ: Presbyterian and Reformed, 1975 (pamphlet).

_____. *What Do You Do When You Become Depressed?* Phillipsburg, NJ: Presbyterian and Reformed, 1975 (pamphlet).

_____. *What Do You Do When You Know that You're Hooked?* Phillipsburg, NJ: Presbyterian and Reformed, 1975 (pamphlet).

_____. *What Do You Do When You Worry All the Time?* Phillipsburg, NJ: Presbyterian and Reformed, 1975 (pamphlet).

_____. *What Do You Do When Your Marriage Goes Sour?* Phillipsburg, NJ: Presbyterian and Reformed, 1975 (pamphlet).

_____. *What to Do about Worry*. Phillipsburg, NJ: Presbyterian and Reformed, 1980.

_____. *How to Handle Trouble: God's Way*. Phillipsburg, NJ: Presbyterian and Reformed, 1982.

_____. *The War Within: A Biblical Strategy for Spiritual Warfare*. Eugene, OR: Harvest House, 1989.

Blanchard, John. *Ultimate Questions*. Durham, England: Evangelical Press, 1987.

Perhaps the single best gospel tract available today. It is well-written, colorful, and forthright. This book is ideal for counselors who work with non-Christians. It presents God, the Scriptures, sin, and the plan of salvation.

Bridges, Jerry. *Trusting God*. Colorado Springs, CO: NavPress, 1989.

This book presents the biblical directive for trusting God, even in the troubles and turmoil of life. It is especially profitable for the counselee going through deep hurt and struggle.

Hodge, Charles. *The Way of Life: A Guide to Christian Belief and Experience*. Edinburgh: Banner of Truth Trust, 1978 (reprinted from the original 1841 edition).

This work opens the Scriptures in a systematic manner and answers the question of how the great doctrines of the Bible must be translated into the everyday life of the believer. This is a book every Christian should read annually.

Kinneer, Jack. *How to Grow in Christ*. Phillipsburg, NJ: Presbyterian and Reformed, 1981.

Klempel, Richard, and Lois Klempel. *Abused? How You Can Find God's Help*. Lima, OH: Fairway Press, 1991 (foreword by Jay Adams).

Mack, Wayne A. *The Bible's Answer to the Question: What is a Christian?* Cherry Hill, NJ: Mack Publishing, 1972.

_____. *Where Are You in Relation to God?* Cherry Hill, NJ: Mack Publishing, 1973.

_____. *Strengthening Your Marriage*. Phillipsburg, NJ: Presbyterian and Reformed, 1977.

Eight units cover the basics of marital unity: God's purpose for marriage, the wife's responsibilities, the husband's responsibilities, communication, finances, sex, raising children, and family religion. Each chapter provides outlined teaching followed by Bible study, self-analysis, and personalized response and application.

_____. *A Homework Manual for Biblical Living.* Vol. 1 and 2. Phillipsburg, NJ: Presbyterian and Reformed, 1979; 1980.

_____. *Your Family God's Way: Developing and Sustaining Relationships in the Home.* Phillipsburg, NJ: Presbyterian and Reformed, 1991.

_____. *Down But Not Out: How to Get Up When Life Knocks You Down.* Phillipsburg, NJ: Presbyterian and Reformed, 2004.

_____. *Reaching the Ear of God.* Phillipsburg, NJ: Presbyterian and Reformed, 2004.

_____, and Nathan A. Mack. *Preparing for Marriage God's Way.* Tulsa, OK: Virgil W. Hensley, 1986.

_____, and Nathan A. Mack. *The Twin Pillars of the Christian Life.* Sand Springs, OK: Grace and Truth Books, 2003.

Matzat, Don. *Christ Esteem: Where the Search for Self-Esteem Ends.* Eugene, OR: Harvest House, 1990.

Mayhue, Richard. *Fight the Good Fight.* Fearn, Ross-shire: Great Britain: Christian Focus, 1999.

This volume emphasizes Christian character building through the study of Old Testament people. By studying various personal cases, some successful and some failed, Christians can learn what to avoid and what to cultivate in their walk with God.

_____. *Seeking God.* Great Britain: Christian Focus, 2000.

Although not a book on counseling per se, it is, rather, a book on the theology and practice of one's Christian life. This is an ideal book to put into the hands of new Christians, those who have not received good initial nurturing in the Christian faith, or those who need to be reminded about what God expects of them.

_____. *Unmasking Satan.* Grand Rapids: Kregel, 2001.

This volume exposes the many tricks of the temptation trade that Satan employs to snare the unprepared or unwary believer. Biblical countertactics are offered, illustrated, and applied for a practical and successful scriptural battle plan. Dependence on God's Word and God's Spirit is emphasized.

Ray, Bruce A. *Withhold Not Correction.* Phillipsburg, NJ: Presbyterian and Reformed, 1978 (foreword by Jay Adams).

Sande, Ken. *The Peacemaker: A Biblical Guide to Resolving Personal Conflict.* Grand Rapids: Baker, 1990.

Whitney, Donald S. *Spiritual Disciplines for the Christian Life.* Colorado Springs, CO: NavPress, 1991.

Wiersbe, Warren W. *Why Us? When Bad Things Happen to God's People.* Old Tappan, NJ: Fleming H. Revell, 1985.

Wiersbe takes on the task of answering the book by Rabbi Harold S. Kushner, *When Bad Things Happen to Good People.* Kushner took the position that bad things were unfortunate, but that God was not able to prevent them. The problem of evil in the world and the suffering of God's children are age old. Wiersbe presents the biblical understanding and the compassion of a godly pastor. This book can be a great help to counselees going through any type of severe trial.

AUDIO AND VIDEO RESOURCES

A large number of audio and video tapes are available to help biblical counselors. Here are some reliable sources for the materials. Many of these sources now have on-line ordering systems.

1. *Strengthening Ministries International* (www.mackministries.org)
   Box 249
   Center Valley, PA 18034
2. *Sound Word Cassettes* (www.soundword.com)
   430 Boyd Circle
   P.O. Box 2035, Mail Station
   Michigan City, IN 46360
3. *Grace to You* (www.gty.org)
   P.O. Box 4000
   Panorama City, CA 91412
   Telephone 800-55-GRACE
4. *Grace Books International* (www.gbibooks.com)
   13248 Roscoe Boulevard
   Sun Valley, CA 91352
   Telephone 818-909-5555

Sessions at the annual NANC (National Association of Nouthetic Counselors) Conference are recorded and made available to those who request copies. Normally a single theme is emphasized each year. These recordings are available through *Sound Word Cassettes,* which also has a large collection of materials for biblical counseling. *Grace to You* is the primary source for tapes and materials by John MacArthur. (While John MacArthur's ministry is one of biblical exposition, his material is invaluable for the counselor.) Grace Book Shack stocks a wide variety of books and materials by John MacArthur, Jay Adams, Wayne Mack, and other biblical counselors. Additional titles by various leaders in the biblical counseling movement are available through the sources listed above.

Periodicals

The Journal of Biblical Counseling (formerly *The Journal of Pastoral Practice*) is the triennial publication of the Christian Counseling and Education Foundation (CCEF). The address for subscription information is 1803 East Willow Grove Avenue, Laverock, PA 19118. Telephone 215-884-7676. Currently subscription rates are eighteen dollars annually.

The Biblical Counselor is the regular newsletter of The National Association of Nouthetic Counselors (NANC). The address for subscription information is 5526 SR 26 East, Lafayette, IN 47905. Telephone 317-448-9100. The newsletter is offered free of charge, although contributions to offset costs are appreciated.

Training Opportunities

The Master's College (www.masters.edu)
21726 Placerita Canyon Road
Santa Clarita, CA 91321
Telephone 661-259-3540

Information about counseling studies and other majors is available on request. Under the direction of Dr. John Street, the Biblical Studies Department offers a degree in Biblical Studies with an emphasis in Biblical Counseling. The eight core courses in Biblical Counseling include: (1) Introduction to Biblical Counseling, (2) The Theological Basis for Biblical Counseling, (3) Methods of Biblical Change, (4) Marriage and Family Counseling, (5) Problems and Procedures in Biblical Counseling, and (6) Counseling Practicum.

Biblical Counseling Foundation (www.bcfministries.org)
42–600 Cook Street, Suite 100
Palm Desert, CA 92211–5143
Telephone 760-773-2667

This foundation trains laypeople and pastors in discipleship methods largely influenced by biblical counseling.

Faith Baptist Counseling Ministries
5526 State Road 26 East
Lafayette, IN 47905
Telephone 765-448-1986

This organization offers counseling in the local area and trains interested persons in the principles of biblical counseling. They also offer assistance to local churches in developing and refining a counseling ministry.

National Association of Nouthetic Counselors (www.nanc.org)
3600 W. 96th Street
Indianapolis, IN 46268–2905

NANC offers seminars throughout the United States featuring key leaders in biblical counseling. It also offers training at the headquarters in Indiana and serves as a resource center for local churches.

Christian Counseling and Educational Foundation (www.ccef.org)
1803 East Willow Grove Avenue
Glenside, PA 19038
Telephone 215-884-7676

CCEF presents extensive training in biblical counseling in several avenues: (1) instruction leading to a lay certificate in biblical counseling, (2) weekend training modules in local churches, and (3) participation in M.A. programs at Biblical Theological Seminary and Westminster Theological Seminary. Mr. John Bettler is the executive director.

The Master's Seminary (www.tms.edu)
13248 Roscoe Blvd.
Sun Valley, CA 91352
Telephone 818-782-6488

The Master's Seminary, as part of its regular Master of Divinity program, offers courses in biblical counseling as part of the required and elective course offering. The seminary also has a Master of Theology, a Doctor of Theology, and a Doctor of Ministry in Expository Preaching program.

19

Frequently Asked Questions about Biblical Counseling

Compiled and Edited by Dennis M. Swanson

The purpose of this book is to help both pastors and laypeople become familiar with the principles of biblical counseling and to apply them in the life of the church. Because the concept of integration has held sway for so many decades and the psychological model for counseling has been virtually unchallenged in the church, Christians have raised many questions regarding the entire concept of biblical counseling. Jay Adams, in his book *What About Nouthetic Counseling* (Baker, 1976), dealt with many questions about this subject, but there have been additional and more pointed questions posed of biblical counseling since then. The questions presented here represent a sample of the questions that are most frequently asked. The answers to these questions have been prepared by various members of the staff and faculty of The Master's College, The Master's Seminary, Grace Community Church, and others who contributed to this book.

Is there any difference between biblical counseling and Christian psychology?

At a superficial glance, it would appear that a biblical counselor and a psychotherapist who is a Christian do many of the same things. Both converse with people; both care about people; both get to know people; both are interested in motivation, thoughts, emotions, and behavior; both explore the various pressures in a person's situation; both give feedback; perhaps both talk about Jesus or a passage of Scripture. So how do they differ?

To understand how Christianized psychotherapy differs from biblical counseling it is necessary to look closely at what each practices and teaches. Here are some of the distinctives of each.

Perspective of the Bible and its contribution to counseling. Most Christian psychologists view the Bible as an inspirational resource, but their basic system of counseling, both theory and methods, is transferred unaltered from secular psychology. Most are self-consciously eclectic, picking and choosing theories and techniques according to personal preference. In contrast, biblical counselors follow the Bible's view of itself as the source of a comprehensive and detailed approach to understanding and counseling people (2 Tim. 3:15–17; 2 Pet. 1:4).

Some Christian psychotherapists use few Scriptures; others use many. But frequency of citation is much less important than the way passages are used, or misused, and in the vast majority of cases the passages cited are completely misused. There is a dearth of contextualized exegesis (a critical interpretation of a text) and an abundance of eisegesis (interpreting a text by reading one's own ideas into it). Biblical counseling is committed to letting God speak for Himself through His Word, and to handling the Word of Truth rightly (2 Tim. 2:15).

Perspective of God. There are many aspects of God that Christian psychologists routinely ignore. In particular, His sovereignty, holiness, justice, kingly authority, and power are virtually unmentioned. The fatherly love of God is the great theme of these psychotherapists, but detached from the entirety of who God is, this love becomes the unconditional positive regard of a great therapist in the sky, indistinguishable from classic liberal theology. Biblical counseling follows the Bible and seeks to minister the love of the true and living God, whose love deals with sin and produces obedience (1 John).

Perspective of human nature and motivation. Almost every Christian psychologist espouses some variety of need theory. Needs for self-esteem, for love and acceptance, and for significance tend to dominate. If these needs are met, it is believed that people will be happy, kind, and moral; if not met, people will be miserable, hateful, and immoral. Christian psychologists borrow their motivation theory directly from humanistic psychology. Scripture flatly opposes such need theories because it teaches that sinful human motivation roots in various cravings and lusts (Gal. 5:16–24; Eph. 2:3; James 1:14–16; 3:13—4:12). Scripture teaches that God changes our desires and that godly motivation is rooted in the desire for God and godliness. If people crave self-esteem, love, and significance, they will be happy if they get it and miserable if they don't, but they will remain self-centered in either case. On the other hand, if people desire God (Ps. 42:1–2; 73:25), God's kingdom (Matt. 6:9–13; 6:33; 13:45–46), godly wisdom (Prov. 3:15; 2 Tim. 2:22), and resurrection glory (Rom. 8:18–25), they will be satisfied, joyous, obedient, and profitable servants of God.

Perspective of the gospel. For most Christian psychologists, Jesus Christ is the provider for built-in psychic needs and the healer of psychic wounds. The love of God at the cross simply portrays how valuable one is to God in order to boost self-esteem and to meet the need to be loved. But in the

Bible, Jesus Christ is the Lamb of God crucified in the place of sinners. The love of God actually demolishes self-esteem and the lust for self-esteem. It produces, instead, a great and grateful esteem for the Son of God, who loved us and gave His life for us, for the Lamb of God who alone is worthy. The love of God does not meet our lust to be loved as we are. It demolishes that deluded craving in order to love us despite who we are and to teach us to love God and neighbor (1 John 4:7—5:3).

Perspective of counseling. Christian psychologists tend to view counseling the same way secular psychologists view it: as a professional activity without any necessary connection to the church of Jesus Christ. A client with a felt-need engages a professional for help in attaining goals of personal adjustment, emotional happiness, stability, self-fulfillment, and the like. But biblical counselors follow the Bible and view counseling as a pastoral activity. Their counseling aims at progressive sanctification and must communicate the true contents of Scripture. Biblical counseling connects logically and structurally to worship, discipleship, preaching, pastoral oversight, use of gifts, church discipline, and other aspects of life in the body of Christ. (David Powlison)

I have heard that those who practice biblical counseling are unsympathetic, mean-spirited, and callous. Is this true?

Biblical counselors are certainly none of these things. In truth, they are just the opposite. Biblical counselors want to come alongside counselees in concern and love as they address the problems. They want to help individuals find biblical solutions; they encourage change for God's glory primarily but also for the counselee's own benefit.

The apostle Paul serves as a good model for biblical counselors. He reminded the elders of the church at Ephesus (Acts 20:20) how he had not held back anything in his teaching that was profitable for them. He had even gone house to house in order to minister to them. Then in verse 31 he showed the spirit of humility in his heart as he said, "Night and day for a period of three years I did not cease to admonish (*noutheteo*) each one with tears." Even though Paul had to admonish these people and tell them the truth, he was not unsympathetic, mean-spirited, or callous with them.

Another passage illustrating Paul's compassion is 1 Thessalonians 2:7–9. There he made the point with his readers that he was gentle with them (v. 7), and that he had imparted not only truth to them but his own life (v. 8). Paul was known for speaking the truth, but speaking it in love (Eph. 4:15, 29). And that is what a biblical counselor does. The counselor establishes involvement in the life of the counselee and gives hope that the person's problem can be overcome. Many counselees have never experienced this type of caring confrontation. They have never experienced true

concern and compassion, traits that are essential prerequisites of a nouthetic counselor.
(Carey Hardy)

Do secular disciplines have absolutely nothing to offer to biblical counseling methodology?

Let us clarify first what we mean by counseling methodology. A counseling methodology is a *system* of theoretical commitments, principles, goals, and appropriate methods. It is a set of interconnected components; it is not a collection of random and eclectic bits of observation or technique. A counseling methodology is an organized, committed way of understanding and tackling people's problems.

Do secular disciplines have anything to offer to the methodology of biblical counseling? The answer is a flat no. Scripture provides the system for biblical counseling. Other disciplines, such as history, anthropology, literature, sociology, medicine, psychology, biology, business, political science, may be useful in a variety of secondary ways to the pastor and the biblical counselor, but such disciplines can never provide a system of understanding and counseling people.

Secular disciplines may serve us well as they describe people; they may challenge us by how they seek to explain, guide, and change people; but they seriously mislead us when we take them at absolute face value because they are secular. They explain people, define what people ought to be like, and try to solve people's problems without considering God and man's relationship to God. Secular disciplines have made a systematic commitment to being wrong.

This is not to deny that secular people are often brilliant observers of other human beings. They are often ingenious critics and theoreticians. But they also distort what they see and mislead by what they teach and do, because from God's point of view the wisdom of the world has fundamental folly written through it. They will not acknowledge that God has created human beings as God-related and God-accountable creatures. The mind-set of secularity is like a power saw with a set that deviates from the right angle. It may be a powerful saw, and it may cut a lot of wood, but every board comes out crooked.

Given this built-in distortion, how might secular observations, ideas, and practices be useful to Christians? They should play *no* role in our *model* of counseling. But, radically reinterpreted, they can play an illustrative role, providing examples and details that illustrate the biblical model and fill out our knowledge. They can also play a provocative role, challenging us to develop our model in areas we have not thought about or have neglected or misconstrued. Jay Adams stated this succinctly in *Competent to Counsel,* where he explained that psychology can be a "useful adjunct" to biblical counseling in two ways: (1) "for the purposes of illustrating, filling in gener-alizations with specifics"; and (2) "challenging wrong human interpretations of Scripture, thereby forcing the student to restudy the Scriptures."[1]

What do secular disciplines have to offer biblical counselors? God is the expert when it comes to people, and He has spoken and acted to change us and to equip us to help others change. Secularists have a twisted and blinkered perceptive that can only be useful to biblical counselors as it is radically reinterpreted according to the counseling methodology revealed in Scripture. (Chapters 8–14 of this book present a biblical methodology for helping people.)

(David Powlison)

Isn't biblical counseling overly simplistic?

If overly simplistic means that biblical counseling does not seem to be as sophisticated as say, psychology or psychiatry, with its intricate terms and methods, then yes, it is more simple. But note that it is not simplistic.

It has been well stated, "Simple language no more indicates simplistic thinking than complex language indicates profundity of thought." In its essence, biblical counseling is simple in that it seeks to find the answers to the problems of sin from the pages of Scripture. It does not seek to find those answers anywhere else except in God's Word, for nowhere else is there a remedy for this desperately needed cure. Lest we be criticized unnecessar-ily at this point, let us clarify that the difficulties of this life are, admittedly, enormous, but they are not impossible to understand and they can provide impetus for growth. To simply assert that the problems of life and sin are simple and then to move on to something else is to miss the point entirely. God's Word has the simple yet profound truths that change people into the very image of Jesus Christ. Those whose commitment is to Scripture and its sufficiency will base their counseling efforts on the foundation of that standard.

Peter's commitment was spelled out in these terms: "His divine power has granted to us everything pertaining to life and godliness, through the true knowledge of Him [through Scripture] who called us by His own glory and excellence" (2 Pet. 1:3). Biblical counseling, then, provides the only sure and superior basis for helping people, and because this is so, it cannot inherently be called simplistic. If so, it would impugn the character of God Himself, as though He were simplistic. The truth is, in the final analysis, biblical counselors are actually the ones who go deep into the region of the soul—into all arenas of mankind's being—whereas others do not go deep enough! Only the man or woman who is equipped with God's tools (His Word and Spirit) can traverse the murky waters of the human heart. Proverbs 20:5 declares: "A plan in the heart of a man is like deep water, / But a man of understanding draws it out." Biblical counselors, not those who pretend to deal with the deep issues, are the ones who can truly draw out the real issues of life.

Counselors who are committed to Scripture alone do not need to bend to the pressure of those who would want them to somehow see complex and intricate issues in every counseling situation. Of course, some situations are going to be more difficult than others, but it cannot be charged that biblical counseling is overly simplistic. Jay Adams deftly countered this charge by stating, "I consider both clarity and simplicity virtues, not vices. In my opinion, whatever darkens understanding is a detriment; whatever lightens it deserves praise. . . . I look on clarity as a sacred obligation of a Christian minister, whether he speaks from the pulpit or whether he writes with his pen. Obscurity is the father of heresy and ambiguity is the mother of all error. Clarity bears a close relationship to truth."[2]
(S. Lance Quinn)

Since the Bible is not a textbook on psychology, don't we need to supplement it with other disciplines to understand and help people with deep psychological needs?

At first glance, this seems like a reasonable question. The scientific disciplines *have* shown us truth that goes beyond the truth of Scripture. All of us have benefited from medical knowledge that is, after all, extrabiblical. Appendectomies, for example, have saved countless lives in the past hundred years or so. Smallpox vaccinations have virtually wiped out the disease. If we limited ourselves in medicine to the remedies specifically revealed in Scripture, we would be at a tremendous disadvantage in the treatment of diseases.

Certainly, Scripture does *not* claim to be a thorough textbook on medicine, or physics, or any of the sciences.[3] But psychology differs from these in two important regards. First, psychology is not a true science. It does not deal with objective, measurable data that can be subjected to reliable tests and confirmed by the scientific method. It is a pseudoscience, and most of its cardinal doctrines are mere speculations, not reliable truth.

Second, and most significant, psychology, unlike medicine and physics, deals with matters that are fundamentally spiritual. In fact, the word *psychology* literally means, "study of the soul." What are deep psychological needs if they are not the spiritual issues the gospel is concerned with? And Scripture certainly does claim absolute sufficiency in addressing those needs: "All Scripture is inspired by God and profitable for teaching, for reproof, for correction, for training in righteousness; *that the man of God may be adequate, equipped for every good work*" (2 Tim. 3:16–17, emphasis added). "The law of the LORD is perfect, restoring the soul" (Ps. 19:7). Scripture itself promises believers the most comprehensive spiritual resources: "everything pertaining to life and godliness" (2 Pet. 1:3).

Is the problem depression? Scripture contains the only reliable remedy. Is the problem guilt? What can psychology offer that goes beyond the perfect solution Scripture suggests: "the blood of Christ . . . [that cleanses] your conscience from dead works to serve the living God" (Heb. 9:14)? Every so-called psychological need that is not traceable to physical causes is, in reality, a spiritual problem, and Scripture does indeed claim to be the only sufficient guide in handling spiritual problems. To attempt to add psychological theory to the unfailing testimony of God's Word is to adulterate God's truth with human opinion.
(John MacArthur)

Is biblical counseling really necessary? Isn't discipleship sufficient?

Christian discipleship is the process of passing the truths of God's Word that one has learned and applied on to another believer (2 Tim. 2:2). It takes time. It may involve the investment of years of teaching, training, encouraging, and rebuking. The goal during this process is to help the disciple grow to maturity in Christ that is, to walk consistently according to God's Word. The discipler equips the individual so that ultimately that person in turn begins to build biblical principles into the lives of others (again, 2 Tim. 2:2). The person who imparts truth about God to someone else will also sharpen and mature through the discipleship process.

From this perspective, it should be apparent that biblical counseling is actually a *part* of discipleship. It is not the distinct entity the world and many Christians make it. In fact, much of what one would say about discipleship could be said equally about counseling. In counseling, though, the discipleship process has progressed to more *specific* application of biblical principles, to more *specific* problems in the life of a believer. Perhaps the individual requires more structure and accountability than a normal discipling relationship might provide. This is especially true if the issues being dealt with are ingrained habits in the counselee's life.

Normally, in a counseling relationship specific problems are dealt with over a much shorter period of time than in a discipling relationship. It is not necessary to counsel an individual for years. In many cases, people who are saved need only a few weeks to understand the biblical principles involved to change their thinking concerning the issue and, thus, to change their behavior or responses to their circumstances.

There are instances in the discipling process when specific problems are identified, and in the course of addressing those issues the discipler counsels the individual. It is also true that in the process of biblical counseling a person may be able to resolve the issue that necessitated the counseling but will want to continue in a discipling relationship with a mature believer for help with further spiritual growth. Thus, discipling at times necessitates

counseling, and counseling at times functions as a concentrated form of discipleship.
(Carey Hardy)

How do God's grace and the gospel fit into biblical counseling?
    The Bible speaks of God's grace in the good news of Jesus Christ. When Jesus opened the minds of His disciples to understand the Scriptures, He explained to them the things concerning Himself. The Bible is *about* Jesus Christ the Savior and Lord; therefore, biblical counseling is *about* Jesus Christ the Savior and Lord. When Jesus opened the minds of His disciples to understand the Scriptures, He spoke of repentance, the forgiveness of sins, and making disciples. The Bible is *about* making sinners into children of the Father; therefore, biblical counseling is *about* making sinners into children of the Father. When Jesus opened the minds of His disciples to understand the Scriptures, He taught them to minister like their gracious Master; therefore, biblical counseling carries a gracious message. Biblical counselors embody a gracious method: loving candor, humility, prayerful dependency, wisdom, gentleness, boldness, kindness, persistence, courage, authority, flexibility, self-sacrifice, and patience. The Bible is *about* equipping counselors to minister the whole counsel of God; therefore, biblical counseling is *about* equipping counselors to minister the whole counsel of God.
    What then is the place of God's grace and gospel in biblical counseling? That is rather like asking, "What is the place of water and oxygen in human physiology?" The gospel is the fundamental material of biblical counseling. Every part of biblical counseling is made of gospel and grace, from understanding people and their problems to solving those problems.
    Why do people wonder whether grace is central to biblical counseling? There are three possible reasons. First, many people think that the purpose of the Bible is to get people saved and tell them what to do. From that perspective, all the counselor can say to people is, "Here is how to accept the gospel and God's forgiving grace so you will go to heaven. Now, until then, do this. Do not do that. Shape up. Just say, 'no.' Be a good person." Such moralizing, however, is antibiblical. The Bible does not tack willpower and self-effort onto grace. The gospel and grace of God are not only about forgiveness for the guilt of sin but about God's power to change believers progressively throughout their lives. The indwelling Spirit intends to change people in the practical details of life. God's self-revelation becomes the environment we live in; God's promises become the food we live on; and God's commands become the life we live out. Can anyone doubt that biblical counseling worthy of the name is a ministry of God's own power in the gospel, changing people both inwardly and outwardly?
    Here is a second reason people ask about the place of grace in biblical counseling. Biblical counselors aim for practical obedience. Many people

think that emphasizing obedience to God's commands means ignoring or contradicting the free grace of the gospel. But free grace is effective grace. It is no treat to be forgiven adultery and yet remain adulterous. It is no glory to God to forgive anger and yet leave people given to angry outbursts. It is no honor to the gospel if anxiety can be forgiven yet people who are nervous wrecks continue to live in unbelief. It is no advance for God's kingdom to forgive self-centered people, if they do not learn in some measure how to consider the interests of others. It is no happiness for a grumbler to be forgiven, if that person remains utterly self-absorbed, demanding, and pessimistic. It does no good to either the world or the church if forgiven war-makers do not learn how to become practical peacemakers. God is in the business of making disciples through the grace of the gospel. The Spirit will produce His desires and His fruit, and biblical counseling is a servant of such practical and sweet-tasting changes.

The third reason people ask about the place of grace in biblical counseling is that would-be biblical counselors sometimes fall short of being biblical. What biblical counselor is not aware of failures in pastoral wisdom when seeking to minister the counsel of God? The solution to this dilemma is short and succinct: biblical counselors need to become more biblical. They need to ask God to reveal their shortcomings; they need to repent of folly; they need to seek the God who gives wisdom without reproaching; and they need to humbly learn from more skilled and mature biblical counselors. Biblical counseling is the ministry of God's grace to individuals, just as biblical preaching is the ministry of God's grace to the multitudes. *(David Powlison)*

Why do biblical counselors refuse to use information from science and psychology?

First of all, biblical counselors are primarily concerned with the problem of sin and how people can change and grow (sanctification) for God's glory. Science (in general), as we now know it, does not concern itself with either the problem of sin or God, so there is no reason for biblical counselors to use science for the purpose of man's sanctification to the glory of God. The question of the use of psychology in counseling is a bit different. It must be said up front that psychology, as such, is not science per se. While psychologists would want people to assume that it is, psychology is the *study* of human behavior, not the *science* of human behavior. Human behavior cannot be scientifically studied, as though someone with a white coat could take a person's attitude and analyze it in a test tube. Even if, somehow, all of the issues of the human heart could be empirically quantified and verified, no psychologist or scientist could provide the proper interpretations or solutions of problems apart from the revealed Word of God and its direct application to the human heart.

It must be stated as clearly as possible that biblical counselors do not object to psychology or to psychologists as such. There are some in the general field of psychology who are performing important tasks, say, in the area of studying sleep patterns of individuals and what profit can be gained from such study. The objection biblical counselors have to psychologists (and even psychiatrists for that matter) is when they attempt to give nonbiblical (and in many cases, patently unbiblical) solutions to people's sin problems. As one of the leaders in the biblical counseling movement, Jay Adams has rightly observed, "When psychologists attempt to change men, although they have no warrant from God to do so, no standard by which to determine what are proper or deviant attitudes or behavior, no concept of what man *should* look like, and no power by which to achieve the inner change of heart and thought that are so necessary, I cannot help but be concerned"[4]

When it comes to true "soul work," only those ordained by God to do so can be used by God to change lives. The apparatus necessary is the Word of God shared through illumination by the Spirit of God and given by and administered through those called by God in the local church. Psychology or psychiatry, though it may purport to be under the aegis of the local church, if it is not under the functioned control of Holy Scripture, is not useful or helpful to the biblical counselor and could even be (and certainly is!) destructive to the counseling process.

We cannot assume that when psychologists make judgments regarding human behavior, they are doing so in a purely unbiased and scientific way if they go on to suggest solutions for change in that behavior apart from the control of God's Word. All proposed solutions to the problem of sin come down to our view of God and His Word. Any attempt to provide solutions apart from biblical exegesis, theology, and the application of the fruit of that study to the heart will result in faulty counseling, whether from psychologists or pastors.
(S. Lance Quinn)

Is it true that biblical counseling de-emphasizes graduate studies and overly emphasizes training in biblical discipleship?

In most professions today a graduate education is either required or highly recommended. If one were to pursue state licensure in any of the helping professions, such as psychology or marriage and family counseling, a graduate education would be required. Normally, this would require at least one year beyond the undergraduate degree, plus numerous hours of supervised internship. This is the normal approach for most Christian psychology programs.

But biblical counseling does not follow this conventional educational track, and because of that is perceived by some as less academically rigorous and, therefore, lacking in substantive content. The question must be asked, however, "What does one study in a Christian psychology curriculum?" If we looked in the catalogue of any Christian college in America, we would readily see that the courses taught at both the undergraduate and graduate levels primarily consist of theory and applied classes in psychology. Typically, students who pursue this curriculum complete a core of lower-division Bible courses along with courses in their major of counseling or psychology, which are taught largely by instructors who have a minimum academic background in biblical studies. But how can instructors who lack theological education properly integrate psychology and the Bible? And how can they possibly use the Bible as the infallible reference point for psychology?

Since biblical counselors believe the Bible is sufficient for dealing with all matters of faith and practice, students who desire to pursue a biblical counseling ministry are encouraged to continue their education at the graduate level in a graduate program that is theologically based and offers courses in biblical counseling ministry and technique. At the heart and soul of biblical counseling are the knowledge and application of God's Word. This must be the foundation of any biblical counseling education at both the undergraduate and graduate level.

All who are committed to the biblical counseling movement must strenuously pursue academic excellence in counselor training. This demands a high level of formal education, which should take place in colleges and seminaries that hold to a high view of Scripture. Faculty at these institutions should be highly skilled in understanding and applying theology, biblical content, and practical theology. Based on this foundation, practical courses in biblical counseling should be taught by faculty who have both biblical and theological skill coupled with practical experience in biblical counseling. The third part of this academic preparation should be an internship in a local church under the guidance of both faculty and pastors. We must produce men and women who, because of their understanding of Scripture and what it reveals about the human condition, are qualified by academic training and commitment to Christ and His Word to counsel others.
(John P. Stead, Ph.D.)

Does biblical counseling deny the existence of mental or emotional illness and the healing that is necessary in these areas?

The concept of mental illness is a theory based upon a medical model of illness. In the medical model an organic illness is the cause of various symptoms in the body. The body is sick because something from without has affected it. Thus, a person has the flu because of a flu virus. It is not that person's fault that he or she has the flu. That person cannot be held responsible for the inability to work since the illness is the result of something that affected the body.

This same logic is used in dealing with behavior that is difficult to explain.

When a person has bizarre behavior and no organic cause for the behavior is found by laboratory studies, nonbelievers have theorized that the person is mentally sick. Just as the body gets sick, they conclude the mind is sick. Since the mind is sick, the person cannot control the behavior and thus is not responsible for any actions. Any time a person functions in an abnormal (irresponsible) way, that person is considered mentally or emotionally ill, with a mind and emotions that are believed to be sick.

The difficulty with this theory is that it cannot be proved. There are tests that measure thinking, but these cannot prove that the mind is sick. Even though the mind uses the brain, the mind is not the brain. Tumors, severe injuries, strokes, etc. can damage part of the brain and may affect how the person thinks and acts, but these are not mental illnesses; they are organic illnesses that can be proved in the laboratory. They can cause the brain to be sick but not the mind. While parts of the brain that are damaged may not be available to the mind, the mind is not sick. There is brain damage, not mental illness. The concept of the mind being sick is a theory with no scientific proof.

Psychiatry uses disease labels to describe different groups of symptoms. When an organic illness is found, it is given a label that describes the problem in the body. For example, it may be found through a medical examination that a person with the diagnosis of depression has an underactive thyroid. In this case, the diagnosis is changed from depression to hypothyroidism. If mental illness had an organic basis the term *mental illness* would be substituted by the name of the physical disease in the body.

One argument for the existence of an organic basis for behavior problems is based on the improvement some people achieve through medications. Yet this logic is unscientific. Two concurrent events do not automatically mean one caused the other. For example, 100 percent of the people who ate carrots in 1825 are now dead. If we followed that argument's reasoning, we would conclude that carrots are a dangerous food—obviously an illogical conclusion. Yet it is also illogical to conclude that because medications improve a person's feelings, the person has an organic illness.

The biblical counselor is accused of denying reality. Yet, who is to say this is reality? Even though the majority of people in our society accept the theory of mental illness as a fact, that still does not make it a fact. Such reasoning is not scientific but philosophical. This is the same logic that says believers deny the existence of Santa Claus or the Easter Bunny. Many people believe they exist, so does that make them real? Since mental illness is a theory and not a fact, biblical counselors do not deny the existence of something that has been proven to exist by empirical data gained in the laboratory. There is no need to deny the existence of something that does not exist.

The behavior and thinking characterized as mental illness totally ignores what the Bible teaches. When people's problems are not handled biblically, the results are confused thinking and bad feelings. These add to the problems that must be handled. When people live by their feelings, their behavior is affected. Attempts are made to improve the feelings and through this to improve the behavior. But when these attempts fail (as they will), further problems are created; the thinking becomes more and more confused attempting to deal with the difficult situations. As this spiral continues, the person ends up with bizarre thinking and behavior. The problem is not the feelings or emotions but the thinking and actions. When the Bible is not used to deal with problems, thoughts, and feelings, the result will be confused thoughts and actions. This continues until the thinking and behavior are bizarre. The emotions do not need to be healed since they are not sick; they are the natural result of unbiblical thinking.

The question also implies that the failure to accept mental illness as a reality is cruel since this means that healing is not available. In reality, however, the opposite is true. Those who label the behavior as illness are cruel since they remove the hope and victory available through the application of biblical principles. When the medical model argues that the person is sick, can it guarantee that a cure is even possible? How is healing to be defined? What happens if it does not occur? Since, in reality, there is no mental illness, to offer healing is to encourage a fraudulent and futile hope. In essence this removes true hope and that is the *truly* cruel action.

Biblical counselors can offer something superior to healing. They can offer victory in the midst of difficult circumstances, rather than improved feelings or attempts to change the circumstances. This is biblical and far superior to a healing that cannot be defined or measured. Biblical counseling is loving because it produces the victory God has promised.
(Robert Smith, M.D.)

Why does biblical counseling hold to a dichotomous rather than a trichotomous view of mankind?
Dichotomy teaches that people are composed of two distinct elements, body and soul. The body represents everything material, while the soul represents everything immaterial. In this case, the terms *soul* and *spirit* are understood as viewing the immaterial aspect of human nature from different vantage points. That is, the numerical essence of *soul* and *spirit* is one.

Evidence for dichotomy can be found in Scripture's interchangeable usage of the terms *soul* (*nephesh* in the Old Testament and *psychē* in the New Testament) and *spirit* (*ruah* in the Old Testament and *pneuma* in the New Testament). For instance, compare Genesis 35:18 and 31:5, as well as John 12:27 and 13:21. Another line of argument is the importance of the *soul* as it is used in various contexts to represent the totality of the immaterial aspect of mankind. For example, see Mark 12:30; Luke 1:46; Hebrews 6:18–

19; and James 1:21. Finally, Scripture uses *body* and *soul* together as a representation for the whole person, such as in Matthew 10:28 and 16:26.

In evaluating dichotomy, the strongest defense is the argument from creation. Genesis 2:7 records that man became a living *soul*. The term is inclusive of everything that constitutes a living, breathing being. It would be more accurate then, to say that man *has* a *spirit,* but *is* a *soul.* Furthermore, the interchangeability of the terms argues for dichotomy. On the negative side are those passages (1 Thess. 5:23; Heb. 4:12) that seem to distinguish between *soul* and *spirit* as advocated by trichotomists.

Trichotomy teaches that humans are composed of three distinct elements: body, soul, and spirit. The *soul* includes the principle of animation and the faculties of human nature, such as mind, heart, and will. The *spirit,* on the other hand, is the spiritual capacity to relate to God. This is what is reborn in salvation.

Evidence for the position is found in some Scripture passages that point to a distinctive function for each, *soul* and *spirit,* such as Matthew 16:26 (what will a man give for his *soul,* not his *spirit*) and Romans 8:16 (the Holy Spirit testifies to our *spirit,* not our *soul*). Furthermore, the terms are distinguished from one another in 1 Thessalonians 5:23. More importantly, Hebrews 4:12 indicates that *soul* and *spirit* are capable of being divided by the Word of God and, therefore, should be understood as comprising different entities.

By way of evaluation, a trichotomy view at first glance appears to best explain how an individual can be physically alive and yet spiritually dead. Accordingly, many gospel presentations are built on a trichotomist view of mankind. But this apparent advantage is offset by the lack of biblical support for the position. Concerning 1 Thessalonians 5:23, it must be observed, first of all, that Paul was engaged in prayer. He was not delivering a discourse on the human constitution. Secondly, the "and" connecting *soul* and *spirit* could be understood as an epexegetical *kai* rather than a simple connective, so that the terms in question would represent different ways of referring to the same immaterial aspect of man. Third, the verb "be preserved" and the modifying adjective "entire" are both singular. Even though a singular verb can modify plural neuter subjects in Greek grammar, the Rule of Concord suggests that "when a collective subject is taken in mass, the verb is singular."[5] Finally, the word "whole" is *holoteleis* rather than *holomereis,* meaning that it has no reference to parts. Thus, the lexical, contextual, and grammatical indicators significantly undercut the trichotomist interpretation of the verse.

The case made for Hebrews 4:12 is equally problematic. The passage is not teaching division of soul *from* spirit, because the prepositions, *ek, apo,* and *kata,* are absent. Also, there is no verb to indicate a division *between* two things. The objects of the participle are a series of genitives, such as "dividing *of* soul and *of* spirit." In other words, what is being affirmed is the ability of the Word of God to divide the soul *from itself* and the spirit *from itself*. Further support for this understanding of the verse is found in the reference "of both joints and marrow." This does not mean a separation of the joints *from* the marrow, since they are unrelated. Rather, the division is of the bones in the joint from one another and the marrow of the bone from the surface of the bone. Consequently, Hebrews 4:12 cannot be used exegetically to defend trichotomy.

The dichotomist has a better way of relating *soul* and *spirit* to one another consistent with biblical interpretation. The *soul* animates the body and is the center of consciousness and personality, including the intellect, affections, and will. The *spirit* refers to the same immaterial faculties in relation to God. A spiritually dead person is one in whom the capacities of the soul are not rightly related to God. In regeneration, the Spirit reorients the faculties of the soul in a godward direction so that the soul is made spiritually alive.

(Ken L. Sarles)

Why are those involved in biblical counseling so critical and condemnatory of other believers who hold differing views?

It would be grossly unfair to characterize the entire biblical counseling movement as critical and condemnatory. Having read much of the literature of the movement, I have been impressed with the balanced, thoughtful, proactive, biblical reasoning employed by men such as Jay Adams, Richard Ganz, Wayne Mack, and others.

The error that the biblical counseling movement seeks to address, however, is extremely serious, dealing with the integrity and authority of the Scriptures. Much is at stake. Those who are committed to biblical counseling understand that to dilute Scripture with foolish worldly wisdom (see 1 Cor. 1:20; 3:19) is to forfeit the power and blessing of God in counseling ministries.

Is it inherently unkind or condemnatory to say someone else's view is errant? Not if one has biblical authority for saying so. In fact, to remain silent and allow error to go unexposed and uncorrected is an abdication of the elder's role (Titus 1:9). The apostle Paul publicly called Peter a hypocrite for compromising biblical principles (Gal. 2:11–15). Peter had been publicly hypocritical; it was right that he be rebuked publicly (see 1 Tim. 5:20).

To disagree with or critique someone's published views does not constitute a personal attack. If the church cannot tolerate polemic dialogue between opposing views, especially if Christian leaders cannot be held accountable for whether their teaching is biblical, then error will have free reign.

(John MacArthur)

What can biblical counseling offer non-Christians who come for counseling?

First, biblical counseling recognizes that believers and nonbelievers cannot be counseled in the same way. We cannot use Scriptures to counsel a nonbeliever who has not been bound to its authority. Indeed, counselees cannot and will not respond to truth if their blinded spiritual eyes are not opened by God. As Paul said, "But a natural man does not accept the things of the Spirit of God; for they are foolishness to him, and he cannot understand them, because they are spiritually appraised. But he who is spiritual appraises all things, yet he himself is appraised by no man" (1 Cor. 2:14–15). So, in order for people to change, they must have submitted their will to the will of God. The only change that can come to a nonbeliever is a superficial change that never changes the heart. And that is precisely what biblical counseling speaks to—changing the heart in order to respond to God.

Then what can biblical counseling offer to the unregenerate person? We can communicate the truth that no one can change to any significant degree without embracing Jesus Christ as Savior and Lord. That is where true change must begin. Biblical counseling can offer the gospel, the answer to the most profound human need. This is the goal and basis of any counseling with nonbelievers. If the person refuses to acknowledge a need for Christ's saving work, there is really no other way to help that person. *(S. Lance Quinn)*

What theological commitments are basic to the nouthetic method of biblical counseling?

The question can be answered in two parts: first, what theological commitments are involved, and second, what theological issues are not involved.

Generally speaking, the biblical counselor seeks to affirm the fundamental doctrines of the faith. Specifically, three doctrinal commitments are foundational to biblical counseling. The first commitment is to the authority and sufficiency of Scripture. This truth, more than any other, distinguishes biblical counseling from all other counseling approaches. The Word of God, used by the Spirit of God, is sufficient to solve all the spiritual, psychological, and relational problems of the child of God (2 Tim. 3:16–17). No other branch of knowledge is to be integrated with the Bible; it stands alone and speaks with absolute and final authority.

The second commitment is to the person and will of God, who is both the author and the subject of Scripture. Every counseling problem can ultimately be traced to wrong thinking about the character and will of God (Is. 55:8–9). Therefore, all heartaches, tragedies, trials, and sufferings are to be placed in proper relationship to His glorious, majestic person. Since He alone is God, and there is no one else besides Him, difficulties of whatever sort must be related to His sovereign plan (Rom. 8:28–30).

The third commitment involves the doctrine of sin, a distinctive of biblical counseling. Only the nouthetic method gives due regard to the radically defective nature of mankind. The most fundamental dilemma is not that people are in pain, or that they lack self-esteem, or that they come from a dysfunctional family; rather, the root problem is that they are fallen (Gen. 3) and are rebellious against God (Rom. 5:10). They worship and serve the creature instead of the Creator (Rom. 1:25).

Though the nouthetic approach is nonintegrationist, that does not eliminate all theological or denominational diversity among those who use the approach. For instance, there are no ecclesiological or eschatological implications in biblical counseling. A biblical counselor could be dispensational, covenantal, or neither. The counselor could be an Episcopalian, Presbyterian, Baptist, or Congregationalist regarding form of church government and could be premillennial, postmillennial, or amillennial concerning the prophetic future. Biblical counseling is nonsectarian and interdenominational. It is not tied to any one individual, church, or organization. Aside from the theological principles that are foundational to nouthetic practice, this method of counseling does not align one with any particular theological camp. As a result, wherever the fundamentals of the faith are affirmed, biblical counseling can be utilized regardless of the church structure or eschatological position.

(Ken L. Sarles)

How can biblical counselors classify drug and alcohol addictions simply as sin when medical science has proven they are diseases?

The idea that addictions are diseases has become so pervasive it seems foolish to speak against it. However, the idea that medical science has proven addictions to be actual organic diseases is entirely without foundation. The medical and scientific communities remain greatly divided over the issue of the disease versus the nondisease models.[6] The California Supreme Court, in its famous Sundance Case (*Sundance versus The City of Los Angeles,* 43 Cal 3rd 1101), sided with the disease model and in so doing legally removed personal responsibility for drunkenness and set in motion governmental and private treatment programs. In fact, what Dr. William Playfair has called the "Recovery Industry" has been so effective in spreading the idea that addiction is a medical disease that a 1990 survey showed 87 percent of Americans holding this view.

On the other hand, the Bible declares that drunkenness—the nonmedical, nonprescribed introduction of chemicals into the body for the purpose of gaining pleasure or altering perceptions of reality in order to cope with or escape from the trials and struggles of life—is sin (Gal. 5:17–21; Eph.

5:18; 1 Pet. 4:3–5). These chemicals are alcohol or drugs of various types. The ingestion of these substances is a personal choice completely within the control of the individual. To postulate otherwise is to suggest a genetic predisposition to addiction or to suggest that as the substance-abuse continues a person gradually loses the ability to choose not to continue in this pattern of life.

The genetic answer is currently the most popular idea, even in Christian circles. In this model a person is born an alcoholic or addict in the same manner as a person might be born with brown or blue eyes. The thing that triggers the pattern of alcoholism or drug addiction is the first drink or first pill. These individuals have no options, they are victims of their genetic makeup. This concept, besides being unbiblical, is also not even agreed upon in the medical community.[7] The other model, which says that a person gradually loses the ability to refrain from abusing these substances, is simply a modification of the disease model, and again, it has no unity of opinion among medical professionals.

When a person is brought under the control of a substance, breaking that bondage is not easy. That is why Paul warns so strongly about being mastered by anything apart from the Holy Spirit (1 Cor. 6:12). The only effective treatment with substance abuse is to recognize that it is sinful behavior, repent of it, and cease doing it. This may not be pleasant or easy. It is well known that the physical withdrawal symptoms of longstanding habits are often uncomfortable. Some extreme cases, such as in the case of heroin addiction, may even require medical supervision. However, the biblical way to deal with these sins is clear: repent and cease the sinful activity. The problem of substance abuse and addiction is not, popular opinion notwithstanding, an undefined disease, genetics, environment, or any other exterior force; it is the willful and sinful choice of a fallen individual. *(Dennis M. Swanson)*

Is it true that the foundation of biblical counseling is rooted in legalism?

Legalism is a term that is frequently tossed around without much thought to its meaning. Essentially, legalism means to attain spirituality by means of what one does or does not do. In legalism someone establishes an external standard of spirituality and then judges everyone by that standard. Since the individual has established the standard, normally that person always achieves it. The apostle Paul denounced this activity in 2 Corinthians 10:12 where he railed against those "who measure themselves by themselves and compare themselves with themselves."

Biblical counseling has been caricatured by its critics as being legalistic, and it must be granted that occasionally, on the part of some, that charge has been true. But biblical counseling is not rooted in legalism. It is narrow in its accepted source of authority—God's revealed truth in His Word—and there is no tolerance for the integration of secular psychological concepts or practices in the area of counseling. But biblical counselors do not set themselves up as the standard for life and godliness. Rather, they point people to the Scriptures so that they may see God more clearly and realize that He has provided for them "every spiritual blessing in the heavenly places in Christ" (Eph. 1:3). The biblical counselor is like Paul, who admitted, "Brethren, I do not regard myself as having laid hold of it yet; but one thing I do: forgetting what lies behind and reaching forward to what lies ahead, I press on toward the goal . . ." (Phil. 3:13). The biblical counselor also points the counselee in the direction that Paul took when he said, "I can do all things through Him who strengthens me" (4:13).

To call biblical counseling legalistic is to deny the truth. Biblical counseling seeks to honor God in all things, to come alongside brothers and sisters in Christ with admonition, counsel, and rebuke when necessary, to demonstrate to non-Christians that their problems are pale compared to their need for salvation in Christ, and to declare to all the omniscient, omnipotent, and omnipresent God who alone is able to save and then empower to serve Him in this world.
(Dennis M. Swanson)

Do you ever refer people to psychologists or psychiatrists for help?
I never make such referrals for counseling unless the person bearing the title is committed to biblical counseling—as such, the professional title is incidental. Many biblical counselors happen to have degrees in psychology, psychiatry, neurology, general medicine, nursing, education, or social work. They studied secular counseling theories and methods that they have rejected in favor of biblical theory and practice.

Would I ever refer to a psychiatrist or psychologist for other reasons? A psychiatrist's medical training could help in determining whether neurological or other organic problems contribute to a person's problems in living, and a psychologist might help by intelligence testing. But, unfortunately, psychiatrists and psychologists too often adopt the role of a psychotherapist. They trespass into the domain of the Spirit, the Word, and ministry because they counsel people in unbiblical ways. A letter from a leading Christian organization contained the following statement:

> Psychologists do far more than engage in the practice of psychotherapy. To whom would you take a six-year-old boy to determine whether he were emotionally and physically ready to enter the first grade? . . . To whom would you turn if your wife became schizophrenic and ran screaming down the street? Would your pastor be able to deal with that situation? What if you wished to make a career change in mid-life, and wanted an objective evaluation of your strengths and inter-

ests? Whom could you ask to help you? To whom would you go to seek help with an adolescent who was extremely rebellious and resentful of his father? In each of these instances, and in a hundred others, you would look for a psychologist whose first love and highest commitment is to Jesus Christ and to the Word of God. And how silly to say, "There is no such thing."[8]

Let me interact with this statement sentence by sentence.

"Psychologists do far more than engage in the practice of psychotherapy." Indeed they do. Of course, psychotherapy is the money-making staple for most Christian psychologists. But such counseling practice is legitimated by a great deal of popular writing and speaking. In fact, psychologists' biggest influence in the Christian church at this time is not through psychotherapy, but through scores of best-selling books, conferences, video tapes, and radio shows. The statement stresses the service roles that psychologists have assumed. But (at least in this quote) it does not mention their biggest role: teachers about human nature and about problems and solutions. In an ominous development for the church, psychologists have gained three kinds of authority: (1) the right to interpret human beings and their problems; (2) the right to work with people experiencing problems in living; and (3) the right to endeavor to solve people's problems.

The dilemma is this: Christian psychologists' interpretations of people are systematically twisted by error. What do they teach? Diverse as they are in the details, popular Christian psychologists are united in teaching that mankind's fundamental problem stems from some lack, emptiness, unmet need, woundedness, or trauma (for example, "low self-esteem," "deep yearnings for relationship," "love hunger," or "search for significance"). In contrast, the Bible teaches that our fundamental problem stems from the active desires, thoughts, and intentions of the heart. Are we basically sinful, or do we simply react sinfully to the failings of primary care givers to meet our needs?

The excerpt cited appeals to the *de facto* institutionalization of psychology within contemporary secular and Christian culture, as if this establishes psychologists' legitimacy. The authority is made to appear self-evident: because people go to psychologists, psychologists are needed. However, each of the examples cited above proves dubious upon inspection.

"To whom would you take a six-year-old boy to determine whether he were emotionally and physically ready to enter the first grade?" Take him to a medical doctor for the physical questions. Take him to the principal and kindergarten and first-grade teachers for the other questions. They have dealt with hundreds of kids over the years. Other parents are also a resource. Experienced people can give you good advice to weigh into *your* determination of your child's readiness.

"To whom would you turn if you wife became schizophrenic and ran screaming down the street? Would your pastor be able to deal with that situation?" If your wife's behavior and thinking became bizarre, between a medical doctor, the police, and your pastor (or otherwise pastoral counselor) you should be able to do what can be done humanly. Psychologists' success with so-called schizophrenics is not noteworthy.

"What if you wished to make a career change in mid-life and wanted an objective evaluation of your strengths and interests? Whom could you ask to help you?" A career counselor could provide interest and aptitude testing, and a knowledge of the job market. Any pastoral counselor worthy of the name could help you think through your motives for considering a change, as well as help you with other aspects of the decision-making process. People who know you well and people in your current and contemplated careers could also offer practical advice.

"To whom would you go to seek help with an adolescent who was extremely rebellious and resentful of his father?" This is bread-and-butter biblical counseling. Bring both the adolescent and the parents into counseling. Find out why the young person is resentful and rebellious, and whether this is due to provocation from the father. Help them both to make necessary changes.

"In each of these instances, and in a hundred others, you should look for a psychologist whose first love and highest commitment is to Jesus Christ and to the Word of God. And how silly to say, 'There is no such thing.'" I honestly cannot think of any instances, except perhaps intelligence testing from a school psychologist, where the title *psychologist* would be significant. Biblically wise people from many walks of life might prove helpful in these instances. My biggest problem with the "psychologists whose first love and highest commitment is to Jesus Christ and to the Word of God" is that most of the ones I have met and read deviate markedly from that professed commitment in both their theory and practice. Verbal commitment to the Word of God coexists with deviant teachings from enemies of that Word.

Christians who are psychologists almost have to deviate in order to define themselves as legitimate professionals with some unique expertise. After all, the territory they are claiming is not theirs by some natural right. It is the territory of parents, pastors, teachers, doctors, friends, and a host of practical advisors who make no pretense to being psychologists. It is the territory of life's problems. And wisdom in that territory lies open on the pages of Scripture. Though hard won through experience in applying truth to life, such wisdom is available to all who seek it.

(David Powlison)

Appendix

Personal Data Inventory Form[1]

GENERAL INFORMATION:

Name _____ Phone _____

Address _____

Occupation _____ Business Phone _____

Sex _____ Height _____

Birth Date _____ Age _____

Marital Status: Single _____ Going Steady _____ Married _____

Separated _____ Divorced _____ Widowed _____

Education (last year completed): _____ (grade)

Other training (list type and years completed) _____

Referred here by _____

Address _____

HEALTH INFORMATION:

Rate your health (check): Very Good _____ Good _____ Average _____

Declining _____ Other _____

Your approximate weight (lbs.) _____

Weight changes recently: Lost _____ Gained _____

List all important present or past illnesses or injuries or handicaps:

_____

_____

Date of last medical examination _____ Reports _____

Your Physician_____ Address _____

_____

Are you presently taking any medication? Yes _____ No _____

What? _____

Have you used drugs for other than medical purposes? Yes _____ No _____

What? _____

Have you ever had a severe emotional upset? Yes _____   No _____

What? _____

Have you ever been arrested? Yes _____   No _____

Are you willing to sign a release of information form so that your counselor may write for social, psychiatric, or medical reports? Yes _____   No _____

Have you recently suffered the loss of someone who was close to you?
Yes _____   No _____

Explain _____

Have you recently suffered loss from serious social, business, or other reversals? Yes _____   No _____

Explain _____

RELIGIOUS INFORMATION

Denominational preference _____   Member _____

Church attendance per month (circle):   1   2   3   4   5   6   7   8   9   10+

Church attended in childhood? _____

Baptized? Yes _____   No _____

Religious background of spouse (if married) _____

Do you consider yourself a religious person? Yes _____   No _____
                                                    Uncertain _____

Do you believe in God? Yes _____   No _____   Uncertain _____

Do you pray to God? Never _____   Occasionally _____   Often _____

Are you saved? Yes _____   No _____   Not sure what you mean _____

How much do you read the Bible? Never _____   Occasionally _____
                                          Often _____

Do you have regular family devotions? Yes _____   No _____

Explain recent changes in your life, if any. _____

_____

PERSONALITY INFORMATION

Have you ever had any psychotherapy or counseling before? Yes _____

No _____   If yes, list counselor or therapist and dates. _____

_____

What was the outcome? _____

Check any of the following words which best describe you now:

active _____   ambitious _____   self-confident _____   persistent _____

nervous _____   hardworking _____   impatient _____   impulsive _____

moody _____   often-blue _____   excitable _____   imaginative _____

calm _____   serious _____   easy-going _____   shy _____

good-natured _____   introvert _____   extrovert _____   likable _____

leader _____   quiet _____   hard-boiled _____   submissive _____

lonely _____   self-conscious _____   sensitive _____   other _____

Have you ever felt people were watching you? Yes _____   No _____

Do people's faces ever seem disoriented? Yes _____   No _____

Do you ever have difficulty distinguishing faces? Yes _____   No _____

Do colors ever seem too bright? _____   Too dull? _____

Are you sometimes unable to judge distance? Yes _____   No _____

Have you ever had hallucinations? Yes _____   No _____

Are you afraid of being in a car? Yes _____   No _____

Is your hearing exceptionally good? Yes _____   No _____

Do you have problems sleeping? Yes _____   No _____

MARRIAGE AND FAMILY INFORMATION

Name of spouse _____   Phone _____

Address _____

Occupation _____   Business phone _____

Your spouse's age _____   Education (in years) _____

Religion _____

Is spouse willing to come for counseling? Yes _____   No _____

Uncertain _____

Have you ever been separated? Yes _____   No _____   When? _____

Date of marriage _____

Your ages when married Husband _____   Wife _____

How long did you know your spouse before marriage? _____

Length of steady dating with spouse _____

Length of engagement _____

Give brief information about any previous marriages. _____

_____

_____

Information about children:

PM*	Name	Age	Sex	Living Y or N	Education in years	Marital status

*Check this column if child is by previous marriage (PM).

If you were reared by anyone other than your own parents, briefly explain:

_____

_____

How many older brothers ____ sisters____ do you have?

How many younger brothers ____ sisters____ do you have?

BRIEFLY ANSWER THE FOLLOWING QUESTIONS:

1. What is your problem?
2. What have you done about it?
3. What can we do? (What are your expectations in coming here?)
4. As you see yourself, what kind of person are you? Describe yourself.
5. What, if anything, do you fear?
6. Is there any other information we should know?

Endnotes

Preface

1. John F. MacArthur et al., *Think Biblically!* (Wheaton: Crossway, 2003).

Introduction

1. Paul Gray, "The Assault on Freud," *Time* 29 November 1993: 47.
2. Cited in Frank B. Minirth, *Christian Psychiatry* (Old Tappan, NJ: Revell, 1977), 27.
3. Sigmund Freud, *New Introductory Lectures on Psychoanalysis,* lecture 35 (New York: Norton, 1977).
4. Vergilius Ferm, *A Dictionary of Pastoral Psychology* (New York: Philosophical Library, 1955), 208 (emphasis added).

Chapter One—Rediscovering Biblical Counseling

1. Much of this chapter has been adapted and expanded from John MacArthur, *Our Sufficiency in Christ* (Dallas: Word, 1991), 55–72.
2. See Martin and Deidre Bobgan, *PsychoHeresy* (Santa Barbara: EastGate, 1987), 53–54. The Bobgans list eight evidences of the "psychologizing of the church."
3. Jay Adams, *Competent to Counsel* (Grand Rapids: Baker, 1970), 17–18. Adams's extraordinarily accurate analysis of the state of counseling in evangelicalism is now more than a quarter of a century old but is more apropos than ever. He has given the Church an indispensable corrective to several trends that are eating away at the Church's spiritual vitality. Christian leaders would do well to heed his still-timely admonition.
4. Jay Adams, *More Than Redemption* (Phillipsburg, NJ: Presbyterian and Reformed, 1979), x–xi.
5. Sigmund Koch, "Psychology Cannot Be a Coherent Science," *Psychology Today* (September, 1969): 66.
6. D. Martyn Lloyd-Jones, *Healing and Medicine* (Eastbourne: Kingsway, 1987), 144–45.

7. Bobgan, *PsychoHeresy,* 5–6.

8. See the comments of a psychological counselor cited in Bobgan, *PsychoHeresy,* 5–6: "At the present time there is no acceptable Christian psychology that is markedly different from non-Christian psychology. It is difficult to imply that we function in a manner that is fundamentally distinct from our non-Christian colleagues."

9. Larry Crabb, *Understanding People* (Grand Rapids: Zondervan, 1987), 54–58.

10. Crabb, *Understanding People,* 129.

11. Ibid., 211.

12. Quoted in Bobgan, *PsychoHeresy,* 23.

13. See Gary R. Collins, *Christian Counseling: A Comprehensive Guide* (Dallas: Word, 1980), 19.

14. Arthur Janov, *The Primal Scream* (New York: Dell, 1970).

15. Daniel Casriel, *A Scream Away from Happiness* (New York: Grosset and Dunlap, 1972).

16. Leo Steiner, "Are Psychoanalysis and Religious Counseling Compatible?" A paper read to the Society for the Scientific Study of Religion, Harvard, November 1958. Cited in Adams, *Competent to Counsel,* 18–19.

17. "Psychiatry on the Couch," *Time* 2 (April 1979): 74.

18. Ibid., 79.

19. Ibid.

20. Ibid., 82.

21. Ann Japenga, "Great Minds on the Mind Assemble for Conference," *The Los Angeles Times* (18 December 1985).

22. Ibid., 17.

23. "A Therapist in Every Corner," *Time* 23 (December 1985): 59.

24. Ibid.

25. Japenga, "Great Minds."

26. "Therapist," 59.

27. Japenga, "Great Minds."

28. Adams responded skillfully to this kind of thinking, citing O. Hobart Mowrer's *The Crisis in Psychiatry and Religion* in Adams, *Competent to Counsel,* xvi–xvii.

29. Nicole Brodeur, "Center Aids Christian Sex Addicts," *Orange County Register* (13 February 1989).

30. Ibid.

31. Ibid.

Chapter Two—Biblical Counseling in Recent Times

1. For a useful introduction to this heritage, see Timothy Keller, "Puritan Resources for Biblical Counseling," *The Journal of Pastoral Practice* 9, no. 3 (1988): 11–44, and chapter 2 of this book.

2. Jay E. Adams, *The Christian Counselor's Manual* (Phillipsburg, N.J: Presbyterian and Reformed, 1973), 130. The first volume of Ichabod Spencer's *A Pastor's Sketches* was published in 1850, the second in 1853. *Sketch* was Spencer's word for a case study. For a more detailed historian's look at Spencer, refer to chapter 4 in E. Brooks Holifield, *A History of Pastoral Care in America: From Salvation to Self-Realization* (Nashville: Abingdon, 1983).

3. Readers interested in the history of the eclipse of the pastorate by the mental health professions can find a provocative analysis by Andrew Abbott, *The System of Professions: An Essay on the Division of Expert Labor,* (Chicago: University of Chicago Press, 1988). Read chapter 10, "The Construction of the Personal Problems Jurisdiction," 280–314, especially 294–314. Abbott wrote of how pastors had the inside track to address people's personal problems in the late nineteenth century. "But clergy analysis remained primitive. The gradual recognition of personal problems as legitimate categories of professional work did not bring a serious clergy effort to conceptualize them. The clergy's failure to provide any academic foundation for their practice with personal problems ultimately proved their undoing" (286). The newborn mental health professions seized the field. Abbott went on to speak of the subsequent "drift of pastoral counseling towards secular psychotherapy" and "the clergy's willful desertion of its traditional work" (310, 313).

4. For example, compare R. A. Torrey's turn-of-the-century *Personal Work: A Book of Effective Methods* (New York: Fleming H. Revell, n.d.) with the earlier writers cited above. Though it has some redeeming qualities, Torrey's book is impoverished in its understanding of people, of Scripture, of pastoral ministry, and of the change process.

5. Jonathan Edwards' method (and subject matter) in *A Treatise on Religious Affections* was taken over by William James in *The Varieties of Religious Experience* (n.p., 1902), one of the foundational monographs in modern psychology.

6. Philip Rieff, *The Triumph of the Therapeutic: Uses of Faith After Freud* (Chicago: University of Chicago Press, 1987), 24.

7. Sociologist and apologist Os Guinness turned Rieff's insight into a multileveled call to repentance. See "America's Last Men and Their Magnificent Talking Cure," in *No God But God,* ed. Os Guinness and John Seel (Chicago: Moody, 1992), 111–132.

8. "The words 'secular pastoral worker' might well serve as a general formula for describing the function which the analyst, whether he is a doctor or a layman, has to perform in his relation to the public." Sigmund Freud, "The Question of Lay Analysis, Postscript," in *The Freud Reader,* ed. Peter Gay (New York: W. W. Norton, 1989), 682.

9. Carl Jung, *Modern Man in Search of a Soul* (New York: Harcourt Brace Jovanovich, 1933), 241. The last two chapters of this book, "The Modern Spiritual Problem" and "Psychotherapists or Clergy," are telling. Jung viewed "neurosis" as a crisis in spiritual meaning, not a medical issue. Psychotherapy sought to give meaning to life. Jung exhorted therapists: what will they do when they see that the patient's problems arise "from his having no love, but only sexuality; no faith, because he is afraid to grope in the dark; no hope, because he is disillusioned by the world and by life; and no understanding, because he has failed to read the meaning of his own existence?" (225f). The psychotherapist needed to embrace the task of providing love, faith, hope, and understanding to a secular people.

10. B. F. Skinner, *Walden Two* (New York: MacMillan, 1948), 199.

11. Charles Rosenberg's seminal article in the history of psychiatry, "The Crisis in Psychiatric Legitimacy," deserves wider readership (in *American Psychiatry Past, Present, and Future,* ed. George Kriegman et al. [Charlottesville: University Press of Virginia, 1975], 135–148; reprinted in Charles Rosenberg, *Explaining Epidemics and Other Studies in the History of Medicine* [New York: Cambridge University Press, 1992]). Rosenberg noted, first, that psychiatry has been assigned and has assumed a huge social role—the varied ills of the human soul—but it has little real knowledge or efficacy to offer. Second, psychiatry depends on its medical identity for legitimacy, yet it is unable to provide either understanding or relief consistent with its pretensions to be a truly medical specialty. Third, psychiatry's most clearly medical activity—caring for patients with chronic organic syndromes in hospitals—is low status; high status psychiatry is precisely where it becomes the most philosophical, pastoral, and quasi-theological. "Much of our century's most influential psychiatric writing has consisted of general statements about the human condition" (142). Rosenberg accepted psychiatry's legitimacy almost by default; by and large there is no other framework of meaning because older religious values "seem no longer compelling to most Americans" (147). But for those who still find the older religious values compelling, who believe in the God and Father of Jesus Christ, the alternative to psychiatry is delightful!

12. See Holifield, *A History of Pastoral Care: From Salvation to Self-Realization.* The book, as the subtitle reveals, is essentially the story of how a psychologized liberalism replaced orthodoxy. Holfield did not tip his own hand, but did make some provocative statements. For example, "When Harry Emerson Fosdick referred to the sermon as counseling on a large scale, he forgot that Protestant sermons, at their best, have interpreted an ancient text that resists reduction to the psychological" (356).

13. I have written at greater length elsewhere on the relationship between modern psychology and conservative Christianity. See David Powlison, "Integration or Inundation?" in *Power Religion,* ed. Michael Horton (Chicago: Moody, 1992), 191–218.
14. Betty Jane Adams, interview by the author, 4 December 1990.
15. Jay Adams wrote about this experience in *The Power of Error,* (Phillipsburg, NJ: Presbyterian and Reformed, 1978).
16. Jay E. Adams' notes from a talk given by the chaplain at Marlboro State Hospital (New Jersey) in the mid-1960s.
17. Jay E. Adams, interview by the author, 4 December 1990.
18. Jay E. Adams, interview.
19. From the Greek word *noutheteō,* literally "place in mind," which means reproof or admonishment or pointedly personal teaching. It is a word linked with bringing specific truth to bear on the details of an individual's life. It is associated with intense love: for example, Paul's "admonishing with tears" in Acts 20:31 and his "as my beloved sons I admonish you" in 1 Corinthians 4:14. It serves as a summary word for verbal edification: whether to one another ("competent to counsel one another," Rom. 15:14), or under pastoral authority (1 Thess. 5:12). It also summarizes the verbal aspects of a parent raising children (e.g., "bring them up in the admonition of the Lord," Eph. 6:4). *Noutheteō* "holds hands" with both teaching and worship in Colossians 3:16, reinforcing the sense of the word as involving a *personal* application of God's truth, expressed in humility and tenderness and submission to God. Adams has been criticized for not picking *parakaleō,* which is more frequently used in the New Testament and is also a summary word for verbal edification (e.g., Heb. 3:13; 10:25). But as Adams has noted, the choice of words is indifferent—they can cover the same semantic field. Both words involve God's truth applied to lives, both words communicate love and concern, and both words communicate an appropriate directness and toughness.
20. Jay E. Adams, *Ready to Restore* (Phillipsburg, NJ: Presbyterian and Reformed, 1981), 9–12.
21. Jay E. Adams, *Insight and Creativity in Christian Counseling: An Antidote to Rigid and Mechanical Approaches* (Grand Rapids: Zondervan, 1982).
22. Westminster Theological Seminary, P.O. Box 27009, Philadelphia, PA 19118.
23. Christian Counseling and Educational Foundation, 1803 East Willow Grove Avenue, Glenside, PA 19038.
24. National Association of Nouthetic Counselors, 3600 W. 96th Street, Indianapolis, IN 46268–2905.
25. Jay E. Adams, *Journal of Pastoral Practice* 1, no. 1 (1977): 1.

26. *The Journal of Biblical Counseling,* 1803 East Willow Grove Avenue, Glenside, PA 19038.
27. Biblical Counseling Foundation, P.O. Box 925, Rancho Mirage, CA 92270.
28. Faith Baptist Counseling Ministry, 5526 State Road 26 East, Lafayette, IN 47905.
29. The Master's College, 21726 Placerita Canyon Road, Santa Clarita, CA 91321. The Master's Seminary, 13248 Roscoe Blvd., Sun Valley, CA 91352.
30. See D. Powlison, "Crucial Issues in Contemporary Biblical Counseling," *Journal of Pastoral Practice* 9, no. 3 (1988): 53–78, for specific areas with a growing edge.

Chapter Three—Why Biblical Counseling and Not Psychology?

1. For a historical discussion of this jurisdictional dispute of who is qualified to give counsel, the psychiatrist or the pastor, see Andrew Abbott, *The System of Professions: An Essay on the Division of Expert Labor* (Chicago, IL: University of Chicago Press, 1988) and David A. Powlison, "Competent to Counsel? The History of a Conservative Protestant Anti-psychiatry Movement" Ph.D. diss., University of Pennsylvania, 1996.
2. See Psalm 1:1–2; 119:50, 92; 2 Timothy 3:15–17; 2 Peter 1:3, 19–21.
3. See Luke 2:35; Hebrews 4:12–13.
4. See Psalm 73:25–28; Romans 11:36; 1 Corinthians 10:31; 1 John 1:3–4.
5. German for a comprehensive worldview.
6. One universal axiom taught to pastoral students regardless of the psychological tradition of the seminary illustrates the jurisdictional encroachment of the therapeutic agenda: "Pastoral counseling is only for the most basic problems of life (e.g. interpersonal struggles, pre-marital counseling). The pastor should never assume the counseling of the weightier issues of "mental diseases" (e.g. manic depression, the suicidal, panic attacks, schizophrenia, sadomasochism, multiple personalities, attention deficient, etc.) for which only a trained psychotherapist is qualified." This reasoning is based upon the fundamental presupposition that the Word of God does not speak to the substance of these problems and referral needs to be made to a trained "professional" in the matters of the *psyche* (i.e. humanistic psychology).
7. Few realize Ladd was appointed the second president of the American Psychological Association before the more well-known William James.
8. Sigmund Koch, "Psychology Cannot be a Coherent Science," *Psychology Today:* (September 1969), 66.
9. The more common are the Minnesota Multiphasic Personality Inventory (MMPI/MMPI-2) and the Taylor-Johnson Temperament Analysis (T-JTA).

10. John F. MacArthur and Wayne A. Mack, *Introduction to Biblical Counseling* (Dallas, TX: Word, 1994), 7.
11. Occurs 101 times in the New Testament and over 900 in the Septuagint, most often translating the Hebrew *nepeš* (soul, breath), but occasionally *lêb* (heart, inner man, 25x), *hayyâh* (life, 5x), *rûah* (spirit, 2x), and *'îš* (man, 1x, Lev. 17:4).
12. Biblical usage of the term *logos* meant "word" or "law" while the Classical stressed the human discipline or study—*ology.* Also see an early distinction of *psychē* (unconscious soul) and *thymos* (conscious soul) in Homer, *Iliad,* 11, 334.
13. Matthew 25:15; Mark 5:30; Romans 1:16; 1 Corinthians 4:19–20; Philippians 3:10.
14. D. A. Carson, *Exegetical Fallacies* (Grand Rapids, MI: Baker, 1984), 32–33.
15. In practice, it is the Bible that ends up supplementing psychotherapeutic theory in Christian psychology, not vice versa.
16. Frank B. Minirth, *Christian Psychiatry* (Old Tappan, NJ: Fleming H. Revell, 1977), 64–65.
17. Jay E. Adams, *A Theology of Christian Counseling* (Grand Rapids, MI: Zondervan, 1979), 116.
18. Proverbs 30:5–6; see Deuteronomy 4:2; 12:32; Matthew 5:18–20; Revelation 22:18–19.
19. Robert C. Roberts, "A Christian Psychology View," *Psychology & Christianity: Four Views* ed. Eric L. Johnson and Stanton L. Jones (Downers Grove, IL: IVP, 2000), 159.
20. Ibid.
21. Ibid, 110. The Bible does not claim to be a textbook on biology, chemistry, physics, astronomy or business administration; but when it speaks in these areas, it speaks infallibly and authoritatively. However, the Bible does claim to be the counsel of God for man.
22. This is Dr. Dave Powlison's term (instructor at the Christian Counseling and Education Foundation and professor at Westminster Theological Seminary in Philadelphia).
23. Robert S. Feldman, *Essentials of Understanding Psychology,* 4th ed. (Boston, MA: McGraw Hill, 2000), 4.
24. Karl Popper, "Science Theory and Falsifiability," *Perspectives in Philosophy,* Robert N. Beck, ed. (New York, NY: Holt, Richart, Winston, 1975), 343.
25. Scott O. Lilienfeld, "The Scientific Review of Mental Health Practice: Our Raison d' Être," *The Scientific Review of Mental Health Practice* (Spring-Summer 2002): 5.
26. See psychologist Harry Harlow's classic study; H. F. Harlow and R. R. Zimmerman, "Affectional Responses in the Infant Monkey," *Science* (1959): 130, 421–32.

27. Edward T. Welch, *Blame it on the Brain?* (Phillipsburg, NJ: P&R, 1998), 91.

28. David Powilson, "Critiquing Modern Integrationists," *The Journal of Biblical Counseling,* XI (Spring 1993): 32.

29. Ibid., 33.

30. 1 Samuel 18:1; Matthew 22:37–40; Mark 12:30–31; Ephesians 5:28–29; see also Jay E. Adams, *The Biblical View of Self-Esteem, Self-Love, Self-Image* (Eugene, OR: Harvest House, 1986) and Paul Brownback, *The Danger of Self Love: Re-examining a Popular Myth* (Chicago, IL: Moody Press, 1982).

31. Sanguine, Phlegmatic, Melancholic, and Choleric have Latin roots that refer to the four bodily humors respectively—blood, phlegm, black bile, and yellow bile. It was believed by the ancient Greeks that an abundance of any of these humors in body determined personality characteristics.

32. National Association of Nouthetic Counselors, 3600 W. 96th St., Indianapolis, IN 46268–2905, www.NANC.org.

33. Lawrence J. Crabb Jr., *Effective Biblical Counseling,* (Grand Rapids, MI: Zondervan, 1977), 36–37.

34. A phrase coined by Jay Adams and heard personally by this author.

35. John H. Coe, "Why Biblical Counseling is Unbiblical?," CAPS 1991 position paper presentation, 7, www-students.biola.edu~jay/bcresponse. html.

36. Ronald Barclay Allen, *Praise! A Matter of Life and Breath* (Nashville, TN: Thomas Nelson, 1980), 140.

37. Ernst Jenni, Claus Westermann, *Theological Lexicon of the Old Testament* Vol. 3, Mark E. Biddle, trans. (Peabody, MA: Hendrickson Publishers, Inc., 1997), 1312–1317.

38. An excellent treatise for instructing counselees enduring unjust suffering is 1 Peter 2:13—4:19.

39. John Calvin, *Institutes of the Christian Religion,* vol. 1, ed. John T. McNeill, trans. Ford Lewis Battles, (Philadelphia, PA: The Westminster Press, rpt. 1960), 72.

Chapter Four—The Godward Focus of Biblical Counseling

1. John N. Oswalt, "*Chabod,*" in *Theological Wordbook of the Old Testament,* ed. R. L. Harris, G. L. Archer, Jr., B. K. Waltke (Chicago: Moody, 1980), 1:426. With all of its derivatives the term occurs 376 times in the Old Testament. Its most concrete usage is as the title for the theophanic glory-cloud that appeared as Israel departed Egypt (Ex. 13:22) and that indwelt the tabernacle (Ex. 40:34); *chabod* is used at least 45 times in the Old Testament of this visible manifestation of God.

2. Gerhard von Rad, *"Chabod* in the Old Testament," in *Theological Dictionary of the New Testament,* ed. G. Kittel (Grand Rapids: Eerdmans, 1964), 2:235.

3. Two times in the Old Testament it is used of literal weightiness: Eli the priest is described as "heavy" in 1 Samuel 4:18, and the hair of Absalom is portrayed as "heavy on him" in 2 Samuel 14:26. Again, the term may be used of "slowness or dullness" as in a heavy (or hardened) heart (Ex. 7:14; 8:15, 18; 9:7); or of ears (Is. 6:10), a tongue (Ex. 4:10), or eyes (Gen. 48:10) that are dull and insensitive. Again, it may signify severity, as when used of work (Ex. 5:9), slavery (1 Kin. 12:10), warfare (Judg. 20:34), or a yoke (2 Chr. 10:4, 11).

4. Oswalt, "Chabod," 426.

5. Note, such material wealth is referred to by the noun *chabod,* not because the term has a primary sense of riches, but because the riches were conceived of as giving the individual some distinctive honor. Thus the basic concept is that of weightiness, or that which distinguishes an individual, setting him or her apart from others.

6. Notice that the word "glory" in these verses is *chabod.*

7. Payne said of the glory-cloud, "[A] man of *kavodh* carries weight in the eyes of his fellows (Gen. 45:13). God's *Kavodh* is, therefore, the visible extension of His divine perfection." J. B. Payne, *The Theology of the Older Testament* (Grand Rapids: Zondervan, 1962), 46. The term is transliterated in the Old Testament name Ichabod, which was given to a child born just after his mother learned that the ark of the covenant had been captured by the Philistines and that the glory-cloud had departed from Israel (1 Sam. 4:21); the term *ichabod* involves a rare usage of the Hebrew particle, but is best understood as meaning "no glory."

8. These two aspects of the concept of God's glory are sometimes distinguished as *intrinsic* glory (that which is inherent to God) and *ascribed* glory (the conscious acknowledgement of God's glory by rational creatures). See, for instance, John F. MacArthur, Jr., *The Ultimate Priority* (Chicago: Moody, 1983), 128–30.

9. Notice that the word translated "honored" in both verses 17 and 18 by the NASB is the verb form of *chabod* in the Hebrew.

10. Notice that it was precisely this captivity in Babylon and the subsequent deliverance effected through the Persian, Cyrus, that was in view when YHWH declared in Isaiah 48:11, "For my own sake . . . I will act . . . and My glory I will not give to another."

11. There is much discussion today as to whether the fall of Lucifer is referenced in Isaiah 14 (and/or in Ezekiel 28). I am persuaded that in those passages conscious reference is made to that primordial insurrection, but the point being made in the text here will stand even if the

characterization of Isaiah 14 is in context restricted only to the wickedness of the king of Babylon.

12. A. H. Strong, *Systematic Theology* (Valley Forge, PA.: Judson, 1907), 572.
This occurs in a section in which Strong was arguing "the essential principle of sin to be selfishness." He insisted that selfishness is "not simply
the exaggerated self-love which constitutes the antithesis of benevolence, but that choice of self as the supreme end which constitutes the
antithesis of supreme love to God" (567). Although there are various
suggestions as to what constitutes the essence of sin in Scripture (unbelief, hardness of heart, pride, sensuality, fear, self-pity, jealousy, greed,
etc.), Strong's point is well taken: given that love of God and man
together constitute the whole law (Matt. 22:37–39; Rom. 13:8–10; Gal.
5:14; James 2:8), it is reasonable to conclude that love of self, which
thus exalts self above God and above others, constitutes the fundamental violation of God's law (2 Thess. 2:3–4). For other biblical arguments
in defense of thus defining the essence of sin, see Strong, 572.

13. S. C. Burn, *The Prophet Jonah* (London: Houghter and Stoughton, 1880;
reprint, Minneapolis: Klock and Klock, 1981), 130. Compare Pusey's
representation of the verb as meaning "to diligently watch, pay deference to, court" in E. B. Pusey, *The Minor Prophets: A Commentary*
(Grand Rapids: Baker, 1950), 1:410.

14. The verb is *shamar,* "to keep, guard, observe, give heed." Austel stated
that the basic idea of the root is "to exercise great care over and that
this meaning "can be seen to underlie the various semantic modifica-
tions seen in the verb" in H. J. Austel, "Shamar," *Theological Wordbook
of the Old Testament* (Chicago: Moody, 1980), 2:939. Pusey emphasized
the fact that the verb means more than just to *do* vanities; it has to do
with "they who observe, guard vanities, or lies, they, into the affections
of whose hearts those vanities have entered; who not only do vanities,
but who guard them, as loving them, deeming that they have found a
treasure." Pusey, *Minor Prophets,* 1:410.

15. Pusey, *Minor Prophets,* 1:410. To understand something of the cruelty
and greed of Assyria is to begin to comprehend Jonah's anxiety to see
that country destroyed, but none of that reduces the guiltworthiness
of Jonah's rebellion and flight.

16. C. F. Keil, "The Twelve Minor Prophets," in *Biblical Commentary on
the Old Testament,* ed. C. F. Keil and F. Delitzsch (Grand Rapids:
Eerdmans, 1949), 1:403. There is some debate as to whether Jonah
was criticizing the idolatrous religion of the pagans who had cast him
overboard or his own wickedness in resisting YHWH. That the noun
translated "vanities" is sometimes used with reference to idols is employed as an argument in favor of the contention that Jonah's focus
is upon the pagan rituals of the sailors. But the spirit of his prayer

demonstrates that the prophet was speaking here of his own sin. Perhaps the reference to "lying vanities" included the admission that in resisting God he was treating his own desire for the destruction of Nineveh as an idol to be worshiped.

17. G. T. Coster, "Jonah," in *The Pulpit Commentary,* ed. H. D. M. Spence and J. S. Exell, 22 vols. (Grand Rapids: Eerdmans, 1958), 55.
18. J. R. Thomson, "Jonah," in *The Pulpit Commentary,* ed. H. D. M. Spence and J. S. Exell, 22 vols. (Grand Rapids: Eerdmans, 1958), 47.
19. Keil, "Minor Prophets," 403.
20. Compare the observation of Eliphaz that man "drinks iniquity like water" (Job 15:16); Solomon's observation, "Like a dog that returns to its vomit is a fool who repeats his folly" (Prov. 26:11, quoted by Peter in 2 Pet. 2:22); Jeremiah's rebuke of his contemporaries because their feet "loved to wander" (Jer. 14:10); Hosea's application of his own unhappy domestic experience, as he rebuked his countrymen because they "direct their desire toward their iniquity" (Hos. 4:8); Jesus' condemnation upon people because they "loved darkness rather than light, because their deeds were evil" (John 3:19); and Paul's statement that people will be deceived by the man of sin because they "did not receive the love of the truth" but took "pleasure in unrighteousness" (2 Thess. 2:10, 12). The univocal testimony of Scripture is that the root cause of sin is not confusion but rebellion, that people obey wicked impulses not because those desires seem morally noble or spiritually credible but because their hearts long to do evil (Rom. 1:18–25).
21. In every one of these passages the word translated "life" (NASB) is *psuche,* the Greek term most often translated "soul." The reference is not to the soul/spirit (i.e., the immaterial aspect of man) as opposed to the body (the material aspect); rather, Jesus was making reference to the "principle of life generally." F. J. A. Hort, *Expository and Exegetical Studies* (Minneapolis: Klock and Klock, 1980; Grand Rapids: Kregel Publications, 1987), 122.
22. Hort, *Expository and Exegetical Studies,*122.
23. J. Morison, *A Practical Commentary on the Gospel According to St. Matthew* (Boston: Bartlett, 1884; reprint, Minneapolis: Klock and Klock, 1981), 291.
24. J. C. Ryle, *Expository Thoughts on the Gospels: John* (Greenwood, SC: Attic Press, 1965), 2:333.
25. A. W. Tozer, *The Pursuit of God* (Camp Hill, PA: Christian Publications, 1982), 104.

Chapter Five—Counseling and the Sinfulness of Humanity

1. Adapted and abridged from *The Vanishing Conscience* (Dallas: Word, 1994).

2. Jerry Adler et al., "Hey I'm Terrific," *Newsweek* (17 February 1992): 50.
3. Charles Krauthammer, "Education: Doing Bad and Feeling Good," *Time* (5 February 1990): 70.
4. Cheryl Russell, "Predictions for the Baby Boom," *The Boomer Report* (15 September 1993): 4.
5. Adler et al., "Terrific," 50.
6. Ibid., "Terrific," 50.
7. Norman Vincent Peale, *The Power of Positive Thinking* (Englewood Cliffs, NJ: Prentice Hall, 1952).
8. Ibid., viii.
9. Ibid., ix.
10. Adler et al., "Terrific," 50.
11. D. Martyn Lloyd-Jones, *The Plight of Man and the Power of God* (Grand Rapids: Eerdmans, 1945), 87.
12. George F. Will, "A Trickle-Down Culture," *Newsweek* (13 December 1993): 84.
13. Dennis Prager, "The Belief that People Are Basically Good," *Ultimate Issues* (January–March 1990): 15.
14. Prager, "People Are Basically Good," 15.
15. J. C. Ryle, *Holiness* (1879; reprint, Durham, England: Evangelical Press, 1991), 9–10.

Chapter Six—The Work of the Spirit and Biblical Counseling

1. Wendy Kaminer, *I'm Dysfunctional, You're Dysfunctional* (Reading, MA: Addison-Wesley, 1992).
2. Ibid., 121.
3. Ibid., 124.
4. Kaminer, *I'm Dysfunctional, You're Dysfunctional,* 124–125.
5. John Murray, *Redemption—Accomplished and Applied* (Grand Rapids: Eerdmans, 1955), 161.

Chapter Seven—Spiritual Discipline and the Biblical Counselor

1. Jay Adams, *What to Do On Thursday* (Nutley, NJ: Presbyterian and Reformed, 1982), 31–49.
2. Jay Adams, *The War Within* (Eugene, OR: Harvest House, 1989), 87–88.
3. Jay Adams, *A Theology of Counseling* (Grand Rapids: Zondervan, 1979), 309–325.
4. Jerry Bridges, *Trusting God* (Colorado Springs: NavPress, 1989), 25–26.

Chapter Eight—Developing a Helping Relationship with Counselees

1. We could discuss at length the necessity of the counselor's involvement with Christ for only when he or she has a vital, intimate relationship

with the Lord can counseling be truly effective (see Matt. 7:3–5; Acts 4:13; 1 Cor. 11:1). But this chapter will primarily discuss the counselor's involvement with the counselee, an involvement intended to develop and maintain a facilitative relationship between the two. Ultimately and preeminently the purpose for that involvement is to enhance the counselee's involvement with Christ. This vertical dimension is what makes biblical counseling different from all other forms of counseling.

2. Adapted from Jay Adams, *The Christian Counselor's Casebook* (Grand Rapids: Zondervan, 1974), 186.

3. Unfortunately, the counselor who does this lends validity to the criticism that biblical counselors merely "throw out Bible verses" or "shove Scripture down people's throats." As we will see later in this chapter, that kind of "biblical" counseling is patently not biblical.

4. Clara's sin in the situation was of utmost importance and needed to be dealt with as the counseling continued. But by taking the approach he did, the counselor gave Clara the impression that he did not consider her husband's sin to be very serious, which immediately created a wall between them because of her preoccupation with her husband's hurtful actions.

5. Of course the counselor cannot *make* the counselee view him or her as a friend or ally. Some people we work with may be so predisposed against us that nothing we do will reverse this attitude. Our responsibility is simply to do whatever we can to be the kind of person that deserves their respect and trust.

6. See Matthew 14:14; Luke 10:33; 15:20.

7. Of course not every counselee will respond with the proper respect for us even if we do all we can to respect them. In some cases, we may deal with people who simply respect no one. But we still must exemplify a godly honor for them and trust that God will use our example to convict them of their own pride.

8. Adapted from Gerard Egan, *The Skilled Helper: Model Skills and Methods for Effective Helping* (Monterey: Brooks/Cole, 1986), 76–77.

9. Gerald Corey, *Theory and Practice of Counseling and Psychotherapy* (Monterey: Brooks/Cole, 1977), 179.

10. Jay Adams, *Handbook of Church Discipline* (Grand Rapids: Zondervan, 1986), 30–32. See also George Scipione, "The Limits of Confidentiality in Counseling," *Journal of Pastoral Practice* 7, no. 2.

11. Philip E. Hughes, *The Second Epistle to the Corinthians,* in *The New International Commentary on the New Testament,* ed. G. D. Fee (Grand Rapids: Eerdmans, 1962), 124.

12. This, of course, does not mean that we should tell our counselees everything about ourselves or volunteer everything we are thinking at any given time. Nevertheless, a willingness to share our thoughts and

experiences with them is a good indicator of the godliness of our attitudes toward them, toward ourselves, and toward God. Reluctance to be open and transparent, even when appropriate and helpful, may indicate pride and a fear of man.

13. Vincent D. Foley, *An Introduction to Family Therapy* (New York: Grune and Stratton, 1974), 84–85.

Chapter Nine—Instilling Hope in the Counselee

1. See sample of Personal Data Inventory form on page 265.

2. Two classic examples of this are people who open a Bible and read whatever verse their eyes first notice, or those who swing a finger over a page with their eyes closed and let it fall on the verse God wants them to read that day. People who do this often end up trying several times because they first happen upon an inappropriate verse such as Exodus 16:36: "Now an omer is a tenth of an ephah."

3. For a discussion of the contextual meaning of this verse, see John MacArthur, Jr. *Matthew 16—23* (Chicago: Moody, 1988); or William Hendriksen, *The Gospel of Matthew* (Grand Rapids: Baker, 1973).

4. Colin Brown, ed., *The New International Dictionary of New Testament Theology* (Grand Rapids: Zondervan, 1976), 240.

5. Paul's attitude is especially meaningful in light of the integral part he played in the foundation of the Church. It would have been easy for him to focus on avoiding prison or death, with the idea in mind that God had called him to apostleship and therefore needed Him to complete the divine plan. But even Paul was expendable, and he knew it. Like him, we should never compromise the truth because we think we are too important to suffer the consequences of standing for it.

6. This includes even the most wicked intents and actions of mankind. See Acts 2:22–23 where Peter says that the crucifixion of Christ was foreordained by God—certainly that was the vilest, most sinful event in world history, yet it produced more good than any other event ever will.

7. Christian Science and the Word/Faith movement essentially deny the reality of bad circumstances (such as sickness). For more information on Christian Science, see Walter Martin, *The Kingdom of the Cults* (Minneapolis: Bethany, 1985). For more information on the Word/ Faith error, see D. R. McConnell, *A Different Gospel* (Peabody, MA: Hendrickson, 1988); and John F. MacArthur, Jr., *Charismatic Chaos* (Grand Rapids: Zondervan, 1992).

8. Tim Stafford, "The Therapeutic Revolution," *Christianity Today* 37, no. 6 (1993): 24–32.

9. The practical implications of that quote are frightening. It implies that a person with problems *must* have the help of another person (besides

God) to choose what is right, and also that the only person who can help is someone who has knowledge beyond that revealed in Scripture. Counselors who persuade people of such helplessness will only succeed in making them dependent upon their counsel.

10. For more information on this issue, see Jay Adams, "What To Do When You Counsel An Unbeliever," in *A Theology of Christian Counseling* (Grand Rapids: Zondervan, 1979), 309–326.

11. For an excellent discussion of both the nature of true faith and the danger of false profession, read John F. MacArthur, Jr., *The Gospel According to Jesus* (Grand Rapids: Zondervan, 1988); and *Faith Works: The Gospel According to the Apostles* (Dallas: Word, 1993).

12. This is not to say that if a person falters in faith during trials we can automatically conclude that he or she is not a Christian. Proverbs 24:10 says, "If you are slack in the day of distress, / Your strength is limited." There could be several reasons for the limit on someone's strength. It could be that the person has true faith but has let it become weak (like the disciples at times in the gospels). On occasion, Jesus spoke of their "little faith." Sometimes weakness in faith is due to the fact that the individual is a young believer, or it could be that the person has neglected the spiritual disciplines that strengthen faith (Rom. 10:17; Eph. 3:16–19; Heb. 3:12–13; 10:24–25; 2 Pet. 1:5–9). Weakness in faith also happens when people take their focus off the Lord and allow themselves to become spiritually dull (Dan. 11:32; Heb. 12:2; Rev. 2:1–7). Or, in some instances, a person is weak because he or she has no true faith and therefore no power to stand during hard times. Because weak faith can be symptomatic of various things, biblical counselors must seek to discover what it signifies and address that particular need.

13. John MacArthur et al., *Think Biblically!* (Wheaton: Crossway, 2003).

14. Psalm 3:1–6; 4:1–8; 127:2; Proverbs 3:13–16; 19:23; Ecclesiastes 5:12.

15. Jerry Bridges, *Trusting God: Even When Life Hurts* (Colorado Springs: NavPress, 1988), 175.

16. For an excellent discussion of the sufficiency of our spiritual resources, see John F. MacArthur, Jr. *Our Sufficiency in Christ* (Dallas: Word, 1991).

17. Not only proactive sin, but reactive sin, that is, unbiblical responses to the manifestations, expressions, or results of sin in our world; not necessarily nor primarily sinful actions but unbiblical attitudes, desires, thoughts, concepts, ideas (Prov. 4:23; James 1:13–16); not necessarily presumptuous or deliberate sins but also sins of ignorance, or secret sins (Ps. 19:12–14; Luke 12:46–47; 1 Tim. 1:13); not merely sins of commission but sins of omission (Rom. 3:23; 1 John 3:4); not merely behavioral sins but motivational sins or idolatrous sins where the primary focus

of life is to please and serve self or other people, where the main concern, confidence, and desire of life is something or someone other than God, where as Romans 1:25 puts it: "They worship and serve the creature rather than the Creator" (Jer. 17:5–10; Ezek. 14:1–9; Rom. 1:18–32; 1 Cor. 10:1–13; Heb. 4:12). Sin may be defined as any thought, action, reaction, response, attitude, ruling desire, motive, choice, feeling, or habit pattern that is contrary to the revealed moral will of God in the Bible, whether known by the person or not, and whether deliberately and consciously chosen or committed as a habitual pattern of response. (See also Ex. 20:1–17; Ps. 51:5; 58:3; Matt. 5:17—7:28; Mark 7:21–23; Rom. 7:21–25; 14:23; Gal. 5:19–21; Eph. 2:1–3; 4:17–22; Heb. 4:12–13; James 4:17.)

Chapter Ten—Taking Counselee Inventory: Collecting Data

1. Pastors, in particular, may find it difficult to listen to counselees. Gifted in teaching and accustomed to speaking from the pulpit, a pastor tends to take a one-sided approach in counseling. Pastors need to be aware of the differences between preaching and counseling and take care not to approach them in the same way.

2. Jay Adams, *The Christian Counselor's Casebook* (Grand Rapids: Zondervan, 1974), 16. Used by permission.

3. This process is usually related to the development of the facilitative relationship we discussed in chapter 8. Counselees with walls built around themselves want to know that they can trust the counselor before they will share the concerns that are central to their problems.

4. Robert Smith, M.D., "Sleep," *The Journal of Pastoral Practice* 4, no. 2 (1980): 36–43, citing Julius Segal, Ph.D., "Missing Sleep Dangerous," *Family Practice News* 2, no. 17 (1972).

5. Following is an excerpt from an article written by Arnold Fox, M.D. called "Caffeine—Unexpected Cause of Fatigue": "Simply put, caffeine is nothing more than a cruel hoax you play on yourself. You take in caffeine to give yourself a 'lift.' You get the lift—but you also set yourself up for fatigue, anxiety, and depression. Fatigue, followed closely by anxiety and depression, is the most common complaint we physicians hear from our patients. Although there are many causes of fatigue, one of the most common, and most often overlooked cause is 'caffeinism'—the consumption of caffeine" (*Let's Live* [April 1982]: 19–20). For other information on the effects of caffeine, see Bob Smith, "Caffeine," *The Journal of Pastoral Practice* 1, no. 1 (1977): 95–96.

6. When you do advise counselees to exercise, however, suggest that they be involved in a form of exercise that is noncompetitive, otherwise they may compound their stress rather than release it. Some people are so competitive they cannot participate in sports without being

obsessed with winning. It is important to understand the individual's tendencies in this area in order to design an exercise plan that will be helpful.

7. For some helpful discussions of this truth, see S. I. McMillen, *None of These Diseases* (Old Tappan, NJ: Revell, 1973); Smith, "Caffeine," 79–92; and Jay Adams, *Competent to Counsel* (Grand Rapids: Zondervan, 1970), chapter 7.

8. Many times a counselor who suspects this will not be able to confirm it alone but will need to advise the counselee to ask a physician about a possible connection.

9. Doctors are issued a new book each year by the drug companies and often will pass along the previous year's book to a counselor who asks for it.

10. For further reading on this issue, see Bob Smith, "The Use of Drugs in Counseling," *The Biblical Counselor* (May 1992): 1, 4.

11. Romans 8:7–8 says that "the mind set on the flesh [the mind of the unsaved person] is hostile toward God; for it does not subject itself to the law of God, for it is not even able to do so; and those who are in the flesh cannot please God." And 1 Corinthians 2:14 says that "a natural man [again, someone who is unsaved] does not accept the things of the Spirit of God; for they are foolishness to him, and he cannot understand them, because they are spiritually appraised."

12. It is not our place to pronounce judgment upon the spiritual state of those who profess to know Christ (1 Cor. 4:5; James 4:11–12), so we must treat them as believers unless they ascribe to doctrinal heresy, are guilty of continuing, flagrant, ungodly conduct (2 John 9–11), or are placed under discipline by the church (Matt. 18:17). But if their responses and conduct cause us to question the validity of their profession, we certainly can and should challenge them to examine their spiritual condition (2 Cor. 13:5). Some materials that are helpful in this process are John MacArthur, Jr.'s tape series *Examine Yourself* (Grace to You) and chapter 5 in his book *Saved Without A Doubt* (Wheaton: Victor Books, 1992).

13. Social resources are particularly important because there may be people in the counselees' environment (such as church or family) who can be enlisted to help with their problems. Many counselors miss such opportunities simply because they fail to gather the appropriate data.

14. The Bible speaks not only of sins of commission but also sins of omission. God is concerned that we exert a positive influence on those around us through good deeds (Matt. 5:13–16; Eph. 4:22–32; James 4:17).

15. Second Corinthians 10:4–5 contains another often overlooked reference to the mind. Here Paul talked about the intense spiritual warfare

we are involved in, and then said we fight it by "taking every thought captive to the obedience of Christ." And in James 4:1–6, describing why people do the ungodly things they do, James said that the source of these problems is in our "pleasures (desires) that wage war in [our] members" (v. 1), in our lusts (v. 2), in our idolatry or spiritual adultery (v. 4), and in our pride (v. 6).

16. Issues that need to be addressed include family of origin, marital history, other significant relationships, problems in school or family, and possible physical or sexual abuse. We need to be concerned about any shaping experience from the past, especially those that the counselee believes are important.

17. For further reading about errors concerning the past, see John Bettler, "Toward A Confession of Faith on the Past," and Steve Viars, "Handling the Past Biblically," both in *The Biblical Counselor* (July 1993): 1–4.

18. Some passages that refer to the effect of our past on our current lives are Genesis 25:27–28; 26:1–5; 2 Chronicles 22:1–4; Proverbs 5:22–23; 22:6; Jeremiah 13:23; Ephesians 6:4; Colossians 3:21; 2 Timothy 1:5; 3:15; and 1 Peter 1:18.

19. We should be willing to listen to the history of those we counsel, if for no other reason than it is important to them. If we conclude from the start that their past is irrelevant and show no concern about it, it will be extremely difficult to establish the necessary facilitative relationship between counselor and counselee (see ch. 10).

20. See Numbers 11—23; Deuteronomy 24:16; Proverbs 6:30–31; Luke 6:27–38; Romans 12:17–21; 14:10–12; Galatians 6:5; James 1:2–5; and 1 Peter 1—5.

21. See Genesis 3:1–4; 4:1–14; 12:10–20; 14:14–23; 22:1–14; 26:1–7; 2 Kings 19:1–28; Psalm 3:1–2; 73:1–28; Proverbs 1:10–19; 13:20; 22:24–25; 30:7–9; 1 Corinthians 15:33; 16:10; 2 Corinthians 1:8–9; Galatians 2:11–12; 1 Timothy 2:1–2; 2 Timothy 2:16–18; Hebrews 10:24–25; Revelation 2 (vv. 2–3, 9, 13, 15, 19–20, 24); 3:8–9, 15–17.

22. An exception to this rule would be when the counselor senses that the discussion is getting too heavy and decides to lighten it up by allowing the counselee to respond to something different for a few moments.

23. Adams, *Casebook,* 90.

24. A study of the questions Jesus asked in the gospels reveals that He asked *what* questions much more often than *why* questions. For instance, in Mark 8—10 Jesus asks twenty questions; seventeen of them are *what* questions.

25. This kind of question is helpful in certain circumstances, such as when you want to get a commitment from a counselee, when you need to clarify what you think he or she has been saying, and when the coun-

selee is getting uncomfortable (because closed-ended questions are usually less threatening than open-ended questions).

26. Those questions followed by an asterisk are adapted from David Powlison's class notes.

27. Halo data can also provide material for questions: "When I asked you that question you seemed upset. Could you help me to understand what bothered you about the question?" "You seem angry with me today. Is there something I have done to upset you?" "You seem a little preoccupied. What are you thinking about?" In many cases the questions inspired by halo data yield key information.

28. For examples of data-gathering homework, see Wayne A. Mack, *A Homework Manual for Biblical Living,* 2 vols. (Phillipsburg, PA: Presbyterian and Reformed, 1979); Wayne A. Mack, *Your Family God's Way* (Phillipsburg, PA: Presbyterian and Reformed, 1991); and Wayne A. Mack, *Preparing for Marriage God's Way* (Tulsa, OK: Hensley, 1987).

29. I suggest that this be done during the session in a limited way—write down important phrases, statements, or ideas for future recollection, reflection, and development. After the session is concluded, the counselor may want to take a few minutes to reflect, evaluate, and record any other significant information. That would also be a good time to plan tentatively what will be done in the next session.

Chapter Eleven—Interpreting Counselee Data

1. Jay Adams, *The Christian Counselor's Casebook* (Grand Rapids: Zondervan, 1974), 162.

2. Perhaps Gus is evaluating himself wrongly in light of what other people can do physically, instead of recognizing that they may have different constitutions. He may think he cannot be useful or successful because he does not have the physical strength that others have.

3. Their involvement may be helpful, even crucial, for Gus to repair the broken relationship with his father.

4. If Gus has accomplished some tasks in his life, and especially if he is successfully carrying out responsibilities in other areas, we can challenge his claim that he lacks "ego strength." We can build on his successful completion of past and present tasks to challenge and encourage him.

5. The reason for questioning Gus about what he thinks God would say is to encourage him subtly to think through his presuppositions rather than blasting him with the truth (see Eph. 4:15). We would need to encourage Gus to think on his own and help him to come to the conclusion that he is seeing things differently than God sees them.

6. See pages 134–135.

7. See 1 Corinthians 3:1–2; Hebrews 5:12–14.

8. Other passages in Proverbs that speak of the fool are 9:7; 13:20; 14:7; 17:10, 12; 22:10; 23:9; 26:3–5, 12; and 27:22.

9. Paul used the term to refer to those who are considered deficient in 1 Corinthians 1:27: "God has chosen the weak things of the world to shame the things which are strong."

10. Proverbs 1:33 also reveals something about fear (and instability and insecurity). It says that those things are often the result of not listening to or obeying God's Word.

11. *Paranoia,* a Greek word found in 2 Peter 2:16, is translated "madness" or "foolishness." It is a combination of two Greek words: one means "to be at or by the side of" and the other refers to the mind. So, literally, a person experiencing paranoia is a person who is "by the side of his or her mind" or "out of his or her mind." That person is not viewing things realistically, rationally, accurately, and is not in touch with reality. As a result, the individual may experience panic attacks and delusions and act in other bizarre ways.

12. See Proverbs 5:22; Jeremiah 13:23; 22:21; and Ephesians 4:22.

13. Another example of bizarre behavior resulting from sin and the judgment of God is found in Deuteronomy 28:28–29.

14. For an excellent discussion of the role of personal discipline in the process of spiritual growth, see John MacArthur, Jr., "A Balance of Faith and Effort," in *Our Sufficiency in Christ* (Dallas: Word Publishing, 1991).

15. For instance, Proverbs 22:24–25 says, "Do not associate with a man given to anger; / Or go with a hot-tempered man, / Lest you learn his ways, / And find a snare for yourself." You may encounter a counselee struggling with anger who is surrounded by a lot of angry people. A change in environment and companions may be an important part of the solution.

16. See H. R. Lewis and M. E. Lewis, *Psychosomatics* (New York: Viking, 1972).

17. Drugs can be very misleading in this area. If medication seems to be helping someone, that does not necessarily mean the problem is organic. The medication may alleviate some of the symptoms but still not solve the root problem. So the fact that drugs are helping does not necessarily prove that the cause is organic.

18. There are seventy-two references to the heart in the book of Proverbs.

19. Other representative passages indicating the crucial significance of the heart are Genesis 6:5; 8:21; Deuteronomy 5:29; 6:5; 10:12; 11:13; 26:16; 30:6; 1 Samuel 16:7; 2 Chronicles 19:3; 30:19; Ezra 7:10; Psalm 27:3; 28:3; 76:5; 101:4; 140:2; Proverbs 3:1–6; 6:14, 18, 25; 7:24; 11:20; 12:2; 15:13–15; 16:23; 20:9; 21:2; Matthew 5:8; 9:4; 12:33; 23:26; Luke 16:15;

Acts 5:3; 16:14; Romans 1:21, 24; 2:5; 8:7; 10:9–10; Ephesians 3:17; 4:17; Hebrews 3:8–15; 8:10; 10:16, 22; and James 3:8.

20. When Moses described the incident Paul was referring to (Numbers 11), he focused on the hearts of the people as well. Verses 4 and 34 both mention "greedy desires" as the source of their sin.

21. First John 2:14–16 provides some clear and helpful direction to biblical counselors for interpreting the motivations of counselees. This passage identifies the three primary areas of heart idolatry: the lust of the flesh (inordinate, controlling desires for sensual pleasure, for ease and comfort, for physical gratification; see Gen.3:6; 19:33, 35; Num. 11:1–34; Prov. 21:17; 23:20–21, 29–35; Eccl. 10:16–17; Luke 21:34; Rom. 13:11–14); the lust of the eyes (covetousness and greed, a controlling desire for profit or for material things: see Deut. 15:19; 1 Sam. 25:11; 1 Kings 21; Joshua 7; Prov. 28:22–23; Eccl. 4:8; 5:9–11; Matt. 6:18–34; Col. 3:5; 1 Tim. 6:9–10); and the pride of life (inordinate ruling desires to be great in one's self and for self, to be accepted and approved, to have power and be in control, to be recognized and respected, to be regarded as successful; Gen. 3:16; Judg. 9:1–21; 1 Sam. 25:36; Ps. 10:3–4; Prov. 13:10; 16:5; 25:27; 27:2; 28:25; 29:25; 30:13; Is. 10:7–11; 37:12–13; Jer. 45:5; Dan. 4:20–27; Amos 6:1–6; Matt. 23:5; 6:1–6; 21:15; Luke 18:11; Acts 12:23; Rom. 12:3; 3 John 9–10). It is often profitable to determine whether a counselee is falling prey to the lust of the flesh, the lust of the eyes, or the pride of life. For a helpful exposition of those areas of sin, see J. Cotton, *An Exposition of 1 John* (Evansville: Sovereign Grace Publishers), 190–205.

22. See T. Keller, "Puritan Resources for Biblical Counseling," *The Journal of Pastoral Practice* 9, no. 3 (1988): 11–41 for an excellent treatment of idolatrous desires.

23. Always inform the counselee that you are doing this. In most cases it is best to ask for the counselee's permission.

Chapter Twelve—Providing Instruction Through Biblical Counseling

1. See Proverbs 6:23; Matthew 22:29; Ephesians 4:11–12; 1 Thessalonians 4:13; 1 Timothy 4:6, 11, 16; 2 Timothy 2:16–18; Titus 1:10–11.

2. Quoted in F. S. Mead, ed., *The Encyclopedia of Religious Quotations* (Westwood, NJ: Revell, 1965), 24.

3. Second Timothy 3:16–17 teaches the same truth when it says that Scripture is able to make us "adequate, equipped for *every* good work."

4. Epistemology is the area of philosophy commonly called "the science of knowing," which seeks to answer the questions "How do we know?" and "What can we know?"

5. R. Pratt, Jr. wrote, "*All* that can properly be called truth, not just so called 'religious truth' resides first in God and men know truly only as they come to God's revelation of Himself as the source of truth, for it is God who teaches man knowledge (Ps. 94:10). . . . This dependence of man on God in the area of knowledge does not mean that men are without true ability to think and reason nor that they are 'programmed' by God in analogy to the way computers 'know.' Men do actually think, yet, true knowledge is dependent on and derived from God's knowledge as it has been revealed to man." *Every Thought Captive* (Phillipsburg, NJ: Presbyterian and Reformed Publishing, 1979), 17.

6. See chapter 3 for more information about epistemological issues.

7. This certainly applies to anything written by an unsaved person, such as a secular psychologist, because even when an unsaved person makes a basic observation about the world or reiterates an idea taught by Scripture, there is still a dangerous tinge of falsehood to what that person says. Richard Pratt, Jr. wrote, "We may speak of such statements as false because they are not the result of voluntary obedience to God's revelation. . . . Beyond this, the statements are falsified by the non-Christian framework of meaning and therefore lead away from the worship of God. If nothing else, the mere commitment to human independence falsifies the non-Christian's statements" (ibid.).

8. J. C. Ryle, *Practical Religion* (Cambridge: James Clark, 1959), 81.

9. A contemporary book that contains helpful discussions of these attributes of Scripture is Noel Weeks, *The Sufficiency of Scripture* (Carlisle, PA: Banner of Truth, 1988). See also John MacArthur, Jr., *Our Sufficiency in Christ* (Dallas: Word Publishing, 1991).

10. Two other verses that emphasize the danger of using the Scriptures inaccurately in our ministry to others are 1 Timothy 1:8 where Paul said that "the Law is good if one uses it lawfully" and Mark 7:13 where Jesus spoke of those who make void the Word of God by adding to it their own traditions.

11. See chapter 9, pages 115–122 for a further discussion of this concept.

12. Two other tools that would be helpful are A. T. Robertson, *Word Pictures in the New Testament,* 6 vols. (Nashville: Broadman, 1930); and *The New International Dictionary of New Testament Theology,* 3 vols. ed. Colin Brown (Grand Rapids: Zondervan, 1975).

13. This is a pertinent example because the book of Proverbs is one of the few books in Scripture where we normally do not have to worry about context (because it is made up of mostly short, unrelated sayings). But this example proves that even when we are quoting a proverb, we need to examine the context to see if we are using it correctly.

14. When we approach a passage, we need to ask the questions "What is the Holy Spirit trying to communicate in this passage?" and "What does

He want to accomplish through it?" And rather than just launching into our study of a passage assuming we are able to ascertain its meaning, we ought to pray, "Holy Spirit, this is Your book, You gave it to us. Please help me to understand this part of it correctly. Help me to learn what You meant to say in it."

15. Governmental authority is similar to a husband's. First Peter 2:13 says, "Submit yourselves to every ordinance of man" (KJV), but it was the author of that book who led the stand against the authorities in Acts 5. For a thorough discussion of the submission required of a wife, see *Rediscovering Biblical Manhood and Womanhood,* ed. John Piper and Wayne Grudem (Wheaton: Crossway Books, 1991); and Wayne A. Mack, *Strengthening Your Marriage* (Harmony, PA: Presbyterian and Reformed, 1977).

16. From *Luther's Works,* vol. 54 (Philadelphia: Fortress Press, 1967), 45.

17. D. Martyn Lloyd-Jones, *Preaching and Preachers* (Grand Rapids: Zondervan, 1971), 76.

18. See chapter 14, endnote 21.

19. This is such an important method of instruction that it is really not optional. Scripture teaches that we cannot truly learn without doing (see James 1:22–25), and so it is never enough for us to simply heap information on our counselees. We need to give them opportunities (in the sessions and through homework assignments) to put the knowledge that they are acquiring into practice.

20. The following verses would be helpful for a further study of the biblical manner of instruction: Proverbs 15:1, 4; 16:21, 24; Acts 20:31; Galatians 6:1; 1 Thessalonians 4:9–10; 1 Timothy 3:3; 4:6; 5:1–2; 6:2, 13; 2 Timothy 1:6; 2:16–17, 23–24; 4:1; Titus 2:6–9, 15; 3:1.

21. It is helpful to accumulate ideas for homework assignments in a similar fashion. Place a list of assignments that relate to a particular problem in a notebook next to biblical information on that problem so those ideas will be easily accessible in the counseling session.

22. NANC's address is 3600 W. 96th Street, Indianapolis, IN 46268. CCEF's address is 1803 East Willow Grove Avenue, Glenside, PA 19118.

23. NANC publishes *The Biblical Counselor* (monthly), and CCEF publishes *The Journal of Biblical Counseling* (quarterly; formerly known as *The Journal of Pastoral Practice*).

24. See chapter 18 for a more complete listing of resources for counselor development as well as resources for counselees.

Chapter Thirteen—Biblical Counseling and Inducement

1. See Psalm 139:13; 51:17; Jeremiah 3:10; 4:4; 29:13; Ezekiel 14:1–9; Joel 2:13; Matthew 5:8; 15:8–9; Acts 8:21; Romans 2:5, 29; 2 Timothy 1:5; Hebrews 4:12; James 4:8.

2. Matthew 19:26; John 15:1–16; 2 Corinthians 3:18; 7:1; 9:8; Ephesians 4:22–24; Philippians 4:13; Colossians 3:1–14; Hebrews 12:1–4; Jude 24–25.

3. See 2 Chronicles 20:13; Psalm 57:7; Matthew 25:24–28; Luke 15:11–18; 1 Corinthians 6:19–20; Galatians 5:1; Ephesians 4:1–3; 1 Peter 4:1–2.

4. *Indicative* refers to statements of fact, as opposed to *imperative* (commands), or *interrogative* (questions).

5. John Murray writes, "The future tense, 'we shall live' does not refer exclusively to the future resurrection state but, as found above (see v. 5), points to the certainty of participation in the resurrection life of Christ here and now; it is the life of Spiritual, mystical union." *The New International Commentary on the New Testament—Romans,* ed. G. D. Fee (Grand Rapids: Eerdmans, 1990), 223.

6. John MacArthur, Jr., *The MacArthur New Testament Commentary: Romans 1–8* (Chicago: Moody, 1991), 336–337.

7. Another helpful illustration of biblical motivation is found in the book of Hebrews. The audience of that book included people who were thinking of entering the Christian life and those who were about ready to give up on it, so the author was trying to motivate them to commit themselves to Christ or to persevere in that commitment. Throughout the book the author exhorted the reader by saying, "Let us . . ." (4:1, 11, 14, 16; 6:1; 10:22–24; 12:1, 28; 13:13, 15). Each of those verses yields additional insights about biblical principles of motivation.

8. Those who exhibit such behavior have probably used this technique many times in the past and have found that it kept them safe from having to be honest and admit their sin.

9. For further details see Chapter 9.

10. For a helpful discussion of this issue, see the chapter entitled "A Balance of Faith and Effort" in John MacArthur, Jr. *Our Sufficiency in Christ* (Dallas: Word, 1991).

11. Consider Christ in the Garden of Gethsemane, for example (Matt. 26:36–44). At that time He certainly did not *feel like* obeying God and facing the agonies of the cross (vv. 37–38), but despite His feelings He prayed, "Not as I will, but as Thou wilt."

12. Tom Carter, *Spurgeon At His Best* (Grand Rapids: Baker, 1988), 263.

13. This is the reason for most marriage counseling. Many couples try without success to solve their problems by themselves and then need to find help outside their relationship. They should not be hesitant or feel ashamed to share their problems with a godly counselor, because in doing so they will be following the command Jesus gave in Matthew 18:16.

14. This is an important reason why biblical counseling is best done in the context of the local church (or at least in cooperation with it).

Counseling outside of that context lacks a certain measure of authority that resides only in the leadership of the church (Matt. 18:18; Heb. 13:17). See Chapter 17 of this book for a discussion of the role of the church in counseling.

15. Richard Baxter, *The Reformed Pastor* (Carlisle, PA: Banner of Truth, 1989), 105.

16. Baxter, *The Reformed Pastor,* 106.

Chapter Fourteen—Implementing Biblical Instruction

1. D. Martyn Lloyd-Jones, *Studies in the Sermon on the Mount,* vol. 1 (Grand Rapids: Eerdmans, 1959), 243 and 249–250.

2. Many times people struggle with feelings of guilt for sins they committed long ago because they recognize that the inner change God wants to accomplish has not occurred. They have ceased the sinful action, but their heart still longs for it from time to time. They have not yet learned to view it, as God does, with a holy aversion.

3. Romans 13:1–4.

4. Acts 19:17–19.

5. Acts 2:41–47; Hebrews 13:17. For more information on the role of the church in counseling, see chapter 17.

6. John 5:39; Luke 24:44–48; Hebrews 10:7. See Wayne A. Mack, *A Homework Manual for Biblical Living,* vol. 1 (Phillipsburg: Presbyterian and Reformed, 1979), 63–71 for helpful suggestions and plans for making devotions meaningful.

7. Romans 12:10, 16; 15:14; 1 Corinthians 12:25; Galatians 5:13; 6:2; 1 Thessalonians 4:18; 5:11, 14; Hebrews 3:13–14.

8. 1 Corinthians 10:31.

9. Psalm 4:8; Psalm 127:2 NKJV; Proverbs 3:21, 23–24; Ecclesiastes 5:12; Matthew 4:1–4; Mark 4:38; 11:19; Luke 6:12.

10. Mark 10:45; John 13:13–17.

11. Romans 12:3–8; Ephesians 4:10–16; 1 Corinthians 12:1–7; 1 Peter 4:10, 11. For more information about spiritual gifts and the way they should be used, see chapter 16 of this book; see also Mack, *A Homework Manual,* 93–99, 161–163, 183–199.

12. John 2:4; 7:6, 8, 30; 8:20, 29; 12:23; 17:3–4.

13. See Mack, *Homework Manual,* vol. 1, 132–43, for a helpful study on planning the godly use of time.

14. Psalm 50:15; 34:4–6; Isaiah 40:31.

15. 1 John 2:15–17. Is the person tempted by the lust of the flesh—a desire for pleasure; the lust of the eyes—a desire for possessions; or the pride of life—a desire for power and/or prestige? Identify the particular idolatrous desire the person is tempted to worship and serve. See also chapter 13 of this book for more details on this issue.

16. Genesis 39:8–9; Deuteronomy 31:6; Psalm 55:21; Isaiah 41:10; 43:1–3; 1 Corinthians 10:13; 2 Corinthians 9:8; Ephesians 3:20–21; 2 Peter 1:3–4; Jude 24–25.

17. 2 Corinthians 5:14–15; Galatians 1:4; Titus 2:11–13; 1 Peter 2:24.

18. Proverbs 15:15–16; 24:16.

19. For a helpful discussion of what it means to confess, see Ken Sande, *The Peacemaker* (Grand Rapids: Baker, 1991), chapter 6. In this chapter Sande referred to what he calls "The Seven A's of Confession": (1) address everyone involved; (2) avoid *if, but,* or *maybe;* (3) admit specifically; (4) apologize for offending or hurting the other person(s); (5) accept the consequences; (6) alter your behavior; and (7) ask for forgiveness.

20. Psalm 32; 103:12; Proverbs 28:13; Isaiah 43:25; 44:22; Micah 7:19; Ephesians 1:7; Philippians 3:10–14; 1 John 1:9.

21. See Mack, *Homework Manual* vol. 1, for other examples of homework assignments that facilitate the practice of biblical principles. Many of these assignments were developed to fulfill the seven key elements of the counseling process presented in Part Three of this book. For example, different parts of the anger study on pages 1 through 11 will be useful in accomplishing all seven phases or elements of the counseling process. Pages 1 through 6 will focus mainly on elements 1 through 5, and pages 7 through 11 will be most helpful in the inducement and implementation phases. Pages 7 through 9 relate mainly to the planning aspect of implementation, whereas pages 10 and 11 highlight the practice phase. Other homework assignments that encourage the practice aspect of the implementation phase of counseling are found in Mack, *Homework Manual* vol. 2; Mack, *Strengthening Your Marriage;* Mack, *Preparing for Marriage;* and Mack, *Your Family God's Way.*

22. Luke 9:23.

23. S. MacMillan, ed., *Complete Works of the Late Rev. Thomas Boston,* 12 vols. (Wheaton: Richard Owen Roberts, 1980), 285.

24. MacMillan, *Complete Works.*, 287.

25. To me, the purposes of counseling are fulfilled and implemented when I observe the following things happen: (1) the counselee understands what caused his/her problems and the biblical way of handling them; (2) the counselee becomes comfortable with the new response pattern; (3) the counselee begins to practice the new pattern automatically; (4) the counselee has failed and can diagnose the reason for the failure and make plans for correcting the problem; (5) the counselee can state specifically how he/she has changed; (6) the counselee has been tested and has been victorious in the test; (7) others have verified the changes in the counselee; (8) the counselee starts to share with others what he

or she is learning in counseling; the counselee becomes an informal and spontaneous counselor to others.

26. Matthew 12:38–45; 2 Peter 2:20–22.

Chapter Sixteen—Spirit-Giftedness and Biblical Counseling

1. Cited in Jay Adams, *Competent to Counsel* (Grand Rapids: Baker, 1980), xvi.
2. John Calvin, *The Epistles of Paul the Apostle to the Romans and to the Thessalonians* (Grand Rapids: Eerdmans, 1960), 269.
3. Richard Baxter, *The Reformed Pastor* (Edinburgh: Banner of Truth, 1979), 68.
4. Baxter, *The Reformed Pastor,* 68.
5. Adams, *Competent to Counsel,* 51.
6. Martin and Deidre Bobgan, *How to Counsel from Scripture* (Chicago: Moody, 1985), 54–55.

Chapter Nineteen—Frequently Asked Questions about Biblical Counseling

1. Jay Adams, *Competent to Counsel,* (Grand Rapids: Zondervan, 1970), xxi.
2. Jay Adams, *What About Nouthetic Counseling?* (Grand Rapids: Baker, 1979), 3–4.
3. Wherever Scripture speaks on any of these matters, however, its revelation is true, reliable, and without error: "All Scripture is inspired by God and profitable for teaching" (2 Tim. 3:16).
4. Adams, *Nouthetic Counseling,* 31.
5. Harvey E. Dana and Julius R. Mantey, *A Manual Grammar of the Greek New Testament* (New York: MacMillan, 1957), 164–65.
6. David G. Benner, ed. *Baker Encyclopedia of Psychology,* (Grand Rapids: Baker, 1985), 38.
7. William L. Playfair, and George Bryson, *The Useful Lie,* (Wheaton: Good News/Crossway, 1991), 45–47.
8. The quotation was presented in a form letter sent out by Focus on the Family, 9 November 1989. The letter was signed by David Tompkins, a personal assistant to Dr. James Dobson.

Appendix

1. This material is taken from Jay Adams, *The Christian Counselor's Manual: The Practice of Nouthetic Counseling* (Grand Rapids: Zondervan, 1986) and is used by permission.

Subject Index

Kaminer, Wendy, 78
Keil, C. F., 57
Kierkegaard, Soren, 32
Knowledge, as a spiritual gift, 219
Koch, Sigmund, 32

Ladd, G. T., 32
Laing, R. D., 12
Legalism, 261
Lloyd-Jones, D. Martyn, 8, 68, 169
Logos, 33
Luther, Martin, 169

MacArthur, John, Jr., 33, 180, 250, 258
Mack, Wayne A., 26, 258
Mailman Research Center, 12
Man: dichotomous view of, 256–57; nature of, 65; trichotomous view of, 256–57
Marxism, xi
Maslow, Abraham, 40
Master's College and Seminary, The, 25, 174, 244
Mental hygiene movement, 20
Mental illness, 254
Mercy, as a spiritual gift, 220
Mesmerism, 11
Minrith-Meier Clinic, 79
Moses, 181
Mowrer, O. Hobart, 22
Murray, John, 84

Narramore, Clyde, 22
National Association of Nouthetic Counselors (NANC), 24, 41, 174, 228
Natural revelation, 204. See also General revelation.
Nebuchadnezzar, 53
Need theory, 245
New birth, as the work of the Spirit, 87

Pastoral counseling, 32
Paul, the apostle: 3, 33, 43, 109–10, 119–20, 130; as counselor, 103; methods of motivation, 179–80; his hope, 119
Peale, Norman Vincent, 65
Perls, Fritz, 108

Person-orientation, 102
Personal Data Inventory Form (PDIF), 140
Phrenology, 10–11
Popper, Karl, 36
Powlison, David, 39, 246, 248, 252
Prayer: proper view of, 89; wrong view of, 89
Preaching, as biblical counseling, 225
Problem-orientation, 102
Problems, nature and cause of, 126–27
Progressive sanctification, 227
Prophecy, as a spiritual gift, 215–16
psyche, 33, 34
Psychiatrists, 262
Psychoanalysis, as a religion, 10
Psychologists, 262
Psychology: definition of, 7; as opposed to Christianity, xii; not a science, 14, 36, 37; as a threat to biblical exposition, 203, 250; usurping sanctification, 80
Psychotherapy: as a business, 13; and the decline of preaching, 203; replacing the church, 20, 80

Quinn, S. Lance, 249, 253, 259

Recovery industry, the, 260
Reiff, Philip, 19
Respect in counseling, 106
Reverse psychology, 111
Rogers, Carl, 19, 22, 32
Ryle, J. C., 78, 165

Sanctification, 87
Sarles, Ken L., 258
Scripture: as a guide to truth, 206–10; inspiration of, 210; knowledge of, 173; memorization of, 89; power of, 205; sufficiency of, 203
Self-esteem: 40, 64; as faith, 65; as an expression of neo-orthodoxy, 66; as an expression of sin, 70–71; as a theological system, 66
Sermon on the Mount, 35

Contributors

Douglas Bookman, M.Div, Th.M., Th.D.	Senior Pastor of Trinity Baptist Church in Pasadena, California
William Goode, D.D. (deceased)	Former Senior Pastor of Faith Baptist Church, Lafayette, Indiana
John MacArthur, D.D., Litt.D.	President of The Master's College and Seminary; Professor of Pastoral Ministries
Wayne A. Mack, D.Min.	Adjunct Professor of Biblical Counseling at The Master's College
David Powlison, M.Div., D.Min.	Staff member at the Christian Counseling and Education Foundation in Laverock, Pennsylvania; Editor of *The Journal of Biblical Counseling*
Robert D. Smith, M.D.	Staff member of Faith Baptist Counseling Ministries; Member and Fellow of the American Academy of Family Physicians
John D. Street, D.Min.	Chairperson, Department of Biblical Counseling at The Master's College; Associate Professor of Biblical Counseling
Dennis M. Swanson, M.Div., M.L.I.S.	Librarian at The Master's Seminary